"The recovery of this work of J. Gresham Machen is not like finding a gold mine in the mountains, it is more like discovering a diamond mine. It is a true treasure—one of sparkling jewels and glorious truth. To mine this treasure is to find a deposit in heaven."
—R.C. Sproul, Founder, Ligonier Ministries

"With the exegetical skills of a renowned New Testament scholar, the passionate precision of a defender of the faith, and the sweet sympathy of a human being, Machen treats theology as urgent life-and-death communication. Some of his references might be dated (by nine decades or so), but the substance remains as relevant as ever. I can think of few teachers of the past who are more reliable and rewarding to read, and now we can read his insights across the whole span of Christian doctrine."
—Michael Horton, J. Gresham Machen Professor of Theology and Apologetics, Westminster Seminary California

"J. Gresham Machen was a man of his times, enmeshed in protracted and penetrating conflict over the triumphant liberalism of his day. He was also a man who transcended his times, because he undertook, with rare learning and clear-sighted understanding, the defense of the faith 'once for all entrusted to God's holy people' (Jude 3). His *Christianity and Liberalism*, for instance, written almost a century ago, still sounds amazingly prophetic. This present volume brings together 50 of Machen's radio talks of the 1930s, preserving Machen's voice and emphases in an idiom that is more popular than his more academic books, but no less important. Machen is always worth reading."
—D. A. Carson, Emeritus Professor of New Testament, Trinity Evangelical Divinity School

"J. Gresham Machen was one of the most prescient and courageous Christian theologians of the early 20th century. During his life, Machen was a clear and consistent voice for Christian orthodoxy and evangelical truth in the face of liberalism. This collection of lectures is a valuable addition to the Machen library. They reflect the heart of Machen's ministry and provide yet another compelling presentation of Reformed Christianity. Machen's works are as relevant now as they were when they were first written. These lectures are no exception."
—Albert Mohler, President, The Southern Baptist Theological Seminary

"These popular essays show the heart of J. Gresham Machen: brilliant, clear, and persuasive, calling everyone to faith and life in Jesus. They will bless and encourage all who read them."
—W. Robert Godfrey, President Emeritus and Professor of Church History Emeritus, Westminster Seminary California

"J. Gresham Machen was one of the best thinkers and writers among Reformed theologians before his untimely death on New Year's Day of 1937. Machen's writing is always crisp and clear, without any compromise of cogent argument. When Machen finishes dealing with an unbelieving argument, I always feel that there is nothing more to be said on the unbelieving side. Even though this work is over eighty years old now, I would not hesitate to give it to someone today seeking to learn about the Reformed system of thought."
—John Frame, Professor of Systematic Theology and Philosophy Emeritus, Reformed Theological Seminary

"All of the qualities that enabled J. Gresham Machen to make such an important contribution to English-speaking Protestantism—theological tenacity, clarity of mind, readability, and courageous conviction—are easy to see in this instructive and edifying collection of essays. These talks show once again that doctrine has consequences, with Machen as a superbly gifted guide to the significance of what the church confesses about Christ."
—D. G. Hart, Distinguished Associate Professor of History, Hillsdale College

"J. Gresham Machen was one of the leading Christian scholarly voices of the last century. His ability to distill theology into clear, direct terms intelligible to a lay readership and to explain the gospel to the uncommitted is nowhere better demonstrated than in these radio broadcasts that have here been put in writing. I hope they obtain as wide a readership as possible."
—Robert Letham, Professor of Systematic and Historical Theology, Union School of Theology

"Reading Machen's *Things Unseen* is like reading C. S. Lewis. At first it feels so simple, the waters seem shallow, then without realizing it, you find yourself in deep waters, enthralled at the mystery of the truth of God's Word."
—Paul Miller, Executive Director, SeeJesus

"In J. Gresham Machen, God gave the church an inimitable champion of biblical orthodoxy and gospel clarity. This book will show you why Machen is one of American evangelicalism's most important 20th-century thinkers. More to the point, this book will ground you firmly in what it means to see in the face of Jesus Christ the grace and truth and glory of God."
—RUSSELL MOORE, President, Ethics & Religious Liberty Commission of the Southern Baptist Convention

"J. Gresham Machen wore many hats in his illustrious career, including New Testament scholar, apologist, seminary founder, and churchman. In this welcome volume, we meet Machen the clear and sturdy catechist of Presbyterian doctrine. On every page, Machen commends 'the pattern of sound words' revealed in Holy Scripture and confessed by the church, bringing the reader into contact with the invisible things of God so that he or she may meet the visible realities of this life in a God-honoring manner."
—SCOTT SWAIN, President and James Woodrow Hassell Professor of Systematic Theology, Reformed Theological Seminary

"J. Gresham Machen's essays are timeless, though set in the swirling currents of his day, because the Christian faith he describes, the faith revealed in the Scriptures by the Spirit, rises above time. His learned rhetoric, his passionate defense of Christian orthodoxy, his love of the Savior and his church make what you will find in these pages a delight to read, a source of spiritual strengthening, and a bulwark against the destructive effects of a contemporary scholarship that continues to denigrate the Creator, Redeemer, and only Judge of mankind."
—JOHN D. HANNAH, Research Professor of Theological Studies and Distinguished Professor of Historical Theology, Dallas Theological Seminary

"The life and teaching of J. Gresham Machen are rightly revered by contemporary Christians who prize Reformed orthodoxy. Machen's compelling voice lives again in the pages of this masterful treatment of Christian doctrine. As a theologian for ordinary Christians, his clear and concise communication of biblical truth will draw new readers into a deeper and more personal knowledge of the risen Christ."
—PHILIP RYKEN, President, Wheaton College

"J. Gresham Machen was a theological titan, a champion of the truth, a guardian of the gospel, and a contender for the faith. In a declining day of spiritual apostasy, he was mightily used by God to teach sound doctrine and refute those who contradicted it. His strong stance, even while others around him were crumbling, marks him as a man to whom we must give strictest consideration. I rejoice to see this long-awaited volume of Machen's collected writings assembled together into one body of divinity. Blessed will be the reader who devours and absorbs these God-exalting truths."
—STEVEN J. LAWSON, President, OnePassion Ministries

"It is not hyperbole to say that J. Gresham Machen is one of the most—some would say the most—significant Christian thinkers of the 20th century. His sobering apologetic against Protestant liberalism was a timely alarm, exposing liberalism's illegitimate claim to the Christian religion. But now, thanks to Westminster Seminary Press, Machen's voice is heard once again— yet this time Machen puts forward a positive presentation of the Christian faith. *Things Unseen* is saturated throughout with doctrinal truth as Machen, with urgency in his voice, calls sinners back to the Bible to hear the voice of God afresh and to receive the eternal life only God himself can give through Christ."
—MATTHEW BARRETT, Associate Professor of Christian Theology, Midwestern Baptist Theological Seminary

"In C. S. Lewis like fashion, Gresham Machen's radio broadcasts were of a caliber unimaginable in today's world. These snapshot portraits of doctrine, delivered in exquisite prose designed to be heard as much as read, are simply breathtaking. An accessible compendium of theology that will prove to be the gold-standard for years to come. An outstanding achievement."
—DEREK W. H. THOMAS, Chancellor's Professor of Systematic and Pastoral Theology, Reformed Theological Seminary

"Here is the provocative premise of this countercultural book: At a time when the world's immediate political, social, and economic crises overwhelm us, the most 'practical' act for us is to attend to our soul and its relation to God. It is, says Machen, impossible to deal successfully with the world's problems until we have come to be right with God. Fifty radio talks spell out what this involves in prose that is as personally engaging and understandable as it is profound in its robust defense of orthodox

Christianity. Machen's vision remains as timely for our day as it was in the 1930s; a time eerily like our own."
—John Bolt, Jean and Kenneth Baker Professor of Systematic
Theology Emeritus, Calvin Theological Seminary

"Professor J. Gresham Machen, first of Princeton, then founder of Westminster Theological Seminary, was writing at a time when his scholarly but profoundly believing testimony made a tremendous difference in both the intellectual and popular mind of the American people, and far beyond them into Britain and Europe. It was written at the height of the fundamentalist-modernist controversy that lasted from before World War I to II. The modernists had taken on board the skeptical principles of the 18th-century European Enlightenment, which openly denied Holy Scripture as a divine revelation of truth from the triune God—as well as miracles and the deity of Christ—and replaced it with the ever-changing ideas of the mind of man. It was their delight to point out that the Fundamentalists were largely uneducated, simplistic, and backward and were thus not worthy to be followed by cultured people. Machen, in this book as well as in others, set them back seriously by demonstrating the good sense made by the ancient truth of the Christian tradition, based upon an assumption of the reliability of the Word of God written. He showed that their Enlightenment principles were, in effect, another sort of faith or religion, and one by no means required by the advances of science and the progress of thought. On the contrary, Holy Scripture made much greater sense of a clear reading of nature, as well as providing an access to the saving grace of God. This volume is typical of the best of Machen's thought: it gives clarity and profundity in its exposition of the great truths that must be faced by any enquiring mind, and therefore, it is absolutely contemporary and is a guide to us today."
—Douglas F. Kelly, Professor of Theology Emeritus,
Reformed Theological Seminary

"J. Gresham Machen enjoys a richly deserved reputation for his unwavering commitment to the historic Christian faith. In the face of devastating attacks upon the foundations of Christian theology in the early decades of the 20th century, Machen stood in the breach and offered a trenchant case against liberalism in his classic work, *Christianity and Liberalism*. With the publication of this volume of Machen's radio talks on Reformed theology, a new generation of believers will be introduced to Machen at his best. Readers will enjoy a rich feast of clear doctrinal instruction in the basic tenets of Reformed theology. But they will also witness a wonderful model of a Christian apologist who was always prepared to give a defense to anyone of the reason for the hope that is in us, 'yet with gentleness and respect' (1 Pet 3:15)."

—Cornelis Venema, President and Professor of Doctrinal Studies, Mid-America Reformed Seminary

"Early in my Christian life I read J. Gresham Machen's classic, *Christianity and Liberalism*, and it did not leave my thinking and life unchanged. What struck me was Machen's thoughtful, clear, biblically rich, theologically faithful, and Christ-centered defense of the Christian faith, which was also evident in all of his writings. I am simply thrilled to see back in print a collection of Machen's talks which set forth the glory and beauty of Christian doctrine for another generation. We all stand on the shoulders of giants and Machen is certainly a giant of the Christian faith. Take up this work and read it with delight as once again Machen reminds us of the glory of our triune God, the authority of his Word, and the wonder of God's grace as given in Christ Jesus our Lord. I hope this book will receive a wide reading for today's church in a day which desperately needs sound theology and there is no one better to do so than J. Gresham Machen."

—Stephen Wellum, Professor of Christian Theology, Southern Baptist Theological Seminary

"This collection of radio talks shows all Machen's qualities as a great scholar, a sure-footed theologian, and a fearless champion of biblical Christianity. These addresses are still remarkably contemporary, covering almost the whole range of Christian truth, and robustly intellectual; the beginner will find them easily accessible, the seasoned thinker will find fresh stimulus, and the defender of the faith will take fresh courage."

—Donald Macleod, Professor of Systematic Theology, Retired, Edinburgh Theological Seminary

"In *Things Unseen* you get vintage Machen: a top-shelf mind, making the deepest truths of Christianity clear and its absolute claims plain to everyone. Something of a Presbyterian C. S. Lewis in this regard, Machen knew that simplicity need not be sacrificed for the sake of profundity. In this first-rate, if sadly unfinished, volume of theology and apologetics you get

both. Take it up and read to learn, to be strengthened and challenged, but most of all to be welcomed into a deeper communion with the living God."
—Derek Rishmawy, Reformed University Fellowship

"Someone said recently that we need 'a new Machen' to speak insightfully to present-day theological confusions. That would be great. But, thank the Lord, the old Machen does continue to teach us. These wonderful essays speak powerfully to all of us today—and with refreshing clarity."
—Richard Mouw, President Emeritus and Professor of Faith and Public Life, Fuller Theological Seminary

"In these still-timely essays we meet profundity wed with clarity. Illustrations from Machen's colorful life abound. His gift for practical expression shines, as does his knack for gentle suasion. Though he died in 1937, Machen sounds like a contemporary pundit in observing that 'we are in the midst of a tremendous emergency.' The response Machen offers: Help in rediscovering 'an old Book that has been sealed by the seals of prejudice and unbelief,' so that readers may 'come into communion with the living God.' This is a model of biblically faithful, creative, and insightful social commentary and theological exposition."
—Robert Yarbrough, Professor of New Testament, Covenant Theological Seminary

"These essays on the Reformed faith were forged long ago in the furnace of debate. They are, however, as fresh today, and as compelling, as they were when they were first delivered. Machen speaks with clarity, conviction, a matchless command of the subject, and with the wind of historic Christianity behind him."
—David Wells, Distinguished Senior Research Professor, Gordon-Conwell Theological Seminary

"J. Gresham Machen is one of a select band of Christian writers of whom it can truly be said that 'he being dead, yet speaketh.' This republication of some of his most important talks will be widely welcomed by those who appreciate his strong and learned defense of orthodoxy, and it will make his thought more accessible to a younger generation."
—Gerald Bray, Research Professor of Divinity, Beeson Divinity School

"I am so delighted that the faculty at Westminster Theological Seminary has decided to compile and publish these theological essays to present to the church this wonderful gift of the substance of Machen's theology. I hope that it gets a wide reading within the contemporary church so that its members might also recognize the present emergency of becoming blind to the things of God and to an 'unseen world.' In a very accessible and engaging way, Machen gives us a needed exhortation to pursue the true knowledge of God."
  —STEPHEN T. UM, Senior Minister, Citylife Presbyterian Church, Boston

"J. Gresham Machen was a hero of the faith and a rare scholar who mastered technical scholarship, popular writing, and dedicated himself to the life of the church. Machen's timeless monograph, *Christianity and Liberalism*, demonstrates that his clear and orthodox voice still resonates today. Readers will find that his almost-lost *Things Unseen* will speak with the same abiding authority."
  —DAN DORIANI, Professor of Biblical and Systematic Theology and Vice President at Large, Covenant Theological Seminary

"I first encountered J. Gresham Machen's work as an undergraduate student grappling with modern challenges to the Christian faith. I found in him a mind passionate for the truth and a heart aflame with the gospel. Both of these traits shine through in these essays from the 1930s. We still need to hear what he had to say."
  —TIMOTHY GEORGE, Distinguished Professor of Divinity, Beeson Divinity School

"Sanity regained in a world gone mad. J. Gresham Machen writes with a heart of love for the Lord Jesus. Cool, clear, and fresh as a mountain stream, he bubbles with living water. Doctrinal indifference, a big issue in his day, is the black plague of ours. The antidote to truth decay is his clarity about who Jesus was, what he said and did, and, above all, how he lives and reigns today."
  —PAUL WELLS, Emeritus Professor of Systematic Theology, Faculté Jean Calvin, Aix-en-Provence

"These gems by J. Gresham Machen are essential reading now for thoughtful Christians. Historians of conservative Protestantism will also greatly benefit from these essays. . . . Machen distills the core doctrines of Christian

theology that he fought so hard to defend against the acids of modernity. Listen for Machen's voice as you read these transcriptions. Lend your ear to this man whose apologetic labors hastened his tragic, early death."
—Douglas Sweeney, Dean and Professor of Divinity,
  Beeson Divinity School

"J. Gresham Machen was one of the lions of Reformed evangelical thought in the 20th century. His clarity of thought and courage borne of a deep conviction and a personal walk with the God about whom he spoke and wrote suffuses this entire book. With disarming simplicity, Machen presents the most important truths in the world and challenges us all to take them seriously. We need more of such clarity and directness today."
—Mark Thompson, Principal, Moore College

"J. Gresham Machen was the towering intellectual defender of historic Christianity during one of the most turbulent periods in American church history. These lectures on Reformed theology, delivered in the heat of the battle, are not merely an important theological voice from the past; they will encourage your faith today."
—Frank James, President and Professor of Historical Theology,
  Missio Seminary

"The church is rightly indebted to Machen for his and his associates' principled stand against the onslaught of liberalism in the academy and church. To these men Christianity was first and foremost about truth and that truth as revealed in Scripture and confessed by the church. It is because truth lies at the heart of true religion that he, in particular, had a passion to share it with lay people. This laypersons' guide to systematic theology proves to be an excellent introduction to the faith once delivered to the saints."
—Liam Goligher, Senior Minister, Tenth Presbyterian Church,
  Philadelphia

"Almost eighty years after his death, J. Gresham Machen's voice still speaks with timeliness. In our day, when people question whether Christians and Muslims worship the same God, Dr. Machen's cogent exposition of Scripture in these essays provides needed clarity."
—William Barker, Professor of Church History Emeritus,
  Westminster Theological Seminary

"Why am I regularly surprised at the way past authors speak powerfully to the present day? This is the way of all gifted authors: though they write in the past and thus in quite different circumstances, their writings have a timeless quality that more often than not makes them far more relevant than so much contemporary ephemera. Thus it is with these rich and lucid theological meditations of Gresham Machen: the 1930s were different in many ways than the present, but again and again his words address modern issues with such aplomb that they could have been written yesterday. Highly recommended."

    —MICHAEL A. G. HAYKIN, Professor of Church History and Biblical Spirituality and Director of the Andrew Fuller Center for Baptist Studies, Southern Baptist Theological Seminary

"This powerful book on Christian theology fully displays what made Machen great. We see his relentless logic in the clarity of his thinking and the lucidity of his prose."

    —THOMAS SCHREINER, James Buchanan Harrison Professor of New Testament Interpretation and Professor of Biblical Theology, Southern Baptist Theological Seminary

"Here is theology that floats like a butterfly and stings like a bee. In these essays Machen defends biblical doctrine with punch and quite stunning verve. Fresh, enlightening, and logically compelling, this is not only good theology but a model of good apologetics."

    —MICHAEL REEVES, President and Professor of Theology, Union School of Theology

THINGS UNSEEN

THINGS UNSEEN

A Systematic Introduction
to the Christian Faith and Reformed Theology

J. GRESHAM MACHEN

Foreword by Sinclair B. Ferguson
Preface by Stephen J. Nichols
Introduction by Timothy J. Keller
Afterword by Richard B. Gaffin, Jr.

Things Unseen:
A Systematic Introduction to the Christian Faith and Reformed Theology

Copyright © 2020 by Westminster Seminary Press
All Rights Reserved

No part of the copyrighted material
may be reproduced without the written consent of the publisher,
except for brief quotations for the purpose of review or comment.

Westminster Seminary Press
2960 Church Road, Glenside, Pennsylvania 19038

Email wsp@wts.edu to contact the publisher

Jacket and Cover Design by Jessica Hiatt
Typeset in Adobe Garamond by Angela Messinger

Printed and Bound by L.E.G.O S.p.A. in Italy.

Unless otherwise indicated, all English Scripture quotations are from
The Holy Bible, English Standard Version® (ESV®), copyright © 2001 by Crossway.
Used by permission. All rights reserved.

Hardcover ISBN: 978-1-7336272-4-5
Ebook ISBN: 978-1-7336272-5-2

Contents

Foreword by Sinclair B. Ferguson xvii
Historical Preface by Stephen J. Nichols xxi
Introduction by Timothy J. Keller. xxix

Part 1: *The Christian Faith in the Modern World*

   Preface. 3
1. The Present Emergency and How to Meet It 5
2. How May God Be Known?. 13
3. Has God Spoken?. 19
4. Is the Bible the Word of God?. 25
5. Do We Believe in Verbal Inspiration? 33
6. Shall We Defend the Bible?. 41
7. The Bible versus Human Authority. .49
8. Life Founded upon Truth 57
9. God, the Creator. 67
10. The Triune God 75
11. What Is the Deity of Christ?. 83
12. Does the Bible Teach the Deity of Christ?. 91
13. The Sermon on the Mount and the Deity of Christ 99
14. What Jesus Said about Himself 107
15. The Supernatural Christ 115
16. Did Christ Rise from the Dead? 123
17. The Testimony of Paul to Christ 131
18. The Holy Spirit. 139

Part 2: *The Christian View of Man*

   Preface. 149
19. The Living and True God 151
20. The Decrees of God 159
21. God's Decrees and Man's Freedom .167
22. What Is Predestination?. 175
23. Does the Bible Teach Predestination? 183

24.	Objections to Predestination	191
25.	God's Works of Creation and Providence	199
26.	God's Works of Providence	207
27.	Miracles	217
28.	Did God Create Man?	227
29.	How Did God Create Man?	235
30.	God's Image in Man	245
31.	The Covenant of Life	253
32.	The Fall of Man	263
33.	What Is Sin?	271
34.	The Majesty of the Law of God	279
35.	Is Mankind Lost in Sin?	289
36.	The Consequences of the Fall of Man	297
37.	What Is Original Sin?	305
38.	Sinners Saved by Grace	315

Part 3: The Final Broadcasts

39.	The Progress of Christian Doctrine	327
40.	The Creeds and Doctrinal Advance	335
41.	God, Man, and Salvation	343
42.	Christ as Prophet, Priest, and King	351
43.	What Is a Prophet?	359
44.	Prophecy and the Gospel	367
45.	The Teaching of Jesus	375
46.	Prophet and Priest	383
47.	Christ Our Redeemer	391
48.	The Doctrine of the Atonement	399
49.	The Active Obedience of Christ	407
50.	The Bible's View of the Atonement	415

Afterword by Richard B. Gaffin, Jr. 423
Indexes 427
Notes and Acknowledgments 445

Foreword

It is a privilege to serve as the herald who calls attention to this new collection of the work of J. Gresham Machen. Westminster Seminary Press certainly deserves to be congratulated for making the contents of *Things Unseen* available in this new form.

John Gresham Machen (1881-1937) was by any measure one of the towering figures in American Evangelicalism in the first half of the 20th century. He was born into a privileged and devoted Presbyterian family in Baltimore, Maryland. His father was a distinguished and scholarly lawyer, an avid reader, a linguist, and a man of theological acuity to boot. His mother—her husband's junior by more than twenty years—was also a great reader and a deeply thoughtful and sensitive Christian lady.

The young Machen was superbly well educated. Not only did he study classics with the leading Greek scholars of the day both at Johns Hopkins University and the University of Chicago, but thereafter went on to study theology under the most significant conservative scholars in the USA. He was thoroughly versed in Scripture and in the Shorter Catechism from his childhood, but his own Christian faith was permanently confirmed only after deep intellectual struggle.

Machen also became personally acquainted with the liberal theology of the continent of Europe and studied with its most impressive and scholarly representatives. He found some of them to be men of outstanding learning, immense commitment and religious conviction, and with considerable natural powers of communication. To that extent he regarded them with appreciation and respect. But he came to the conviction that the Jesus of whom they spoke was not the Christ of Scripture. He could not therefore save and transform. Partly as a result of this, for the rest of his life Machen sought to lay his very considerable intellectual and academic gifts at the feet of the living Christ, and devoted himself to expressing the gospel as clearly and fully as he could, whether in the pages of learned journals and books, or in more popular form.

The depth of Machen's conviction that liberal theology is not Christianity and the clarity and boldness with which he expressed this, eventually led him to sacrifice the immense privileges of professorship at Princeton Theological Seminary, along with his emotional connection to its history, for the humble beginnings of Westminster Theological Seminary. He would also give up the dignity of being a mainstream Presbyterian minister for the indignities of leadership in what would become the small Orthodox Presbyterian Church.

Although his life was cut short before his fifty-sixth birthday, Machen had already published works of permanent significance such as *The Virgin Birth of Christ* (1930)—a topic on which he had already written in his final year at Princeton—and his powerful manifesto, *Christianity and Liberalism* (1923). It is not difficult to see the providential hand of God in his life preparing him to write this latter volume, which continues to make a decisive impact on readers today. He had heard liberal theology "from the horse's mouth" as it were. He had admired some of its greatest exponents and assessed it with intellectual seriousness. Having weighed it in the balances he found it not only wanting but also capable of bankrupting both individual Christians and indeed the entire church. This helps to explain the vigor and power of his writing.

It is not always the case that an individual with such massive learning is as gifted a popular communicator as Machen. In fact, much of his published material was addressed not to theologians and scholars but to ordinary men and women. Thus, *What is Faith?* (1925) draws on sermons he had preached during the year it was published, while the posthumous *God Transcendent* (1949) contains an eight-message series preached in Princeton in 1923.

In addition to being frequently invited to preach in churches around the country, Machen became a relatively early entrant into the world of Christian broadcasting, and during what would prove to be the closing years of his life he delivered several series of weekly radio addresses. These messages are reprinted here, and they make for nourishing reading. They are talks of a straightforward, personal, serious and biblically literate kind, addressed to intelligent, thinking Christians.

Things Unseen covers many areas of systematic theology. Here you will find pieces on revelation and Scripture, as well as on God as Triune and as Creator, and on man created as his image but, alas, now fallen, with all the tragic entail of human sin. Machen also handles the themes of creation and providence, and the person, ministry, and work of Christ. He did not attempt to deal in comprehensive detail with all these topics. But it is clear from the contents of this book that he recognized the importance in the contemporary world, as well as in first century Ephesus, of teaching "the whole counsel of God" (Acts 20:27).

There is no dichotomy or schizophrenia here between the preacher, the biblical scholar, and the systematic theologian. Indeed, although a New Testament scholar, Machen at times discussed the themes of these radio sermons with his younger Westminster colleague and systematic theology professor, John Murray. In preparation for his penultimate radio message on December 20, 1936, Machen consulted with Murray about the nature and significance of Christ's whole life of obedience. Less than two weeks later, as he lay dying in a hospital bed in Bismarck, North Dakota, where he had gone to preach, he sent a brief telegram to Murray: "I'm so thankful for active obedience of Christ. No hope without it." It was his final personal testimony to the wonderful comfort of a theology that is rooted in Scripture and to his own faith in Christ.

Profound scholarly learning, deep personal faith, and God-created courage characterized Machen's mature life. For that reason alone, everything he published is worth reading. This book provides a wonderful sample. Those who already love his work will rejoice to see these chapters in print again. And if this is your first exposure to him, and you are wondering whether a scholar's words may fly far above your head, you will soon discover that—like his Savior—Machen was able to speak and preach in such a way that ordinary people heard him gladly.

Much of what Gresham Machen wrote was prophetic and remains relevant to the church in our own day. Indeed, the messages in this volume are timeless. For orthodoxy, clarity, and sheer gospel verve they are hard to beat. If they do not at first strike you that way, remember that they were originally scripts. They were written with a view to being spoken, and so the best way to feel their force may be to read them out loud to yourself or to someone else.

Do this and it will almost certainly become clear that you are listening to clear-headed biblical Christianity at its finest. And you will perhaps sense why it is that Machen's personal presence made such an impression on people and why they followed his lead. Here then, "through his faith, though he died, he still speaks" (Heb 11:4). That is indeed a cause of thanksgiving. But it is also the best reason to encourage you now to read on in the pages that follow. Be instructed, encouraged, humbled, strengthened, and best of all—as Machen would have wished—be brought to a deeper knowledge of, trust in, and love for the Lord and for his Word.

> Sinclair B. Ferguson
> Visiting Scholar of Systematic Theology
> Westminster Theological Seminary, Philadelphia

Historical Preface

The most effective way to be timely is to be timeless. Perhaps no Christian leader in the modern age personifies this maxim more than J. Gresham Machen. The first lines of the first address in this book attest to the timelessness of Machen's aims. The first address is entitled, "The Present Emergency and How to Meet It." This sounds like Machen will be holding the newspaper as he speaks into the microphone in the studio at WIP in Philadelphia. That is not, however, what he's up to. Machen, in fact, tells us that he will not be talking "about the topics that are usually regarded as most timely just now."[1] Instead of addressing the headlines and emergencies of 1935, he addresses a timeless emergency and points to an eternal solution.

From the beginning, Machen says he will be talking about two things: God, and the unseen world. In these talks, Machen reminds us of what is absolute, what is eternal, and what is ultimately real. God—not modern man—is ultimate. The unseen world is eternal; the space and time of 1935 and 1936 was passing. This is not to say that Machen was unengaged and out of touch with his time. It is to say that he knew what his time needed most—and it is exactly what we need to hear in our time too.

When, as an incoming student, Machen first arrived at Princeton in 1902, he was greeted by tree-lined streets and ivy-covered walls well suited to a bucolic scholarly life. He studied divinity at Princeton Seminary and philosophy in the graduate school at Princeton University. He cut classes to watch football games. He took the train to New York City to take in a Broadway show. After his master's degrees at Princeton, he spent time in Germany in doctoral studies. He returned in 1906 to take a position as instructor at the seminary and moved into his apartment on the top floor of Alexander Hall. It was, as Edith Wharton's novel put it, the age of innocence. Soon, however, just as it does in Wharton's novel, the age of innocence at Princeton would pass.

The stalwart at Princeton in those days was none other than B. B. Warfield, who would become a mentor to Machen. Warfield's funeral in

1. See page 5 of this volume

1921, in Miller Chapel on the campus of Princeton Seminary, prompted a legendary line from Machen. As the pallbearers walked Warfield's casket down the aisle and out the chapel doors, Machen observed, "They're carrying 'Old Princeton' with him."[2] The observation was astute. From then on, Machen found himself at odds with his seminary and, then, with his denomination. Wave upon wave of controversy would find him, from the mid-1920s until the time he started airing these addresses in 1935.

Much good came from all that conflict. The first to come from it was Machen's *Christianity and Liberalism*, published in 1923. In this book, Machen offers an argument both timeless and timely for a contemporary crisis. The crisis was liberalism, ricocheting through the church. Liberalism was a response to modernism. Modernism gave a high place to man, man's achievements, and man's potential. The grandeur of man loomed so large that little room, if any, was left for God. Leadership in the denominations and seminaries panicked. Until now they had enjoyed a seat at the table, as it were, in American culture, and they feared these new modern sensibilities would cut them out. Hoping to keep their seat at the table and their influence, they accommodated Christianity to these new sensibilities. Put another way, they compromised. Harry Emerson Fosdick personified this. His sermon, "Shall the Fundamentalists Win?" paved a way forward for liberals. He offered a new way of thinking about the Bible, about sin, about salvation, and about Christ.

Fosdick's sermon also paved the way for *Christianity and Liberalism*, which argued that liberal Christianity was not Christianity at all, but an entirely different religion, cunningly crafted to undermine biblical orthodoxy. With the publication of that book, Machen's bucolic days at Princeton were over. From here on in, even to the end of his life on January 1, 1937, Machen would remain in the throes of controversy and conflict.

The first major wave of conflict came in 1926. The board of Princeton Seminary approved Machen's appointment to the chair of apologetics. The decision then was passed along to the General Assembly for approval, by what should have been a purely perfunctory vote. The committee at the Assembly, however, delayed voting on the matter. This action on behalf of the denomination thinly veiled a growing distrust of Machen. The

---

2. In a letter to his mother the day after Warfield's funeral, Machen wrote "It seems to me that the old Princeton—a great institution it was—died when Dr. Warfield was carried out," Machen Archives, Westminster Theological Seminary.

denomination was influenced by moderates who sought peace at the expense of confessional fidelity. Machen and his message were not welcome. The action of the denomination caught the attention of the media, even *The New York Times*.³ Neither did it escape the attention of all those in the denomination, including Machen's former students. One of those former students sent Machen a telegram: "The love, devotion, and loyalty of hundreds of your former students go out to you at this bitter hour."⁴ More bitter hours were to come.

The second major wave of conflict came with the reorganization of the board of Princeton Seminary in 1929. Immediately on the heels of the reorganization, Machen packed up his belongings from 39 Alexander Hall, moved across the Delaware River, and opened the doors of Westminster Theological Seminary in a Center City Philadelphia brownstone. The name of the institution signaled a commitment to confessional orthodoxy. Machen's seminary would stand firmly against accommodating the timeless teaching of Scripture to winds of cultural favor.

The third major wave came in 1935, when Machen was defrocked of his ministerial credentials because of his founding the Independent Board for Presbyterian Foreign Missions. In response he formed a new denomination that would be, like the seminary, firmly committed to the confessional standards: the Orthodox Presbyterian Church.

Out of all of these bitter hours in Machen's life, good things had come. These conflicts spawned the most well-known aspects of Machen's legacy: *Christianity and Liberalism*, Westminster Theological Seminary, and the Orthodox Presbyterian Church. Another major aspect of his legacy—his confidence in the Truth and his devotion to faithful communication of the Truth—is exemplified by the radio addresses presented in this volume.

Edwin H. Rian, a former student of Machen's and member of the board of trustees of Westminster Seminary, arranged for the broadcasts in the hope that they would help to promote the seminary. Colleges and seminaries trade on their legacy, rely upon their alumni, and lean on their reputation. Start-ups need to cultivate all constituencies, from prospective

---

3. "Dr. Machen Keeps Silent: Refuses to Comment on Action of the General Assembly." *New York Times*, June 3, 1926.
4. Cited in Stephen J. Nichols, *J. Gresham Machen: A Guided Tour of His Life and Thought* (Phillipsburg: P&R, 2004) 56. Original telegram in Machen Archives, Westminster Theological Seminary, Philadelphia.

students to a donor base. The broadcast would help in those areas. In the hands of Machen, however, they would accomplish much more. Tuning in to WIP became part of the daily routine for many Philadelphians, and Machen had something he wanted to say to them.[5]

Machen grew up surrounded by books. He read the Greek poets in Greek. He read the Latin classics in Latin. Modernist critics, with no dog in the fundamentalist-liberal fight, noted the brilliance of Machen's books.[6] He knew words well, and the power of words even better. He could craft a sentence. But as you read these addresses you begin to realize how well he understood the timbre of words and the rhythm of spoken English. These addresses were meant to be heard by someone leaning in to their Philco or Victor radio. Machen gets personal and direct in these messages. Read them and you will *hear* Machen.

There's a great deal of sympathy in Machen's voice. He relates, without pandering. Sample this paragraph:

> What is true about humanity as a whole is also true, I venture to think, about you. The world is weary and perplexed today. Well, how is it with you? Are you contented with your lives as they are now? I suppose that many of you are. But some of you, I know, are discontented, and are looking for something entirely different from that which you now possess. That is true of rich as well as of poor; it has little to do with your particular situation in the world. To such hungry souls I think I have something to say in this little series of talks; and there are many hungry souls today.[7]

Machen here echoes his ending to *Christianity and Liberalism*, in which a soul, hungry for truth and "weary with the conflicts of the world," is seen wandering into the church, seeking refreshment.[8] And what is this soul given? Stones instead of bread. Machen pleads with the church to proclaim the

---

5. WIP was founded by the Gimbel brothers, the namesake of Gimbels Department Store, which opened in Philadelphia in 1894. In 1922, they began the radio station with the antenna high atop their building at Ninth and Market Streets. The radio station soon had its own success and moved out from the auspices of the department store. In 1935, when Machen began recording, the studio moved into its own quarters on South Ninth Street.

6. See H. L. Mencken's obituary for Machen: "Dr. Fundamentalis" *Baltimore Evening Sun*, January 18, 1937.

7. See page 10 of this volume.

8. J. Gresham Machen, *Christianity and Liberalism* (Grand Rapids: Baker, 1946), 179.

gospel, and simply to be the church, "in sole reliance upon the Savior who bought us with his blood." For, he declares with conviction, "from under the threshold of that house will go forth a river that will revive the weary world."[9]

The compassion detectable in Machen's voice stems from his sympathy with the true condition of his audience. He knew that, apart from the gospel, God was far off. Weary and hungry souls were Machen's audience. God, and the unseen world, were Machen's solution.

Consider Machen's second address, "How May God Be Known?" This world "presents pressing problems," he readily admits. But those problems will never be solved "unless you first face the question of your relation to God."[10] God—not what we see—is ultimate.

When Machen says "God," he means, of course, nearly the whole scope and complex of theology. He discusses the Bible, the Trinity, the person and work of Christ, the decrees of God, and even predestination. In these short radio addresses intended for a general audience (which means there will be "secular" people listening in), he talks about predestination not once but three times. Machen had a deeply-rooted conviction that theology alone could deliver that urgently needed timeless message, because all of our problems are ultimately theological, and all of the solutions are, consequently, ultimately theological.

Machen had many demands on his time. The infant seminary required all the attention he could give it and more. He was in constant demand as a speaker. He was the *de facto* leader of fundamentalism's more intellectual wing. Yet he chose to devote time to these talks for the people of Philadelphia.

R. C. Sproul has said that the one thing that sets the Reformers apart is that they were not "Ivory Tower" theologians, but they were "Battlefield" theologians. And more, the Reformers took the message to the people. The same is true of Machen. Although he lived in something like an ivory tower for a time—in ivy-covered Alexander Hall at Princeton—Machen was a fighter. In the preface to the second collection of essays in this book, he says that he "believes that the Reformed faith should be preached as well as taught in the classroom, and that the need for the preaching of it is particularly apparent at the present time. The author is trying to preach it in this little book, and preach it very specifically to the people of our generation."[11]

Machen, like the Reformers of the 16th century, lacked no boldness

---

9. Ibid., 180.
10. See page 13 of this volume.
11. See page 149 of this volume.

or courage in defending and contending for the doctrines of grace. Ned Stonehouse, his colleague at Westminster and his biographer, called him "Valiant for Truth."[12] An homage to *Pilgrim's Progress*, the reference also speaks to what animated Machen—that people would know the Truth. Machen was a battlefield theologian who took the message directly to the people—the very message contained in the fifty addresses collected here.

In addition to being a preacher, at one point Machen also self-identifies as an apologist. It may be recalled that Princeton Seminary appointed Machen as a chair of apologetics. While Machen never held the title of professor of apologetics, that did not keep him from the vocation. He says, "I believe with all my soul, in other words, in the necessity of Christian apologetics—the necessity of a reasoned defense of the Christian faith, and in particular a reasoned defense of the Christian conviction that the Bible is the Word of God."[13] And although Machen served as pulpit supply and preached regularly, he never held a pastorate. In fact, he was reluctant to seek ordination. But this did not keep him from the vocation. Machen was a preacher-apologist.

What we need to notice is the content that Machen felt so compelled to preach and defend. We have already mentioned that when Machen says he's going to talk about God what he means is that he will talk about a wide range of theological topics. Machen's content was theology, even specific points of theology.

At the end of these addresses Machen turns his attention to the work of Christ. The next to the last address concerns the active obedience of Christ. Machen explains that theologians use the expressions of the passive obedience and the active obedience of Christ to explain the full extent of what Christ accomplished in his life and death. Keep in mind these were short, weekly radio addresses for a general audience. After walking through the corridors of this particular doctrine, Machen pulls all the threads of the discussion together in this clear and succinct paragraph: "We can put it briefly by saying that Christ took our place with respect to the law of God. He paid for us the law's penalty, and he obeyed for us the law's commands. He saved us from hell, and he earned for us our entrance into heaven. All that we have, then, we owe unto him. There is no blessing that we have in this world or the next for which we should not give Christ thanks."[14]

---

12. Ned B. Stonehouse, *J. Gresham Machen: A Biographical Memoir* (Grand Rapids: Eerdmans, 1954), 7.
13. See page 43 of this volume.
14. See page 410 of this volume.

When the fall semester of 1936 ended, Machen forwent much needed rest. Word of disputes in some of the fledgling churches of the new denomination in North Dakota came to Machen's attention. His colleagues pleaded with him not to go but to take some well-deserved time off. He went. While there Machen developed pleurisy, which then developed into pneumonia. He spent the very last moments of his life in a hospital in Bismarck. He died on January 1, 1937.

Just before his death he sent a telegram to John Murray, his colleague back at Westminster: "I'm so thankful for the active obedience of Christ. No hope without it."

Read the final lines of the very last address in this book. That address aired on the last Sunday afternoon of 1936. He lets his listeners know how encouraged he has been by them. He then says, "I trust that you have had a very joyous Christmas and I trust that the new year which is so soon to begin may be to you a very blessed year under the mercy of God."[15] While Machen only lived into the first few hours of 1937, he knew the blessing of living—and dying—under the mercy of God. The gospel is the timeless message that is always timely. That was true for Machen in 1935 and 1936, and it was true for him on January 1, 1937, as he drew his final breath.

These addresses, originally aired on WIP in Philadelphia in the 1930s, helped to promote Westminster Theological Seminary. Then it was a start-up. Now it is in its third generation, continuing to stand for the same timeless Truth that Machen proclaimed and defended in these addresses some eighty years ago. Machen said he started the seminary to train specialists in the Bible. That's what he was. But he was not your ordinary specialist. He was the kind of specialist who knew how to take the message to the people. May this publication of Machen's addresses find a whole new audience of weary and hungry souls in need of the refreshing river of life of the gospel. May they also inspire a whole new generation to take up the task Machen did so ably nearly a century ago, and to take this message directly to the people.

>   Stephen J. Nichols
>   President and Professor of Apologetics,
>   Reformation Bible College
>   Chief Academic Officer,
>   Ligonier Ministries

---

15. See page 422 of this volume.

Introduction

Machen's Rhetorical Approach

This book presents J. Gresham Machen's popular radio addresses, delivered over station WIP in Philadelphia on Sunday afternoons during 1935 and 1936. He wrote and gave fifty such "little talks," as he often referred to them. According to John Murray, he had envisioned at least four series that would have been published in four volumes.[1] The first series, of eighteen messages, was broadcast over the first four months of 1935, covering the doctrines of the knowledge of God, of the Word, of God, of Christ's person, and of the Holy Spirit. It was published in February 1936 as *The Christian Faith in the Modern World*. The second series, of twenty messages, was broadcast in late 1935 and early 1936, covering the doctrines of the decrees of God, creation and providence, of man, and of sin and grace. These were published in early 1937 as *The Christian View of Man*, just after Machen's death. He had begun a third series in the fall of 1936, and broadcast twelve of them. Five of these were published in a volume of sermons and addresses, *God Transcendent*, in 1949. The remaining seven were published in *The Presbyterian Guardian* in 1940.[2]

The word "innovative" is not a term we usually associate with J. Gresham Machen, but he was carefully breaking new ground with these messages. Not that he was the first minister to go on the air. Radio preachers had been doing that since the early 1920s, and they were not just fundamentalists and Pentecostals. Sunday broadcasts were delivered by prominent mainline Protestants such as S. Parkes Cadman, Ralph W. Sockman, and Harry Emerson Fosdick. But these were all *sermons*, even sometimes aired on Sunday mornings, which enabled Americans to get their inspiration in the comfort of their homes without the need for church participation. Machen was much more judicious. His Sunday afternoon talks were not sermons but expositions of doctrine—a layman's systematic theology, as it were. And

---

1. John Murray, "Foreword to the British Edition," in J. Gresham Machen, *The Christian View of Man* (London: Banner of Truth, 1965), 7.
2. "The Progress of Christian Doctrine," in *The Presbyterian Guardian*, January 1940; "God, Man and Salvation," in *The Presbyterian Guardian*, March 1940; "Christ as Prophet, Priest and King," in *The Presbyterian Guardian*, April 1940; "What Is a Prophet?" in *The Presbyterian Guardian*, May 1940; "Prophecy and the Gospel," in *The Presbyterian Guardian*, June 1940; "The Teaching of Jesus," in *The Presbyterian Guardian*, July 1940; "Prophet and Priest," in *The Presbyterian Guardian*, August 1940.

Machen was the only first-class theologian and scholar I know of who took to the airwaves to popularize historic Christian truth without watering it down in the slightest, and to do so with a strong apologetic bent, including a direct appeal to skeptics.[3]

We know this much about the material. What are less well-known are Machen's aims and motives for engaging in such an ambitious project while he was under so much pressure. Indeed, he began these broadcasts the very year he was being tried by the Presbytery of New Brunswick and suspended from the ministry. He continued writing and delivering them as he was founding a new denomination and leading the still new Westminster Seminary in Philadelphia, founded in 1929. The talks aired right up to Sunday, December 27, just five days before he died.[4]

Why did he do it? The basic idea came from his young friend Edwin H. Rian, a member of Westminster's Board of Trustees, and a chief fundraiser and recruiter for the school.[5] Machen only mentions the seminary four times in the talks, but by the beginning of the final series he calls the broadcast the "Westminster Seminary Hour," a title that does not appear earlier. It's likely that Rian and Machen hoped to use the radio addresses to promote the seminary, and it does appear that increasing the profile of Westminster loomed larger in Machen's mind over the two years he was writing them. In early 1936 nearly half of the seminary's Board of Trustees resigned in a dispute over Machen's establishment of the Independent Board for Presbyterian Foreign Missions. With that loss, the importance of promoting the seminary and finding new students and supporters became even more crucial. Several times in the talks Machen takes the opportunity to make his case that "the more Christian scholarship you have, so much the more evangelism. Out of real theological seminaries, where the Bible is expounded and defended, come ministers and evangelists who know what they believe and why they believe it."[6]

Machen himself tells us something about his motives is in the preface

---

3. The only parallel that springs to mind is C.S. Lewis' radio broadcasts over BBC during World War II. But while Lewis was a world-class scholar like Machen, also doing apologetics on the air, Lewis was a layman, not a theologically trained minister. Interestingly, Machen's junior colleague Paul Woolley reviewed Lewis's published radio talks in 1944, critiquing them rightly for doctrinal missteps, but nonetheless calling them a "brilliant statement" of reasons to believe in Christianity. See his review in *Westminster Theological Journal* 6, no. 2 (1944): 210–14.

4. Ned B. Stonehouse, "Introduction," in J. Gresham Machen, *God Transcendent* (Edinburgh: Banner of Truth, 1982), 13.

5. See pages 3 and 149 of this volume.

6. See page 45 of this volume.

to *The Christian View of Man*, where he writes that he is not content simply to teach Christian doctrine "in the classroom." Rather, in these talks he tries "to preach it . . . and preach it very specifically to the people of our generation."[7] In the very next sentence he clarifies that the addresses are not sermons, yet he can still call it "preaching" because he is here showing that solid and clear doctrine is "not something useful merely to the theologian but a matter of the most vital concern to every man."[8] Machen's comment that he was especially aiming at this "generation" is echoed in Stonehouse's observation that these were "popular expositions of Christian doctrine" in which he was seeking to be "helpful especially to college students."[9]

This explains Machen's style of speaking in these addresses. It is remarkably jargon-free, clear, personal, reasonable, and calm—all traits that make the talks highly accessible. They are indeed *talks*, not merely essays read over the air. There are plenty of oralisms (e.g., "but wait a minute"). He speaks dialogically—stopping to pose typical objections and questions and then answer them, giving the hearers the sense that they are engaged in a back and forth conversation with Machen. He deploys down-to-earth illustrations and references to his own personal experiences. And even though each talk is still more like an instructor's lesson than a preacher's sermon, Machen continually breaks into expressions of admiration and even wonder at God and his truth.

While these are the marks of his style throughout the fifty talks, as we read them in order, it becomes clear that there is a change in the primary audience he is addressing across the three series.

The early chapters most frequently speak to people who do not believe in the Christian faith, or at least not in orthodoxy. His first talk uses the darkening world situation of 1935 to argue that human understanding and knowledge is inadequate to deal with our problems, and that we need a revelation from God. Throughout this first series Machen makes his case for the authority of the Bible, the deity of Christ, and the resurrection, using arguments similar to the classical apologetics of Old Princeton.[10] But while he may have gotten his basic lines of reasoning from Warfield and the Hodges, he presents them with such easy-to-grasp, compelling clarity that (I believe but cannot prove) later popular apologists in the 20th century

---

7. See page 149 of this volume.
8. See page 149 of this volume.
9. Stonehouse, "Introduction," 13.
10. See Dennison, available at www.wts.edu/ThingsUnseen

got their basic approaches from him. Even though he is rigorously logical, he also reaches at times for the heart. When he makes the case for the Bible being the inspired Word of God, he certainly asserts it as an objective truth, but he is not above recommending it for its sublime, subjective comfort: "[I]f a man founds his life upon it he can be very joyous and quite undismayed in all the sorrows and all the battles that may come upon him in this world."[11] Here he addresses primarily listeners who do not believe the basic doctrines of the Word and of God, and he always distinguishes the historic and orthodox view from modernist substitutes.

The most striking thing about this first series is how directly evangelistic Machen is. He ends the talk on "God, the Creator" with a call to find peace with God through his Word.[12] He ends "Does the Bible Teach the Deity of Christ?" with a word to "that great army of persons who stand outside the household of faith." He urges them to pray to God, saying "help my unbelief."[13] He ends "The Sermon on the Mount" with an appeal that listeners not see Jesus as merely "a religious genius" but rather that they would fight through their doubts to say with Thomas, "My Lord and my God."[14] At the conclusion of "What Jesus Said about Himself," he confronts listeners: "Which are you, my friends? . . . Do you belong to those who rely upon the wisdom of this world and turn aside from Christ? Or . . . will you come to him that he may give you rest?"[15] Of the last ten talks in the first series, eight end with an evangelistic call, some gentle, others remarkably forceful.

When we get to the second series, however, his primary audience are Christians. Only one of these twenty talks ends with any reference to those who may not yet believe.[16] And while in the first series Machen quotes the Shorter Catechism several times, he never uses the term "Reformed" to talk about his faith or doctrine in either his introduction or his addresses. That changes completely in the second series. His Preface says that these talks present the "Reformed Faith" and that the doctrines he is expounding are

---

11. See page 28 of this volume.
12. See page 74 of this volume.
13. See page 106 of this volume.
14. See page 106 of this volume.
15. See pages 113–114 of this volume.
16. Machen says: "The world is lost in sin, and you too are lost in sin unless the Holy Spirit has led you or is leading you at this hour to have recourse to God's grace which has been extended to your freely and wonderfully in Jesus Christ our Lord." See page 296 of this volume.

the "Reformed doctrines" of man, sin, and grace.[17] Within this second series Machen expounds the Reformed doctrines of predestination and providence. In the second to last talk, after citing Charles Hodge's *Systematic Theology*, Machen says that "for my part I rejoice greatly in trying to stand in the great current of the Reformed faith. If I can show you a little bit of what that great system of doctrine is and a little bit of the basis for it in the Word of God, the purpose of these talks will have been fully attained."[18]

Why the change in audience-focus? I believe it was appropriate and inevitable with the change in topics. In general, the doctrines of the first series were doctrines held by all Protestants. In *Christianity and Liberalism* Machen says that while "a Calvinist is constrained to regard the Arminian theology as a serious impoverishment of the Scripture doctrine of divine grace . . ." and adds that Arminians think Reformed thought is similarly impoverished, "yet . . . true evangelical fellowship is possible between those who hold, with regard to some exceedingly important matters, sharply opposing views."[19] That passing comment helps us understand the difference between the first and second series. There is no need to publicly call the deity of Christ a "Reformed" doctrine, since it is held in common by Christians in all theological traditions. To convince people who do not believe is to evangelize them, and that is exactly what Machen does, with vigor. But in the second series Machen gets to the topics of the character of our fallen condition and how God's grace saves us, and here we arrive at contested territory *within* the Christian church. When Machen seeks to convince people who do not believe in total depravity and electing grace, he rightly speaks to Christians. They are the people who are in a position to believe these doctrines because they accept the doctrines in the first series.

In short, when Machen makes his case for the doctrines of the Word, of God, and of Christ, he is seeking to turn non-Christians into Christians. But when he makes his case for the doctrine of sin and the need for God's predestination and grace, he is trying to bring Christians into the Reformed faith.

In the third, unfinished series, Machen continues to speak largely to

---

17. See page 149 of this volume.
18. See page 310 of this volume.
19. J. Gresham Machen, *Christianity and Liberalism* (Grand Rapids: Eerdmans, 1968), 51–52. It is worth reflecting on Machen's belief that he could have "true evangelical fellowship" with Arminians. He may have meant that he regarded Arminians as fellow evangelical Christians or perhaps more generally that he shared a belief with them in the evangel or the gospel. There is an interesting balance here, in which Machen expresses his view that Arminianism has an "impoverished" gospel, and yet claims that it has the gospel nonetheless.

believers and to show them the beauties of the Reformed understanding of grace. Even when he returns to a "gospel invitation" at the end of "God, Man, and Salvation," he does so in a way that differs from the earlier ones. He says, "if any one of you has not received Jesus as your Savior you may do so at this very moment," but immediately adds, "God grant that some of you within the sound of my voice today may receive the message and may show thereby that from all eternity you have been foreordained unto adoption as God's children through Jesus Christ our Lord."[20] Unlike the earlier invitations to put faith in Christ, this one assumes the listener has much more understanding of—and even agreement with—the doctrine of predestination. And yet in these very last talks on the atonement Machen returns to touching gospel appeals even when teaching rather advanced lessons in doctrine. At the end of "The Active Obedience of Christ," he says:

> People sometimes say, indeed, that it makes little difference what theory of the atonement we may hold. Ah, my friends, it makes all the difference in the world. When you contemplate the cross of Christ, do you say merely, with modern theorists, "What a noble example of self-sacrifice: I am going to attain favor with God by sacrificing myself as well as he." Or do you say with the Bible, "He loved me and gave himself for me; he took my place; he bore my curse; he bought me with his own precious blood." That is the most momentous question that can come to any human soul.[21]

What then, can preachers and communicators of God's Word today learn from Machen?

I believe we can learn a great deal, but first we may need to do some ground clearing. Contemporary readers should not be put off by the somewhat antiquated language, which may strike our ears as flowery or patronizing at times. Nor should we be too troubled by the places where he seems to emphasize classical argumentation more than his own successors, such as Cornelius Van Til, would have. Despite the influence of Scottish "common sense realism" on Machen,[22] he is too biblically grounded to have his

---

20. See page 349–350 of this volume.
21. See pages 414 of this volume.
22. See "Understanding J. Gresham Machen," in George M. Marsden, *Understanding Fundamentalism and Evangelicalism* (Grand Rapids: Eerdmans, 1991), 182–201. See also Dennison's discussion in his essay at www.wts.edu/ThingsUnseen

evangelistic appeals depend on human reason. He continually reminds his audience that none of his arguments will make any sense without the intervention of the Holy Spirit.[23]

One more thing to keep in mind is this: Even though Machen speaks directly to non-believers, mid-1930s American society was still heavily influenced by Christianity. Critics of the faith, too, were more traditional in their ways of thinking and particularly in their views of morality than they are today. Machen was indeed unusually far-sighted about the implications and potential consequences of modernist thinking, but the "triumph of the therapeutic" and the sexual revolution had not yet happened. So, the skeptics and non-believers of his day were not in every way like the skeptics that we encounter today. And yet unbelief in any age shares enough common elements that Machen's exhortations and arguments remain an enormous help.

So, what should we learn from him?

First, we should learn to both propagate *and* defend the faith, rather than only one or the other. When we look at the old purpose statement of Princeton Seminary, namely to produce graduates who "propagate and defend" the Reformed faith, we can say Machen is one of the few who could do both. We marvel at how easily Machen goes back and forth from being an incisive apologist in evangelism to the skeptics (not just writing about apologetics but doing it), to being a profound instructor in Reformed doctrine to the baptized. I can't think of any of his peers or even successors who combined these abilities so successfully. We should not look at his gifts and be discouraged, however. We should learn from him and emulate him to the degree we are able. We who are academics should strive to propagate the faith, not just defend it with scholarship. We who are practitioners should not despise the scholarly defense of the faith, but incorporate it into our evangelism.

Second, we should freely glean from him. On virtually every page these addresses bristle with ideas for preaching and communicating the great doctrines of the faith. Machen's talks have been an enormously formative influence on my preaching, especially after I came to New York City. While seven of his messages here are new to me, I have returned to the rest of them repeatedly over the years as an unparalleled storehouse of great illustrations, delineations, and arguments for Christian doctrines. There is

---

23. For example: "Do you know that triune God as your God, my friends? . . . We pray that the Holy Spirit may enable you to believe in the Son, and that, redeemed by His precious blood, you may stand in the Father's presence for evermore." See page 145 of this volume.

nothing quite like it, except for C.S. Lewis' own broadcast talks. But Lewis never provided a case for the Reformed faith.

For years I have used Machen's illustration of Paul in the storm (Acts 27) to explain the congruence of divine sovereignty with human responsibility.[24] There is another place in the early talks were Machen makes a startling rhetorical move. He confronts the view that the Bible is only true regarding its moral ideals but not necessarily true when it deals with history. Instead of merely refuting the objection using rational arguments, he gets intensely personal. He tells any listeners who hold that view they are actually "mocking" him and failing to give him what he really needs as a flawed, sinful man: "What *I* need first of all is not exhortation but a gospel, not directions for saving myself but knowledge for the way God has saved me. Have you any good news for me? . . . your exhortations will not help me."[25] Those who have heard my preaching know that this approach and way of describing the contrast between moralism and grace has been crucial to how I've worded my appeals over the years.

Another, more controversial way in which Machen can be a guide (and has been for me) is in how he approaches science, and particularly the area of creation and evolution. Remember that this is the author of *Christianity and Liberalism*, in which it was argued that modernist Christianity is not really Christianity at all but a different religion altogether. There is no more staunch and uncompromising defender of orthodox Christianity than Machen. And yet he writes: "It is certainly not necessary to think that the six days spoken of in that first chapter of the Bible are intended to be six days of twenty-four hours each."[26] In "Did God Create Man?" he contradicts both what today is called Young Earth Creationism *and* theistic evolution. He argues both for an old earth and for the special creation of Adam and Eve. This shows that Machen was not afraid to use innovative arguments when speaking to issues of science and faith.[27]

---

24. See pages 195–196 of this volume.
25. See page 39 of this volume.
26. See page 228 of this volume.
27. Scientists argue that "the most minute similarity" exists between humanity and lower animals, making it appear certain that we evolved from those lower animals by a natural process. Machen points out that Jesus' body, in the virgin birth, was produced by a supernatural act of God yet would not, if it had been examined by a doctor, have appeared to been produced by anything other than natural processes. Then he asks why God's supernatural, special creation of the first man could not have been the same? "If there was an entrance of the immediate power of God in connection with the origin of the human life of Jesus, why may there not have been also an entrance of the immediate power of God in the case of the first man who ever appeared on the earth? If similarity of bodily structure does not disprove that occurrence of the miracle in the one case, why should it do so in the other?" See page 233 of this volume.

Another thing we can learn from him is this: We should be as ready as Machen was to be open to new ways of reaching people with gospel truth. Machen was by no means prone to like new technologies just because they were new and "cool" (a word that for him, thankfully, had not yet been given its new meaning). Indeed, his temperament seems to have made him ordinarily skeptical of modern developments. Yet he was open to this new technology of radio. He didn't reject it even though its use was dominated by Pentecostal, Catholic, and liberal ministers. He envisioned accomplishing something new and ambitious with it, namely, the popularization of orthodox, Reformed Christian doctrine and, on its basis, doing direct evangelism to the masses. None of his Princeton colleagues and predecessors in the academy had ever tried anything like it. Nor, really, were any of his contemporaries in the gospel ministry of the church capable of it, even if they were motivated to try.

There has always been a pessimism among conservative Reformed people that our doctrine simply can't be expressed in a fashion that has any kind of broader appeal. Machen, on the other hand, did not refrain from media just because it had been misused. He did not fear or oppose innovation even though he was judicious in his use of it. And he was not pessimistic about the popular appeal of orthodox doctrine, even as he was experiencing heart-breaking rejection on so many fronts because of his stand for it.

Finally, we should learn from Machen that we must not just hold our doctrine intellectually—we must let it shape our inward life and heart. Repeated readings of this material have impressed me with how much Machen simply rejoiced and exulted in the doctrines of the Reformed faith. Despite his being a very rational thinker, he is constantly, spontaneously falling into expressions of gratitude and amazement at the truths he is presenting. The greatest testimony to this is the now well-known way that Machen faced death itself recalling the doctrine presented in the second last talk, "The Active Obedience of Christ." On the day of his death he sent John Murray a telegram message dictated through his nurse. "I'm so thankful for the active obedience of Christ. No hope without it."[28] Indeed.

Timothy J. Keller
Founding Pastor, Emeritus
Redeemer Presbyterian Church, New York City

---

28. Stonehouse, "Introduction," 14

THINGS UNSEEN

Part 1

The Christian Faith in the Modern World

Preface to *The Christian Faith in the Modern World*

During the first four months of the year 1935, the author of this book delivered a course of radio addresses over Station WIP, the arrangements for which were made by the Rev. Edwin H. Rian on behalf of Westminster Theological Seminary. The addresses are here published in a form very similar to that in which they were delivered. The resulting book may perhaps lay claim to a larger degree of unity than that which is usually possessed by published addresses because these addresses proceeded in logical sequence. Little more than a beginning, however, is made of the treatment of the subject indicated in the title. The Christian view of the Bible and a part of the biblical doctrine of God are presented (of course only in summary fashion), whereas other great elements in the Christian faith—the Christian view of man and the Christian view of salvation—are left for future treatment.

The author desires to express his heartfelt gratitude to his friend, the Rev. Edwin H. Rian, of the Board of Trustees of Westminster Theological Seminary, to whom the plan for the delivery of such a course of lectures was due, and whose unfailing encouragement and help made possible the carrying out of the plan. The author is also indebted to colleagues in the Faculty of the Seminary—particularly to Mr. John Murray, who is in charge of the Department of Systematic Theology—for counsel generously given him with regard to certain of the subjects treated in the lectures.

J. Gresham Machen

1

The Present Emergency and How to Meet It

At the very beginning, I may as well tell you plainly that I am not going to talk about the topics that are usually regarded as most timely just now; I am not going to talk to you about the gold standard or about unemployment or about the NRA or about the Brain Trust.[1] Possibly some of you may discover that certain things I may say have a bearing upon those topics, but those topics are not the topics about which I am going to talk.

Instead, I am going to talk to you about God and about an unseen world.

May I reasonably expect you to be interested in such very intangible topics as these?

There are many persons who say "No." We are living, say these persons, in the midst of a serious emergency. One economic system, they say, seems to have broken down, and another is not quite ready to be put into its place. Everywhere are to be found unemployment and distress, almost everywhere there are wars or rumors of wars. In the midst of such distresses, who, these persons say, could be so heartless as to spend his efforts upon doubtful speculations regarding a life beyond the grave? Time enough to deal with that other world when we have set this world in order! Let us deal bravely—so the argument runs—first with the problems that we can see; and then, when we have done that, we may possibly find opportunity afterward to deal with the unseen and intangible things.

I have much sympathy with persons who speak in that way. I do not mean that I agree with them. On the contrary, I disagree with them with

---

1. The National Recovery Administration was a controversial Great Depression-era federal agency. The "Brain Trust" was a popular term for President Roosevelt's advisors.

all my soul. But I do say that I can sympathize with them, and I think I can recognize the element of truth in what they say.

It is certainly true that circumstances do alter a man's choice of the things to which he shall turn his attention. If you were living at Little America along with Byrd[2], I could hardly advise you to go in to any great extent for landscape gardening. What is true, moreover, of different positions on the earth's surface is true also of different times. There *are* times of emergency when work that is needed in ordinary times is no longer in place.

The World War, of course, gave us a stock example. In time of war, people turned their attention to things very different from the things that they did at ordinary times. If I may use the very humblest of all examples, the example of myself, I may say that in the time of peace before the war, I taught Greek; in the time of war, I made what I am afraid was the world's worst effort at running a small delicatessen store. Other persons did things that were more useful but were even more remote from their ordinary occupations. It was a time of emergency, and things that were ordinarily needed were no longer in place.

I am perfectly ready to admit, moreover, that although the World War is now over, the emergency remains with us to the full. Indeed, the emergency is far more serious than we could ever have imagined it would be. Little did I think, for example, as I walked through the little town of Zingem on the Scheldt River in Belgium on the morning of November 11, 1918, and saw the dead lying beside the road and went out into the positions across the river so recently occupied by the enemy, and as I gloried in the strange peace of that November morning when the noise of war that had so long seemed to be an inevitable part of human existence gave place to a strange, eloquent, unbelievable silence—little did I think, and little did men far wiser than I think, that the peace then vouchsafed to humanity would result after sixteen years in a condition like that which faces us today. Little did I think that a war supposed to make the world safe for democracy would be followed by an era in which, in Italy and in Germany, as well as in Russia, democracy and liberty would be openly despised and would be replaced by a tyranny far more crushing and soul-killing, in many respects, than the cruder tyrannies of the past. Little did I think that

---

2. Little America was a series of Antarctic exploration bases, the first of which was established by Richard Byrd in 1929.

even in America the civil and religious liberty which was our dearest possession and which was won by our fathers at such cost would be threatened as it is being threatened today.

No thoughtful man can possibly look out upon the world today without observing that we are in the midst of a tremendous emergency. It does seem perfectly clear to thoughtful people, whether they are Christians or not, that humanity is standing over an abyss.

At such a time, is it any wonder that this world with its pressing problems would seem to many persons quite sufficient to occupy all our thoughts? Is it any wonder that the pressing problems that are before our very eyes should crowd out attention to God and to an unseen world?

Persons who adopt that attitude may, with some plausibility, argue that the most important thing that you have to do for a man is not always the first thing that you must do for him. If a man is in the water, drowning, the most important thing to do for him is to preach the gospel to him for the saving of his soul. But that is not the first thing to do for him. The first thing to do for him is to pull him out of the water. He cannot even attend to the gospel for the saving of his soul when his ears are full of salt water. The first thing that you have to do for him—even though it be not the most important thing—is to pull him out of the water and give him artificial respiration. Then and then only can you preach the gospel to him for the saving of his soul.

It might seem to be the same way with humanity as a whole. Humanity is drowning in the water, or, to change the figure slightly, is sinking in the mire. The first thing to do might seem to be to pull it out, in order that after it has been pulled out we may ask it to deal with the unseen things. Let the church show what it can do with the plain emergency as it actually exists in this world—the argument might run—and then, if it proves able to do that, the world may think it worth listening to if it talks about God.

Plausible reasoning this is—plausible, but utterly untrue.

In the first place, the program that this reasoning proposes will not work. It proposes that we shall first deal with the political and social emergency and then afterward deal with the unseen things. But what was it that brought the emergency upon us in the first place? Was it something in the realm of that which can be seen? Not at all. The physical resources of the world were amply sufficient for the world's needs. No, the thing that brought the emergency upon us was something in the realm of the unseen things. It was an evil that was found within the soul of man.

That evil was not quite so simple as was at first supposed. Not many of us, I think, would now hold that the war was due solely to the sins of the Kaiser or the German military machine. The evil, alas, was considerably more widespread than that, but at least it clearly lay within the realm of those intangible unseen things. It lay within the soul of man and within the sphere of the relations between man and the unseen world.

Moreover, if it was something within that realm that brought the emergency to us in the first place, it is also something in that realm that keeps the emergency with us today. The distress of the world is due clearly to an evil that is within the soul of man.

Hence these so-called practical men who would neglect the realm of the soul and of the soul's relations to God in order to deal with the economic problems of the day are the most impractical people that could possibly be imagined. They always remind me of a man who tries to run a gasoline engine that is not producing a spark. You may have your engine in fine working order; there may be a good flow of gasoline; there may be the most perfect lubrication: but if there is something wrong with the ignition system, your engine will not run. I think I remember trying the experiment inadvertently sometimes in those heroic days before the invention of self-starters when a Ford was still a Ford. I cranked my engine until I was very red in the face and until my temper suffered considerable strain. I imagined that I needed an expert capable of discoursing on the most intricate principles of dynamics. But despite all my efforts and despite all my search for mechanical learning, the miserable engine would not start. Why? Because there was anything wrong with the engine? Not at all. Henry Ford had done his work well. But because I had forgotten to turn on the switch, it would not start. So it is with these practical men who are not interested in the human soul or in God. They are cranking the engine of society furiously; they are proposing all sorts of radical changes in the machinery. But there is one little thing that they have forgotten. They have forgotten to turn on the switch. The engine is not producing a spark; and until it produces a spark, it will not run.

The truth is that the analogy of the drowning man does not apply to the evils of society. To pull a drowning man out of the water is a simple physical effort. But to pull society out of the mire into which it has fallen today is not a simple physical effort at all, but a highly complex matter; and at the very heart of it is that mysterious portion of the mechanism known as the soul of man.

It is impossible, therefore, to deal first with the social and political evils of the day and then deal afterward with the unseen things for the simple reason that without dealing with the unseen things you cannot deal successfully with those social and political problems at all.

In that point I am particularly anxious to avoid any misunderstanding of what I am saying. I certainly do not mean by what I have been saying that religion is to be regarded merely as a means to a higher end. I certainly do not mean that God is to be dragged in merely to help us out in the troubles that face us at the present emergency. If I meant that, I should be rejecting the central things of the Christian religion and should be saying something quite contrary to the Bible.

We ought to be perfectly clear about this point. If you regard religion merely as a means to attain worldly ends, even the highest and noblest of worldly ends—if you regard religion, for example, merely as a means of meeting the present emergency in this world—then you have never begun to have even the slightest inkling of what the Christian religion means. God, as he is known to the Christian, is never content to be thus a mere instrument in the hands of those who care nothing about him. The relation to God is the all-important thing. It is not a mere means to an end. Everything else is secondary to it.

But what I do mean is that God has so ordered the course of this world that in this case—unlike that case of the drowning man—it is impossible to attain the lower end until the higher end has been attained. It is impossible to deal successfully even with these political and social problems until we have come to be right with God. No emergency can possibly be so pressing as to permit us to postpone attention to the unseen things.

Indeed, the emergency ought to have exactly the opposite effect; the evils of the time, instead of leading us away from God, ought to lead us to him. There was a time not so very long ago when this world might have seemed to a superficial observer to be a fairly satisfactory place. Even then the evil was there, but it was covered up; the abyss over which we were standing was concealed by the amenities of modern life. When I was a student in Germany in the years 1905–1906, the world might have seemed to a superficial observer to be getting along fairly well without God. It was a fine, comfortable world, that godless, European world before 1914. And as for another European war, that seemed to be about as far beyond the bounds of possibility as that the knights should don their armor and set their lances again in rest. The international bankers, we supposed, obviously would prevent an anachronism so absurd. But we have since discovered our mistake. That godless European and American world proved to be not so comfortable after all.

Today the world is in a state far more disquieting than that which prevailed in 1918. Europe is armed to the teeth. Russia stands under the most systematic and soul-crushing tyranny that the world has ever seen. In Germany, fiendish wickedness is being practiced in the name of science, and in that country as well as in Italy, even the form of liberty—to say nothing of the reality of it—has been abandoned. Civil and religious liberty are being treated openly as though they have been merely a passing phase in human life, well enough in their day but now out-of-date. In America, the same tendencies are mightily at work. Everywhere there rises before our eyes the specter of a society where security, if it is attained at all, will be attained at the expense of freedom, where the security that is attained will be the security of fed beasts in a stable, and where all the high aspirations of humanity will have been crushed by an all-powerful state.

Is this a time when we ought to be contented with things as they are? Is it not rather a time when we ought seriously to ask ourselves whether there is not some lost secret which must be regained if humanity is to be saved from the abyss?

What is true about humanity as a whole is also true, I venture to think, about you. The world is weary and perplexed today. Well, how is it with you? Are you contented with your lives as they are now? I suppose that many of you are. But some of you, I know, are discontented and looking for something entirely different from that which you now possess. That is true of rich as well as of poor; it has little to do with your particular situation in this world. To such hungry souls I think I have something to say in this little series of talks; and there are many hungry souls today.

But why is it that I have something to say to you? Is it because I am an expert in religion and because I can draw upon great resources of wisdom and experience in order to help you deal with the problems of your lives? Is it because I am a skillful soul-physician who can point you to hidden resources in your own souls upon which you yourselves can then draw? I may as well say at once that if that is the program of these addresses, I cannot expect you to attend to them anymore. There are many persons in the world, there are many persons speaking "over the air," who are far wiser and more learned and in every way more gifted than I. No, I certainly cannot expect you to listen to me because of any wisdom of mine, for I have none. I cannot expect you to be particularly interested in any opinions of mine that I may be bold enough to present.

There is just one reason why I may possibly expect you to listen to me. I may expect you to listen to me if I can bring to you a message from God. If I can do that, then the very insignificance of the speaker may in a certain sense be an added inducement to you to listen to him, since it may help you to forget the speaker and attend only to the message.

It is just this that I am trying to do. I am asking you to turn away from me and my opinions; I am asking you to turn away from yourself and your opinions and your troubles; and I am asking you to turn instead that you may listen to a word from God.

Where can I find that word? I am going to try to tell you in the next one of these little talks. Not in myself and not in you, but in an old book that has been sealed by the seals of prejudice and unbelief but that will, if it is rediscovered, again set the world aflame and show you, be you wise or unwise, rich or poor, the way by which you can come into communion with the living God.[3]

---

3. These talks have been reprinted in Hart, D.G, *J. Gresham Machen: Selected Shorter Writings* (Phillipsburg: P&R, 2004).

2

How May God Be Known?

In the first talk of this little series, I tried to tell you why I think you cannot postpone attention to God and to an unseen world. It is true that this world presents pressing problems, but you can never solve even those problems aright unless you first face the question of your relation to God. That is the all-important thing, and the distresses of the present time only serve to press it still more insistently upon our attention.

But if it is important for us to face the question of our relation to God, how can God be known to us? How can we discover whether there is a God at all, and then, if there is, what sort of being he is?

I have something rather simple to say about that question at the very start. It is something that seems to me to be rather obvious, and yet it is quite generally ignored. It is simply this: that if we are really to know anything about God, it will probably be because God has chosen to tell it to us.

Many persons seem to go on a very different assumption. They seem to think that if they are to know anything about God they must discover God for themselves.

That assumption seems to me to be extremely unlikely. Just supposing, for the sake of the argument, that there is a being of such a kind as that he may with any propriety be called "God," it does seem antecedently very improbable that weak and limited creatures of a day, such as we are, should discover him by our own efforts without any will on his part to make himself known to us. At least, I think we can say that a god who could be discovered in that way would hardly be worth discovering. A mere passive subject of human investigation is certainly not a living God who can satisfy the longing of our souls.

Some years ago, I was asked to contribute to a composite volume which had as its general title, *My Idea of God*.[1] Various writers told, each of them, what his own idea of God was. One said, "I think of God so"; another said, "I think *so*." Now I shall not presume to say whether the essay that I contributed to that volume had any particular merit at all. Perhaps it was a rather poor effort. But I do very deliberately maintain that I was right at least in saying at the beginning of it that if *my* idea of God were really mine I should attach very little importance to it myself and could reasonably expect even less importance to be attributed to it by others.

A divine being that could be discovered by my efforts, apart from his gracious will to reveal himself to me and to others, would be either a mere name for a certain aspect of man's own nature, a God that we could find within us, or else at best a mere passive thing that would be subject to investigation like the substances that are analyzed in a laboratory.

I think we ought to stick to that principle rather firmly. I think we ought to be rather sure that we cannot know God unless God has been pleased to reveal himself to us.

How, then, has God revealed himself to us?

In the first place, he has revealed himself by the universe that he has made. How did the world come into being? It is here. That cannot be denied. But how did it come to be?

The question forces itself upon the attention of every thinking man. We may try to evade it. We may just say that it is unanswerable. We may try to put it out of our minds. But it continues to haunt us all the same, and for ages it has haunted the human race.

I think the universe itself provides the answer to that question. The answer is itself a mystery, but it is a mystery in which we can rest. The answer is a very simple answer. The answer is that the world came into being because God made it. It is the work of an infinite and all-wise and all-powerful God.

That answer presses itself upon different people in different ways. It has been defended by philosophers and theologians by way of detailed reasoning. That reasoning has been divided logically into what are called the "theistic proofs"—indications in the world itself that point to the existence of a personal God, Creator and Ruler of the world.

I am not going to speak of them here except just to say that I think they are good proofs, and that the Christian man, whether he has a detailed

---

1. *My Idea of God: A Symposium of Faith*, ed. Joseph Fort Newton, Litt.D., D.H.L., 1926.

knowledge of them or not, ought never to depreciate them or regard as a matter of no importance the debate about them among philosophers and learned men.

But I am not going to attempt any exposition of those proofs. What I do want to do is just point out that the testimony of nature to nature's God comes to different people in different ways. I remember listening some time ago to a lecture by an eminent man of science. The lecturer traced the progress of scientific investigation and pointed out, if I remember aright, its material benefits. But then he paused to speak of another product of the scientific spirit; the true scientist, he said, is brought face to face at last with the ultimate mystery, and at that point he becomes a religious man. There is endless diversity in the world, said he, but the progress of investigation has revealed the electron; and the electrons, said he, are all alike—they are machine-made—and their marvelous likeness reveals the existence of a mystery into which man cannot penetrate; in truly religious awe the man of science stands at length before a curtain that is never lifted, a mystery that rebukes all pride.

I am not saying that the man of science had a true knowledge of God. I do not think that he had. I should have liked, if he had been willing to listen to me, to tell him of the way in which, for little children as well as for learned men of science, that dreadful curtain of which he spoke has been pulled gently aside to give us at least a look into the mysteries beyond. But at least there was one aspect of nature that brought the scientist to the threshold of a knowledge of God.

To some men the testimony of nature to nature's God comes by such precise knowledge of nature as was possessed by that scientist. To others it comes by a reasoned consideration of the implications of nature's existence. But to still others it comes by what Browning calls "a sunset-touch."[2] To one man in one way, to another in another.

To me nature speaks clearest in the majesty and beauty of the hills. One day in the summer of 1932, I stood on the summit of the Matterhorn in the Alps. Some people can stand there and see very little. Depreciating the Matterhorn is a recognized part of modern books on mountain-climbing. The great mountain, it is said, has been sadly spoiled. Why, you can even see sardine cans on those rocks that so tempted the ambition of climbers in Whymper's[3] day. Well, I can only say that when I stood on the Matterhorn

---

2. Robert Browning, "Bishop Blougram's Apology," in *Men and Women*, 1855.
3. Edward Whymper (1840–1911) was an English mountaineer and explorer.

I do not remember seeing a single can. Perhaps that was partly because of the unusual masses of fresh snow which were then on the mountain, but I think it was also due to the fact that, unlike some people, I had eyes for something else. I saw the vastness of the Italian plain, which was like a symbol of infinity. I saw the snows of distant mountains. I saw the sweet green valleys far, far below, at my feet. I saw the whole glorious round of glittering peaks, bathed in an unearthly light. And as I see that glorious vision again before me now, I am thankful from the bottom of my heart that from my mother's knee I have known to whom all that glory is due.

Then I love the softer beauties of nature also. I wonder whether you love them with me. Some years ago, in the White Mountains, I walked beside a brook. I have seen, I suppose, hundreds of brooks. But somehow I remembered particularly that one. I am not going to tell you where it is, because if I did you might write to the C.C.C.[4] or the National Park Service about it and get them to put a scenic highway along it, and then it would be forever ruined. But when I walked along it, it was untouched. I cherish the memory of it. It was gentle, sweet, and lovely beyond all words. I think a man might travel through all the world and never see anything lovelier than a White Mountain brook. Very wonderful is the variety of nature in her changing moods.

Silence too, the silence of nature, can be a very revealing thing. I remember one day when I spent a peaceful half-hour in the sunlight on the summit of a mountain in the Franconia range. I there experienced something very rare. Would you believe it, my friends? It was really *silent* on that sunny mountain top. There was not the honk of a motor horn; there was no jazz music; there was no sound of a human voice; there was not even the rustling of the leaves. There was nothing but a strange, brooding silence. It was a precious time indeed. I shall never forget it all my life.

Please do not misunderstand me. I am not asking that everyone should love the beauties of nature as I love them. I do think, indeed, that the love of nature ought to be cultivated. At least, I do not think that government ought to go into the business of crushing it out of a people's soul as the United States government is doing by some of the artificialities and regularities of its National Parks. I think some sweet and delicate little things ought to be left untouched. But I well understand that there are many people who do not love the beauties of nature. Are they shut off from finding God revealed in the world that he has made?

---

4. Civilian Conservation Corps, a Great Depression-era federal work program.

Indeed, that is not so, my friends; indeed, it is not so. The mystery of the existence of the world presses itself upon different people in different ways. I remember, for example, a talk that I heard from a professor at an afternoon conference service many years ago. I do not know just why I should remember it, but I do remember it. The professor said that he had a friend who had come to a belief in God, or had come back to a belief in God, by—what do you suppose? Well, by a trip through Europe! As he went from city to city and observed the seething multitudes, the throngs upon throngs of men and women, somehow, he said, the conviction just seemed to come over him: "There is a God, there is a God."

Was that a foolish fancy? Were those experiences in my own life of which I have been bold enough to speak merely meaningless dreams? Or were they true testimonies to something marvelous beyond? Were they moments when God was graciously revealing himself to me through the glory of the world that he has made?

I think a Christian ought not to be afraid to give the latter answer. The revelation of God through nature has the stamp of approval put upon it by the Bible. The Bible clearly teaches that nature reveals the glory of God.

In a wonderful passage in the first chapter of the Epistle to the Romans, the apostle Paul says that God's "invisible attributes, namely, his eternal power and divine nature, have been clearly perceived, ever since the creation of the world, in the things that have been made" (Rom 1:20). Here the Bible approves the arguments of those who in systematic fashion argue from the existence of the world to the existence of a divine Maker of the world. But the Bible also approves those more unreasoned flashes of knowledge in which suddenly we see God's workmanship in the beauty and the majesty of his world. "The heavens declare the glory of God, and the sky above proclaims his handiwork," says the psalmist (Ps 19:1). And what said our Lord Jesus Christ? "Even Solomon in all his glory," said he of the lilies of the field, "was not arrayed like one of these" (Matt 6:29).

All that is true. The revelation of God through nature is a very precious thing. But then a serious question arises: if God has revealed himself through the things that he has made, why do so very few men listen to the revelation? The plain fact is that very few men arrive by a contemplation of nature at a true belief in a personal God. Even those scientists whose religious views are sometimes being incautiously welcomed by Christian people are often found, upon closer examination, to believe only in a God who is identical with a spiritual purpose supposed to inhere in the world process itself and are found not to believe at all in a living and holy God—the true God who created the heavens and the earth.

Why is that so? If God has revealed himself so plainly through the world that he has made, why do men not see?

Well, when men do not see something, there are two possible explanations of the fact: one is that there is nothing there to see and the other is that the men who do not see are blind.

It is this latter explanation which the Bible gives of the failure of men to know God through the things that he has made. The Bible puts it very plainly in that same passage already quoted from the first chapter of Romans. "Their foolish hearts," says Paul, "were darkened" (Rom 1:21). Hence, they did not see. The fault did not lie in nature. Men were "without excuse" (Rom 1:20), Paul says, when they did not see what nature had to show. Their minds were blinded by sin. That is a hard saying, but like many other hard sayings it is true. You will never understand anything else that I may say unless you understand that we, all of us, so long as we stand in our own right and have not had our eyes mysteriously opened, are lost and blind in sin.

3

Has God Spoken?

At the beginning of this little series of talks, I tried to tell you why you cannot postpone attention to an unseen world and to God. This world presents very pressing problems just now, but even the problems of this world cannot be solved aright if you neglect the other world and the great question of your relation to God. Then I began to tell you how you can come into relations with that unseen world; I tried to begin to tell you how God may be known. He may be known, I said, through the universe that he has made; the existence of the world shows that there is a Maker and Ruler of the world.

That revelation of God through nature, I said, is wonderfully confirmed by the Bible, but it does not come only from the Bible. It is spread out before men so that all might be expected to see.

But in the last of these talks I was not able to finish, even in bare outline, what ought to be said about that general revelation of God which is given to us outside of the Bible. I spoke of the way in which God has spoken to us through the majesty and beauty of the world that he has made. But there is another way, still apart from the Bible, in which God has spoken to his creatures. He has spoken not only in the wonders of the world outside of us but also through his voice within—he has planted his laws in our hearts. He speaks to all men through the voice of conscience. He speaks through the majestic words which all but the most degraded men utter: the words "I ought." He speaks through the majesty of the moral law. A law implies a lawgiver. Conscience testifies of God.

There are some people, even people who are not Christians, to whom that revelation seems particularly to appeal. Some years ago, I remember hearing an informal lecture by a well-known professor of philosophy. The speaker told us about the present state of philosophical opinion. It was, he said, overwhelmingly in favor of naturalism—that is, very few philosophers believed in any reality beyond and above the universe in which we live. He himself, the speaker said, disagreed with this naturalism. He did believe in a transcendent reality. Why? He believed in it, he said, because he observed that certain people sacrifice their own interests for the sake of other people or for the sake of duty. What could possibly lead them to act so if there is no transcendent principle of right? How could they possibly act in a way so contrary to all worldly interests unless there is a reality beyond this world?

The Bible sets the stamp of its approval upon that revelation of God through conscience, as we have seen that it sets the stamp of its approval upon the revelation that comes through the external world. Paul says, for example, in the second chapter of the Epistle to the Romans: "For when Gentiles, who do not have the law, by nature do what the law requires, they are a law to themselves, even though they do not have the law. They show that the work of the law is written on their hearts, while their conscience also bears witness, and their conflicting thoughts accuse or even excuse them" (Rom 2:14–15). Here the apostle does seem clearly to teach that the voice of conscience, which speaks in the very constitution of man's nature, is the voice of God. He does not mean that men really obey that law as it ought to be obeyed. On the contrary, he is very clear indeed in teaching that all have disobeyed. They have disobeyed the law, but at least the law is there, in their hearts. Because of their disobedience, they are under the condemnation of the law; the law can therefore of itself never give them any hope. But that is not the fault of the law; the moral law is written in the very constitution of their being, and if they do not heed it, they are without excuse.

Thus God the great lawgiver is revealed in the voice of conscience as he is in the wonders of the world without. These two may be grouped together as constituting the revelation of God through nature, if nature be taken to include the nature of man. The philosopher Immanuel Kant is said to have summed it up when he spoke of the starry heavens above and the moral law within as being the two things which fill the heart of man with awe. I do not mean that those two things gave to Immanuel Kant a true knowledge of God. I do not mean even that he had a true notion of what knowledge itself is. But what I mean is that he made a correct summary of those things which, apart from the Bible, ought to give us a knowledge of God. The wonders of the universe without and the moral law within—those are the two great elements in God's revelation of himself through nature.

But he not only revealed himself through nature; he has also revealed himself in an entirely different way. That other revelation of God, different from his revelation of himself through nature, is not natural but supernatural.

When we say "supernatural," we are not speaking about something contrary to nature. Nothing that is contrary to nature could possibly come from God, for God is the author of nature, and he cannot contradict himself.

But when we say that anything is "supernatural" we are saying that it is "above nature."

There is an existing order of nature; the order of nature does not consist merely in our observation of certain regularities in God's working, but it is something that truly exists.

That does not mean that nature exists apart from God. On the contrary, it would not continue to exist for one moment except by God's will. God is not isolated from the world; he does everything that nature does and he says everything that nature says.

But what we mean is that God acts and speaks in two very different ways. In the first place, he acts and speaks by means of the world that he has made; and in the second place, he acts and speaks directly, without the use of natural means.

It was in this latter way that God acted when he first created the world, and it was in this latter way that he acted when he wrought the miracles recorded in the Bible and when he spoke to men in the supernatural revelation with which we are dealing just now.

Why was this supernatural revelation needed?

It was needed for two reasons. In the first place, God's revelation of himself through nature has been hidden from our eyes by sin. We saw in the last talk how that is the case with the revelation given by the wonders of the external world. Those wonders reveal the glory of God, but men are blinded so that they do not see. That is even more clearly true of the revelation of God through his voice within. Have you ever experienced, my friends, the way in which conscience can become blunted? Have you never first looked upon some foul thing with horror, and then slipped into that thing by insensible degrees, so that what seemed wrong to you before is now treated as a matter of course, until at some sad hour you come to yourself and see that you are already wallowing in the mire? Ah, yes, the voice of conscience is silenced by a life of sin. We can detect that dreadful hardening process in ourselves, and very terribly is it set forth in the Bible as a punishment for sin. How terrible, too, are the perversions of the conscience among men! It is certainly true that the revelation of God through conscience has been hidden from men's eyes by sin.

There is need of supernatural revelation, therefore, to show us again those things which sin has hidden from our eyes.

But is that all the supernatural revelation that there is? If it were, we should be of all men most miserable. Suppose we had revealed to us the terrible majesty of God; suppose the voice of conscience had spoken to us with perfect clearness of the justice of God and of our disobedience. How terrible that revelation would be!

No, thank God. He has also, in his supernatural revelation, told us other things. He has told us again in supernatural fashion things that we ought to have learned through nature, but then he has told us other things of which nature gives not the slightest hint. He has told us, namely, of his grace. He has told us of the way in which sinners, who have offended against his holy law and deserve nothing but his wrath, have been made his children at infinite cost and will live as his children forevermore.

Where shall we find that supernatural revelation? I want to say very plainly that I think all that we can know of it now is found in the pages of one book.

There have, indeed, been men in our day who have claimed to be the recipients of supernatural revelation, who have claimed to be prophets, who have said as they have come forward: "Thus says the Lord; God has spoken directly to me, and my voice therefore is the voice of God."

But those who have said that in our times are false prophets one and all; the real supernatural revelation that we know is recorded in one blessed book: the Bible.

It is no wonder that that is the case, because there is a marvelous symmetry and completeness in that revelation of God which the Bible records. I should love to speak to you about it if there were time. When sin came into the world, the Bible tells us that there was a revelation of salvation to come; the seed of the woman should bruise the serpent's head. I should love to tell you of the unfolding of that promise. I should love to tell you of Abraham and of Moses. I should particularly love to tell you of the great prophets, because in their words we see so plainly what supernatural revelation is. They spoke of judgment; they spoke of the terror and the majesty of God. But they also spoke, very tenderly, of God's grace. As when at some solemn sunset hour there are dark clouds above but low on the horizon a deep, clear, unearthly light, despair of every artist's brush, so in the great prophets there are warnings of the day of vengeance of our God but mingled with the warnings are strange gleams of a heavenly tenderness and peace. "For to us a child is born, to us a son is given; and the government shall be upon his shoulder, and his name shall be called Wonderful Counselor, Mighty God, Everlasting Father, Prince of Peace" (Isa 9:6). "Behold, the virgin shall conceive and bear a son, and shall call his name Immanuel" (Isa 7:14).

Only, our figure was not altogether right; those passages reveal to us not a sunset glow but the glory of a far-off dawn. Then, as we read the Bible, we see the dawn drawing nearer. It is like that solemn hour when all nature is hushed before the appearance of the day. Shepherds kept watch over their flocks by night. There came to them a heavenly word: "For unto you is born this day in the city of David a Savior, who is Christ the Lord" (Luke 2:11). I should love to tell you of that Savior. He spoke as never a man spoke. But I suppose his whole life can be called a supernatural revelation. He was true man but he was not only man. He came into this world by a supernatural act of God, and in his death and resurrection he wrought a supernatural work. I should love to tell you of the way in which, through the apostles, supernatural revelation was gloriously continued after his saving work was done. I should love to tell you how, by heeding the revelation contained in the epistles of the New Testament, you can have that glorious Savior as your Savior today. I should love to tell you of the last book of the Bible, with its promises of things to come, with its promises of the time when we shall see our Savior face-to-face.

Yes, there is a wonderful symmetry and completeness in the supernatural revelation recorded in the Bible. But one question may trouble us. Have we a true *record* of that revelation? The revelation came to men of long ago. How do we know that the account which we have of it is true? And how do we know that those saving acts of God which went with the revelation really did happen? The revelation is one thing, it might be said, and the record of the revelation is another. How do we know that the record is true?

I want to talk to you about that question in the next one of these addresses. I want to talk to you about inspiration—the inspiration of the Book in which the revelation is recorded. I want to talk to you about the question, "Just exactly what do we mean when we say that the Bible is the Word of God?"

4

Is the Bible the Word of God?

In the last two talks in this series, I have been speaking to you about the question of how God may be known. He may be known, I said, only as he has been pleased to reveal himself. But he has been pleased to reveal himself in two ways. In the first place, he has been pleased to reveal himself through nature—by the wonders of the world and by his voice within, the voice of conscience—and, in the second place, he has been pleased to reveal himself in an entirely different way that we call "supernatural" because it is "above nature." We were talking about that supernatural revelation in the last talk. In that supernatural revelation, God has spoken to men not only through the wonders of the world that he has made and not only through his voice planted in our hearts, the voice of the conscience, but directly and specially, in a way analogous to the way in which one person here on earth gives a piece of information to another.

I said at the close of the little talk that all the "supernatural" or special revelation that we know is contained within the pages of one book: the Bible. Was I right in saying that?

Well, I think that I was just about right. Supernatural revelation, along with the miracles, ceased when the last of the apostles of Jesus died. If you want information as to why the miracles ceased, and with them supernatural revelation, I think you will find it if you will turn, for example, to the admirable book by the late B. B. Warfield entitled, *Counterfeit Miracles*.[1]

But why should we not obtain information, in addition to that recorded in the Bible, about supernatural revelation given, indeed, not later, but in Bible times? Well, it is perfectly conceivable, for example, that there

---

1. B. B. Warfield, *Counterfeit Miracles*, 1918, 1–33.

might turn up in Egypt bits of papyrus affording true information about words of Jesus not contained in the four Gospels. But the bits of papyrus which have actually turned up so far hardly seem to provide such information. It is, for example, on the whole, unlikely that Jesus really spoke the words recorded in one such fragment: "Lift up the stone, and there thou shalt find me; cleave the wood, and there I am."[2] On the whole, speaking broadly, we can certainly say that all the supernatural revelation we can be at all certain about, although no doubt other supernatural revelation was given in Bible times, is recorded in the pages of one book: the Bible.

But then the question forces itself upon our attention: "How about *that* record?" We have said that the record of supernatural revelation outside the Bible is uncertain, to say the very best for it. But is the record *in* the Bible any better? Can we really depend upon the record?

I want to try to answer that question today. I want to try to tell you what I think the right view of the Bible is.

In doing so, I am perfectly well aware of the fact that in the opinion of a good many people I shall be putting my worst foot forward. I shall be giving expression to views which put me out of accord with the main trend of opinion both outside the church and inside of it. Should I not be wiser if I took this thing more gradually, if I adopted a more apologetic line of approach, if I decided, in the first part of my little series at least, to conceal somewhat the full unpopularity of my opinions?

In reply, I just want to say that I do not think that if I adopted that method I should be treating you quite fairly. Here we are, sitting down together quietly. Cannot we at least be friends? Cannot we at least try to understand each other, whether we can agree with each other or not? I do not think that I should be doing my part toward that mutual understanding if I concealed from you the real basis of what I am going to say.

Hence I am going to tell you at once, just as briefly and as plainly as I can, what I think about the inspiration of the Bible.

As I do that, I am afraid I shall have to relinquish any ambitions of being brilliant or sparkling or eloquent. A simple summary presentation of a large subject does not lend itself to the exercise of these qualities, so I must resist the temptation of exhibiting my eloquence. That is just too bad! But I do not think I can estimate my self-sacrifice in this particular too

---

2. For text and translation, see Hugh G. Evelyn White, *The Sayings of Jesus from Oxyrhynchus*, 1920, 35f.

highly. You see, I am greatly assisted in my battle against the temptation of exhibiting my eloquence by the fact that I have no eloquence to exhibit.

At any rate, whether because of necessity or because of choice, I am subordinating all other ambitions in these little talks to the one ambition of being plain. I do want to try to help you get certain things straight. They may seem to be simple and even elementary, and yet there is the strangest confusion about them today. You may not agree with me about these things, but at least I hope that if you are broadminded enough to listen to me at all you may obtain a fairer conception about what certain much-abused people—we who believe in the inspiration of the Bible—really hold. After all, there are a good many people in the world who believe, as I do, that the Bible is the Word of God; and you cannot really be broadminded, you cannot really have an intelligent view of the state of humanity as a whole, if you listen only to what is said about these people by their opponents and never take the trouble to listen to what they have to say for themselves.

Of course, I cannot conceal from you the fact that I have also another and a higher purpose in these little talks. I want not only to clear away misconceptions from your minds as to what we believe, but I want to win some of you to believe the same thing yourselves. I want not only to show you what are the views of people who believe that there is a God and that he has spoken to men, but also to try to lead some of you to listen to the voice of God for yourselves. I know I cannot do that by any mere persuasions or arguments of mine. I can do it only if I have the blessing of God. But if I can just be the instrument, in these little talks, to clear away the mists and enable you to see God, above all if I can bring you a message from God's Word as to how you can come into God's presence and become his child—if I can do that even for a single one of you—then these little talks will have been well worthwhile.

What, then, shall we think about the Bible? I will tell you very plainly what I think we ought to think. I will tell you very plainly what I think about it. I hold that the biblical writers, after having been prepared for their task by the providential ordering of their entire lives, received, in addition to all that, a blessed, wonderful, and supernatural guidance and impulsion by the Spirit of God, so that they were preserved from the errors that appear in other books and thus the resulting book, the Bible, is in all its parts the very Word of God, completely true in what it says regarding matters of fact and completely authoritative in its commands.

That is the doctrine of full or "plenary" inspiration of Holy Scripture.

It is not a popular doctrine. It is not in accordance with the wisdom of this world. A man cannot hold to it seriously (and really act in accordance with it) and at the same time enjoy the favor of the world or the favor of the ecclesiastical authorities in many of the churches of the present day. Yet it is a very blessed doctrine all the same, and if a man founds his life upon it he can be very joyous and quite undismayed in all the sorrows and all the battles that may come upon him in this world.

Now I want to talk to you a little about that blessed doctrine of the inspiration of the Bible. It is certainly worth talking about because it belongs not to the superstructure but to the foundation. If a man really holds to it, everything else for that man is changed.

But can a man hold to it? Is it a reasonable thing to believe in the plenary inspiration of the Bible? And if it is a reasonable thing, how can we show that it is a reasonable thing? I cannot attempt to answer that latter question with any fullness in the rest of the present little talk. But I do believe that some of the objections to the doctrine of the plenary inspiration of the Bible disappear the minute a man observes clearly what that doctrine is, and, in particular, the minute he observes what that doctrine is not. The strangest misconceptions prevail, even among people who otherwise are educated people, about what we believers in the plenary inspiration of the Bible really hold. Perhaps I can perform a service by clearing away one or two of those misconceptions now.

In the first place, then, let it be said that we believers in the plenary inspiration of the Bible do not hold that the Authorized Version or any other form of the English Bible is inspired. I beg your pardon for saying anything so obvious as that, but, do you know, my friends, it is necessary to say it. There are scarcely any limits to the ignorance which is attributed to us today by people who have never given themselves the trouble to discover what our view really is. Let it be said, then, very plainly, that we do not hold that the Authorized Version or any other form of the English Bible is inspired. We are really quite well aware of the fact that the Bible was written in Hebrew and in Greek. The Authorized Version is a translation from the Hebrew and the Greek. It is a marvelously good translation, but it is not a perfect translation. There are errors in it. The translators were not supernaturally preserved from making mistakes. It is not inspired.

In the second place, we do not hold that any one of the hundreds, even thousands, of the Greek and the Hebrew manuscripts of the Bible is free from error. Before the invention of printing, the Bible was handed down from generation to generation by means of copies made by hand. Those copies were written out laboriously by scribes. Before one copy was worn out or lost, another copy would be made to take its place, and so the Bible was handed down. Hundreds of thousands, perhaps—no one knows how many—of such copies or "manuscripts" were made. Several thousand of them, some of these containing, of course, only parts of the Bible or only parts of either Testament, are now in existence. These are just remnants from among the vast number that are lost. Now we believers in the inspiration of the Bible do not believe that the scribe who made any one of these manuscripts that we have was inspired. Every one of the manuscripts contains errors; no one of them is perfect. What we do believe is that the *writers* of the biblical books, as distinguished from scribes who later copied the books, were inspired. Only the autographs of the biblical books, in other words—the books as they came from the pen of the sacred writers, and not any one of the copies of those autographs which we now possess—were produced with that supernatural impulsion and guidance of the Holy Spirit which we call inspiration.

At this point, an objection to the doctrine of inspiration arises in the minds of many people. I am inclined to think it is a widespread objection, and I am inclined to think it troubles many thoughtful and intelligent people. "What is the use of the inspiration of the Bible," people say, "if no form of the Bible that we now have is inspired? Why should God have worked a stupendous miracle in order to preserve the writers of the biblical books from error and make the autographs of their books completely true if he intended then to leave the books thus produced to the mere chance of transmission from generation to generation by very human and often careless copyists?"

Such is the objection. I have deep sympathy with the people who raise it or who are troubled by it. It is such a very human objection. We are, all of us, so prone to say, "If God did this, why did he not also do that?" We are, all of us, so apt to demand of God just a little bit more than he has given us. We are, all of us, so reluctant to say to ourselves that perhaps God's way is best, and that in not giving us all he has given us just exactly what it was good for us to have.

But, human though such reasoning is, it is very wrong. What we ought to do as a matter of fact is to take with thankfulness what God has been pleased to give us and not say that because he has not been pleased to give us something else therefore what he has been pleased to give us is of no use.

Certainly, in this case with which we are dealing now, what he has been pleased to give us is a very great deal, and it is far more than some people seem to think. He has given us the supernatural inspiration of the writers of the biblical books. That is much. But, according to our view of the Bible, that is not all that he has given us. He has also, according to our view, given us a marvelously accurate, though not a supernaturally accurate, transmission, from generation to generation, of what those inspired writers wrote.

The objector says to me, "How strange, according to your view, the view of you believers in the plenary inspiration of the Bible, that God should leave the transmission of a supernaturally inspired book to the chance of transmission by fallible human copyists!" What do I say in reply? I say: Hold on there, brother; what is that you said? Did you say that, according to our view, God left the transmission of the Bible to chance? If you said that, you said something that is quite wrong. That is not our view at all. No, God certainly did not, according to our view, leave the transmission of the Bible to chance. He did not leave anything to chance; but it is particularly plain that he did not leave *that* to chance. Was it by chance that in the early days the text of the New Testament books was so diligently copied from one piece of papyrus to another that knowledge of what the sacred writers had written was not lost during the period when that very perishable writing material was used? Was it by chance that about the beginning of the fourth century the wonderfully durable writing material, vellum, or parchment, came into use, so that two great manuscripts of the Bible made in that century are for the most part just as clear and easy to read today as if they had been made yesterday? Was it by chance that one of these manuscripts, the great Codex Sinaiticus, was so strangely preserved in the monastery of St. Catherine on Mount Sinai until it was found by Tischendorf in 1859? Was it by chance that a perfect photographic reproduction of that manuscript has been made, so that although the manuscript itself was well worth the half-million dollars that the British Museum is said to be paying the Soviet government for it, you can obtain to all intents and purposes just as much information about the manuscript as if you had the manuscript itself in your hands any time you will just come to the library of Westminster Theological Seminary, for example, and look at the photographic reproduction? Is it by chance that the evidence for the original text of the Bible is so vastly more abundant than for the text of other ancient books in the case of which, nevertheless, nobody doubts but that we have a very close approximation indeed to what the authors wrote?

Was it by chance that the King James Version or Authorized Version of the English Bible was made in the most glorious period of the English language and by men so wonderfully qualified for their task?

No, my friends, these things did not come by chance. God did these things. He did not do them by a miracle. But it was just as much God that did them as it would have been if he had done them by a miracle. He did them by his use of the world that he had made and by his ordering of the lives of his creatures. Very wonderfully and very graciously, according to our view of the Bible, has God provided for the preservation, from generation to generation, of his holy Word.

What is the result for you, my friends? The result is that you can take down your Authorized Version from the shelf, the version hallowed, for many of you, by many precious associations, and be very sure that it will give you good information about that which stood in the autographs of the Word of God. The study of the manuscripts of the Bible is a wonderfully reassuring thing. The Greek text of the New Testament, for example, from which the Authorized Version is taken, is based not upon the best manuscripts but upon inferior manuscripts. Yet how infinitesimal is the difference between those inferior manuscripts and the best manuscripts—how infinitesimal in comparison with what they have in common! I do not mean that we ought not to take care in the use of the Bible; I do not mean that we ought not to try by every means within our power to determine what the exact wording of the autographs was. I do think that careful Christian scholarship is a very important thing. Yet God has provided very wonderfully for the plain man who is not a scholar. You do not have to depend for the assurance of your salvation and the ordering of your Christian lives upon passages where either the original wording or the meaning is doubtful. God has provided very wonderfully for the transmission of the text and for the translation into English. The Bible is perfectly plain in the things that are necessary for your souls. God will make other things in it clearer to you as the years go by. Read it, my friends. It is God's book, not man's book. It is a message from the King. Read it, study it, trust it, live by it. Other books will deceive you, but not this book. This book is the Word of God.

Many things have been left unsaid this afternoon. Many things are left at loose ends. I do not like to leave things at loose ends when I am talking about the Bible. This theme is so momentous that I always wish when I talk about it that I could say everything at once. I am so afraid of leading somebody astray by telling just a part of the truth, so I do hope you will listen to me in the next one of these talks. I want to say certain things that simply must be said. I want to say something more about what the inspiration of the Bible means. Does it mean a mechanical treatment of the biblical writers as so many people say it does? In what sense is it, and in what sense is it not, "verbal" inspiration? I want to talk to you about that question. I also want to talk to you about the question whether it is enough to say that the Bible contains a record of supernatural revelation or whether we ought rather to say that it is, as a whole, itself a supernatural revelation from God.

5

Do We Believe in Verbal Inspiration?

In the last talk I was speaking about the inspiration of the Bible. The writers of the biblical books, I said, received a blessed, wonderful, and supernatural guidance and impulsion by the Spirit of God, so that they were preserved from the errors that appear in other books and thus the resulting book, the Bible, is in all its parts the very Word of God, completely true in what it says regarding matters of fact and completely authoritative in its commands. That is the great doctrine of the full or plenary inspiration of Holy Scripture.

I had to break off what I was saying to you about that doctrine. In fact, almost all that I had time to do was to clear away certain misconceptions. Now we get more into the heart of the subject.

I think I can help you to get into the heart of the subject if I just ask you to consider with me, for a minute or two, what I suppose is one of the commonest if not the very commonest of the objections to the doctrine of full or plenary inspiration. You see, this business of considering objections is a good thing in more ways than one. Not only may it possibly help people who are actually troubled by the objections, but also it may enable all of us to get the thing more nearly straight in our minds. There are few better ways of seeing clearly what a thing is than the way of setting it off sharply in contrast with what it is not.

Well, what is this common objection to the doctrine of plenary inspiration? It is that the doctrine of plenary inspiration represents God as acting upon the biblical writers in a mechanical way, a way that degrades those writers to the position of mere machines.

People who raise this objection sometimes ask us: "Do you believe in the 'verbal' inspiration of the Bible?" When they ask us that, they think that they have us in a dreadful hole. If we say: "No, we do not believe in verbal inspiration," they say, "How then can you hold to your conviction that the Bible is altogether true? If God did not exercise some supernatural control over the words, then the words will surely contain those errors which are found in all human productions." If, on the other hand, we say: "Yes, we do believe in verbal inspiration," then they hold up their hands in horror. "How dreadful, how mechanical!" they say. "If God really provided in supernatural fashion that the words should be thus and so, then the writers of the biblical books are degraded to the position of mere stenographers; indeed, they are degraded even lower than that, since stenographers are human enough to err and also to help, whereas in this case the words would be produced with such perfect accuracy as to show that the human instruments in the production of the words were mere machines. What becomes of the marvelous beauty and variety of the Bible when the writers of it are regarded as having been treated in this degrading way?"

Such is the hole into which we are thought to be put; or, if I may change the figure rather violently, such are the horns of the dilemma upon which we are thought to be impaled.

How can we possibly escape? Well, I think we can escape very easily indeed. You ask me whether I believe in the verbal inspiration of the Bible. I will answer that question very plainly and quickly. Yes, I believe in the verbal inspiration of the Bible; but I do insist that you and I shall get a right notion of what the word "verbal" means.

I certainly believe in the verbal inspiration of the Bible. I quite agree with you when you say that unless God provided in supernatural fashion that the words of the Bible should be free from error, we should have to give up our conception of the Bible as being, throughout, a supernatural book.

Yes, inspiration certainly has to do with the words of the Bible; in that sense, I certainly do believe in verbal inspiration. But if you mean by verbal inspiration the view that inspiration has to do *only* with the words of the Bible and not also with the souls of the biblical writers, then I want to tell you that I do not believe in verbal inspiration in that sense. If you mean by verbal inspiration the view that God moved the hands of the biblical writers over the page in the way in which hands are said to be moved over a Ouija board—in such a way that the writers did not know what they were doing when they wrote—then I hold that that kind of verbal inspiration does utterly fail to do justice to what appears in the Bible very plainly from Genesis to Revelation.

The writers of the Bible did know what they were doing when they wrote. I do not believe that they always knew all that they were doing. I believe that there are mysterious words of prophecy in the prophets and the Psalms, for example, which had a far richer and more glorious fulfillment than the inspired writers knew when they wrote. Yet even in the case of those mysterious words, I do not think that the sacred writers were mere automata. They did not know the full meaning of what they wrote, but they did know part of the meaning, and the full meaning was in no contradiction with the partial meaning but was its glorious unfolding.

I believe that the biblical writers used ordinary sources of information; they consulted documents, they engaged in research, they listened to eyewitnesses.

I do not, indeed, believe that they were limited to such sources of information. They were sometimes, as they wrote, the recipients of fresh supernatural revelation—supernatural revelation not previously given to others but given for the first time to them in the very moment of their writing. I believe also that sometimes, even when they used ordinary sources of information or when they consulted their memory, their use of such means of information went far beyond what is possible, except with supernatural assistance, to the human mind.

In one sense, of course, their use of such sources of information always went beyond what is possible to the human mind. To err is human, and these men did not err. They were always protected, in supernatural fashion, from the errors which appear in ordinary books.

But what I mean is that sometimes that supernatural heightening of human powers consisted not only in the invariable prevention of error in matters where uninspired writers might in any individual case have avoided error, but also in the prevention of error in matters where uninspired writers could not possibly have avoided error.

I am thinking, for example, of the discourses of Jesus reported in the Gospel according to John. It is often urged as an objection against the authenticity of those long discourses that no one who heard the discourses could possibly have remembered them so long afterward with anything like accuracy. That objection no longer troubles me as much as it formerly did. Did not our Lord himself tell the apostles, including the writer of this gospel, that after his departure the Holy Spirit would bring to their remembrance whatsoever he had said unto them? May we not suppose that the report by the beloved disciple, writer of this gospel, of the things that Jesus had said when he was with the disciples on earth goes far beyond what is possible to the unaided human memory and is due, in part, to that mysterious and supernatural work of the Holy Spirit of which Jesus spoke?

But such considerations ought not to obscure the fact that the biblical writers did use ordinary sources of information where they were reporting things that had been said and done on this earth. Indeed, they often lay great stress on the fact that they used such ordinary sources of information. The author of that very gospel about which we have just been speaking, and in which we were inclined to find something that goes far beyond what is possible to the unaided human memory—even the author of that gospel lays particular emphasis on the fact that he was an eyewitness of the life of Jesus. He reported what he had seen and heard. He did not tell these things just because they had been revealed to him at some later time in some supernatural experience. No. He was there when Jesus said certain things and did certain things. As an eyewitness, he insists that he is worthy of belief. Even before his hearers or his readers should come to believe in any supernatural inspiration of which he was the recipient, they ought to believe him as men believe a credible witness when he takes his seat on the witness stand.

So the apostle Paul appeals to the witness of the five hundred brethren who had seen the risen Lord. So the evangelist Luke tells in the prologue of his gospel about the historical research in which he had been engaged. Yes, the biblical writers used ordinary sources of information, and when they were eyewitnesses, they used their own memory of what they had seen and heard.

It is very important indeed to insist upon these facts, because they give the Bible such evidential force. Suppose a man comes to the reading of the Bible without any belief in inspiration. Even then he ought to give credence to what he reads. It can be shown him, even before any acceptance on his part of the doctrine of plenary inspiration, that the writers were men who had opportunities of knowing the facts, that they were honest men, that they knew how to distinguish truth from falsehood. If he will only consider these biblical books with the same fairness as that with which he approaches other sources of historical information, he will accept what they say as being substantially true. Then, on the basis of that conviction that they are substantially true, he will go on to see that the books are not only substantially true in the way in which other good books are true, but that they are altogether true because of the supernatural work of the Spirit of God.

We do not therefore merely *admit* that the biblical writers used ordinary sources of historical information; we *insist* upon it. It is tremendously important for the witness which the Bible renders to those who have not yet come to believe.

What is more, the biblical writers did not merely use ordinary means of obtaining information, but also followed their own individual habits of style. When people say that the doctrine of plenary or full inspiration of the Bible fails to do justice to the individuality of the biblical writers, they simply show that they do not know what they are talking about. Yes, what a wonderful variety there is in the Bible. There is the rough simplicity of Mark, the unconscious yet splendid eloquence of Paul, the conscious literary art of the author of the Epistle to the Hebrews, the matchless beauty of the Old Testament narratives, the high poetry of the prophets and the Psalms. How much we should lose, to be sure, if the Bible were written all in one style!

We believers in the full inspiration of the Bible do not merely admit that; we *insist* upon it. The doctrine of plenary inspiration does not hold that all parts of the Bible are alike; it does not hold that they are all equally beautiful or even equally valuable; but it only holds that all parts of the Bible are equally true, and that each part has its place.

That wonderful variety in the Bible did not come by chance. It came by the gracious providence of God. It was God who superintended the varied education of those writers to prepare them the better for their mighty task. It was God who watched over the prophet Amos when he was "a herdsman and a dresser of sycamore figs" (Amos 7:14). It was God who watched over Paul when he sat at the feet of Gamaliel. When I consider the wonderful variety among the biblical writers and the wonderful unity of the book amid this variety, I am tempted to use a figure of speech to describe what is really beyond all human figures. I am tempted to think of the writers of these sixty-six books as though they were a great orchestra, not composed of poor mechanical strummers but of true musicians, carefully chosen, carefully trained, individual, different, yet contributing by their very differences to the unity of some glorious symphony under a great Director's wand. In that marvelous harmony of Holy Scripture, even the least-considered parts of the Bible have their place. None could be lacking without offending the great Musician's ear.

But, you say, this doctrine of inspiration is certainly a great paradox. It holds that these men were free, and yet that every word they wrote was absolutely determined by the Spirit of God. How is that possible? How could God determine the very words that these men wrote and yet not deal with them as mere machines?

Well, my friend, I will tell you how. I will tell you how God could do that. He could do it simply because God is God. There is a delicacy of discrimination in God's dealing with his creatures that far surpasses all human analogies. When God deals with men, he does not deal with them as with machines or as with sticks or stones. He deals with them as with men.

But what needs to be emphasized above all is that when God dealt thus with the biblical writers, though he dealt with them as with men and not as with machines, he accomplished his ends. He ordered their lives to fit them for their tasks. But then, in addition to that providential ordering of their lives, in addition to that use of their individual gifts of which we have spoken, there was a supernatural work of the Spirit of God that made the resulting book not man's book but God's book.

That supernatural work of the Spirit of God extends to all parts of the Bible. People say that the Bible is a book of religion and not a book of science, and that where it deals with scientific matters it is not to be trusted. When they say that, if they really know what they are saying, they are saying just about the most destructive thing that could possibly be imagined.

Is religion really independent of science? Well, "religion" is a very broad term. I will not say just how broad a term it is. Possibly it is even broad enough to include an attitude of the human soul that is independent of all facts with which science may legitimately deal. I am not saying whether such an attitude may or may not be called "religion." I am not much interested in the question. What I am interested in and what I am certain about is that whatever may be true of religion in general, the *Christian* religion is most emphatically dependent upon facts—facts in the eternal world, facts with which science, in the true sense of the word, certainly has a right to deal.

When you say that the Bible is a true guide in religion but that you do not care whether it is a true guide when it deals with history or with science, I should just like to ask you one question. What do you think of the Bible when it tells you that the body of the Lord Jesus came out of that tomb on the first Easter morning nineteen hundred years ago? That event of the resurrection, if it really happened, is an event in the external world. Account would have to be taken of it in any ideally complete scientific description of the physical universe. It is certainly a matter with which science, in principle, must deal. Well then, is that one of those scientific matters to which the inspiration of the Bible does not extend, one of those scientific matters with regard to which it makes no difference to the devout reader of the Bible whether the Bible is true or false?

There are many people who say just that. There are many people who do not shrink from that logical consequence of their division between religion and science. There are many people who say that the Bible would retain its full religious value even if scientific history should show that it is wrong about the resurrection of Jesus and that as a matter of fact Jesus never rose from the dead.

I say there are many people who say that, but the people who say that are not Christians. We Christians know that we are sinners; and we look to the Bible for something far more than inspiring poetry, soul-stirring exhortation, or expert instruction in the art of being religious. We look to the Bible for facts.

What good does it do to tell me that the type of religion presented in the Bible is a very fine type of religion and that the thing for me to do is just to start practicing that type of religion now? What good does it do to tell me that I have a fine pattern of religion in the account of Jesus in the Gospels, whether that account is history or an inspiring ideal? What good does it do to tell me to cultivate my religious nature in the manner in which the religious nature was cultivated with such eminent success by Jesus, by Paul, or by Isaiah?

I will tell you, my friend. It does me not one tiniest bit of good. You are mocking me when you talk to me like that. You are ignoring my true condition. You are ignoring the fact that in my own right I am a sinner under the wrath and curse of God, and that in my own strength I am under the awful bondage of sin. What *I* need, first of all, is not exhortation but a gospel, not directions for saving myself but knowledge of the way God has saved me. Have you any good news for me? That is the question that I ask of you. I know your exhortations will not help me. But if anything has been done to save me, will you not tell me the facts?

The Bible does tell me the facts. It tells me Jesus died on the cross to save me; it tells me he rose from the dead to complete his saving work and be my living Lord. What do I say when it tells me that? Do I say: "That is history and not religion. I am not interested in it; it may be true or it may not be true for all I care; the Bible is a book of religion and not a book of science or a book of history?" No, my friends, I do not say that. I say rather:

"Praise be to God for that blessed story of the resurrection and the cross; upon the truth of it all my hope depends for time and for eternity; how I rejoice that God himself has told me in his holy book that it is true!"

Here is a rule for you, my friends: no facts, no good news; no good news, no hope. The Bible is quite useless unless it is a record of facts.

Thank God it is a record of facts. The Spirit of God, in infinite mercy, was with the writers of the Bible not merely when they issued God's commands, but also—and just as fully— when they wrote the blessed record of what God had done.

What a dreadfully erroneous thing it is to say merely that the Bible *contains* the Word of God. No, it *is* the Word of God. It is the Word of God when it records the facts. It is the Word of God when it tells us what we must do.

Hear it as the Word of God, my friends. It will probe very deep into your life. It will reveal the dark secrets of your sin. But then it will bring you good tidings of salvation as no word of man can do.

6

Shall We Defend the Bible?

In the last few talks in this little series, I have been speaking to you about the inspiration of the Bible. I have been saying that the Bible is the Word of God and that, as such, it is completely true in matters of fact and completely authoritative when it issues commands.

That is certainly a good deal to say; it is certainly a large claim for me to make on behalf of a book that many people regard merely as a collection of Hebrew religious literature.

The question arises whether the claim is justified, whether the Bible is really and truly the Word of God.

I have a great deal of sympathy for those who raise that question, and I do not think that it is a question that ought to be dodged. If you should come into the classes that I try to conduct at Westminster Theological Seminary, I do not believe that you would charge me with dodging the question. I do try as best I can—only I wish my best were better—to show the students how we can deal with people who do not yet believe in the inspiration of the Bible. We cannot help them very much if we just assume that they already believe what we believe. Instead, we ought to try to understand their present position and then lead them logically from one thing to another until finally we can show them that the Bible is, as we believe it is, the Word of God.

When I say that, I do not mean that everyone who comes to believe in the inspiration of the Bible passes successively through those logical steps. In countless cases, conviction as to the divine authority of the Bible comes in very much more immediate fashion. A man hears some true preacher of the gospel who speaks on the authority of a book which lies open there on the pulpit. As the words of that book are expounded, the man who listens finds that the secrets of his heart are revealed. It is as though a cloak had been pulled away. The man suddenly sees himself as God sees him. He suddenly comes to see that he is a sinner under the just wrath and curse of God. Then from the same strange book there comes a wonderful offer of pardon. It comes with a strange kind of sovereign authority. The preacher, as he expounds the book, seems to be an ambassador of the King, a messenger of the living God. The man who hears needs no further reflection, no further argument. The Holy Spirit has opened the doors of his heart. "That book is the Word of the living God," he says. "God has found me out, I have heard his voice, I am his forever."

Yes, it is in this way, sometimes, and not by elaborate argument, that a man becomes convinced that the Bible is the Word of God.

Yet that does not mean that argument is unnecessary. Even that man in our illustration may meet criticism of his newfound conviction. People may tell him that the book which he thinks to be the Word of God is really full of errors and absurdities. How is he going to meet such criticism? Well, that depends. He may be able, because of his intellectual gifts, to meet the criticism squarely; he may be able to meet the critics on their own ground and show that, as a matter of fact, the Bible is *not* full of errors and absurdities. Or, he may be a simple soul unable to say any more to the critics of his newfound conviction than that which was said by that man in the ninth chapter of John: "One thing I do know, that though I was blind, now I see" (John 9:25).

But whatever may be possible to that converted man in our illustration, it is perfectly clear, when you take the Christian world as a whole, that convictions are held by but a precarious tenure if those who hold them continue, on principle, to ignore objections. After all, truth is essentially one. I may be convinced with my whole soul that the Bible is the Word of God; but if my neighbor adduces considerations to show that it is really full of error, I cannot be indifferent to those considerations. I can, indeed, say to him: "Your considerations are wrong, and because they are wrong I can with a good conscience hold on to my convictions." Or I can say to him: "What you say is true enough in itself, but it is irrelevant to the question whether the Bible is the Word of God." But I do not see how in the world I can say to him: "Your considerations may be contrary to my conviction that the Bible is the Word of God, but I am not interested in them; go on holding to them if you want to do so, but do please agree with me also in holding that the Bible is the Word of God."

No, I cannot possibly say that. This last attitude is surely quite absurd. Two contradictory things cannot both be true. We cannot go on holding to the Bible as the Word of God and at the same time admit the truth of considerations that are contrary to that conviction of ours.

I believe with all my soul, in other words, in the necessity of Christian apologetics—the necessity of a reasoned defense of the Christian faith, and in particular a reasoned defense of the Christian conviction that the Bible is the Word of God.

Some years ago, I attended a conference of Christian students. Various methods of Christian testimony were being discussed, and particularly the question was being discussed whether it is necessary to engage in a reasoned defense of the Christian faith. In the course of the discussion, a gentleman who had considerable experience in work among students arose and said that, according to his experience, you never win a man to Christ until you quit arguing with him. Well, do you know, my friends, when he said that I was not impressed one tiny little bit. Of course a man never was won to Christ *merely* by argument. That is perfectly clear. There must be the mysterious work of the Spirit of God in the new birth. Without that, all our arguments are quite useless. But just because argument is insufficient, it does not follow that it is unnecessary. What the Holy Spirit does in the new birth is not to make a man a Christian regardless of the evidence, but, on the contrary, to clear away the mists from his eyes and enable him to attend to the evidence.

So I believe in the reasoned defense of the inspiration of the Bible. Sometimes it is immediately useful in bringing a man to Christ—it is graciously used by the Spirit of God to that end. But its chief use is of a somewhat different kind. Its chief use is in enabling Christian people to answer the legitimate questions, not of vigorous opponents of Christianity, but of people who are seeking the truth and are troubled by the hostile voices that are heard on every hand.

Sometimes, when I have given a lecture in defense of the truth of the Bible—a lecture, for example which has adduced considerations to show that Christ really did rise from the dead on the third day—somebody has come up to me afterward and has said very kindly something to the following effect: "We liked your lecture all right, but the trouble is that the people who need it are not here; we who are here are all Christian people, we are all convinced already that the Bible is true, so we are not the ones who really needed to listen to what you had to say."

When people have told me that I have not been too much discouraged. It is true, I do wish that those persons who do not agree with me might occasionally give me a hearing. It does seem rather surprising that people who pride themselves in being so broadminded should take their information about what is called by its opponents "fundamentalism" from newspaper clippings instead of reading what these so-called fundamentalists—these conservatives, these Christians— have published in serious books over their own signatures or listening to what they have to say when they lecture. But although I do wish that my opponents in this debate would give me a fairer hearing, yet I am not too much discouraged when they are not present at one of my lectures. You see, what I am trying to do in such a lecture is not so much to win directly people who are opponents of the Bible as to give to Christian parents who may be present, or the Christian Sunday school teachers, materials that they can use, not with those whose backs are up against Christianity, but with the children in their own homes or in their Sunday school classes— the children who love them and want to be Christians as they are Christians, but are troubled by the voices against Christianity that are heard on every side.

Yes, I certainly do believe in Christian apologetics; I certainly do believe in the necessity of the reasoned defense of the truth of the Bible, and I have felt it to be my duty to engage in it myself, to the very best of my limited ability. But what is really important is that many persons far, far abler than I should engage in this great work.

Certainly, neglect of this work will be to the loss of countless precious souls. Some years ago, a kind of anti-intellectualism prevailed widely in the church. Scholars were despised by evangelists; theological seminaries were regarded either as nurseries of unbelief or as places where men engaged in dry-as-dust pursuits remote from living reality.

Well, many theological seminaries today *are* nurseries of unbelief; and because they are nurseries of unbelief, the churches that they serve have become unbelieving churches too. As go the theological seminaries, so goes the church. That is certainly true in the long run. Look out upon the condition of the church throughout the world today, and you will see that it is true.

But why is it that so many theological seminaries have become nurseries of unbelief and have dragged the churches that they serve down with them? It is partly because of that anti-intellectualistic attitude of pastors and evangelists, of which I spoke just now. Despising scholarship as they did and leaving it in possession of the enemy, they discover today that in the long run they cannot get along without it. When real revival comes in the church, we may be perfectly sure of one thing. We may be perfectly sure that with it, and as a vital part of it, will come a revival of Christian learning. That was true of the Reformation of the sixteenth century, and it will be true of every reformation or revival that does any more than merely scratch the surface.

I do wish people would read the twelfth chapter of First Corinthians more often than they seem to do—that chapter where Paul speaks of the diversity of gifts and of that one Spirit who "apportions to each one individually as he wills" (1 Cor 12:11). If they did read that great chapter more carefully, they would see that what was true of the supernatural gifts of the Spirit in the apostolic age is also true of the gifts which the Holy Spirit still graciously bestows upon the church. It is still quite true that one gift cannot do without the others. Certainly, it is true that evangelism cannot do without Christian scholarship. I do not like to think of the relationship between Christian scholarship and evangelism as being a balance between the two things. I do not like to say: "Let us have evangelism, but not so much evangelism as to crowd out Christian scholarship." No, the true state of the case is that you can hardly have evangelism unless you have Christian scholarship; and the more Christian scholarship you have, so much the more evangelism. Out of real theological seminaries, where the Bible is expounded and defended, come ministers and evangelists who know what they believe and why they believe it; and the preaching of such ministers and evangelists is graciously used of God for the salvation of precious souls. There is no guesswork about that. Look about you today, and you will see that it is simply a fact.

Well, perhaps you may say that I have said enough about the necessity of defending the Bible and ought now to go on and defend it. Obviously, I cannot do so today, since my time is nearly up. Also, I am not going to be able to do so in any great detail in the following talks of this series because, in this particular series, I am going to talk about what the Bible teaches rather than about the reasons which impel us to believe that the Bible is true. At some future time, I should particularly love to study the New Testament with you, for example, in order to show you how wonderful are the evidences of its truth, and how wonderfully those evidences of truthfulness confirm our conviction that the whole Bible is indeed the Word of God.

But even now, even in the present talk, I cannot leave you without saying just a word about the way in which we come to that great conviction about the Bible. I want just to indicate very briefly one great argument for the inspiration and divine authority of Holy Scripture. Mind you, it is not the only argument; but I am just singling it out by way of example this afternoon.

That argument is found in the testimony of Jesus Christ. In the first century of our era, there lived in Palestine a man called Jesus of Nazareth. We have certain records of his life in the New Testament. I want you to study them at least as historical documents. If you are not yet ready to take them as part of the inspired Word of God, as I do, study them at least, fairly, as historical documents.

If you do study them thus fairly, you will be impressed by the picture which they give of Jesus Christ. That picture is evidently the picture of a real person; of that there can be no doubt. But it is also the picture of a very strange person. The Jesus of the Gospels advanced stupendous claims and substantiated those claims by a sovereign power over the forces of nature. He seemed to command nature as nature's Maker and nature's God. He was clearly a supernatural person.

Modern men have tried to separate the supernatural from the natural in the gospel picture of Jesus. "We shall just remove these antiquated supernatural trappings from the picture," they have said to themselves, "and then we shall have a picture of the real Jesus, a great religious genius and nothing more." But the effort to make that separation has been a failure. The supernatural element in the gospel picture of Jesus has proved to be an integral part of the whole. It cannot be separated from the rest in that easy, artificial way. The gospel picture of Jesus is supernatural through and through.

Some radicals of the present day are drawing the logical conclusion. Because the supernatural is inseparable from the rest, and because they will not accept the supernatural, they are letting the whole go. They are telling us that we cannot know anything at all with any certainty about Jesus.

Such skepticism is preposterous. It will never hold the field. You need not be afraid of it at all, my friends. The picture in the Gospels is too vivid. It is too incapable of having been invented. It is evidently the picture of a real person.

So the age-long bewilderment of unsaved men in the presence of Jesus still goes on. Jesus will not let men go. They will not accept his stupendous claims; they will not accept him as their Savior. But he continues to intrigue and baffle them. He refuses to be pushed into their little molds. They stand bewildered in his presence.

There is only one escape from that bewilderment. It is to accept Jesus after all. Refuse to believe that the picture is true, and all is bewilderment and confusion in your view of the earliest age of the church; accept the picture as true, and all is plain. Everything then fits into its proper place. The key has been found to solve the mighty riddle.

The supernatural Jesus is thus the key to a right understanding of early Christian history. But he is also the key to far more than that. Mankind stands in the presence of more riddles than the riddle of New Testament times. All about us are riddles—the riddle of our existence, the riddle of the universe, the riddle of our misery and our sin. To all those riddles, Jesus, as the New Testament presents him, provides the key. He is the key not to some things but to everything. Very comprehensive, very wonderfully cumulative, very profound, and very compelling is the evidence for the reality of the supernatural Christ.

But if we are convinced by that evidence, we must take the consequences. If we are convinced that Jesus is what the New Testament says he is, then the Word of Jesus becomes for us law. We cannot then choose whether we will believe him when he speaks. We *must* believe. His authority then must, for us, be decisive in all disputes.

On many questions, our records do not record any decision of Jesus. But on one question his decision is plain. It is plain to us not only after we have become convinced that the records of his life are divinely inspired and therefore altogether without error, but it is plain even when we take those records merely as reasonably accurate history. If one thing is clear to the historian, it is that Jesus of Nazareth held to the full truthfulness of the Old Testament Scriptures; it is that Jesus held that high view of the divine authority of the Old Testament which is held by despised believers in the Bible today.

That is admitted even by those who have a low opinion of the truthfulness of the Gospels. Jesus, they admit, held that view of the Bible which was held generally by the Jews of his day. They are sorry to admit that. "Too bad," they say, "that Jesus, whom we admire so much, was in this respect a child of his time!" But admit it, if they are scholars, they must. Jesus did certainly believe that the Old Testament was the very Word of God, and he certainly placed that belief at the very heart of his life as a man.

But if he thus pointed back to the Old Testament and founded his human life upon it, he also pointed forward to the New. He chose apostles. He endowed them with a supernatural authority. In exercise of that authority, they gave the New Testament books to the church. No man who believes what Jesus says can, if he is consistent, help taking the whole Bible as the very Word of God.

When we do take the whole Bible thus as the very Word of God, we find rich and manifold confirmation of our decision. We find it in the marvelous unity of Holy Scripture—what the Westminster Confession calls "the consent of all the parts" (WCF 1.5). We find it in the countless evidences of truthfulness in detail. We find it in the utter dissimilarity of this book to other books. We find it in the sweetness and peace of a life grounded upon what this book tells. Yes, my friends, very rich and varied, yet marvelously convergent, is the evidence that bids us take the Bible as the Word of God.

7

The Bible versus Human Authority

If the Bible is really the Word of God, as we have said it is, a question arises: what does it actually mean in our lives to take the Bible in that way?

I want to talk to you for a little while about that question now.

The answer to the question ought not to be so very difficult, however difficult some of the implications of the answer may turn out to be. If we take the Bible as the Word of God, then the Bible becomes our standard of truth and of life. When we are asked whether we can support any kind of message or engage in any course of conduct, what we do is simply compare that message or that course of conduct with the Bible. If it agrees with the Bible, we can support it or follow it; if it does not agree with the Bible, we cannot support it or follow it, no matter what we may be told by other authorities to do.

I really think it is very important that this should be perfectly clear. We are living at a time when a very serious difference of opinion has appeared in the church. The first question in dealing with any difference of opinion is the question of what standard of judgment is to be applied to the question at issue. Unless people can agree about that preliminary question, it is not likely that they will agree about anything else.

Suppose I have an engagement with a businessman in Philadelphia in the summertime. The engagement is for eleven o'clock. I come in from the country and appear at the office promptly at eleven. But when I get there, I find the man with whom I have the engagement considerably perturbed. "What do you mean," he says, "by keeping me and these other gentlemen waiting in this way? The engagement was for eleven o'clock, and it is now exactly twelve. You are exactly an hour late." I then reply in kind. "You surprise me," I say; "in fact, I should really hesitate to characterize the impropriety of your words. My watch says exactly eleven o'clock, and I would back my watch against any cheap office clock in the whole city of Philadelphia." Then, after we have disputed about the matter vigorously for a good while, I discover that Philadelphia is on daylight saving time. You see, we could not come to any agreement because we were applying different standards to the question under dispute.

It is somewhat that way with the difference of opinion in the church. There, too, the disputing parties cannot come to an agreement because they are operating with different standards. In one very important particular, however, our illustration of daylight saving time and standard time does not apply to the situation in the church. In the case of my imaginary dispute with that businessman, both parties to the dispute could be right because it did not make any particular difference which of the two standards should be applied. It did not make any very great difference whether we should go on daylight saving time or on standard time, just so we were, both of us, perfectly clear as to which was being used. But in the case of the situation in the church, both parties to the dispute are laying claim to the same thing—namely, truth. Therefore, they cannot both be right. In this case, the standard that is sought is not just some arbitrary method of dividing up the day, but it is a standard of truth, and truth is not relative but absolute.

However, the illustration does at least show that if two parties to any dispute are to understand each other—to say nothing of coming to an agreement—the first question they must discuss is the question of what standard is to be used. Certainly, that principle applies in fullest measure to the difference of opinion in the church. Here we find perfectly earnest and sincere people differing from each other in the sharpest possible way. What one holds to be true, the other holds to be false; what one holds to be wise and beneficent, the other holds to be destructive. Discussion between the contending parties sometimes seems only to make matters worse; it sometimes seems only to lead to greater irritation and greater confusion. The reason for this unfortunate state of affairs—at least one important reason for it—is perfectly plain. It is found in the fact that the contending parties do not see clearly that the real ground of their difference of opinion is that they have totally different standards of truth and of life.

I have already said what our standard is. It is the Bible. When we are deciding whether we can support any propaganda or engage in any course of conduct, we simply ask whether that propaganda or that course of conduct agrees with the Bible.

I think I can best explain what it means to take the Bible thus as one's standard of truth and of life if I set this standard over against some of the other standards that are being proposed today.

Many persons, for example, are taking human experience as their standard. They are saying that they will adhere to that kind of religion which works the best and which shows itself to be the best in actual practice.

I remember that some years ago I preached a baccalaureate sermon at a college. When I got through, a member of the graduating class asked me what I thought of a certain religious movement, the name of which is entirely aside from our present point. I intimated that I could not support it. In reply, he told me that he, for his part, thought it was the most "vital" thing in the religious world today. That young man and I did not get very far in our discussion because we were applying different standards. He was applying the standard of experience; I was applying the standard of the Bible.

That young man favored the religious movement that we were discussing because it was "vital." Well, in one sense noxious weeds in a garden are vital. They often grow up more rapidly than the flowers. But the careful gardener is inclined to pull them up. So also we refuse to make mere rapidity of growth or enthusiasm of adherents the criterion by which any religious movement shall be judged. Instead, we test every movement by the Bible. If it agrees with the Bible, we approve it; if it disagrees with the Bible, we oppose it, no matter what external successes it may attain, and no matter even what apparent graces it may seem to our superficial human judgment to induce here and there in its adherents. Those apparent graces, we are sure, will, if the movement is contrary to the Bible, never stand the test to which they will be subjected at the judgment seat of God. God does not contradict his own Word.

That same use of experience as the standard of truth and of life underlies what I believe has been called somewhere "the great inquiry racket." There has arisen in recent years a perfect craze for questionnaires on the subject of religion, open forums and inquiries of various kinds. The thing has become one of the major nuisances of the day. When one contemplates the unscientific character of many of these enterprises and their begging of the real underlying questions, one is tempted to dismiss them as being unworthy of consideration. Many of them are not really inquiries at all, but are merely agencies carrying on propaganda through the particular device of question-begging questionnaires. The people who conduct them are, of course, honest. They are trying to get at the truth; but, the trouble is, they are so completely out of sympathy with the Christian religion that when they formulate their questionnaires they do not know how even to give a Christian man the opportunity of casting his vote or of giving expression to his convictions.

But absurdly unscientific and question-begging though many of these inquiries and questionnaires are, a serious purpose, even though it be a mistaken purpose, does, I think, underlie them. The purpose underlying them is, I think, that through an examination of various types of religion we may arrive, by a process of comparison and elimination, at that type of religion which is best adapted to the age in which we are living and which therefore is the type of religion which it is thought we ought to adopt. Those who engage in these inquiries and questionnaires, or at any rate many of those who engage in them, are making human experience the standard of truth and of life.

That standard is quite different from the standard to which we hold. These persons are advocating a "managed currency" in religion, whereas we are on the gold standard. Our standard is not a flexible standard. Far from holding that what is true today becomes false tomorrow, according to the shifting needs of human life, we find our standard both of truth and of conduct in the Bible, which we hold to be not a product of human experience but the Word of God.

And so we reject the first alternative view that we are considering in this little talk. We reject experience as our standard.

In the second place, we reject as our standard what is wrongly called "the teaching of Jesus" or "the teaching of Christ." At that point I am particularly anxious not to be misunderstood. I certainly hold that the real teaching of Jesus is all completely true. I hold that everything that Jesus said in the sphere of fact is true and that his commands are all completely valid. But my point is that those who make the teaching of Jesus their authority, *as distinguished from the Bible*, are not really holding to the teaching of Jesus at all. We have seen how clearly Jesus testified to the authority of the Bible. How then, if you reject the authority of the Bible, can you possibly claim to be true to Jesus's teaching?

What is the underlying notion of those who make what they call the teaching of Jesus their authority instead of the Bible? I am afraid that question is not hard to answer. It is the notion that Jesus was primarily a teacher, that we honor him because, by his word and by his example, he taught us how to practice the same type of religion as that which he practiced. Jesus, according to this way of thinking, was the founder of Christianity because he was the first Christian. Other men honor Buddha or Confucius as the great teacher and example; we, say the men of this way of thinking, are Christians because we take Jesus, as distinguished from Buddha or Confucius, as *our* teacher and example.

That notion is, of course, radically contrary to the Bible, but it is also radically contrary to the real Jesus's own teaching. Jesus, according to the Bible and according to his own teaching, came, as has well been observed, not primarily to say something, but to do something. He came not just to teach us true general principles of religion and ethics but to redeem us from sin by his death upon the cross.

His teaching is indeed very precious. How wonderfully precious it is, my friends! But its preciousness is altogether lost when it is separated from the rest of the Bible. We miss the very heart and core and substance of it if we take it out of its organic connection with that grand sweep of supernatural revelation that runs through the Bible from Genesis to Revelation and if we separate it from that mighty saving work which culminated in the cross and resurrection of Christ.

Thus we reject this notion that the teaching of Jesus as distinguished from the Bible is the seat of authority. It is profoundly dishonoring to the teaching of Jesus itself. It degrades Jesus to the level of a mere religious teacher, the founder of one of the world's religions.

I am inclined to think that most of those who begin by saying that the teaching of Jesus is their authority are, if they reflect about the matter, obliged to modify their position. Jesus obviously said many things which they do not regard as true. But if Jesus said many things that are untrue, how can his teaching be authoritative?

Well, a great many of these men respond, with more or less clearness, that it is not the teaching of Jesus as such—or, as they would put it, not the "letter" of his teaching—but the underlying "spirit" of his teaching which they regard as authoritative.

That brings us to the third of the alternatives to the authority of the Bible which we are now passing under review. It is the alternative of those who say that their authority is "the spirit of Jesus."

Of course when they use the phrase "the spirit of Jesus," they do not mean at all what the Bible means by it. The Bible means by it the Holy Spirit, the third person of the blessed Trinity. They, on the other hand, spell the word "spirit" with a small letter, not with a capital, and they mean by "the spirit of Jesus" simply the inner temper or quality of Jesus's life. We are Christians, according to the advocates of this view, not because of any particular thing that Jesus did nineteen hundred years ago, not even because we obey any particular commands that he uttered, but because we have caught the inner spirit or temper of his life. The spirit of his life has been handed down from generation to generation. It is a kind of contagion. One who has caught that spirit passes it on to another. To catch that spirit, a man does not need to have any particular view about Jesus; indeed, he does not even need to know that Jesus ever lived. All that he needs to do is to take into his life the peculiar spirit of Jesus's life no matter how it is mediated to him, no matter from what particular Christian he receives it, no matter whether he knows that it is the spirit of Jesus or has ever heard of Jesus at all. So that, we are told in accordance with this view, if a missionary is not permitted to proclaim Christ by his words, he may at least proclaim him by his life; he may be a true missionary merely by "living Christ" as distinguished from preaching Christ; those who come into contact with him can catch from him "the spirit of Jesus" or "the spirit of Christ" even if he is not allowed to tell them anything about the cross of Christ or about the God in whom Jesus believed. And if people, through such missionaries, have caught the spirit of Jesus, what more could possibly be desired?

Such, carried to its logical conclusion, is the view which makes "the spirit of Jesus," in distinction from the Bible, the test of truth and of life.

What is wrong with it from the Christian point of view? Many things, no doubt. But at the heart of what is wrong with it is this: it ignores the fact of sin. All that we need, say the advocates of it, is to catch the spirit of Jesus. If we catch the spirit of Jesus, we can live the life that Jesus lived and then all will be well. Very different is what the real Christian says. The real Christian knows that unlike Jesus he is, of himself, under the guilt and power of sin, subject to the just wrath of God, unable to do any good, without hope, save as Jesus has redeemed him by his precious blood. Can we catch the spirit of Jesus in the manner that is so glibly regarded as possible by those who have never been convicted of sin? Ah, no. We know only too well that we were dead in our trespasses and sins, and that only as we have been made alive by the mysterious act of the Spirit of God can we even begin to be true followers of the holy Jesus.

These two things are poles apart. I do not think that there can be any clearness in our thinking so long as we confuse the one of them with the other. The man who thinks that all we need is to catch the spirit of Jesus and that we can catch that spirit without knowing what Jesus did for us on the cross and without the supernatural act of the Spirit of God in the new birth—that man takes Jesus as just a teacher and example. A Christian man, on the other hand, takes Jesus primarily as a Savior. Where is he presented to us as our Savior? The answer is, "In the whole Bible"; and that is the reason why the Bible is to us such a very precious book.

I have not time to speak at any length of other things which are being proposed as substitutes for the authority of the Bible. But before I leave you, I do want to say just a word or two about one of these. It is the view that takes as the test of truth and of life the pronouncements and regulations of the church.

Those who hold to this view as to the seat of authority do not usually deny the authority of the Bible in so many words. What they do is say—by implication if not in words—that the Bible is interpreted authoritatively by the "living church." "When a man becomes a minister or a member of a church," they say in effect, "it is his duty to support the program of that church. He may think that it is contrary to the Bible but never mind, it is not his business in this particular matter to think; he must submit his judgment to the judgment of the councils of his church; he must let them interpret the Bible for him and must make the message that he supports conform to their shifting votes."

In sharp distinction from that view, we make the Bible, and the Bible only, the test of truth and of life. There is no living authority to interpret the Bible for us. We must read it, everyone for himself, and ask God to help us as we read. A church that commands us to support any program on the authority of the decisions of the church is usurping in the interests of fallible men an authority that belongs only to God.

But is it not a dangerous thing to reject other authorities in this fashion and submit ourselves unreservedly to the authority of this one book? Yes, it is a very dangerous thing. It puts us sharply in conflict with the whole current of the age. But if it is a dangerous thing, it is also a very blessed thing. It is a very blessed thing to hear the Word of the living God.

It is also a very blessed thing to proclaim that Word to others. Every Christian has the duty and the inestimable privilege of proclaiming it to others. But that duty and that privilege belong particularly to ministers.

What do you ministers do—if any of you are attending to me now—when you enter into your pulpits on Sunday mornings? Do you tell the people about your religious experiences? Do you give them the benefit of your expert advice? Do you express to them your views on the great questions of the day? Do you make yourselves the promotion agents of some human organization? If you do these things, you may have very rich rewards, but there is one thing that you will miss. You may be great orators, but never will you be ministers of Jesus Christ. You may proclaim man's word with marvelous eloquence, but never can you proclaim the Word of God.

Oh, may God send us ministers of another kind! God grant that you, my brothers, may be ministers of another kind! May God send us ministers who come forth into their pulpits from a secret place of meditation and prayer, who are servants of Christ and not servants of men, who be they ever so humble are ambassadors of the King; who, as they stand behind the open Bible and expound its blessed words, can truly and honestly say, with Micaiah the son of Imlah: "As the Lord lives, what the Lord says to me, that I will speak" (1 Kings 22:14).

8

Life Founded upon Truth

Having considered with you the question of what kind of book the Bible is, I think it is now high time that we should open that book together and find out what is in it. We have shown that the Bible is worth reading because it is the Word of God. Well, if it is worth reading, let us now begin to read it and see whether we can discover what it contains. What does the Bible teach?

I had in mind a very good answer to that question when I was so very young as to have very little else in my mind. It is the answer to the third question in the Shorter Catechism, and it seems to me to be a very good thing. There are 106 other good things in that catechism. Those are the answers to the others of the 107 questions. I should certainly not go quite so far as to say what some Presbyterian is accused of having said—that the Shorter Catechism is more important than the Bible because the Shorter Catechism is "the Bible boiled down"—but all the same, I am a convinced Presbyterian too, and I do maintain that the Shorter Catechism, with its marvelous comprehensiveness, its faithfulness to Scripture, and its solemnity and tenderness, is the truest and noblest summary of what the Bible teaches that I have ever seen.

The third question in the Shorter Catechism is the question in which I am interested just now: "What do the Scriptures principally teach?" The answer is: "The Scriptures principally teach what man is to believe concerning God, and what duty God requires of man" (WSC Q&A 3).[1]

The thing that I want you to notice about this answer is that it makes

---

1. Machen cites the Westminster Shorter Catechism frequently in these addresses. See the back of this volume for a complete index of these references.

the Scriptures principally teach, first, what man is to believe and, second, what man is to do. It puts truth before conduct, doctrine before life. It makes truth the foundation of conduct and doctrine the foundation of life.

Today, the order is commonly reversed. Life comes first, we are told, and doctrine comes afterward. Religion is first an experience and only secondarily a doctrine. Doctrine is merely an expression of religious experience, and although the experience remains essentially the same, its doctrinal expression must change as the generations pass. So, it is said, we value the great creeds of the church not at all because we regard as true—in the plain man's sense of the word "true"—the things that they contain, but because they expressed, in the language of a bygone day, an experience which we can still share. So it is also, we are told, with the Bible. It is a great mistake, we are told, to take what the Bible says about Jesus as being true in the ordinary sense of the word "true"; but it is a still greater mistake to miss the experience which underlies what the Bible says. Thus when the Bible says that Jesus was born of a virgin, we do not, of course, it is said, believe that any physical miracle took place in connection with the birth of Jesus nineteen hundred years ago. But we do think that the men of that day were giving expression to something very precious when they said that, and we ought not to miss that very precious thing. Thus also, it is said, when people of long ago said that Jesus was God, they of course meant by that expression something that we do not at all accept. They meant that a heavenly person who had existed from all eternity came into this world by a voluntary act when Jesus of Nazareth was born. We do not at all believe that, say the persons whose views we are now summarizing; on the contrary, we believe that the person Jesus never existed before he was born in that Jewish family. Well, then, shall we just reject what those persons said when they declared Jesus to be God? Not at all, it is said; they were giving true expression in the language of their day to something that is just as precious to us as it was to them. They could not possibly give expression to it in any other language. If they had tried to give expression to it in our language, that would for them have been utterly false and futile. Do we then still believe in the deity of Christ? Oh, yes—as the expression of a great experience. That experience is the really essential thing, but the intellectual expression of it must necessarily change from age to age.

Such is the attitude that is dominant in the religious world of our day—religion as an experience and doctrine as just the necessarily changing expression of the experience; life first and creed as just the changing expression of it. Those are the shibboleths that designate the prevailing attitude.

What shall we think of that attitude? Well, in the first place, I think we ought to face clearly the fact that it is an attitude of the most complete unbelief that could possibly be imagined. It denies not this truth or that but truth itself. It denies that there is any possibility of attaining to a truth which will always be true. There is truth, it holds, for this generation and truth for that generation, but no truth for all generations; there is truth for this race and truth for that race, but no truth for all races.

I remember some years ago that I read a paper at a conference of theological professors on the subject of revelation. I read a paper, and then another professor read a paper, and then still other professors made remarks about the papers. One of those latter professors said that although he disagreed with me completely, and agreed much more with my opponent, yet he was bound to say he thought that, so far as the definition of terms was concerned, I was a good deal nearer than my opponent to the historic meaning of the term "revelation." I thought that was very encouraging. But then he went on to say that even I did not mean the same thing by that term as people used to mean by it. Then he developed, with more or less clearness, the view that, in general, words are bound to change their meaning so that we never mean by the words that we use what past generations meant by them.

At any rate, whether that was what that particular professor said or not, I think it does represent what a good many people are saying. A good many people seem to think that every generation lives in a sort of intellectual watertight compartment, without much chance of converse with other generations. Every generation has its own thought-forms and cannot by any chance use the thought-forms of any other generation. Do you know what I think of this notion? I think it comes very near being nonsense. If it were true, then books produced in past generations ought to be pure gibberish to us.

Take any book of Aristotle, for example. Aristotle lived some three and a half centuries before Christ. That book of Aristotle is composed of thousands of words. When Aristotle wrote the book, it made sense because the writer knew the meaning of every one of those thousands of words. Knowing the meaning of those words, he could fit them together so that the resulting book would make sense. But then, according to the theory with which we are now dealing, the meaning of every one of those words began to wobble, and has been wobbling for twenty-two centuries. Of course, the words would not all wobble to just exactly the same extent and in exactly the same direction. That would be a chance too remote to be considered. The probabilities against it would be ten billion or more to one. Very well, then. What will inevitably be the result? The result, after twenty-two centuries of wobbling, will be that all those thousands of words will be completely out of alignment and the resulting book will be a meaningless jumble.

Yes, that will be the inevitable result if that professorial theory as to the inevitable shift in the meanings of words is correct. But the trouble is that that inevitable result is not the actual result. As a matter of fact, that book of Aristotle is just as limpidly clear and logical today as it ever was. What does that show? It shows that the theory that we have been dealing with is untrue. It shows that, as a matter of fact, words do not change their meaning in that kaleidoscopic way. It shows that there is an intellectual gold standard which enables us to carry on commerce perfectly well with the men of past generations.

What is true of different ages in the history of mankind is also true of different races coexisting today. People say that Western creeds ought not to be forced upon the Oriental mind. The Oriental mind, they say, ought to be allowed to go its own way and give its own expressions to the Christian faith. Well, I have examined one or two of those supposed expressions of the Oriental mind, and I am bound to say that they look to me uncommonly like the expressions of the mind of the south side of Chicago. But how about it? Ought we to give our Western creeds to the Oriental mind? I shall just pass over the question whether those so-called Western creeds are really Western. Let us call them "Western creeds" in quotation marks and for the sake of the argument. Ought those "Western creeds" to be given to the Oriental mind? What is our answer?

The answer is: "Certainly." Of course those Western creeds ought to be given to the Oriental mind. But that ought to be done only on one condition—that those Western creeds are true. If they are not true, they ought not to be given to the Oriental mind or to any other kind of mind; but if they are true, they are just as true in China as they are in the United States.

The truth is that although I am thought by some of my friends to be very gullible, believing as I do that the Bible is true and that miracles really happened, there are some things about which I am a confirmed skeptic. Frankly, I do not believe in the separate existence of an Oriental mind or an occidental mind or an ancient mind or a medieval mind or a modern mind. I do believe, indeed, that different races of mankind have different aptitudes or talents. It is perhaps that French writers have the special gift of clearness, while Germans are characterized by a power of metaphysical speculation and by a certain solidity and thoroughness of learning. It must be admitted, indeed, that some German writers are admirably clear and some French writers, on the other hand, are awfully muddled. But still I suppose it is true to a very considerable extent that clearness is especially a French virtue of style. I have a great respect also for the intellectual gifts of Oriental peoples. I have no doubt but that those peoples are contributing something very valuable, and are going to contribute something still more valuable, to the intellectual life of the world.

But the really important thing is that under all fluctuations between this age and that age, between this nation and that nation, there is a gold standard of truth. We may misunderstand ancient writers, but our very recognition of the possibility of misunderstanding them shows that there is also a possibility of understanding them. I may have difficulty in understanding the mental processes of the Chinese and the Japanese, as they may have difficulty in understanding mine; but the very fact that we can both detect that difficulty affords hope that the difficulty may be overcome, since the fact that we can detect that difficulty shows that there is a common, intellectual ground upon which we can stand.

I think, therefore, that we can safely resist the bottomless skepticism which holds that all that remains constant from generation to generation is an experience that must clothe itself in ever-changing intellectual forms. I think that we may safely resist the skepticism which holds that the convictions of one generation can never by any chance be the convictions of another.

But are convictions important? Many people say that they are not. It does not make much difference, they say, what a man believes; life is the thing that counts. But merely saying a thing often does not make the thing true. As a matter of fact, it does make a tremendous difference what a man believes.

A modern French novelist wrote, in 1889, a very interesting book to show that that is the case. I have just been re-reading it, and I find it almost as impressive as I found it when I read it the first time. The novelist who wrote it is hardly to be put in the first rank of French writers. But this one book of his is certainly worth reading. Some years ago I was talking about it to a French lecturer and critic who was inclined to be very severe upon this writer. But then I said that I had read one book of this writer and that it seemed to my poor judgment to be a masterpiece. "Yes," said the critic with whom I was talking, "that particular book of this writer is indeed a masterpiece." The book that I am referring to is the novel by Paul Bourget entitled *Le Disciple*, "The Disciple." It describes, with a delicacy of touch in which French writers excel, the simple and austere life of a noted philosopher and psychologist. He was engrossed altogether in the things of the mind. His lodging was up four flights of stairs. His daily existence was an invariable routine. Coffee at six o'clock, lunch or breakfast at ten, walk until noon, work again until four, visits of scholars and students three times a week from four to six, dinner at six, short walk, work, bed promptly at ten. An inoffensive, scholarly man if there ever was one, a man who, in the words of his caretaker, "wouldn't hurt a fly."

But one day this peaceful routine was strangely broken into. The philosopher was summoned to a criminal inquest. A former pupil of his was accused of murder. He had been a brilliant young man, who had climbed those four flights of stairs full of enthusiasm for what he regarded as liberating doctrines. He had drunk in those doctrines only too well. In the prison, he wrote an account of his life for the eye of his revered master. In it the abstract becomes concrete. The terrible story is told of the way in which those supposedly liberating doctrines work out in actual practice.

It is rather a tremendous little book, that study of "The Disciple" by Paul Bourget.

But the same tragedy as that which is so powerfully depicted in that little book is appearing on a gigantic scale in the whole history of our times. Fifty or even twenty-five years ago, certain views about God and about the Bible might have seemed to a superficial observer to be perfectly respectable and perfectly innocent—as harmless and as remote from anything like tragedy as Bourget's philosopher up his four flights of stairs. It was such a sweet, pleasant thing—that older Modernism, or "Liberalism," as it was euphemistically called. But today it is having its perfect work. It is destroying civil and religious liberty; it is defiling the sweetness and gentleness of the Christian home; it is causing contracts public and private to be explained away, until the man or the nation that swears to his own hurt and changes not is regarded as a curious relic of the past. Do you look with complacency upon this world where purity and honesty and liberty are regarded as out-of-date? Do you think it is going to be a pleasant world to live in? If you do, you are blind. You have to be blind not to see that mankind is today standing over an abyss.

Do not be deceived, my friends. This notion that it does not make much difference what a man believes, this notion that doctrine is unimportant and that life comes first, is one of the most devilish errors that is to be found in the whole of Satan's arsenal. How many human lives it has wrecked, how many mothers' hearts it has broken! That French novelist is entirely right. Out of the Pandora box of highly respectable philosophy come murders, adulteries, lies, and every evil thing.

Well, I have been talking about various things. It might look as though I had forgotten all about the thing I started out to talk about. It might look as though I had forgotten all about the Bible. But indeed that is not the case. I have been talking about these other things, I have been talking about the snarl into which men have come, only in order that at the last I may lead you to the place where that snarl may be straightened out. What does the Bible say about the question that we have been discussing this afternoon? What does the Bible say about the question whether doctrine is merely the changing expression of life or whether—the other way around—life is founded upon doctrine?

You do not have to read very far in the Bible in order to get the answer. The answer is given to you in the first verse. Does the Bible begin with exhortation; does it begin with a program of life? No, it begins with a doctrine. "In the beginning, God created the heavens and the earth" (Gen 1:1). That is the foundational doctrine upon which everything else that the Bible says is based.

The Bible does present a way of life; it tells men the way in which they ought to live, but always when it does so it grounds that way of life in truth.

Run through the Bible in your minds, my friends, and see whether I am not right.

In the Old Testament, a wonderful program of life is presented. It is called the Ten Commandments. But do the Ten Commandments begin with commandments? Not at all. They begin with doctrine: "I am the LORD your God, who brought you out of the land of Egypt, out of the house of slavery" (Exod 20:2). That is the preface to the Ten Commandments. It is not a commandment. It is not a program. It is a doctrine. Only because that doctrine is true—only because the one speaking in the commandments is the Lord God—have the commandments any authority.

The Old Testament contains another wonderful presentation of the way in which men should live. Like the Ten Commandments, it was quoted by Jesus. It reads: "You shall love the Lord your God with all your heart and with all your soul and with all your might" (Deut 6:5). That is a wonderful commandment indeed, that commandment of love. But does it begin with a commandment? Not at all. It begins with a doctrine. It is grounded upon a doctrine. "Hear, O Israel: The Lord our God, the Lord is one. You shall love the Lord your God with all your heart and with all your soul and with all your might" (Deut 6:4–5). Only because that doctrine is true has the commandment any meaning. Only because there is one God, and only because that one God is Jehovah, are God's people commanded to love that one God with all their heart and soul and might.

Turn then to the New Testament. The New Testament tells us how Jesus came. Did he come in the modern fashion, telling people that it made no difference what they believed and that the thing for them to do was just to live life first and then afterward give doctrinal expression to the life?

Well, he did come presenting to them a life that they should live. "Repent," he said, when he came forward in his public ministry in Galilee. But is that all that he said? Did he just say: "Repent, repent, repent, repent, repent"? Not at all. He said: "Repent, for the kingdom of heaven is at hand" (Matt 4:17). "The kingdom of heaven is at hand" is not a command or a program. It is a doctrine; and upon that doctrine the command of Jesus to repent is based.

Jesus sat one day by the well and talked to a sinful woman. In the course of the conversation, he laid his finger upon the sore spot in that woman's life. "You have had five husbands," he said; "and the one you now have is not your husband" (John 4:18). Then, apparently to evade the disconcerting question of the sin in her own life, the woman asked Jesus a theological question about the right place in which to worship God—whether on Mount Gerizim or in Jerusalem. What did Jesus do with that woman's theological question? Did he brush it aside after the manner of certain modern religious workers? Did he say: "You are evading the real question; we will take up your theological question afterward, but now let us come back to the question of the sin in your own life." No, he did nothing of the kind. He answered that woman's theological question with the utmost fullness, as though the woman's soul depended on her getting the right answer. Not Gerizim, he said, but Jerusalem is the place in which to worship God, but the time is coming when the worship of God will be bound to no set places. And then, in response to that sinful, unconverted woman's question, Jesus engaged in some of the profoundest theological teaching in the whole of the Bible. Apparently, Jesus regarded a right doctrine of God not as something that comes along after salvation but as something necessary to salvation.

At the beginning of the book of Acts, Jesus is said to have told his disciples to be witnesses unto him. On the day of Pentecost, a few days later, Peter arose to obey that command. He preached that great sermon which is found in the second chapter of Acts. What did he say in that sermon? He had not had some advantages which men have today. He had not had the inestimable advantage of modern religious education. If he had, no doubt he would have told the people that it did not make any difference what doctrine they held about Jesus or about anything else, and that life was the only thing that mattered. But poor Peter! He had not had the advantage of modern religious education. He had to content himself with another advantage—he had just been filled with the Holy Ghost. The result is that his sermon is doctrinal through and through. He just gave them the facts about Jesus. Not a bit of exhortation, nothing about a program. Just facts, facts, facts, doctrine, doctrine, doctrine. What was the result? They were "cut to the heart" (Acts 2:37). Then Peter told them what to do. Three thousand were saved.

So it is everywhere in the Bible, my friends. First doctrine, then life. The Bible, from Genesis to Revelation, gives not a bit of comfort to the skeptical notion that doctrine is the mere changing and symbolic expression of the Christian experience. The Bible founds living everywhere squarely upon truth. God grant that you may all receive that truth for the saving of your souls, and that, having been saved, you may live true Christian lives upon this earth and then live in God's presence forevermore!

9

God, the Creator

We have seen that the Bible is doctrinal through and through. It gives not the slightest bit of comfort to the skeptical notion, so much in vogue today, that doctrine is merely the necessarily changing form in which Christian experience expresses itself. The Bible, unlike this skepticism, grounds life squarely in truth. Christianity, according to the Bible, is not a life as distinguished from a doctrine and it is not a life that has doctrine as its changing expression, but—just the other way around—it is a life founded upon a doctrine.

That doctrine upon which the Bible grounds life is not one isolated doctrine, and it is not a mere series of doctrines, but it is a system of doctrine. If the Bible contained a number of divergent systems, it could not possibly be the Word of God, because it could not possibly be true throughout. The ordination pledge to which all ministers and elders in the Presbyterian Church in the United States (PCUSA) have subscribed is quite right in speaking of *the* system of doctrine taught in the Holy Scriptures.

I think great stress ought to be laid upon that fact. A great deal of harm is done when people take one part of the teaching of the Bible out of its connection with the rest, or when they leave gaps in their presentation of what the Bible teaches. It is very important to see that the Bible does far more than present isolated truths. It is very important to see that it presents a system of truth, and it is very important to view that system not in part but as a whole.

As we study that system here together, let us remember, above all things, that it is not a system which man has devised but a system which God has revealed graciously in his holy Word.

Where shall we begin in our study of that great system of revealed truth that the Bible contains? I think we ought to begin where the Bible begins. I think we ought to begin with a consideration of what the Bible teaches about God as the Creator and Ruler of the world.

There are many today who insist that we ought to begin at another place. There are many who tell us that we ought to begin with a consideration of the human life of Jesus. In fact, these people often tell us that that is where we ought not only to begin but also to end. They are telling us that is all we really need to know.

All that we need to know about God, they tell us, is that God is like Jesus. We do not need to know how the universe came into being, they tell us, or whether there is a God who governs it in its course. These things belong to metaphysics, they say, not to religion. We are not interested, they say, in the question of whether God is powerful, but are only interested in conceiving of him as good.

Such is the view of those who use the phrase "the Christlike God." That phrase, as it is commonly used, grates upon Christian ears. It grates upon the ears of those who believe not that God is *like* Jesus, but that Jesus himself *is* God.

But what is wrong with that view? Aside from the terminology that is used to set it forth, what is wrong with the view itself? What is wrong with this notion that all that we know about God is that he possesses the moral excellency that is found in the man Jesus?

Two things at least are wrong with it. In the first place, it is terribly degrading to Jesus. That may seem strange at first sight. It may seem strange that a view which holds that all we need to know about God is that God is like Jesus should be derogatory to Jesus, but a little reflection will show that it *is* derogatory to Jesus in the extreme.

It is derogatory to Jesus because it does despite to the deepest things in Jesus's teaching and example. At the very heart of the life of Jesus was just that view of God which is being so contemptuously rejected by those who say that the moral life of the man Jesus tells us all that we need to know about God.

Jesus certainly believed that God is the Creator and Ruler of the universe, and that belief belonged to the foundation of everything that he believed. Not a sparrow, he said to his disciples, shall "fall to the ground apart from your Father" (Matt 10:29). It is God, according to Jesus, who clothes the lilies of the field (Luke 12:27–28), and it is God who makes the sun to rise on the evil and on the good (Matt 5:45). There can be no doubt whatever but that Jesus held just that view of God which the persons of whom we have been speaking reject as being mere metaphysics. He put at the very foundation of his teaching and his life that divinely revealed metaphysic which is found in the first verse of Genesis. Everything that he did and everything that he said was based upon this great truth: "In the beginning, God created the heavens and the earth" (Gen 1:1). God, according to Jesus, is the Creator and the absolute ruler of the universe, bringing all things to pass in accordance with the counsel of his will. You may not like that view of God, but if you are a historian who sees things as they are, you will be obliged to recognize the fact that it was certainly the view held by Jesus of Nazareth.

Moreover, Jesus certainly held that men had a true knowledge of God before he appeared upon the earth. He held that they had the true knowledge of God from the Old Testament. We have already observed in previous talks in this little series that Jesus regarded the Old Testament as the very Word of God and that he put that conviction about the Old Testament at the very heart both of his teaching and of his life. How, then, if you reject that conviction, can you possibly think that you are honoring Jesus? If you hold that the revelation of God contained in the Old Testament is valueless and that all that we need to know about God is found in the moral character of the man Jesus of Nazareth, what will you do with the fact that the Jesus to whom you appeal put at the very basis of that moral character which you so much admire a view of the Old Testament and a view of God which you contemptuously reject?

Jesus did, indeed, present himself as revealing God and as being in his very person the revelation of God. "Whoever has seen me," he said, "has seen the Father. How can you say, 'Show us the Father'?" (John 14:9) But that certainly does not mean that the disciples who were with our Lord on earth were told by our Lord suddenly to regard as of no value the knowledge of God which they already had. The key to what our Lord meant when he said, "Whoever has seen me has seen the Father" is to be found, I am inclined to think, in the words in John 1:18: "No one has ever seen God; the only God, who is at the Father's side, he has made him known." Devout readers of the Old Testament had *known* God, but they had not *seen* him, since God is invisible. But now the one who is both God and only-begotten, the eternal Son, has become flesh, and because he has become flesh can actually be seen with men's eyes. A man who sees him sees the Father, since he is himself one in substance with the Father. Thus, in Christ, the longing of men to actually *see* God is satisfied.

At any rate, what is perfectly clear is that everywhere Jesus presupposed the knowledge of God which his disciples had from the Old Testament. He just assumed that his disciples had that knowledge and then, building upon that knowledge, he led them on into a fuller and more glorious knowledge through his intercourse with them upon earth.

To hold, then, that all that we need to know about God is found in the moral character of the man Jesus of Nazareth and that we can be indifferent to the question of whether God is the Maker and Ruler of the world is to treat Jesus himself with contempt, since it means that we reject what he himself put at the very foundation of his life and of his teaching.

But that view is not only derogatory to Jesus, it is also derogatory to God. What a low view of God it is, to be sure, when men say that they are not interested in the question of whether he is powerful, whether he is the Creator or Ruler of the world, but are only interested in the question whether he is good!

Is that view of God really right? Has all our trust in the infinite power of our God been wrong when, in the midst of storms and trials and a host of enemies, we have quoted the words of Scripture: "If God is for us, who can be against us?" (Rom 8:31) Was Isaiah wrong when he turned his eyes to the starry heavens and said: "Lift up your eyes on high and see: who created these? He who brings out their host by number, calling them all by name; by the greatness of his might and because he is strong in power, not one is missing" (Isa 40:26)? Was Jesus wrong when he bade his disciples trust in him who clothes the lilies of the field (Luke 12:27–28), and when he said: "Fear not, little flock, for it is your Father's good pleasure to give you the kingdom" (Luke 12:32)?

To these questions philosophers may return this answer or that, but the answer of the Christian heart is plain. Away with all these pale abstractions, it cries; away with this strange theory that speaks of the goodness of God but deprives him of his power! If God is good only and not powerful, we are of all men most miserable. We had trusted him so implicitly; we had felt so safe in his everlasting arms. But now you tell us that our confidence was misplaced and that God really had no power to save his children when they called! Shall we believe you? Ah no, my friends. Not if we are Christians. Others may heed these voices that bid us lose confidence in the power of our God, but as for us Christians, we will say still—though ten million times ten million universes unloose against us all their mighty power, though we stand amid the clash of falling systems and contemplate a universal ruin—we will say still that it is God's world which he can create and he destroy, and that through Christ's grace we are safe forever in the arms of our heavenly Father.

But, people say, even if God is not thus all-powerful, even if we can no longer think of him as the sovereign Creator and Ruler of the world, even if we relegate these things to the realm of mere metaphysics, have we not at least something left? Have we not goodness left? We do not know how the world came into being; we do not know what will be our fate when we pass through the dark portals of death. But can we not find a higher and more disinterested worship—far higher, it would seem, than that which Jesus practiced—in the reverence for goodness stripped of the old, vulgar trappings of power?

It sounds noble at first. But consider it for a moment and its glory turns to ashes and leaves us in despair. What is meant by a goodness that has no power? Is not goodness a mere abstraction except as it belongs to persons? And does not the very notion of a person involve the power to act? Goodness altogether divorced from power is therefore no goodness at all. The truth is that if you try to make God good only and not powerful, both God and goodness have been destroyed.

We insist, then, that in order to know God it is not sufficient to examine the moral life of the man Jesus of Nazareth. To regard that as sufficient is to do despite to Jesus himself, and it leaves us with a God who is no God at all.

What then is the view of God which the Bible presents to us when we take the Bible—as we ought to take it—as a whole?

If you will let me answer that question in one word, and if you will not forbid me to make that one word a convenient word which philosophers use, I will just say that the view of God which the Bible presents is the view which philosophers call "theism"—that is, it is the view which holds that there is a personal God who is Creator and Ruler of the world. That is the view which Jesus presents with particular clearness, and that is the view which the Bible presents as a whole.

To understand just what that view of God is, we cannot do better than to contrast it with two other views which men have often held.

In the first place, there is the view called deism. According to that view, God created the universe but then left it alone to run by itself like a machine. That view, affirming the existence of a personal God but denying his presence in the world and his active governance of it, used to be held widely by unbelievers of past generations; but today it is dead. I do not know whether there are any real deists at the present time.

A second view is, however, very much alive; in fact, in different forms, and with greater or less modification, it is the view underlying the modernism that is stifling the life of such large portions of the church today. That is the ancient error called pantheism. It is held in very many different forms and with many degrees of consistency. According to the strict meaning of the term, it is the view that all is God, the view that simply identifies God with the totality of existing things.

I suppose that the first impulse of the ordinary man, untrained in philosophy, is to regard that view as absurd. It was in that way that I regarded it when I first heard of it when I was at school or college. It seemed to me almost more preposterous than the idolatry of the heathen who bows down to idols of wood and stone.

But here is the strange thing, my friends—a great many people who regard pantheism as wrong, even if the meaning of the term is explained to them, are practically pantheists themselves. They are not aware of the fact, but they are pantheists all the same.

We find ourselves in the midst of the mighty process of nature. It manifests itself in the wonders of the starry heavens and the equal wonders that the interior of the atom now reveals. It is seen in the revolving seasons and also in the achievements of the human mind. In the presence of that mighty process of nature, we stand in awe; we are impressed with our own littleness; we understand that we are but infinitesimal parts of the mighty whole. And to that mighty whole, to that stupendous world process, whose vastness we moderns have come to understand as never before, the pantheist applies the dread name of God. God is thus no longer thought of as an artificer apart from his machine; he is thought of rather as the universe itself, conceived of not in its individual manifestations but as a mighty whole.

Such is pantheism in the strict sense of the word. We can well understand the appeal which such a view has for many minds. It has stimulated some of the most brilliant thinking and inspired some of the grandest poetry of the race. But it contains no comfort whatever for oppressed and burdened souls. If God be merely another name for the totality of things and if we possess him, we have nothing that we did not have before. There is for us now no more appeal from nature to nature's God. We are now nothing but the playthings of blind force.

Feeling, perhaps, the defects of the stark pantheism which identifies God with all that exists, some men have sought for a "higher pantheism" of various kinds. No, they say to themselves, God is not simply another name for the universe as a whole but is to be identified rather with the spiritual purpose that runs through the universe. Some of them have said that God is the soul of the universe. As the human body has a human soul, so the universe has a soul, they say, and that soul is to be called God.

Two profound defects are found in all these forms of pantheism, high and middling and low. In the first place, they give us a God who is in some kind of necessary connection with the world. Not only does the world not exist apart from God, they tell us, but God does not exist apart from the world. What becomes, then, of the holiness or separateness of God? Clothe such a view with all the beauty of language with which it has been celebrated by poets and philosophers, and still it gives us a God who is merely a function or an aspect of the world. Such a God can never bring us into contact with that dread and mysterious realm of the beyond into which our souls long to enter.

In the second place, pantheism, high or low, can never really give us a personal God. A God of which we are parts can never be a God with whom we can have communion. We can never stand in the presence of such a God as one person stands in the presence of another. We can never say "Thou" to such a God, and such a God can never say "Thou" to us. We can never love such a God, and such a God can never love us. An abstraction can neither love nor be loved. Never could we say to a "world process" or to a "spiritual meaning" or to a principle of goodness: "Our Father in heaven" (Matt 6:9).

How gloriously are those two defects of pantheism avoided in the teaching of Holy Scripture!

The former of the two defects is certainly avoided. What is it that stands out sharply in the Bible from beginning to end? Is it not the awful holiness or separateness of God, the awful distinction between the finite and the infinite, between the creature and the Creator?

The Bible does indeed teach us that God is immanent in the world. He is not a God far off. He is not a God who stands aloof from the universe as an artificer stands aloof from his machine. The devout reader of the Bible can say with Tennyson: "Closer is He than breathing, and nearer than hands and feet."[1]

But if God is thus immanent in the world, he is also transcendent. The world is dependent upon him, but he is not dependent upon the world.

---

1. Alfred Tennyson, "The Higher Pantheism," 1869.

He has set bounds to the world, but the world has set no bounds to him. It is the work of his hands, but he is from eternity. "Before the mountains were brought forth, or ever you had formed the earth and the world, from everlasting to everlasting you are God" (Ps 90:2). Running all through the Bible is the awful separateness of God from the world. That is what the Bible calls the holiness of God. The Bible, unlike the pantheists, presents to us a holy God.

But the Bible also—and again unlike the pantheists—presents to us a personal God. The God of the Bible is not just another name for the universe itself, nor is he a name for a spiritual purpose supposed to run through the universe, nor any impersonal principle of goodness. No, he is a person. That much is clear at the start. We shall speak in a subsequent talk of the deeper mystery of the three persons in one God. But at least it is clear that God is personal. He is not a force or a principle or a collective something of which we are parts. He is a person to whom we can say "Thou," a person who can, if he will, speak to us as a man speaks to his friend, and who can, if he will, become to us a heavenly Father.

But what is needed, first of all, is that we stand in awe before his throne. We are living in an age when men have forgotten God. They have become engrossed in their own affairs. They have been puffed up in their pride. They have put God out of their thoughts. The result is that our boasted civilization is rushing rapidly to its fall. Oh, that men would turn to God while yet there is time!

How is it with you, my friends? Have you been walking in your own paths? Have you forgotten God? If so, I bid you read the blessed book that will tell you how he may be found. If you heed his Word, you may first stand in awe before his throne and then, by the way that he has provided, you may come to be at peace with him and be his child forevermore.

10

The Triune God

I wish to open this little series of talks by discussing what the Bible teaches about God. The Bible tells us there is a personal God, Creator and Ruler of the world. God, according to the Bible, is not another name for the mighty process of nature, and he is not some part or aspect of the process. He is a free and holy person, who created the process of nature by the fiat of his will and who is eternally independent of the universe that he has made.

Now we ask more in detail what the Bible tells us about God. When we ask that, I know we shall be met with an objection. We are seeking to know God. Well, there are many people who tell us that we ought not seek to know God. The knowledge of God, they say, is the death of religion. Instead of seeking to know God, they tell us, we ought simply to feel him; putting all theology aside, they say, we ought just to sink ourselves in the boundless ocean of God's being.

Such is the attitude of the mystics, ancient and modern. But it is not the attitude of the Christian. The Christian, unlike the mystic, knows him whom he has believed.

What shall be said of a religion that depreciates theology, that depreciates the knowledge of God?

One thing that can be said of it is that it hardly possesses any moral quality at all. Pure feeling, if such a thing exists, is nonmoral. That can be observed in the sphere of human relationships. What makes my affection for a human friend such an ennobling thing is the knowledge that I have of the character and the needs of my friend. Am I indifferent to such knowledge? Am I indifferent to base slanders which are directed against my friend's reputation? Not if I am a friend worthy of the name. Human affection, apparently so simple, is in reality just bristling with doctrine; it depends upon a host of observations, stored up in the mind, regarding the object of affection.

That is true, I think, even with regard to those human affections that are often thought of as instinctive. Take, for example, the love of a mother for a child. That love is no doubt independent of excellence in the child; it is impossible to kill a mother's love, no matter what one may do. But is a mother's love independent of some knowledge of the child, independent of some knowledge of the child's sufferings and needs, independent of some ability to enter into the soul of the child in order to sympathize and understand? If it is thus independent of all knowledge, I am inclined to think that it is hardly human affection at all; it has descended to an almost subhuman level.

It is to that subhuman, impersonal level that the mystic seeks to degrade our communion with God. Very different is the love of God as the Bible sets it forth. According to the Bible, we love God because he first loved us; and he has told us of his love in his holy Word. We love God, if we obey what the Bible tells us, because God has made himself known to us and has thus shown himself to be worthy of our love.

I do not mean to say that the Christian in his communion with God is always rehearsing consciously the things that God has told us about himself. There are times, as someone has observed, when a child of God, weary with the battle of life, can say only as he lies down to rest: "Lord, you know, we are on the same old terms." There are times when the Christian can be strangely conscious of the presence of God, even though he is not for the moment thinking in detail about the things that he knows regarding God. Certainly, the Bible does offer to us an immediate communion with God, which is like no other experience a man can possibly have; and certainly the Bible does make a distinction between knowing God and merely knowing about God. But underlying that sweet and blessed communion of the Christian with his God there is a true knowledge of God. A communion with God which is independent of that knowledge of God is communion with some other god and not with the living and true God whom the Bible reveals.

Every true man is resentful of slanders against a human friend. Should we not be grieved ten times more by slanders against our God? How can we possibly listen with polite complacency, then, when men break down the distinction between God and man, and drag God down to man's level? How can we possibly say, as in one way or another is so often said, that orthodoxy makes little difference? We should never talk in any such way about a human friend. We should never say with regard to a human friend that it makes no difference whether our view of him is right or wrong.

How, then, can we say that absurd thing with regard to God?

The really consistent Christian can have nothing whatever to do with such doctrinal indifferentism. There is nothing so dishonoring to God, he will say, as to be indifferent to the things that God has told us about himself in his holy Word.

What, then, has God told us about himself in his Word? I certainly cannot now answer that question with any fullness. But there are a few things that I do want to say, and if by saying them I can be helpful to you in your own reading of the Bible, the purpose of this little series of talks will have been attained.

In the Shorter Catechism of the Presbyterian churches, there is the following answer to the question, "What is God?": "God is a spirit, infinite, eternal, and unchangeable, in his being, wisdom, power, holiness, justice, goodness, and truth" (WSC Q&A 4). That answer is certainly in accordance with the Bible. I think it will help us a little bit to get straight in our minds what the Bible says about God.

Notice that God is here said to be infinite, eternal, and unchangeable. What is meant by saying that he is infinite? Well, the word "infinite" means without an end or a limit. Other beings are limited; God is unlimited. I suppose it is easy for us to fall into our ordinary spatial conceptions in trying to think of God. We may imagine ourselves passing from the earth to the remotest star known to modern astronomy—many, many light-years away. Well, when we have gotten there, we are not one slightest fraction of an inch nearer to fathoming infinity than we were when we started. We might imagine ourselves traveling ten million times ten million times farther still, and still we would not be any nearer to infinity than when we started. We cannot conceive a limit to space, but neither can we conceive of infinite space. Our minds faint in the presence of infinity.

But we were really wrong in using those spatial conceptions in thinking of infinity, and particularly wrong were we in using spatial conceptions in thinking of the infinite God. It may help us to the threshold of the truth to say that God pervades the whole vast area of the universe known to science, and then infinitely more; it may help us to the threshold of the truth to say that God inhabits infinite space: but when we look a little deeper, we see that space itself belongs to finite things and that the notion of infinite space is without meaning. God created space when he created finite things. He himself is beyond space. There is no near and no far to him. Everything to him is equally near.

So it is when we try to think of God as eternal. If the word "infinity" is related, by way of contrast, to the notion of space, so the word "eternity" is related, by way of contrast, to the notion of time. When we say that God is eternal, we mean that he had no beginning and that he will have no end. But we really mean more than that. We mean that time has no meaning for him, save as it has meaning to the creatures whom he has made. He created time when he created finite creatures. He himself is beyond time. There is no past and no future to him. The Bible puts that in poetical language when it says: "For a thousand years in your sight are but as yesterday when it is past, or as a watch in the night" (Ps 90:4). We, of course, are obliged to think of the actions of God as taking place in time. We are obliged to think of him as doing one thing after another thing; we are obliged to think of him as doing this today and that tomorrow. We have a perfect right so to think, and the Bible amply confirms us in that right. To us there is indeed such a thing as past and present and future, and when God deals with us he acts in a truly temporal series. But to God himself all things are equally present. There is no such thing as "before" or "after" to him.

It is very important to see clearly that God is thus infinite, eternal, and unchangeable. These attributes of God are often denied. Those who have denied them have told us that God is a finite God. We must not blame him, they tell us, if things are not just right in the world. He is doing the best he can, they say; he is trying to bring order out of chaos, but he is faced by a recalcitrant material which he did not create and which he can mold only gradually and imperfectly to his will. It is our business to help him, and while we may at first sight regret that we have not the all-powerful God that we used to think we had, yet we can comfort ourselves with the inspiring thought that the God that we do have needs our help and indeed cannot do without it.

What shall we say of such a finite God? I will tell you plainly what I think we ought to say about him. He is not God but a god. He is a product of men's thoughts. Men have made many such little gods. Of the making of gods, as of the making of books, there is no end. But, as for us Christians, with our Bibles before us, we turn from all such little gods of man's making, out toward the dread mystery of the infinite and eternal, and say, as Augustine said with a holy fear: "Thou has made us for thyself, and our heart is restless until it finds its rest in thee."[1]

---

1. Augustine, *Confessions*, I.i.

The definition in the Shorter Catechism, which we are taking to give us our outline of what the Bible tells us about God, says not only that God is infinite, eternal, and unchangeable in his being and in his power and in his holiness, but also that he is infinite, eternal, and unchangeable in his wisdom and in his justice, goodness, and truth (WSC Q&A 4).

Does that seem surprising to you in the light of what we have just been saying? Well, perhaps it might seem to be surprising. These qualities—wisdom, justice, goodness, and truth—are such startlingly human qualities. Can we ascribe them to that infinite, eternal, and unchangeable God of whom we have just been speaking? If we do try to ascribe them to that God, are we not guilty of a naïve anthropomorphism? Are we not guilty of the childish error of thinking of God as though he were just a big man up in the sky? Are we not guilty of making a god in our own image?

The answer is: no, we are not guilty of that. If we think of God as having some attributes which we also possess, we may conceivably be doing it for one or the other of two reasons. In the first place, we may be doing it because we are making God in our own image. But, in the second place, we may be doing it because God has made us in his image.

The Bible tells us that this second alternative is correct. God made man in the image of God, and that is the reason why God possesses some attributes which man also possesses, though God possesses them to an infinitely higher degree.

The Bible is not afraid of speaking of God in a startlingly tender and human sort of way. It does so just in passages where the majesty of God is set forth. "It is he who sits above the circle of the earth," says the fortieth chapter of Isaiah, "and its inhabitants are like grasshoppers" (Isa 40:22). "All the nations are as nothing before him, they are accounted by him as less than nothing and emptiness" (Isa 40:17). But what says that same fortieth chapter of Isaiah about this same terrible God? Here is what it says: "He will tend his flock like a shepherd; he will gather the lambs in his arms; he will carry them in his bosom, and gently lead those that are with young" (Isa 40:11).

How wonderfully the Bible sets forth the tenderness of God! Is that merely figurative? Are we wrong in thinking of God in such childlike fashion? Many philosophers say so. They will not think of God as a person. Oh, no. That would be dragging him down too much to our level! So they make of him a pale abstraction. The Bible seems childish to them in the warm, personal way in which it speaks of God.

Are those philosophers right or is the Bible right? Thank God, the Bible is right, my friends. The philosophers despise children who think of God as their heavenly Father. But the philosophers are wrong and the children are right. Did not our Lord Jesus say: "I thank you, Father, Lord of heaven and earth, that you have hidden these things from the wise and understanding and revealed them to little children" (Matt 11:25)?

No, God is no pale abstraction. He is a person. That simple truth—precious possession of simple souls—is more profound than all the philosophies of all the ages.

But now we come to a great mystery. God, according to the Bible, is not just one person, but he is three persons in one God. That is the great mystery of the Trinity.

The Trinity is revealed to us only in the Bible. God has revealed some things to us through nature and through conscience but the Trinity is not among them. This he has revealed to us by supernatural revelation and by supernatural revelation alone.

We can, it is true, detect something in the doctrine of the Trinity that serves to render clearer and richer even what nature and conscience reveal. Nature and conscience reveal—in a revelation which, it is true, sinful man seldom receives—a personal and holy God, Creator of the world. But how can a personal and holy being exist entirely alone? The thing is difficult for us to understand. That difficulty is wonderfully overcome by the doctrine of the Trinity, which tells us that even before God had created the world there was a personal interrelation within the Godhead.

But we ought to be exceedingly cautious about such considerations. Though God is a person, he is a person very different from us finite persons, and I am not sure that we could ever have said, on the basis of any general revelation in nature and conscience, that an infinite person could not have existed entirely alone. Let us put such considerations, then, aside. When we are engaging in them we are venturing upon holy ground, where we can walk, at best, with trembling and halting footsteps. The thing that is perfectly clear is that we should not have had any real knowledge of the holy mystery of the Trinity had not that mystery been revealed to us in the written Word of God.

Within the Word of God, it is in the New Testament that the doctrine of the Trinity is taught. There are hints of it in the Old Testament, but they are only hints, and it was left to the New Testament for this precious doctrine to be clearly revealed.

In the New Testament, the doctrine is taught with the utmost clearness; the doctrine is presupposed even more than it is expressly taught, as has well been pointed out by B. B. Warfield in a splendid article, "The Biblical Doctrine of the Trinity." That is, the New Testament is founded throughout on the doctrine of the Trinity, and the doctrine was really established by the great facts of the incarnation of the Son of God and the work of the Holy Spirit even before it was enunciated in words.

Only the smallest part of the teaching of the New Testament about the Trinity is found in passages where the doctrine is stated as a whole. What the New Testament ordinarily does is to state parts of the doctrine, so that when we put those parts together, and when we summarize them, we have the great doctrine of the three persons and one God.

For example, all passages in the New Testament where the deity of Jesus Christ is set forth are, when taken in connection with passages setting forth the deity and personality of the Holy Spirit, passages supporting the doctrine of the Trinity. In the next talk, I hope to deal with some of those passages.

But what needs to be observed now is that although by far the larger part of the biblical teaching about the Trinity is given in that incidental and partial way—presupposing the doctrine rather than formally enunciating it as a whole—yet there are some passages where the doctrine is definitely presented by the mention, together, of Father, Son, and Holy Ghost.

The most famous of such passages, I suppose, is found in the Great Commission, given by the risen Lord to his disciples according to the twenty-eighth chapter of Matthew: "Go therefore and make disciples of all nations, baptizing them in the name of the Father and of the Son and of the Holy Spirit" (Matt 28:19). There we have a mention of all three persons of the Trinity in the most complete coordination and equality—yet all three persons are plainly not three Gods but one. Here, in this solemn commission by our Lord, the God of all true Christians is forever designated as a triune God.

We think also, for example, of the apostolic benediction at the end of the Second Epistle to the Corinthians: "The grace of the Lord Jesus Christ and the love of God and the fellowship of the Holy Spirit be with you all" (2 Cor 13:14). Here the terminology is a little different from that in the Great Commission. Paul speaks of the Son as "the Lord." But the word "Lord" in the Pauline epistles is plainly a designation of deity, like the other Greek word which is translated into English by the word "God." It is the Greek word used to translate the holy name of God, "Jehovah," in the Greek translation of the Old Testament which Paul used, and Paul does not hesitate to apply to Christ Old Testament passages which speak of Jehovah.

That brings us to something supremely important in the teaching of the whole New Testament about the Trinity. It is this: the New Testament writers, in presenting God as triune, are never for one moment conscious of saying anything that could by any possibility be regarded as contradicting the Old Testament teaching that there is but one God. That teaching is at the very heart and core of the Old Testament. It is every whit as much at the heart and core of the New Testament. The New Testament is just as much opposed as the Old Testament is to the thought that there are more Gods than one. Yet the New Testament with equal clearness teaches that the Father is God and the Son is God and the Holy Spirit is God, and that these three are not three aspects of the same person but three persons standing in a truly personal relationship to one another. There we have the great doctrine of the three persons but one God.

That doctrine is a mystery. No human mind can fathom it. Yet what a blessed mystery it is! The Christian's heart melts within him in gratitude and joy when he thinks of the divine love and condescension that has thus lifted the veil and allowed us sinful creatures a look into the very depths of the being of God.

11

What Is the Deity of Christ?

We have been talking about the great mystery of the Trinity. We have seen that according to the Bible there is one God in three persons—the Father, the Son, and the Holy Ghost. There are some places in the New Testament where all three persons of the Godhead are mentioned in the same verse. But the much more important or extensive part of the biblical proof of the doctrine of the Trinity is found in those passages where parts of the great doctrine are so mentioned as that, when they are put together, the completed doctrine inevitably appears. I want to begin to talk to you today about one great central part of the doctrine. I want to talk to you about the deity of our Lord Jesus Christ.

But before I can say a single word to you about the deity of Christ, I must tell you what that term "the deity of Christ" means, or rather, I must make perfectly clear to you what it does not mean. I must make perfectly clear to you the fact that the term "deity of Christ" and the assertion "Jesus is God" are often so employed today as to mean something quite contrary to the Bible and to the Christian faith.

Do you not see, my friends, that when a man says he believes in the deity of Christ, or when he says he believes that Jesus is God, the significance of such assertions depends altogether upon what the man who makes them means by the term "deity" or the term "God"?

If a man has a low view of deity, then, when he says that he believes in the deity of Christ, that means that he has a low view of Christ; and if he has a low view of God, then, when he says that he believes that Jesus is God, that means that he has a low view of Jesus.

But here is where the confusion comes in. A Christian man, hearing some unbeliever say that he believes in the deity of Christ or believes that

Jesus is God, attributes to that unbeliever the Christian definition of the term "deity" or the term "God." He simply assumes that the term "deity" or the term "God" means what Christians have always taken those terms to mean. That is, he assumes that those terms refer to a personal God, Creator and Ruler of the world, separate by a mighty gulf from all finite things. The consequence is that he is very much impressed when those terms are used about Jesus by a man who otherwise seemed to be very far from the Christian faith. "Did you not hear that man say," he exclaims, "that he believes in the deity of Christ; did you not hear him call Jesus 'God'? Well, if he believes in the deity of Christ, if he is willing to call Jesus 'God,' he cannot be so very wrong. He may be unorthodox in some particulars, but surely the root of the matter must be in him."

When I hear Christian people talking in that fashion about one of the noted unbelievers of the day, I have the sad feeling that those Christian people are, if I may use plain language, being deceived.

I am not a bit ashamed of laying stress upon this point, because I think it is a matter of profound importance. If I were sure I could get it really straight in your minds, I should think it worthwhile to devote not merely a part of one lecture to it, but a whole series of lectures. The more I look out upon the condition of the church, the more I am convinced that untold harm is being done by this double use of the term "deity" and of the term "God." The willingness of unbelievers to use the terms in their sense, coupled with the proneness of Christians to understand them in their own, is causing the great issue in the church between Christianity and unbelief to be obscured. What is the result? The result is that the church is being undermined from within. Christian people are being lulled to sleep by this use of orthodox terminology. Unbelievers are quietly gaining control. The young people of the church are being trained up in unbelief. Precious souls are being destroyed.

What ought we to do in such a situation? I will tell you what we ought to do, my friends. We ought to seek light, and we ought to pray to God for light. We ought to pray to God that people may cease to be satisfied by a word, but may insist on looking at the meaning of the word.

Now the Christian meaning of the term "deity of Christ" is fairly clear. The Christian believes that there is a personal God, Creator and Ruler of the universe, a God who is infinite, eternal, and unchangeable. So, when the Christian says that Jesus Christ is God, or when he says that he believes in the deity of Christ, he means that that same person who is known to history as Jesus of Nazareth existed, before he became man, from all eternity as infinite, eternal, and unchangeable God, the second person of the Holy Trinity.

Very different is the use of the term "deity of Christ" or the term "God," as it is applied to Jesus by many leaders in the modern church.

You can tell that they are using the term in some sense entirely different from the Christian sense because of the things that they say about Jesus in detail, or, more, because of the things that they will not say. They will not say that Jesus was born of a virgin. They will not say that he worked miracles. They will not say that the things that he said were always true; they will not say that he died as our substitute on the cross; they will not say that he rose from the tomb on the third day. Yet, they say, he was God.

When they say he was God, are they saying something orthodox? Is that orthodox assertion of theirs to be put to their credit over against the unorthodox assertions that they have made?

We answer: "No, a thousand times no!" When these men say that they believe in the deity of Christ or that they believe Jesus is God, that is not the most orthodox but the least orthodox thing that they say. It is an orthodox and a blessed thing to say that the Jesus of the Bible is God; but to say that this poor, deluded enthusiast of modern reconstruction is God is horrible blasphemy. How low these men must think of God if they can use his name in that way!

But in what sense do these men use the term "God" or the term "deity" when they apply it to the purely human Jesus—their purely human Jesus whom they have reconstructed after their rejection of the New Testament account?

Sometimes they mean by calling Jesus "God" merely that they try to enter into the same religious experience as the religious experience of those who in past generations called Jesus God. In the creeds of the church, they say, Jesus is called God. We do not believe, they say, that he is God in the sense in which the authors of those creeds believed it. Shall we then cease to use the creeds? Not at all, they say. When the authors of the creeds called Jesus "God," they were expressing in the language of their day a very precious experience which we also can share. So, they say, we can use the creeds still. We do not, of course, take them literally. But we can use them as expressions of the historic faith of the church. We can still hold to the underlying spiritual meaning of the doctrines that they contain—including the doctrine of the deity of Christ.

Such repetitions of the creeds and such professions of belief in the deity of Christ are doing untold harm in the church today. No doubt they are comforting to the men who practice them. I have sympathy with those men. To those men this use of traditional terminology seems like the stained glass in an old cathedral. It puts everything in a sort of dim religious light; it seems to impart a solemn glow of sanctity to what would appear to be bald unbelief if it were viewed in the cruel light of day.

But the trouble is that ordinary people in the church are being deceived. They hear a man repeating the creeds. He seems to be repeating them with the utmost fervor. He is particularly fervent in expressing his belief in the deity of Christ. They simply assume that he means by the deity of Christ what people have always meant by it. So, they tolerate him in the church and put him in a position of authority. Time goes on. Many such men are put into positions of greater and greater authority. They undermine the faith of the church, partly by their words, but more particularly by their silence. A deadly vagueness gradually affects the church's witness. The young people of the church are not soundly indoctrinated. People do not know what is wrong, but the church loses its power. Finally, the mask is thrown off. The people who really believe in the Bible and in the creed of the church and who are in dead earnest about that belief are treated as troublemakers. The church sinks down into a merger with the world.

That has been the process in many churches of our day. But it is not in that way that we believe in the deity of Christ. When we say we believe in the deity of Christ, when we repeat the great creeds, we are not just using a form of words that meant something to somebody of long ago. No, we are saying something that we do honestly hold ourselves to be true. We are not just giving expression to the historic faith of the church, but we are giving expression to our faith. We are saying that the historic faith of the church is what we ourselves believe.

But aside from a merely traditional use of ancient terms, what is the actual meaning attributed to the terms "deity" and "God" by those who have given up the meaning that is found in the Bible and in the great creeds of the church? What do modern unbelievers mean by speaking of the "deity of Christ" and what do they mean by calling Jesus "God"?

I think a twofold answer will have to be given to that question. Unbelievers who use the term "deity of Christ" and the term "God" as applied to Jesus mean usually one or the other of two things by those terms.

In the first place, some of them use the terms in what may be called a pantheizing sense. That is, they are willing to call Jesus "God" because they hold that all of us are God. They put only a difference of degree and not a difference of kind between Jesus's deity and ours. God, they say, is not a far-off God. His life pulsates through the life of all the world. He has always been incarnating himself in men and women. At one point, he incarnated himself with particular fullness—namely, in Jesus of Nazareth. But that incarnation was not different in kind from the incarnation in other men. It was different in degree but not in kind. What is revealed by the appearance of such a man as Jesus on the earth is that God and man are essentially one.

It is needless to say that this view of the deity of Christ is just about the diametrical opposite of the Christian view which the Bible teaches. According to the Bible, what is revealed by the appearance of Jesus upon the earth is not that God and man are one, but rather that God and man are not one. God is God and man is man. There can be no confusion between the two. Moreover, man is separate from God by the awful abyss of sin. Hence—just because of that separation between God and man—the eternal Son of God, second person of the Holy Trinity, took upon himself our nature, by an act that was done not many times but once and once only, and so because of that one act "was, and continueth to be God and man, in two distinct natures, and one person, forever" (WSC Q&A 21).

I am not going to try to speak today of the relation between the divine nature and the human nature in the person of Christ. That belongs to a later talk in this series. But what I want now to do is simply to say that the words, "Jesus is God," have no real meaning, certainly no biblical or Christian meaning, unless they go with the supplementary belief that we most emphatically are not God.

In the second place, other unbelievers use the terms "deity of Christ" or the term "God" as applied to Jesus in what may be called an antimetaphysical or positivistic sense. I trust you have some spirit left in you when I use words as long as those. I do not expect all of you to understand the word "positivistic" right at the start, but I do hope to make you understand the thing that I mean by that word. I mean to designate by it the view of people who regard the human life of the man Jesus as the only God that they know. People used to believe, they say, that there is a personal God, Creator and Ruler of the world. But we no longer believe that—at least we are quite uncertain about it. It belongs to the realm of metaphysics, which is a very doubtful realm. The only things that we can be really certain about are the things that we can see and hear, the things that are found here in this world in which we live. So, if we are to have a God, a modern God, we must find him here in the midst of us—here in this plainly visible realm.

Now we want to find a God, say the men of this way of thinking. People who used to believe in that old metaphysical God, Maker and Ruler of the universe, had something that we are in danger of losing. They had religion. They had a Being who could call forth ennobling emotions of reverence and awe. We need those emotions. We need something to call them forth. We need something to worship.

Where shall we find something to call forth these emotions? Where shall we find something to worship? Where shall we find an adequate object of religious devotion to take the place of that personal Creator in whom we no longer believe? We must find it here upon this earth, say these people of whom we are now speaking. Where then shall we find it?

Why, we find it, they say, in the life of a certain man named Jesus. He was not, of course, the Creator of the world. He was a man like the rest of men. But his moral life can call forth the same reverence as past generations used to give to the supposed Creator of the world. So, although metaphysics is gone, religion remains. Men used to have the ennobling emotion of reverence as they turned to the starry heavens and said: "The heavens declare the glory of God, and the sky above proclaims his handiwork" (Ps 19:1). We no longer believe all that. But we can experience those same ennobling emotions by contemplating the human life of the man Jesus.

Such is a very common view of what men call "the deity of Christ." What shall we say about that view? What shall we say about that way of worshiping Jesus? I will tell you what I think we ought to say about it. I think we ought to say that it is a terrible sin.

Please do not misunderstand me. It is not a sin to worship Jesus. On the contrary, it is the highest and noblest privilege and duty ever given to man. It is not a sin to worship the real Jesus. It is not a sin to worship the Jesus who is God and man. But it is a sin to manufacture a Jesus who was man only and not God, and then after you have manufactured that purely human Jesus to bow down and worship him.

Do you not see what that kind of worship of the moral life of a supposedly purely human Jesus, a Jesus who is regarded merely as the ideal man— do you not see what that worship of such a purely human Jesus really means? It means that the man who engages in it has committed the ancient and terrible sin of worshiping humanity. It means that he has worshiped and served the creature rather than the Creator, and that is a sin indeed.

The upshot of what I have been saying is this: when men today say that Christ is God, they often do so not because they think highly of Christ but because they think desperately low of God.

That is not at all the way in which the Bible says that Christ is God. When the Bible says that Christ is God, it does not do that by dragging God down. It does not ask us to forget a single thing that it has said about the stupendous majesty of God. No, it asks us to remember every one of those things in order that we may apply them all to Jesus Christ.

The Bible tells us in the first verse that God in the beginning created the heavens and the earth. Does it ask us to forget that when it tells us that Jesus Christ is God? No, it asks us to remember that. It says of Jesus Christ: "All things were made through him, and without him was not any thing made that was made" (John 1:3).

The Bible tells us that God is infinite, eternal, and unchangeable. Does it ask us to forget that when it tells us that Christ is God? No, it tells us to remember that. "I am the Alpha and the Omega," says Christ, "the first and the last, the beginning and the end" (Rev 22:13). "Before Abraham was, I am" (John 8:58). "In the beginning was the Word" (John 1:1). "He is before all things, and in him all things hold together" (Col 1:17).

The Bible tells us that God is holy. Does it ask us to forget that when it tells us that Christ is God? Let the whole New Testament give the answer.

The Bible tells us that God is mysterious. Does it ask us to forget that when it tells us that Christ is God? No, it tells us that there are mysteries in Christ which only God can know. "No one knows the Son except the Father, and no one knows the Father except the Son" (Matt 11:27).

The Bible tells us that God is the final Judge. Does it ask us to forget that when it tells us that Jesus is God? No, Jesus himself said, in the Sermon on the Mount, that he would sit upon the judgment throne to judge all the earth.

Everywhere it is the same, my friends. The Bible from Genesis to Revelation presents a stupendous view of God, and then it tells us that Jesus Christ is all that God is.

What interest has the Christian man in all that? What interest has the Christian man in knowing that Jesus Christ is very God? What interest in knowing that it was through him that the worlds were made? What interest in knowing that he pervades the remotest bounds? What interest in knowing that he is infinite in knowledge and in power?

No interest, say modern unbelievers; these things are mere metaphysics.

Every interest, say Christians; these things are the very breath of our lives.

We have trusted in Jesus. But how far can we trust him? Just in this transitory life? Just in this little speck that we call the earth? If we can trust him only thus far we are of all men most miserable. We are surrounded by stupendous forces; we are surrounded by the immensity of the unknown. After our little span of life there is a shelving brink with the infinite beyond. And still we are subject to fear—not only fear of destruction but a more dreadful fear of meeting with the infinite and holy God.

So we should be if we had but a human Christ. But now is Christ our Savior, the one who says, "Your sins are forgiven" (Luke 5:23), revealed as very God. And we believe. Such a faith is a mystery to us who possess it; it seems folly to those who have it not. But if possessed, it delivers us forever from fear. The world to us is all unknown; it is engulfed in an ocean of infinity. But it contains no mysteries to our Savior. He is on the throne. He pervades the remotest bounds. He inhabits infinity. With such a Savior we are safe.

12

Does the Bible Teach the Deity of Christ?

In the last talk I began to speak about the deity of Christ. But I had to point out the disconcerting fact that in contemporary parlance the term "deity of Christ" and the term "God" as applied to Jesus mean practically nothing. They are used in so many different senses that the use of these terms has in itself lost all significance. Unbelievers who have a very low view of Jesus indeed are perfectly willing to say that Jesus is God. They are willing to say that Jesus is God not because they have a high view of Jesus but because they have a low view of God.

It is a relief to turn from such intellectual quagmires, where words no longer mean what they say, to the Bible. In modern parlance, with its boundless degradation of formerly lofty terms, there is no solid footing; but it is not so in the Bible. The Bible defines its terms with the utmost clearness, and therefore when the Bible says that Jesus is God, we readers of the Bible know exactly where we stand.

Just now, therefore, we have a much pleasanter task than that which we had in the last talk. We are going to try to begin to set forth in positive fashion a little bit at least of what the Bible says about the deity of Christ.

If we are going to do so with any completeness, we should have to begin with the Old Testament. It is true, the Old Testament does not set forth the doctrine of the deity of Christ with any fullness. I do not suppose that either the prophets or their hearers knew in any clear fashion that the coming Messiah was to be one of the persons in the Godhead. Yet there are wonderful intimations of the doctrine of the deity of Christ even in the Old Testament. The outstanding fact is that the hope of a coming Messiah, as it appears with increasing clearness in the Old Testament books, goes far beyond any mere expectations of an earthly king of David's line. The

Messiah, according to the Old Testament, is clearly to be a supernatural person, and he is clearly possessed of attributes that are truly divine.

It has often been observed that, before the time of Christ, there were two types of Messianic expectation among the Jews. According to one type, the Messiah was to be a king of David's line; according to the other, he was to be a heavenly being suddenly appearing in the clouds of heaven to judge the world.

Both of these types of later Jewish expectation are rooted in the Old Testament. The Old Testament represents the Messiah both as a king of David's line and also as a supernatural person to appear with the clouds of heaven. The former of these two representations appears, for example, in the seventh chapter of Second Samuel, where a never-ending line of kings to be descended from David is promised; and it appears even more clearly in the passages where the coming of one supreme king of David's line is promised. The latter of the two representations appears, for example, in the seventh chapter of Daniel, where a mysterious person "like a son of man" is seen, in the prophet's vision, in the presence of the "Ancient of Days"—a mysterious person to whom is given a universal and everlasting dominion (Dan 7:13).

These two types of Messianic expectation in the Old Testament are by no means sharply distinguished from one another. When we examine closely the expected king of David's line, we find that he is to be far more than an ordinary earthly king—we find that he has distinctly supernatural attributes; and, on the other hand, the supernatural figure of the seventh chapter of Daniel is by no means separate from Israel but appears as the representative of the Old Testament people of God.

This possession of both divine and human attributes by the Messiah appears with particular clearness in the ninth chapter of Isaiah. There the coming deliverer is spoken of as one who shall sit upon the throne of David. Yet his kingdom is to be everlasting, and he himself is actually called, "Mighty God, Everlasting Father, Prince of Peace" (Isa 9:6). There we have the deity of the coming Messiah presented in the Old Testament in so many words.

Now the glorious thing is that in the New Testament we find these two types of Old Testament promises about the Messiah united, in the fulfillment, in the same person. How is it that one person can on the one hand be a man, a king of David's line, and at the same time be the mighty God? The question is not fully answered in the Old Testament. But the New Testament answers it most wonderfully in the great central doctrine of the two natures in the one person of our Lord. Yes, the coming deliverer was indeed to be both mighty God and a king of David's line, because the mighty God in strange condescension and love became man for our sakes "and so was, and continueth to be God, and man, in two distinct natures, and one person, forever" (WSC Q&A 21).

But we are not now speaking about the relation between the divine nature and the human nature in Christ. What we are interested in saying is that the Old Testament does teach the deity of the coming Messiah. Here, as at so many other points, there is a wonderful continuity between the Old Testament and the New.

The continuity is fully recognized by the New Testament. The New Testament does not present the doctrine of the Trinity, including the doctrine of the deity of Christ, as though it meant the introduction of a new idea of God. On the contrary, it presents it as being a revelation of the same God as the God who had revealed himself to Israel in Old Testament times. That is finely brought out in the article on the Trinity by B. B. Warfield, to which we have already referred. The Jehovah of the Old Testament is presented in the New Testament as being a triune God; but he is the same God throughout both the Old Testament and the New.

Hence it is only what is to be expected when we find that the New Testament applies to Christ Old Testament passages where the God of Israel is called by his holiest and most precious name, "Jehovah." Could there be any clearer testimony to the full deity of Jesus Christ?

Warfield rightly calls attention also to the matter-of-course way in which this identity of the triune God of the New Testament with the covenant God of Israel appears in the New Testament books. The New Testament writers are apparently not conscious of saying anything revolutionary. They assume the doctrine of the deity of Christ more than they expressly teach it. Why do they assume it? Warfield gives the answer. They assume it because it had already been established by the fact of the coming of the Son of God in the flesh. The doctrine was established by the fact of the incarnation before it was set forth in words. When the eternal Son of God became man in order to redeem sinners on the cross, and when the Holy Spirit was sent to apply that redeeming work of the Son of God to those who should be saved, then the doctrine of the Trinity was made known to men. The church from the very beginning was founded upon that doctrine; it was the factual revelation of that doctrine by the coming of the Son and the coming of the Spirit that ushered in the new dispensation.

However, although it was the factual revelation of the doctrine which in a true sense came first, yet the doctrine is taught also in words, and taught in the plainest possible way. In setting forth the way in which it is taught, one great difficulty is the difficulty of selection. The whole New Testament teaches the deity of Christ, and that is what makes it hard for us to decide what individual passages we should mention. Where the store is so very rich, it is hard to make a selection from it.

Let us begin with the point of time at which the New Testament narrative begins. Let us begin with the annunciation of the birth of John the Baptist, as it is recorded in the first chapter of Luke. The angel promises to Zacharias that he will have a son who will, in accordance with the prophecy in Malachi (Mal 3), go before the Lord to make ready his people for him (Luke 1:16–17). There is here no clear reference to the Messiah as a distinct person. The promised son of Zacharias is to go before Jehovah, or, in the Greek form, "the Lord," but it is not said that he is to go before the Messiah. Yet there is no doubt but that the author of the Gospel according to Luke, when he quotes the angel's words, identifies that coming of Jehovah with which the Malachi prophecy dealt and to which the angel alludes with the coming of Jesus Christ. The coming of Jehovah is the coming of Christ. There is also no doubt but that in making that identification, the author of this gospel is in accordance with the whole New Testament and in accordance with the real meaning of what the angel said. We have here just one instance of that stupendous fact of which we have already spoken—the fact that the New Testament writers apply to Jesus things that the Old Testament says of Jehovah. The whole New Testament is based upon the thought that there is some strange essential unity between Jesus Christ and the covenant God of Israel.

Then we have the annunciation of the angel to the virgin Mary (Luke 1:30–38). The annunciation is partly in Old Testament terms. Mary's son is to sit on the throne of David; and when it is said that of his kingdom there is to be no end, that also does not go beyond what the Old Testament had promised about the Messiah. But then a great mystery is revealed. The promised child is not to have a human father by ordinary generation, but is to be conceived by the Holy Ghost in the womb of a virgin mother. Even that—at least the part of it that sets forth the fact that the mother is to be a virgin—is found in Old Testament prophecy in Isaiah 7:14 but had not been understood among the Jews. Now, just before the fulfillment, the prophecy is repeated in fuller and more glorious terms. The conception of this child in the womb of the virgin Mary is to be a miracle wrought by the immediate power of the Spirit of God. That miracle is one of the things that will show the child to be rightly called "holy" and "Son of God."

Evidently the term "Son of God" is here used in some very lofty sense. It does not designate the promised child merely as the Messiah, though sometimes the Messiah was called "Son of God." Evidently the term is used here in some unique and stupendous sense.

At twelve years of age, the child Jesus was found in the temple. Joseph and Mary had sought him, sorrowing, and at last they found him among the doctors, hearing them and asking them questions. "Son," Mary said, "why have you treated us so? Behold, your father and I have been searching for you in great distress." Then came the strange answer of the boy Jesus: "Did you not know that I must be in my Father's house?" (Luke 2:48–49) When Mary spoke of the father of that twelve-year-old boy, she meant his human father, the one who stood to him in a relation more like that of a father than did any other human being. When the boy Jesus spoke of his Father in reply, he meant God. Notice that he did not say, "our Father," when he spoke of God. No, he said, "my Father." He was Son of God in a sense entirely different from that which would apply to any other person who ever lived upon this earth.

That brings us to one of the strangest things about the way in which Jesus all through the Gospels speaks of God. This strange thing appears not only in the Gospel according to John, which modern unbelief rejects so radically as untrue, but also in the Synoptic Gospels. The strange thing is that Jesus, according to all four of the Gospels, never speaks of God as "our Father," classing himself with his disciples in that word "our." He says, "my Father" and he says to his disciples, "your Father," but never does he say, "our Father," classing himself with his disciples in that filial relationship to God. The Lord's Prayer begins with those words "our Father," but Jesus certainly did not pray that prayer with his disciples, because that prayer contains a confession of sin, and Jesus never had any sin to confess. It was a prayer that he taught his disciples, not a prayer that he prayed himself. The significant fact remains, therefore: Jesus never appears in the Gospels as saying, "our Father" to God together with his disciples. God was his Father and God was their Father, but he was Jesus's Father in an entirely different sense from the sense in which he was their Father. Jesus was the Son of God in an entirely unique way.

At the beginning of the Gospel according to Mark, with the parallel passages in Matthew and Luke, we are told about the beginning of Jesus's public ministry. That event was marked by a miracle. The Spirit descended upon Jesus, and there was a voice from heaven that said: "You are my beloved Son; with you I am well pleased" (Mark 1:11; cf. Matt 3:17; Luke 3:22). It is possible that the good pleasure of God which is here spoken of is the definite act of approval accomplished at the moment when Jesus was sent forth into his public ministry. Yet, even so, that divine act of approval is evidently regarded as rooted in a unique relationship in which the person thus approved had always stood toward God. Jesus did not become Son of God because he had divine approval, but he had that divine approval because he had always been Son of God.

For a further discussion of that question and similar questions I may refer you incidentally to the learned and most illuminating book, *The Self-Disclosure of Jesus*, by Geerhardus Vos.

At any rate, Jesus now comes forward in his public ministry. In what light does he present himself in that public ministry?

Here one great central fact stares us in the face. I think it would hardly be possible to lay too much stress upon it. It is this: Jesus does not present himself merely as an example for faith but presents himself as the object of faith. That fact appears not merely in the Gospel according to John, which unbelievers reject as altogether unhistorical; but it appears also in the three Synoptic Gospels, and in the Synoptic Gospels it appears even in those parts which are supposed by modern criticism, rightly or wrongly, to come from the earliest sources underlying the Gospels. You cannot get away from it anywhere in the Gospels. It is all-pervasive. That fact has been demonstrated in particularly convincing fashion by James Denney in his book, *Jesus and the Gospel*. I do not commend that book to you in general because, in some respects, it is a sadly mistaken book. But it does show in a singularly convincing way that everywhere in the New Testament, including the Synoptic Gospels, and including the sources supposed, rightly or wrongly, to underlie the Synoptic Gospels, Jesus is represented not as a mere example for faith but as the object of faith.

What do we mean by saying that? What do we mean by saying that Jesus is presented not primarily as an example for faith but as the object of faith? We mean something very simple and at the same time something very stupendous. We mean that Jesus did not come forward merely saying: "Look at me; I am practicing the true religion, and I bid you practice the same religion as that which I am practicing." We mean that he did not come forward merely saying: "Look at me; I have faith in God, and I bid you have faith in God like my faith in God." We mean that he did not come forward merely saying: "Look at me; I regard God as my Father, and I bid you to regard God as your Father too in the same sense as that in which I regard him as my Father."

It is so that modern unbelievers represent Jesus. They regard him as a guide out into a larger type of religious life. They regard him as being the founder of Christianity because he was the first Christian. They regard Christianity as consisting in imitation of the religious life of Jesus. So they love to speak of "the religion of Jesus." They love to speak of the gospel of Jesus in distinction from a gospel about Jesus. Thus they degrade Jesus to the position of a mere teacher and example. They turn away from the gospel that has him as its substance to a gospel which was merely the gospel that he preached.

When they do that, it is evident that they are turning away from what has been known as Christianity for the past nineteen hundred years. But they are also turning away from Jesus himself as he is presented to us in all the sources of historical information that we know anything about. According to the four Gospels, and according to all the supposed sources which modern criticism has tried to detect back of the four Gospels, Jesus put himself into his gospel; the gospel of Jesus was also a gospel about Jesus; the gospel that he preached was also a gospel that offered him as Savior. He did not say merely: "Have faith in God like the faith that I have in God," but he said, "Have faith in me."

That appears of course with the utmost clearness in the Gospel according to John. But it also appears in the Synoptic Gospels. There was, indeed, according to the Synoptic Gospels, a period in the public ministry of Jesus when he did not ordinarily make his own person the express subject of systematic discourse. But if you look a little deeper, you see that everywhere Jesus was offering himself as the Savior of men and asking them to have faith in him.

That appears, for example, in his miracles of healing. "Your faith has saved you," he says; "go in peace" (Luke 7:50). Well, faith in whom? Perhaps we might be tempted to say merely, "Faith in God like the faith which Jesus had in God." But I bid you read the narratives with care and ask yourselves whether that interpretation really does justice to them. I think you will find that it does not. No, Jesus was presenting himself when he worked those miracles as one in whom he was bidding men have confidence. No doubt he was bidding them have confidence in God the Father. But the point is that this confidence in God the Father was also confidence in him. The faith that saved those people was faith in Jesus Christ.

He was saving those people from bodily ills, but he was also saving their souls from sin. That becomes explicit in the healing of the paralytic borne by four, where Jesus says not only, "Rise and walk," but "Your sins are forgiven you" (Luke 5:23). But it is really implied in the cases where it is not expressed. Jesus, according to all the Gospels, saves men from sin, and the means which he uses to save them from sin is the faith which he bids them have in him, the Savior.

Thus Jesus, according to all the Gospels, presents himself as the object of a truly religious faith. Well, who is the object of a truly religious faith? The answer is very simple. He is God. The way in which Jesus presents himself as the object of faith in all the Gospels—and even in the sources supposed, rightly or wrongly, to underlie the Gospels—is a tremendous testimony by Jesus himself to his own deity. That testimony does not appear merely in individual passages. It is a kind of atmosphere that pervades the whole picture, or, to change the figure, a foundation that sustains the whole building. If you ignore it, the whole account which the Bible gives of Jesus becomes a hopeless puzzle.

In the next talk, I want to continue to deal with the deity of Christ. Today I have been able to do no more than make a beginning in the presentation of that great subject. I wonder what you think about it. What do you think of Jesus Christ? Do you think of him, with modern unbelievers, merely as the initiator of a higher type of religious life, the discoverer of certain permanent facts about the fatherhood of God and the brotherhood of man? Or do you think of him, as Christians do, as the Lord of glory, the eternal Son of God become man to save you from your sins? Or, finally, are you undecided with regard to him? Are you undecided on which of these two views you will hold? Do you belong to that great army of persons who stand outside the household of faith and look longingly at the warmth and joy within? Are you hindered from entering in by gloomy doubts? If you belong to that third class, we pray to God that you may be led to say at least: "I believe; help my unbelief!" (Mark 9:24) If you do say that, the Lord will help your unbelief, as he helped the man who said it so long ago, and will bring you into the clear shining of faith.

13

The Sermon on the Mount and the Deity of Christ

We are now in the midst of our discussion of the great theme, the deity of Jesus Christ. Was Jesus a mere man, a leader into a higher and better type of religious experience, or was he the eternal Son of God become man to save us from the guilt and power of sin?

We have already begun to point out what the Bible says about this question. In particular, we have pointed out that all four of the Gospels, and even the sources supposed, rightly or wrongly, to underlie the Gospels, represent Jesus not merely as an example of faith but as the object of faith. They represent Jesus not as saying merely, "Have faith in God like the faith which I have in God," but as saying, "Have faith in me." But that means that the four Gospels teach the deity of Christ and represent Jesus himself as teaching it. The object of a truly religious faith is none other than God.

I want now to show you how extraordinarily pervasive in the Gospels is the lofty view of Jesus Christ which necessarily goes with his offer of himself as the object of faith. People try to escape from that lofty view of Christ. They like to regard Jesus just as a teacher and example; they say that this whole notion about his deity is an unfortunate metaphysical notion that has nothing to do with vital religion. Let us get away from metaphysics and theology, they say, and, instead, just get up and obey Jesus's commands; if we obey his commands we are honoring him more than we could honor him by any amount of intellectual convictions regarding his deity.

Well, my friend, I will say to a man of this way of thinking, Where will you turn in the Gospels to get away from a lofty view of the person of Christ? Where will you turn to find a Jesus who simply gave men directions for the ordering of their lives and did not demand that they should have any particular view about him? Here is a New Testament, my friend; will you just open it anywhere you like in order to prove your point?

I suppose that if I should say that to one of the advocates of this nondoctrinal Christianity, he would be most apt to turn, among all the passages in the New Testament, to the Sermon on the Mount. In the Sermon on the Mount, it is often said, we have a program for Christian living that is quite independent of the niceties of orthodox theology, and if we should just be willing to live that kind of life it would be a great deal better than disputing about theological questions or even being too anxious to get a completely orthodox notion about Jesus himself.

Well, my friend, you have turned to the Sermon on the Mount. I did not choose it. You chose it. It is your favorite passage. You cannot object therefore if we examine it a little for ourselves to see whether it really teaches that kind of nondoctrinal religion that you so enthusiastically advocate. In particular, you cannot object if we examine it to see whether it is really silent about those stupendous claims of Jesus which so trouble you in other parts of the New Testament.

All right, then; we are going to put preconceived opinions aside and examine the Sermon on the Mount for ourselves.

What happens to us when we do that? I will tell you very plainly. We find that the Sermon on the Mount teaches and presupposes that same stupendous view of Jesus Christ which underlies all the rest of the Gospels.

The Sermon on the Mount (Matt 5–7) might seem to begin in a way unfavorable to that view and favorable to the advocate of a nondoctrinal Christianity who is not interested in the question of what sort of person Jesus was. It begins with the Beatitudes, and the Beatitudes might seem at first sight to be independent of any particular view regarding the one who spoke them. "Blessed are the poor in spirit, for theirs is the kingdom of heaven"—does not that remain true whatever we think of the person who uttered it?

Well, I am not sure even about that. I am not sure but that in all of the Beatitudes we detect a strange note of authority which would be overwrought and pathological in any other person than the Jesus of the Bible. Who is this who tells with such extraordinary assurance what sort of persons will be in the kingdom of God? Who is this that announces to men rewards that only God can give?

But let that pass for the moment. The thing that is clear is that Jesus does not finish the Beatitudes before he comes to speak in the most stupendous way about himself. What is the last of the Beatitudes? Is it merely a blessing pronounced upon people who possess a certain quality of soul? Not at all. It is a blessing pronounced upon people who stand in a certain relation to Jesus himself. Here is what it is: "Blessed are you when others revile you and persecute you and utter all kinds of evil against you falsely on my account" (Matt 5:11). Notice those words "on my account." They contain a tremendous claim on the part of Jesus. Men are to be willing to bear his name, and if they are not ashamed to bear his name they are to stand in the final judgment. Imagine any mere man saying that! Imagine anyone other than Jesus saying: "Blessed are you if you suffer on account of me." We have here the words of the same Jesus as was the one who said: "If anyone comes to me and does not hate his own father and mother and wife and children and brothers and sisters, yes, and even his own life, he cannot be my disciple" (Luke 14:26), the same Jesus as the one who said: "For whoever is ashamed of me and of my words in this adulterous and sinful generation, of him will the Son of Man also be ashamed when he comes in the glory of his Father with the holy angels" (Mark 8:38). Who can claim such an exclusive devotion as that—a devotion which shall take precedence of even the holiest of earthly ties, a devotion upon which a man's eternal destiny depends? God can, but can any mere man?

Then comes that great section of the Sermon on the Mount where Jesus declares himself to have come not to destroy the law or the prophets but to fulfill. "You have heard that it was said to those of old," he says, and then makes several quotations. Those quotations contain, in part, sentences found in the Old Testament. Over against those quotations, Jesus in every case puts in something of his own: "You have heard that it was said . . . but I say to you" (Matt 5:21–22). No doubt it may be held that Jesus in none of these instances is setting what he says over against what the Old Testament says, but in every instance is merely setting what he says over against what the Jewish teachers had wrongly held that the Old Testament said. But even then the fact remains that what he sets forth against the wrong interpretation of the Old Testament passages is not just a right interpretation but something wonderfully fresh and new. Plainly, Jesus puts his own sayings here on a level with the Old Testament pronouncements which he certainly regarded as the very Word of God.

I ask you to consider for a moment that authority with which Jesus speaks, that authority which causes him to put his own pronouncements fully on a level with the Old Testament pronouncements. What is the nature of that authority which Jesus here claims?

Well, prophets claimed authority. They asked that people should receive what they said as a message from God. Was then the authority which Jesus is here claiming merely the authority of a prophet? No, most emphatically it was not merely that. The prophets spoke with a divine authority. But it was a delegated authority, and it was delegated to them in a temporary way. There were times when the prophets became spokesmen of God, but they were spokesmen of God merely because they became for the moment channels for the Holy Spirit. They were not in general infallible. They had no authority granted to them as a permanent possession to be used as they saw fit. When they came forward as prophets they were careful to give all honor to God.

Thus, the characteristic way in which the prophets introduced their utterances was with the words, "Thus says the Lord." By that they meant to say: "I am not saying this as my own word, but it is God who is saying it; I am merely the mouthpiece of God."

Now unquestionably Jesus was a prophet. Undoubtedly the catechism that I learned in childhood was right when it told me that he was a prophet as well as a priest and a king (WSC Q&A 23).

But although Jesus was a prophet, he was also vastly more than a prophet. So, he does not introduce these utterances of his in the Sermon on the Mount in the way in which the utterances of a prophet are introduced. He does not say, "Thus says the Lord." No, he says, "I say." He comes forward with his own authority, and that authority he places fully on a level with the authority of God as it was found expressed in the Old Testament.

I am not forgetting the places in the Gospels where the dependence of the man Jesus upon God is set forth. Those passages are found just in the Gospel according to John—the Gospel where the deity of Christ is set forth, I will not say more clearly (since it is set forth with the utmost clearness in all the Gospels), but more expressly and fully, than in the other Gospels. Jesus, according to the Gospel of John, did what he saw God doing, and he said what God told him to say. All the same, despite this subordination of the man Jesus to God, his authority went far beyond the authority of a prophet. It was an authority which was his own personal right, as belonging to the one who was not merely man but God. You can search all through the words of the prophets and not find anything in the remotest degree resembling that stupendous "I say to you" of the Sermon on the Mount.

Then, I bid you read on to the end of that Sermon on the Mount.

"Not everyone," says Jesus, "who says to me, 'Lord, Lord,' will enter the kingdom of heaven, but the one who does the will of my Father who is in heaven" (Matt 7:21). That is one of the favorite texts of unbelievers. If the whole Sermon on the Mount is their favorite passage, this perhaps, within the Sermon on the Mount, may be regarded as their favorite text.

It is a favorite text with unbelievers not because of its real meaning, but because of the meaning which they wrongly attribute to it. They take it as meaning that if a man is what the world calls a good, moral man then he will enter into the kingdom of God no matter what his attitude toward Jesus may be. But, of course, that is not what the text says. The text does not say that if a man does the will of God he will enter into the kingdom of God whether he says "Lord, Lord" to Jesus or not. It does not say that any man who does not say "Lord, Lord" to Jesus will enter the kingdom. But what it does say is that even among those who say "Lord, Lord" to Jesus there are some who will not enter in. Those are the ones who say "Lord, Lord" only with their lips and not with their hearts, and who show that they have not said it with their hearts because they do not say it with their lives.

However, though for bad reasons, it is a popular text among unbelievers. They ought then to be willing to examine carefully what it says, and we all ought to examine it with them.

When we do examine it, we discover that it involves the most stupendous claim on the part of Jesus. For one thing, it provides an instance of the strange way in which Jesus speaks of God as being his own Father. "Not everyone who says unto me, 'Lord, Lord,' will enter the kingdom of heaven," he says, "but the one who does the will of my Father who is in heaven" (Matt 7:21). "My Father," says Jesus, not "our Father" or "the Father." We spoke of that in the talk just preceding this one. We noticed how it appeared in the answer of the twelve-year-old Jesus in the temple, and how it runs all through the Gospels. Well, here it is again, in the Sermon on the Mount. You cannot get away from it. We do not particularly notice it as we read this verse, because we have become so used to it. But that does not destroy its tremendous significance. Indeed, it vastly increases it. Everywhere Jesus thinks of himself as being Son of God in some entirely unique sense.

But now let us look at what this verse itself says. We must take it in connection with the following two verses. Those verses also are favorites with the unbelievers of our day. They read as follows: "On that day many will say to me, 'Lord, Lord, did we not prophesy in your name, and cast out demons in your name, and do many mighty works in your name?' And then will I declare to them, 'I never knew you; depart from me, you workers of lawlessness'" (Matt 7:22–23).

Unbelievers, I suppose, interpret those words as disparaging miracles, and as disparaging the active profession of religion. They interpret them as teaching that if a man leads what the world calls a moral life he does not need to accept any creed or make any definite profession of faith.

That interpretation is of course quite wrong, in the same way as that in which the corresponding interpretation of the preceding verse is wrong. These verses do not say that miracles were unimportant in the apostolic age (when miracles still happened) or that orthodoxy was unimportant then or is unimportant now. They only say that nothing else matters unless a man's heart is changed and unless that change of his heart is shown in a good life. They do not say that orthodoxy is unnecessary or that mighty works in the external world are unimportant, but they only say that orthodoxy without right living is a sham, and that real orthodoxy results in obedience to the commands of God.

But the fact remains that these verses are favorites with unbelievers; they are favorites with those who think that it does not make any difference what a man thinks about God or about Christ and that all that is needed, according to Jesus, is to live what is ordinarily called a moral life.

All right. Let us just look at these verses so popular among unbelievers. Do they really teach that it does not make any difference what a man thinks about Jesus Christ? I tell you, my friends, the exact reverse is the case. These verses, like all the rest of the New Testament, present a stupendous view of Jesus Christ, and, like other sayings of Jesus, they present a stupendous claim made by Jesus himself.

What is the scene to which we are transplanted in these verses? Is it some scene in the course of ordinary history or some scene of merely local or temporary significance? No, it is nothing of the kind. It is the tremendous scene of the last judgment, the court from which there is no appeal, the final decision that determines the eternal destinies of men.

In other words, it is the judgment seat of God. Well, who is it that is represented here as sitting on the judgment seat of God? Who is it that is represented here in this supposedly pleasant, purely ethical, practical, ultra-modern, nontheological Sermon on the Mount, and by this supposedly simple teacher of righteousness who kept his own person out of his message and was careful not to advance any lofty claims? Who is it that is represented here in this supposedly purely ethical discourse and by this humble Jesus as sitting one day upon the judgment seat of God and as determining the eternal destinies of all the world? There can be no doubt whatever about the answer to that question. The one represented here as sitting on the judgment seat of God is Jesus himself.

We may not like the answer to that question, but the answer is as plain as plain can be. "Many will say to me," Jesus says, "'Lord, Lord' . . . and then will I declare to them, 'I never knew you; depart from me, you workers of lawlessness'" (Matt 7:22–23). Who is that "I," and who is that "me"? Is it God the Father? No, it is Jesus; it is the one who speaks these words. Upon Jesus's decision depends the fate of all men. And what is that fate? What is the meaning of that "depart" which is Jesus's sentence upon those who work iniquity? About this question also there can be no doubt. The Sermon on the Mount itself gives the answer: "If your right eye causes you to sin, tear it out and throw it away. For it is better that you lose one of your members than that your whole body be thrown into hell" (Matt 5:29). The answer is given also in the whole teaching of Jesus, and it is implied even in the verses with which we now have to do. No, there can be no doubt whatever about what Jesus meant by that word "depart"; he meant that those upon whom he would pronounce that sentence to depart would be cast into hell.

The thought of hell, as well as the thought of heaven, runs all through the teaching of Jesus; it gives to his ethical teaching that stupendous earnestness which is its marked characteristic. But how is hell here designated? It is described elsewhere in the Gospels; and never let us forget, whether we call the language "figurative" or not, that it means an eternal and terrible punishment, a punishment of which there is no end. But how is hell designated in this particular passage? The answer may be surprising to some people, but it is perfectly plain. Hell is designated in our passage as banishment from Jesus.

I do just beg you to think of that for a moment, my friends. Jesus of Nazareth certainly did believe—no good historian can deny it—that he would sit upon the judgment seat of God at the terrible last Judgment Day, that his word would be final, and that life in his presence would be heaven and departure from him would be hell.

What has become of the weak, sentimental, purely human, purely ethical Jesus of modern reconstruction? What has become of your Jesus who was a simple teacher of righteousness and advanced no claim to be God?

Have you found your purely human Jesus? Have you escaped from the divine Christ of the creeds by appealing from the Gospel according to John to the Sermon on the Mount? No, indeed, my friend. The Jesus of the Bible is everywhere exactly the same.

What will you do with Jesus? Will you treat him with a mild approval? Ah, people are so patronizing in the presence of Jesus today. They say such kind, polite things about him. They are good enough to say that his ethics will solve the problems of society; they are good enough to say that he enunciated some maxims that are better than Jefferson's ten rules and go far beyond Socrates, Confucius, and Buddha. They are perfectly ready to let him influence some departments of their life. But they will not receive him as their Savior; they are not interested in his atoning blood, but they are so complacent in his presence.

God grant that it may not be so with you, my friends! God grant that you may never treat Jesus with this polite, patronizing approval! God grant that you may not treat him as a religious genius or as the founder of one of the world's religions! God grant that, instead, you may say to Jesus, with doubting Thomas, "My Lord and my God!" (John 20:28)

14

What Jesus Said about Himself

We have discussed the deity of Christ as it is attested by Jesus himself in the Sermon on the Mount. We have seen that in the very passage to which unbelievers appeal in support of their view that Jesus kept himself out of his gospel and merely presented a program of life to be followed first by him and then by his followers—in that very passage, Jesus presents himself as possessed of an authority that goes far beyond that of any prophet and is in truth an authority that belongs only to God. At the close of our last talk, we were speaking particularly of the passage near the end of the Sermon on the Mount where Jesus presents himself as the one who is to sit at the last day on the judgment seat of God and determine the eternal destinies of all the world.

This is by no means the only passage in the Gospels where Jesus so presents himself as the final Judge. Indeed, it is probably because of this thought of himself as the final Judge that he uses one of his favorite titles to designate himself—namely, the title "the Son of man."

Our first impulse might be to say that the title is a designation of the humanity of Jesus as distinguished from his deity. He was both God and man, and that, we may be tempted to say, is what he meant when he called himself "Son of man" as well as "Son of God."

If that view of the title were correct, it would certainly be a very lofty title, and it would certainly not be in any contradiction with the deity of Christ. But, as a matter of fact, it is unlikely that the title "the Son of man" on the lips of Jesus has this meaning at all. It is unlikely that it is intended to designate the humanity of our Lord as distinguished from his deity. It is on the whole unlikely that there is any contrast in the Gospels between the title "Son of man" and the title "Son of God." People who use these titles to designate the two natures of Jesus as both man and God, who call attention, in other words, to the fact that he was both "Son of man" and "Son of God," are probably wrong in their interpretation of the title, right though they unquestionably are in holding that Jesus was both God and man.

The true key to the title "Son of man" on the lips of our Lord is probably to be found in the seventh chapter of the book of Daniel, where "one like a son of man" (Dan 7:13) appears in the presence of the "Ancient of Days" and receives an everlasting dominion. When this person is said to be "one like a son of man," that is not said because he is a man in contrast with God. The contrast is rather with the beasts—lion, bear, leopard, and unnamed beast—that represent the world empires preceding the kingdom of the one like a son of man. After the successive appearance of those kingdoms represented by figures designated as being each like the figure of some beast, there arises a kingdom whose ruler appears in the vision as a man. That kingdom, unlike those other kingdoms, is to be everlasting.

This passage in the book of Daniel had an important influence upon subsequent Messianic expectations among the Jews. In the so-called Ethiopic book of Enoch, for example—a book which of course is not in the Bible and does not at all deserve to be there—the title "the Son of man" occurs frequently as the designation of a heavenly personage already existing in heaven but destined to appear in great glory to be the Judge of all the world. Now we certainly do not mean for one moment that our Lord made any use of that so-called book of Enoch. But it is likely that the book does give evidence of the use among the Jews of the great passage in the seventh chapter of Daniel. On the basis of that passage, the coming Deliverer had come to be called—in certain Jewish circles at least—"the Son of man," and had come to be thought of as destined to appear with the clouds of heaven and be the Judge of all the earth. What our Lord did when he called himself "the Son of man" was to place the stamp of approval upon this Jewish expectation because it was really in accordance with the Old Testament, and then to apply it to himself.

It is altogether probable, then, that the title "the Son of man" on the lips of Jesus is distinctly a Messianic title. It does not designate the humanity of Jesus as distinguished from his deity, but it designates him as being that transcendent, heavenly person who was to come one day with the clouds of heaven and be the final Judge of all the world.

A notable passage in the book of Acts confirms this view of the title "the Son of man." In Acts 7:55–56, it is said, of the dying martyr Stephen: "But he, full of the Holy Spirit, gazed into heaven and saw the glory of God, and Jesus standing at the right hand of God. And he said, 'Behold, I see the heavens opened, and the Son of Man standing at the right hand of God.'"

Here the reference to the seventh chapter of Daniel is perfectly plain. Stephen sees essentially the same vision as that which the prophet Daniel had seen; he sees that heavenly figure, the Son of man, appearing in glory in the presence of God.

As Jesus uses the title, the origin of the title is just as clear as it is in the words of the dying Stephen. So, for example, in Mark 8:38: "For whosoever is ashamed of me and of my words in this adulterous and sinful generation, of him will the Son of Man also be ashamed when he comes in the glory of his Father with the holy angels." So also in Mark 13:26: "And then they will see the Son of Man coming in clouds with great power and glory." In such passages, the reference to the great scene in the seventh chapter of Daniel is perfectly clear.

In other passages, it is true, the reference to that scene is not so direct. Jesus sometimes uses the title "the Son of man" when he is speaking not of his exaltation but of his humiliation. So it is in Matthew 8:20 where it is said that "the Son of Man has nowhere to lay his head." So also in the great passage, Mark 10:45, in which Jesus says, regarding his atoning death, that "the Son of man came not to be served but to serve, and to give his life as a ransom for many." But we may fairly hold that the use of the title in these passages is intended to contrast the stupendous dignity properly belonging to the Son of man, the Judge and Ruler of all the world, with his present humble life. The real pathos of those passages is found in the fact that it was not any ordinary man who had nowhere to lay his head, and that it was not any ordinary man who came not to be ministered unto but to minister to, but the heavenly Son of man, that stupendous figure, who was now more homeless than the foxes and the birds!

Here and there, as Jesus uses the title, there may possibly be a special reference to the humanity of the one so designated, but such passages at the most are rare, and the prevailing significance of the title is that it identifies Jesus with the heavenly Messiah, the stupendous figure spoken of in the seventh chapter of Daniel whose kingdom would be an everlasting kingdom.

That, I may say in passing, is the prevailing opinion today among scholars of widely different shades of opinion, both believers and unbelievers.

Here and there a defender of another view of the title appears, but I think it may be said that the prevailing view among careful scholars is what I have just indicated. For a full discussion of this subject, I want to refer you to a book to which I have been much indebted—*The Self-Disclosure of Jesus* by Dr. Geerhardus Vos.

What particularly needs to be said, however, is that whatever view be taken of the origin and meaning of the term "the Son of man," it is at any rate clear that Jesus of Nazareth certainly did claim that he would one day sit on the judgment seat of God to decide the eternal destinies of men. That claim appears, as we observed very clearly, in the Sermon on the Mount. You cannot get away from it even in the supposedly purely ethical parts of Jesus's teaching. It runs all through the Gospels. Every historian, whether he is a Christian or not, ought to take account of this strange fact—that a certain Jesus, a man who lived in the first century in Palestine, was actually convinced, as he looked out upon the men who thronged about him, that he would one day sit on the judgment seat of God as their Judge, as the Judge and Ruler of all the world.

What are you going to do with that claim of Jesus? If you hold it to be true, then Jesus is your King and Lord. If you hold it to be false, then I do not see how in the world you can go on taking him as a worthy example for your life.

The conviction of Jesus that he would at the last judgment decide the eternal destinies of men was joined with the conviction that he could determine those eternal destinies here and now. He claimed to be able to forgive sins. His opponents got the point of that claim; they got it far better than certain modern persons who trip along so lightly over the things that the Gospels contain. "Why does this man speak like that?" they said. "He is blaspheming! Who can forgive sins but God alone?" (Mark 2:7) They were right. None can forgive sins but God. Jesus was a blasphemer if he was a mere man, and that point his enemies saw clearly. You may accept the lofty claims of Jesus. You may take him as very God or else you must reject him as a miserable, deluded enthusiast. There is really no middle ground. Jesus refuses to be pressed into the mold of a mere religious teacher.

Thus we have seen that Jesus's claim of deity runs all through the Gospels. It does not appear merely in this passage or that, but is really presupposed in every word that Jesus uttered and in everything that he did.

There was, it is true, a period in his ministry when he did not make his own person the express subject of his teaching. It was always the background of his teaching and his work; without it everything that he said and did becomes unintelligible. But during a large part of his Galilean ministry, as described by the Synoptic Gospels, he seems not often to have set forth the mystery of his own person in any detailed way.

That lack is wonderfully supplied by the Gospel according to John, which was written by a man who stood in the innermost circle of the disciples of our Lord. But what I want you to observe particularly is that there is no opposition at this point between the fourth Gospel and the other three. The Christ who is so gloriously set forth in the Gospel according to John is exactly the Christ who is everywhere presupposed in the Synoptic Gospels. Far from being in any contradiction with the Synoptic Gospels, the Gospel according to John, with its rich report of the teaching of our Lord about his own person, provides the key which enables us the better to understand what we are told in Matthew, Mark, and Luke.

Here and there, moreover, we have in the Synoptic Gospels just the kind of teaching of our Lord about himself as that which appears so fully reported by the beloved disciple in the Gospel according to John. That is notably the case with a famous passage in the eleventh chapter of Matthew, which has a close parallel in the tenth chapter of Luke. "All things have been handed over to me by my Father," says Jesus, "and no one knows the Son except the Father, and no one knows the Father except the Son and anyone to whom the Son chooses to reveal him" (Matt 11:27). Here we have not only the substance of the teaching that appears so fully in the fourth Gospel but even the form of it: "the Father," "the Son"—how often those terms appear set over against each other in the Gospel according to John, just exactly as they are set over against each other here!

Just consider how wonderfully rich is the content of this verse in its report of the teaching of Jesus about himself! "No one knows the Father except the Son"—that in itself is a very stupendous utterance. It designates Jesus as truly knowing God, and as the only one who knows him. We think instinctively, as we read, of the words in the Gospel according to John: "No one has ever seen God; the only God, who is at the Father's side, he has made him known" (John 1:18). How wonderful is such a knowledge of God! Think of it, my friends. Jesus of Nazareth, a man walking upon this earth, said, as he talked to his contemporaries, "No one knows the Father save me." How is such rich knowledge of God possible to any but God himself?

But that is not all that there is in this saying. No, the saying goes far beyond that. "No one knows the Father except the Son"—that is wonderful enough. But that is not all. There is something still more stupendous in this verse. It is this: "No one knows the Son except the Father."

Just think what these words mean, my friends. They mean that there are mysteries in the person Jesus which none but the infinite and eternal God can know. The two persons, the Father and the Son, are here put in a strange reciprocal relationship. They are both mysterious to all others, but they are known, and fully known, to each other. The Son knows the depths of the Father's being, and the Father knows the depths of the being of the Son. An ineffable mutual knowledge prevails between these two.

What does that mean? It means what is really implied in the Gospels from beginning to end. It means that the strange man who is known to history as Jesus of Nazareth was no mere man, but the infinite and eternal and unchangeable God. In this wonderful verse, the twenty-seventh verse of the eleventh chapter of Matthew, we have in summary and in implication the great doctrine of the deity of our Lord, and when we put it together with Jesus's teaching regarding the Holy Spirit we have the full wonderful teaching of Scripture regarding the three persons in one God.

I have not time in the present talk to speak to you longer about that doctrine; I have not time to set forth further the richness of the Scripture's testimony to the deity of our blessed Lord. But there is one thing that I do want to drive home at once.

It is this: this mysterious verse of which we have just been speaking does not appear as some excrescence in the Gospel picture of Jesus but as an integral part of the whole. When we come upon this "Christological" passage in our reading of the Gospel of Matthew, this passage which has been called "the Johannine passage" because it is so much like the Gospel according to John, do we feel anything like a shock? Do we feel as though we were transplanted into another atmosphere? Do we feel as though we were suddenly dealing with another Christ?

I tell you, my friends, we do not. No, we are dealing with that same Christ with whom we have been dealing all through the Gospel according to Matthew; we are dealing with exactly that same Christ who spoke, for example, the Sermon on the Mount. We are dealing with that same Christ who, according to all four Gospels, spoke words of solemn warning but also words of an infinite tenderness and grace.

What is the context of this verse with which we have been dealing in the present talk—this verse which sets forth in such stupendous fashion the majesty of the person of our Lord? Just let me read it to you before we part: "I thank you, Father, Lord of heaven and earth, that you have hidden these things from the wise and understanding and revealed them to little children; yes, Father, for such was your gracious will" (Matt 11:25–26). Follow the words of which we have spoken, the words in which Jesus speaks of that ineffable relation between the Father and the Son. Then what follows? Does something follow that reveals some later theology of the church, something that fails to show the unmistakable, characteristic, inimitable quality of Jesus's authentic teaching? Judge for yourselves, my friends. Here is what follows upon that stupendous testimony to the deity of Christ: "Come to me, all who labor and are heavy laden, and I will give you rest. Take my yoke upon you, and learn from me, for I am gentle and lowly in heart, and you will find rest for your souls. For my yoke is easy, and my burden is light" (Matt 11:28–30). Are those the words of some falsifier who put upon the lips of Jesus words that he never spoke? Are those the words of some religious genius who used the name of Jesus as the medium through which he might convey his teaching to the world?

Oh, no, my friends; no religious genius ever spoke words like these. These are words such as never a man spoke.

How sweet these words are on the lips of Jesus! How abominable they would be on the lips of any other! "Come to me, all who labor and are heavy laden, and I will give you rest"—who could speak those words without mocking and deceiving those who hear? I will tell you. Only he who said in the same breath: "No one knows the Son except the Father, and no one knows the Father except the Son." The plain fact is that the gracious invitation of Jesus—an invitation so sweetly repeated again and again in the Gospels by him who was sent to seek and to save that which was lost—is a divine invitation. The one who uttered it was a deceiver or he was God.

Yet, it is objected, there are so many who will not accept the invitation; there are so many learned men who will not believe Jesus when he advances these stupendous claims. Yes, I know. They are very many and they are very learned.

But did not Jesus himself say so; did not Jesus himself say that there were many learned persons who would ever learnedly reject him when he offered himself as their Savior and Lord? "I thank you, Father, Lord of heaven and earth, that you have hidden these things from the wise and understanding and revealed them to little children."

Which are you, my friends? Do you belong to the wise and prudent, of whom our Lord spoke? Do you belong to those who rely upon the wisdom of this world and turn aside from Christ? Or are you among the babes? Will you come to Jesus weak and helpless? Will you come to him as a very little child? Are you weary and heavy laden? Will you come to him that he may give you rest?

15

The Supernatural Christ

I have been talking to you about the deity of Christ and have shown you that Jesus's testimony to his own deity is not found merely in the Gospel according to John. It is found in all four Gospels and it pervades all parts of the Gospels. Even in the so-called ethical parts of the Gospels like the Sermon on the Mount, the stupendous claim of Jesus is really presupposed.

We must now, however, notice something else. We must notice that this claim of Jesus is everywhere supported by his power to work miracles. That is the way in which the Gospels represent the miracles. They represent them as attestations to show that Jesus spoke the truth when he came forward with his stupendous claim.

This biblical estimate of the miracles has often been reversed in the minds of modern men. The miracles, men tell us, even if they really happened, are at best an obstacle to faith rather than an aid to faith. People used to believe, they tell us, because of the miracles; they now believe, if they believe at all, in spite of the miracles.

A curious confusion underlies this way of thinking. In one sense, of course, it is true that the miracles are an obstacle to faith. Unquestionably, a narrative that has no miracles in it is easier to believe than a narrative that contains miracles. Of course that is so. Who ever denied it? A perfectly trivial narrative is easier to believe than one that contains an account of extraordinary happenings. So, if I should tell you that when I walked down the street today I saw a Ford car, my narrative would have at least one advantage over the narratives in the New Testament—it would certainly be far easier to believe. But then it would also have one disadvantage. It would be far easier to believe, but then, you see, it would not be worth believing.

So, if the Gospels contained no miracles they would in one sense be easier to believe than they are now. But, do you not see, the thing that would be believed would be entirely different from the thing that is believed now when we take the Gospels as they stand. If the Jesus of the Gospels was a purely natural and not a supernatural person, then we should have no difficulty in believing that such a person lived in the first century of our era. Even skeptics would have no difficulty in believing it. Defenders of the faith would have an easy victory indeed. Everybody would believe. But then there would be one drawback. It would be this: the thing that everybody would believe would not be worth believing.

A purely natural, as distinguished from a supernatural, Christ would be just a teacher and example. There have been many teachers and examples in the history of mankind. It would place no particular demands upon our faith if we were told that this teacher and example was a little better than any of the others. But then, you see, we are not looking for a teacher and example. We are looking for a Savior. And a purely human, a merely natural, as distinguished from a supernatural, Christ can never be our Savior. He would merely be one of us. He would need a Savior for himself before he could save others; he, just as much as we, would need a supernatural Savior.

We have such a Savior presented to us in the Gospels, a Savior who is not merely man but God. The really difficult thing to believe is that such a Savior really entered into this world. It is a very blessed thing, but it is certainly not a trivial thing. It is not one of those trivial things that are so easy to believe because they occur every day. It is certainly not a thing that can be believed without a mighty revolution in all a man's thinking and all a man's life.

If now you ask whether it would be easier to believe that thing without the individual miracles narrated in the Gospels than it is to believe it with those individual miracles, we answer emphatically, "No." It would be easier to believe the story of a mere religious teacher without the miracles—certainly, that goes without saying—but not to believe the story of the life upon earth of the incarnate Son of God. The whole appearance of such a divine person upon earth is itself a stupendous miracle. The individual miracles, with their individual attestation, do make it easier to believe that great central miracle. They are proofs of it. They are exactly what the Bible represents them as being—true testimonies to the truth of that stupendous claim of Jesus to be very God.

If you examine carefully the views of those who reject the individual miracles, you will discover that they do not really hold on to the great central and all-pervading miracle. They may seem to do so. They use the old terminology. They love to speak of "incarnation"; they love to speak of God as having become man. But when you come to look at them closely, you discover that this use of traditional terminology on their part only serves to mask from themselves and from others a profound difference of thought. They mean by "incarnation" just about the opposite of what the Bible means by it. They do not really mean by it that the eternal Son of God, the second person of the Trinity, became man this once, and this once only, "and so was, and continueth to be God, and man, in two distinct natures, and one person, forever" (WSC Q&A 21). No, they mean something entirely different. They are very far indeed from believing in Christ for salvation as he is offered to us in the gospel.

The truth is that the Bible picture of Jesus possesses a wonderful unity. Without the miracles as the Gospels narrate them, the unity would be sadly destroyed. Every one of the miracles, with its historical attestation, adds its quota of evidence to our great central conviction that this Jesus is indeed the Son of God.

It is interesting to observe the way in which the miracles of the life of Christ have been treated in the history of modern unbelief. The cardinal principle of unbelief is that miracles have never happened. What, then, shall be done with the accounts of miracles that are found in the Gospels?

The first impulse of a skeptic might be to say that since the gospel picture of Jesus contains miracles, and since miracles never happened, therefore the whole picture is untrue. But that, of course, will not do at all. It is perfectly clear that we have in the Gospels an account of a real person who really lived in Palestine in the first century of our era. The picture is entirely too lifelike ever to have been the product of invention. That is admitted by all except a few extremists. Very well, then. If the picture is the picture of a real person, what shall be done with the miracles that it contains? Those miracles, according to the initial assumption of our skeptical investigator, never happened; yet they are narrated in an account of a real historical person. What shall be done about it?

The obvious answer of unbelievers is that the miracles must be rejected in order to leave the rest. In this way, it is supposed, we shall be able to sift the material in the Gospels in order to arrive at the modicum of truth that they contain. When, it is said, we have removed from the gospel picture of Jesus these gaudy colors of the supernatural, we shall have Jesus as he actually was.

Well, it sounds easy. Surely it must have been accomplished long before now—the removal of the miracles from the picture of Jesus in the Gospels. Many of the most brilliant of modern men have been engaged in it during the past hundred years. Surely their efforts must have been successful.

That is certainly what one might expect. But in this case, expectations are not borne out by the fact. The plain fact is that this "quest of the historical Jesus," as it has been called—this effort to take the miracles out of the Gospels—has proven to be a colossal failure. It is being increasingly recognized as being a failure even by the skeptical historians themselves. The supernatural is found to be far more deeply rooted in the gospel account of Jesus than was formerly supposed.

At first, it seemed to be quite easy to get the miracles out of the Gospels. All we shall have to do, said the skeptical historians, is just take the miracles out and leave all the rest. Even the miracle incidents themselves, they said, can be accepted as historical; only, we must observe that they were not really miraculous. So, Luke tells us in the first chapter that Zacharias the father of John the Baptist went into the temple at the hour of incense and received an announcement about the birth of a son. Is that incident historical? Did Zacharias really go into the temple that day? Certainly, said the men of this way of thinking, the incident is historical; certainly Zacharias went into the temple. Of course, he was slightly mistaken about what he saw! He thought he saw an angel when what he really saw was just the smoke rising from the altar in that dim religious light. But such mistakes do not cast any general discredit upon the narratives in which they stand.

So also all four of the Gospels say that Jesus one day fed five thousand men. Is that incident historical? Did Jesus really feed those five thousand men? Certainly the narrative is historical, said the men of the way of thinking with which we are now dealing; certainly Jesus fed those five thousand men. What he did was just to take those five loaves and two fishes and set a good example by distributing them to the people immediately around him. That led the other fortunate people among the crowd to do likewise. His good example was contagious. People who were fortunate enough to have any food distributed it to those around them and so everybody was fed. Thus the incident is perfectly historical but was not really miraculous. The whole trouble has come from the fact that readers of the Gospels have insisted on putting a supernaturalistic interpretation upon an incident that was really quite natural.

It is all perfectly easy and simple, is it not? How nicely the task has been accomplished—miracles as neatly extracted as an appendix is extracted in a modern hospital, everything else allowed to remain "as was," the general trustworthiness of the Gospels rescued, and Jesus made to keep within the bounds of nature's laws! What was all the bother about? It was all so perfectly simple!

Such was the so-called "rationalizing" method of dealing with the miracle narratives, as practiced by Paulus[1] and others one hundred years ago. It had considerable vogue in its day. But its vogue was of short duration. God raised upon a besom of destruction for it in the person of a disconcerting young man named David Friedrich Strauss.

Strauss published his book *The Life of Jesus* in 1835. It was unquestionably one of the most influential books of modern times—a very important book to have been written by a young man of twenty-seven years of age.

I said that Strauss's book was influential. I did not say that its influence was good, and as a matter of fact, it was not good but very bad. Strauss did not write in the interests of the truth of the Gospels; he did not write from the point of view of a real Christian believer. On the contrary, he wrote from the point of view of extreme unbelief. His book remains to the present day perhaps the fullest compendium of what can be said against the truthfulness of the Gospel narratives.

Yet such a book had at least the use, in the providence of God, of demolishing the rationalizing method of dealing with the miracle narratives in the Gospels. In those narratives, Strauss said, the miracles are the main thing—they are the thing for which all the rest exists. How absurd, then, to say that the narratives have grown up out of utterly trivial events upon which a supernaturalistic interpretation was wrongly put! No, said Strauss, we must give up all attempts at finding a modicum of historical truth in these narratives; they are simply myths—that is, they are popular expressions, in narrative form, of certain religious ideas; they are merely the way in which popular fancy expressed the great debt which the early Christian church owed to Jesus.

At first, Strauss's book caused great consternation. He had not, indeed, denied the historical existence of Jesus, and of course he really held that much that is narrated about Jesus in the Gospels is true. But so radical was his criticism, and so completely did he fail to put together into any continuous positive account of Jesus what was left after his criticism had done

---

1. Heinrich Paulus, 1761–1851

its work, that it was quite natural for people to feel that Strauss had almost removed Jesus of Nazareth from the pages of history.

Then, however, an attempt was made to repair the damage. I am not referring to the defense of the Gospels by believing scholars, but I am referring to the attempt by men of Strauss's own way of thinking—men who, like Strauss, denied the occurrence of miracles—to discover and make use of the modicum of truth that might be thought to remain in the Gospels after criticism had been given its rights.

Possibly, it was supposed, that modicum of truth might be discovered by what is called "source criticism." The Gospels, it was admitted, contain much that is untrue, but if we could discover the earlier sources used by the writers of the Gospels we might get much nearer to the facts. Well, an imposing attempt was made in that direction. The Gospel according to John was rejected as almost altogether unhistorical, and then the two chief sources of Matthew and Luke were held to be (1) Mark and (2) a lost source composed chiefly of the sayings of Jesus as distinguished from the accounts of his deeds. That was the famous "two-document theory" for the sources of the Gospels.

On the basis of that theory, a supposedly historical account of a purely human Jesus was constructed. People became quite enthusiastic about it. The troublesome miracles, it was supposed, were all removed; the theological Christ of the creeds was done away. But, it was said, something better had been rediscovered—a really and purely human Jesus, a Jesus who was one of us, a Jesus who started where we started and won through to sonship with God, a Jesus who kept his own person out of his gospel and simply taught—by word and by life—the great liberating truths of the fatherhood of God and the brotherhood of man.

Such was the so-called "Liberal Jesus." It was an imposing reconstruction indeed. It was thought to offer great promise to the human race. The shackles of dogma, it was supposed, had been removed. A new Reformation would soon take place.

But alas for human hopes! Nothing has been seen of the new reformation, and the imposing reconstruction of the Liberal Jesus has fallen to the ground. I think the first thirty-five years of the twentieth century might almost be called, in the sphere of New Testament criticism, the period of the decline and fall of "the Liberal Jesus." That is a great outstanding fact. I think that it is a fact that will loom up very large to future historians when the history of the period in which we are living comes finally to be written.

The great trouble is that the miraculous in the Gospels is found to be much more pervasive than it was at first thought to be. It runs through the Gospels as we now have them. That is clear. But it also is found to run through the sources supposed, rightly or wrongly, to underlie the Gospels. All right, then; suppose we go even back of those earliest written sources and examine supposed detached bits of oral tradition out of which they are sometimes supposed to have been composed. Alas, we obtain no relief. Those supposed detached bits are found themselves to contain the objectionable miraculous element. There seems to be no escape from the supernatural Christ. At the very beginning of the church—not at some later time, but at the very beginning—Jesus was regarded not just as a religious teacher or a prophet but as a supernatural deliverer.

That is the result at which ultramodern criticism has arrived. It is a far cry from the cheerful, rationalizing days of Paulus one hundred years ago. It is a far cry from the time when men thought they could explain away this miracle narrative and that, and have a perfectly good account left of a great religious teacher.

The outstanding result of a hundred years of effort to separate the natural from the supernatural in the early Christian view of Jesus is that the thing cannot be done. The two are inseparable. The very earliest early Christian account of Jesus is found to be supernaturalistic to the core.

Very well, what shall we do about it? The earliest view of Jesus that we know anything about represents him as a supernatural person. It is found to exhibit a remarkable unanimity at this point. What shall we do with it? There are only two things to do with it. We can take it or we can leave it.

Modern skeptical historians are saying we must leave it. All our information about Jesus is supernaturalistic, they are saying; therefore, all our information about Jesus is uncertain. We can never disentangle the real Jesus from the beliefs of his earliest followers. The only Christ we really know is the supernatural Christ of Jesus's earliest followers. We can never rediscover the portrait of the real Jesus.

Are you afraid of skepticism like that? I am not afraid of it a bit. It is easily refuted by a mere reading of the Gospels. I beg you just to read the Gospels for yourselves, my friends, and then ask yourselves whether the person here presented to you is not a living, breathing person. The extreme skepticism of the day will always be refuted by common sense.

That being so, the extreme skepticism of our day is very instructive. I get great comfort from it. Do you not see, my friends? That extreme skepticism of Bultmann[2] and others is the inevitable result of trying to reject the miracles in the Gospels. That extreme skepticism is absurd. What is the conclusion? The conclusion is that the process which inevitably led to that extreme skepticism was wrong from the beginning. We never ought to have tried to reject the miracles in the Gospels at all.

I wonder when men are going to draw this conclusion. It does seem to lie so very near at hand. When will they cease to be blind to it? The Gospels present to us just one Christ—the supernatural Christ. They do so with overwhelmingly self-evidencing force. When shall we just accept their witness? When shall we just say that God did walk upon this earth? When shall we just come to that divine Christ and ask him to be the Savior of our souls?

---

2. Rudolf Karl Bultmann, 1884–1976

16

Did Christ Rise from the Dead?

In the last of these talks, I was speaking to you about the miracles of Christ. But a treatment of the miracles would be incomplete unless we singled out for special examination the central or crowning miracle, which is the miracle of the resurrection.

In treating the resurrection, I suggest that we might begin with things about which everybody is agreed in order that we may go on from them to speak of things with regard to which Christian people differ from those who are not Christians.

Nineteen hundred years ago there lived in an obscure corner of the Roman Empire one who would have seemed to a superficial observer to be a remarkable man. He engaged in a career of religious teaching accompanied by a ministry of healing. At first, he had the favor of the crowd, but since he would not be the kind of leader the people demanded he soon fell victim to the jealousy of the rulers of his people and to the cowardice of the Roman governor. He died the death of criminals of that day, on the cross.

At his death, his followers were discouraged. They had evidently been far inferior to him in discernment and in courage, and now what little courage they may have had was gone. His death meant the destruction of all their hopes. Never, one might have said, was a movement more completely dead than the movement begun by Jesus of Nazareth.

Then, however, a surprising thing happened. It is a fact of history, which no real historian denies, that those same weak, discouraged men, the followers of Jesus, began—within a very short time after the shameful death of their leader, in Jerusalem, the scene of their cowardly flight—the most remarkable religious movement that the world has ever known, the movement commonly called the Christian church.

At first, that movement was obscure. But it spread like wildfire. In a few decades at the most it was firmly planted in the chief cities of the civilized world and in Rome itself. After a lapse of less than three centuries it conquered the Roman Empire. Incalculable has been its influence upon the whole history of the world.

What caused that remarkable change in those followers of Jesus? What caused those weak and cowardly men suddenly to become the spiritual conquerors of the world? At that point the difference of opinion arises. Yet even with regard to that point there is a certain measure of agreement. It is now admitted by historians both Christian and non-Christian that those followers of Jesus became the founders of what is commonly known as the Christian church because they became honestly convinced that Jesus was risen from the dead.

But what in turn produced that conviction? What produced the belief of the first disciples in the resurrection of Christ? Here is where the difference of opinion comes in.

The New Testament, of course, has a perfectly clear answer to the question. The belief of the disciples in the resurrection, according to the New Testament, was due simply to the fact of the resurrection. Those disciples came to believe that Jesus had risen from the dead for the simple reason that Jesus had risen from the dead. He had risen from the dead; and they had not only seen his tomb empty but had seen him alive after his death on the cross.

If that explanation of the belief of the first disciples in the resurrection be rejected, what shall be put into its place? The answer to that question, which is given today by all or practically all unbelievers, is that those first disciples of Jesus became convinced that Jesus had risen from the dead because they experienced certain hallucinations, certain pathological experiences in which they thought they saw Jesus before their eyes when in reality there was nothing there. In a hallucination, the optic nerve is really affected but it is affected not by light rays coming from an external object, but by some pathological condition of the bodily organism of the subject himself. This is the so-called "vision theory" regarding the origin of the Christian church. It has held the field among unbelievers inside of the church and outside of the church since the days of Strauss about one hundred years ago.

I think we ought to understand just exactly what that vision theory means. It means that the Christian church is founded upon a pathological experience of certain persons in the first century of our era. It means that if there had been a good neurologist for Peter and the others to consult there never would have been a Christian church.

I am perfectly well aware of the fact that advocates of the vision hypothesis refuse to look at the matter just exactly in that way. The really important thing, they say, was not the pathological experience which those men had, but it was the impression left upon them by Jesus's character. They never would have experienced those hallucinations, they say, unless their minds and hearts had been filled with the thought of the radiant personality of Jesus. It was because they were so much impressed with him that they came to have those hallucinations. Thus the hallucinations, say the advocates of the vision hypothesis, were merely the temporary form which was necessary in that day and among men of that kind of education in order that the influence of Jesus could continue to make itself felt. We, they say, can get rid of that form. We no longer need to believe that Jesus rose from the dead and appeared to the eyes of his disciples. But we can still let the influence of Jesus be felt in our lives. In the changed lives of men who have been influenced by him, Jesus has his truest resurrection.

So the thing is represented by the advocates of what is misleadingly called a "spiritual resurrection." This representation altogether ignores the real character of the first disciples' faith. What those men had from the appearances of the risen Christ was not merely the conviction that Jesus was still alive. No, what they had was the conviction that he had risen. It was not merely the state of Jesus resultant upon the resurrection which was valuable for them, but the act of the resurrection. At the heart of their faith was the conviction that Jesus had done something for them by his death and resurrection. The Christian religion, in other words, is rooted in an event.

If that supposed event really took place, as the Bible says it did, then the Christian religion is true. If it did not take place, as the dominant vision theory holds, then the Christian religion is false, and a church that professes it is merely an empty shell.

But is the message upon which the Christian church is founded really true? Did Christ rise from the dead?

I want to say just a few words to you about that subject now. Two things are to be noted about the account of the appearances which the New Testament contains.

The first thing concerns the manner of the appearances. The appearances, according to the New Testament, were of a plain bodily kind. Jesus did not, it is true, simply resume the conditions of his life before the crucifixion. There was something mysterious about his coming and going. Yet he is plainly represented as being with his disciples in body. They could touch him. He partook of food in their presence. He held extended conversations with them.

The second feature of the appearances, as they are described in the New Testament, concerns the place of the appearances. The appearances, according to the New Testament, were both at Jerusalem and in Galilee; and the first appearances were at Jerusalem.

Both these features of the New Testament account of the appearances are rejected by advocates of the vision hypothesis. The former feature is always rejected by them, the latter usually.

The advocates of the vision hypothesis hold, with regard to the manner of the appearances, that, contrary to the New Testament, the appearances were only of a momentary kind. The disciples who experienced the appearances did not experience any extended intercourse with Jesus. They not only did not really have any extended intercourse with him, but they did not even think they had any extended intercourse with him. All they even thought they had was a momentary sight of him in glory or perhaps the sound of a word or two of his ringing in their ears. The New Testament is quite wrong in saying they even thought they saw or heard any more than that.

The second point at which the advocates of the vision hypothesis, or most of them, reject the New Testament account of the appearances concerns the place of the appearances. Most of the advocates of the vision hypothesis hold that the first of the appearances—which they of course regard as hallucinations—took place a considerable time, perhaps weeks, after the crucifixion, in Galilee; the New Testament says that the first of the appearances took place at Jerusalem on the third day after the death of Jesus.

At first sight it might look as though this were a mere difference in detail. But that is not so. As a matter of fact, it is a difference of a very important kind.

If the first appearances, the first of these supposed hallucinations in which the disciples thought they saw Jesus alive after his death, took place at Jerusalem and on the third day after the death, then the question arises why the tomb of Jesus was not investigated to see whether the story of the resurrection was really true—why it was not investigated by foes as well as by friends. If the resurrection was not a fact, then the investigation of the tomb of Jesus would refute the story, and the beginning of the Christian church would have been prevented.

If, on the other hand, the first appearances took place in Galilee weeks after the death of Jesus, then, it might be said, when the disciples finally did return to Jerusalem it would be too late for the tomb to be investigated. Thus the so-called Galilean hypothesis as to the place of the first appearances might be thought to remove the difficulty which a consideration of the tomb of Jesus has always placed in the way of a denial of the fact of the resurrection.

What shall be said about that? Two things are to be said about it.

In the first place, even the Galilean hypothesis does not really remove the difficulty, since it does seem strange even on the Galilean hypothesis that the tomb of Jesus was not investigated, and, in the second place, the Galilean hypothesis is not true.

Where shall we turn to test the hypothesis of unbelievers, not only on this point regarding the place of the appearances but also on the point regarding the manner of the appearances?

Well, we can of course turn to the Gospels. We can show that the low view which unbelievers hold regarding the Gospels is not justified and that these documents are really trustworthy accounts of what the first disciples of Jesus said with regard to the founding of the church.

But obviously it would be a good thing also if we could find some source of information which is admitted to be good not only by believers but also by unbelievers. Can we find such a source of information? Can we find a source of information with regard to which there is some common meeting ground between ourselves and our opponents in this debate?

The answer is, "Yes." We can find such a source of information in the First Epistle to the Corinthians. It is generally admitted by foes of our view as well as by friends that this epistle was really written by the apostle Paul and that it was written at about AD 55, approximately twenty-five years after the death of Jesus. It is also generally admitted that when Paul says in this epistle that he had "received" the information that he gives in the fifteenth chapter regarding the resurrection and appearances of Jesus he means that he had received it from the early Jerusalem church—particularly, perhaps, from Peter, with whom he tells us in another of his epistles that he spent fifteen days only three years after his conversion. What we have here, then, in the fifteenth chapter of this epistle, in verse eight and the following verses, is a precious bit of what modern historians call "primitive tradition." It is usually admitted by friends and foes of our view that we have here a summary of what the very earliest Jerusalem church said about the events that lay at the beginning of its life.

Well, then, is this account by the primitive Jerusalem church of the resurrection and related events favorable to the contention of unbelievers—the contention that at the beginning the appearances were regarded as independent of what had become of the body of Jesus? Volumes have been written about this question. But the answer, if we may put it plainly and briefly, is most emphatically, "No." This passage is not favorable to the contention of unbelievers at all.

What does Paul say exactly when he summarizes that precious tradition of the earliest Jerusalem church? Here is what he says: "For I delivered to you as of first importance what I also received: that Christ died for our sins in accordance with the Scriptures, that he was buried, that he was raised on the third day in accordance with the Scriptures" (1 Cor 15:3–4).

I want you to notice the mention of the burial of Christ in this passage. What does it mean? I will tell you, and then I just want you to read the passage for yourselves to see whether you do not agree with me. When Paul mentions the burial, he means that the resurrection of Christ about which he is speaking is a bodily resurrection. The thing that was laid in the tomb in the burial was the body; and the thing that was laid in the tomb was the thing that came out of the tomb in the resurrection. "He died, he was buried, he rose." We follow here, as we read, what happened to the body of Jesus. If a man will just read the words without prejudice he will see that they are at this point as plain as day.

It is quite clear that Paul does not mean, and the Jerusalem church as quoted by him did not mean, that the body of Jesus remained in the tomb. The bodily resurrection is the only resurrection that the New Testament knows.

In fact, when we come to think about it, a resurrection that is not a bodily resurrection is a contradiction in terms. Did those first disciples, when they began the work of the Christian church, merely believe in the continued personal existence of Jesus? Was that what gave them their strange new confidence and power? Such a view is really quite absurd. They had that conviction even in the sad hours immediately after the crucifixion. They were not Sadducees. They believed in the personal survival of all men after death; and so they believed, even just after the crucifixion, in the personal survival of Jesus. But that conviction left them in despair. What changed their despair into joy was the substitution, in their minds, of a belief in the continued personal existence of Jesus with a belief in his resurrection. It is quite absurd, then, to say that the two things, in their view, were the same. Our sources of information about the beginnings of the Christian church know nothing whatever of a resurrection that is not a bodily resurrection.

The second thing that I want you to notice in the report by Paul of the tradition of the Jerusalem church is the mention of the third day. "He was raised on the third day in accordance with the Scriptures," he says. There are few words in the whole Bible that are more uncomfortable to modern unbelief than those words, "the third day," in the primitive Jerusalem tradition recorded here by Paul.

Those words demolish the whole edifice of the Galilean hypothesis as to the place of the appearances. They show, by the testimony of the very first disciples, that the first appearance did not take place in Galilee weeks after the crucifixion but on the third day and in Jerusalem. I know that attempts are made to evade the plain implications of these words. The first appearances, it is said, took place only weeks afterward, but when they did take place the disciples who experienced them hit upon the notion that Jesus had risen long before and merely had not chosen to appear to them until then. But why in the world did they hit upon just the third day as the day of the resurrection if nothing in particular happened to them on that day? Various answers have been given to that question, but they are vain. No, the mention of a third day in the primitive Jerusalem tradition interposes a mighty barrier against the whole attempt to explain the appearances of the risen Christ as hallucinations experienced at a time when it would be too late to investigate the tomb of Jesus to see whether the resurrection had really happened or not.

The truth is that the origin of the church in Jerusalem is explicable if Jesus really rose from the dead, and it is not explicable if he did not so rise. The very existence of the Christian church is a mighty testimony to the resurrection of our Lord.

But, it will be objected, that is all very well, but the trouble is that the thing we are asked to believe is really unbelievable. We are asked to believe that a dead man rose from the dead, and we have never seen a man who did that.

What is our answer to this objection? It is very simple. You say, my friend, that you have never seen a man who rose from the dead after he had been laid really dead in the tomb? Quite right. Neither have I. You and I have never seen a man who rose from the dead. That is true. But what of it? You and I have never seen a man who rose from the dead; but then you and I have never seen a man like Jesus.

Do you not see, my friends? What we are trying to establish is not the resurrection of any ordinary man, not the resurrection of a man who is to us a mere x or y, not the resurrection of a man about whom we know nothing, but the resurrection of Jesus. There is a tremendous presumption against the resurrection of any ordinary man. But when you come really to know Jesus as he is pictured to us in the Gospels, you will say that whereas it is unlikely that any ordinary man should rise from the dead, in his case the presumption is exactly reversed. It is unlikely that any ordinary man should rise; but it is unlikely that this man should not rise; it may be said of this man that it was impossible that he should be held in death.

The point is that this thing hangs together. We have in the Gospels an account of a person who was entirely unique. He was totally different from other men in his moral purity and strength. Yet he made the most stupendous claims—claims that place him beyond the bounds of sanity unless the claims were true. The claims are true if the resurrection really happened; they are a hopeless puzzle if the resurrection did not happen.

Do you see what I am driving at, my friends? The evidence of the truth of Christianity must be taken as a whole. The direct evidence for the resurrection must be taken together with the total picture of Jesus in the Gospels, and then that must be taken in connection with the evidence for the existence of God and the tremendous need of man which is caused by sin. If you take the Bible as a whole you have a grand consistent account of God, of the world, and of human life. If you reject the Bible, and particularly if you reject the fact of the resurrection, you have a jumble of meaningless and detached bits of information that dance before your imagination in a wild and riotous rout.

Oh, that God would open men's eyes that they might see, that they might detect the grand sweep and power of his testimony to himself in his Word! Oh, that he would take away the terrible blindness of men's minds! Has he taken away the blindness of your minds, my friends? Do you know the risen Christ today as your Savior and your Lord? If you do not yet know him, will you not bow before him at this hour and say, "My Lord and my God!"

17

The Testimony of Paul to Christ

In our presentation of the testimony of the New Testament to the deity of Christ, we have dealt so far only with the Gospels. But now it becomes necessary to consider also the other New Testament books and particularly the epistles of Paul.

The reason why the epistles of Paul are particularly important in this connection is that we find a common meeting ground with those who deny the deity of Christ and are opposed to the Christian religion. Practically all serious literary critics today admit that the principal ones of the Pauline epistles were really written by the man whose name they bear.

In the case of the four Gospels, it is not so easy to find a common meeting ground with our opponents. We did not indeed altogether give up the hope of finding it. We tried to point out that there is a certain amount of agreement even with regard to the Gospels between those who are friends and those who are foes of Christianity. It is universally admitted, for example, by serious historians, that the picture of Jesus in the Gospels is a picture of a real, historical person. We tried to point out certain important consequences that follow from that admission. But, after all, the common meeting ground which we can find with our opponents is, so far as the Gospels are concerned, not very extensive.

In particular, there is disagreement with regard to questions of what is known as "literary criticism." There is disagreement, namely, with regard to the authorship and date and historical value of each of the Gospels. If, therefore, we begin by assuming that any one of these Gospels was written by the man whose name has been attached to it in the opinion of the church, we shall be accused at once of begging the question. The traditional view of the authorship of all four of these books is disputed by our opponents in this great debate.

Now, mind you, I do not think it is rightly disputed. I am perfectly willing to defend the traditional view of the authorship of the Gospels. I think it is immensely important to defend it. I think it can successfully be defended. But the point is that it *needs* to be defended. Rightly or wrongly, the traditional view of the authorship of the Gospels is disputed by modern skeptics.

About the epistles of Paul, on the other hand, there is no such dispute. Even the most skeptical critics—except a few extremists who are altogether without influence upon the current of modern thought—admit that the principal ones of the Pauline epistles were really written by the apostle Paul and written in the first generation of the Christian church.

That is a very important admission indeed. I think it is very important that we should use it in our effort to lead the men who make it to accept the claims of Christ. You see, we do not regard the people who differ from us regarding these great concerns of the soul as our enemies. On the contrary, we long to help them. Having known something of the misery of doubt ourselves, we long to help others out of that misery. Hence we do like, if we can, to find a common meeting ground with our opponents in the debate, in order that we may lead them on from the things about which they agree with us to an acceptance of the things about which they disagree.

It is to be welcomed, therefore, that friends and foes of Christianity are agreed in holding that the principal ones of the Pauline epistles were really written by the apostle Paul.

The man, Paul, who wrote those epistles, was a contemporary of Jesus. That can be shown from the accepted epistles themselves, because Paul in the Epistle to the Galatians says that he himself had met a brother of Jesus and it is very clear that this meeting took place only a short time after Jesus's death. Paul had abundant opportunities to learn the facts about Jesus. He spent fifteen days, as he tells us in Galatians, with Peter, who was in the innermost circle of Jesus's friends, and at the same time he also saw James, who was Jesus's brother. Contact with the same men was also established at the later time that is referred to in the second chapter of Galatians, and at that later time, John, who, like Peter, belonged to Jesus's innermost circle of friends, was also present. Barnabas and Silas, who, according to the book of Acts, came from the early Jerusalem church, were associated with Paul through long periods of time on the missionary journeys; and while it may be objected that our knowledge of their original connection with the Jerusalem church comes only from the book of Acts and not from the universally accepted epistles of Paul, still the historical basis of such concrete personal details in the book of Acts will likely be admitted by most critics. At any rate, it is perfectly clear, in view of all the conditions of Paul's life, that Paul had abundant contacts with those who had known Jesus when he was on earth.

The testimony of Paul to Jesus becomes, therefore, a matter of the highest importance to every careful historian who is interested in the beginnings of the Christian church. It becomes very important for us to ask what sort of person Paul held Jesus to be.

The answer to that question is very surprising to anyone who approaches the subject with ordinary analogies in his mind because it becomes perfectly clear at once that Paul regarded Jesus in a very extraordinary way. He regarded him as a supernatural person and he regarded himself as standing to Jesus in the relation in which a man stands to God.

He does, it is true, speak of Jesus as a man. But when he speaks of him as a man, we may well hold that he regarded it as something extraordinary, something unexpected, that he should be a man. The really outstanding thing in the way in which Paul speaks of Jesus is that he separates Jesus very clearly from ordinary humanity and places him on the side of God.

So, at the beginning of the Epistle to the Galatians, for example, he says that he, Paul, is an apostle "not from men nor through man, but through Jesus Christ and God the Father" (Gal 1:1). Man is one thing, Christ another; and Christ, over against man, is placed with God the Father. Could there be any clearer testimony to the deity of Christ?

In one place, at least, Paul applies to Jesus the Greek word which is translated by the English word "God." I am referring to Romans 9:5, where Christ is spoken of as the one "who is God over all, blessed forever." Attempts have been made to avoid holding that the word "God" in this passage refers to Christ, but it is more than doubtful whether any of those attempts can be regarded as successful. According to the plain construction of the words—the construction which in any other case would be regarded by every reader as a matter of course—Paul here calls Jesus "God."

It is true that ordinarily he does not use that word in speaking of Christ. He does not ordinarily apply to Christ the word which is translated "God" in our English Bibles. But what of it? He does apply to Christ constantly another word which can clearly be shown to be a word designating deity— namely, the word "Lord." That word had, indeed, its uses in ordinary life; it designated a master of slaves and the like. But it had also a widespread religious use, and—what is vastly more important—it is the word used in the Greek translation of the Old Testament (which was the form of the Bible that Paul ordinarily employed) to translate the word "Jehovah," the holiest name of the covenant God of Israel. Paul does not hesitate to apply to Jesus Old Testament passages that speak of Jehovah.

In view of this lofty significance of the word "Lord," B. B. Warfield is surely justified when he suggests that the title "the Lord" may almost be designated as Paul's "Trinitarian name" of Jesus Christ.[1] Paul teaches the doctrine of the Trinity—only, as Warfield points out, he uses a somewhat different terminology from that to which we have become accustomed. Instead of speaking of "God the Father, God the Son, and God the Holy Ghost," he speaks of "God," "the Lord," and "the Spirit"; but he teaches exactly the same doctrine as that which is taught when men use that other terminology. And his doctrine of the Trinity includes, of course, the doctrine of the deity of Christ.

The doctrine of the deity of Christ is all-pervasive in the epistles of Paul. It is by no means an isolated thing. You do not have to search for it to find it. On the contrary, you cannot get away from it. Open the epistles where you will and you will find the deity of Christ.

Take, for example, the way in which Paul speaks of Christ in the openings of almost all of his epistles. "Grace to you and peace," he says, "from God our Father and the Lord Jesus Christ." Those words often make little impression on our minds. We trip along very lightly over them. But why is it that they make no impression on our minds; why is it that we trip along so lightly over them? Simply for the reason that we have become accustomed to them. They do not stand out in any way in the epistles of Paul because they are so completely in accord with all that Paul says elsewhere about Christ. But in themselves they are really most extraordinary words. Imagine it being said about any other man who ever lived, the greatest of reformers or the holiest of saints—"Grace to you and peace from God our Father and Martin Luther, or the apostle Paul himself or John the beloved disciple"—and I think you will see at once how blasphemous such a form of words would be. Why is it not blasphemous, then, when Paul says, "Grace be with you and peace from God our Father and the Lord Jesus Christ"? For one reason and one reason only, my friends. Because Jesus Christ is God. Being God, and for that reason only, he can be linked in this

---

1. B. B. Warfield, *The Lord of Glory*, 1907, 231.

stupendous fashion with God the Father and can be separated from the whole universe of created things.

The reason why we think nothing of those stupendous words as we come to them at the beginnings of the epistles is that they are in exact accord with *everything* that Paul says about Jesus. The reason why they do not stand out like mountain peaks in the epistles is not that they are not high but that everything else that Paul says about Christ is equally high.

Then I want you to understand something else about the way in which Paul teaches the deity of Christ. It is this: that Paul's teaching about the deity of Christ is not found merely in this passage or that. It is not found merely in any number of passages where Paul ascribes divine honor and glory to Christ—no matter how numerous you may find those passages to be. No, Paul teaches the deity of Christ by the inmost heart and core of his own religious life.

What was the religion of Paul really like? We ought to be able to get the answer to that question because Paul had a remarkable gift of self-revelation. Someone, I believe, has said that he is the best-known man of antiquity. He has bared his heart to us in his epistles. He appears there not as a cold academic teacher but as a man of flesh and blood, and he has let us know what were the inmost springs of his life.

Evidently those springs of his life were in his religion. There never was a more intensely religious man.

What then was that religion of Paul that is so wonderfully presented to us in those revealing documents, the epistles?

Did that religion of Paul consist of having faith in God like the faith which Jesus had in God? Was Jesus, for Paul, just an example for faith—just a pioneer in the religious life, just one who attained sonship with God and inspired others to attain it?

Well, some people have tried to look at the thing in that way. But they have done so only by closing their eyes to what actually stands in the documents from which our information is to be derived. If you simply close your eyes and construct out of your own inner consciousness what you think Paul *ought* to have said, then of course you can make Paul out to be an adherent of what men call "the religion of Jesus"; you can make him out to be a man whose religion consisted primarily in an imitation of the religious experience through which Jesus himself had passed; you can make him out to be a man whose religion consisted in an effort to have the same kind of faith in God as that faith which Jesus had in God.

But the moment you allow yourself to be hampered in the flight of your imagination by some knowledge of the facts, the moment you seek to view Paul not as you think he ought to have been but as he was, you will observe that his religion did not consist merely in the effort to have the same kind of faith in God as the faith which Jesus had, but that it consisted in having faith in Jesus. Jesus, according to Paul, was no mere example for faith but was the object of faith. He was the object, for Paul, of a faith that was truly religious. What does that mean? It means plainly one thing. It means that Paul stood toward Jesus not just in the relation in which a disciple stands toward his teacher, but in the relation in which a man stands toward his God. The deity of Christ was the foundation of Paul's life.

In the light of this fact, we are not surprised to read what Paul says about Christ in detail. Jesus Christ, according to Paul, existed from all eternity. He was the one through whom the universe was made. He came into this world as a man, not as other men come but by a voluntary act of wonderful condescension and love. His death was not just a noble martyrdom but an act of cosmic significance. It meant the redemption, from the wrath and curse of God, of a great multitude of men of all nations. After his death, he rose from the dead and is now exalted far above all principalities and powers. He belongs with God the Father in a category entirely distinct from that of all created things.

Have you ever stopped just to think how extraordinary that Pauline doctrine of the deity of Christ would seem to you if you came to it for the first time? Here was Jesus, a man who had lived only a few years before and had died a shameful death. Here was Paul, a contemporary of Jesus, an associate of Jesus's intimate friends, yet attributing to Jesus the highest divine attributes, and standing to him always in the relation in which a man stands to God.

Have you ever heard of anything like that anywhere else in the history of the human race? Perhaps you might be tempted to say, "Yes." Perhaps you might be tempted to say that this was not the first time or the only time in the history of the world when one man has attributed deity to another. There was the deification of the Roman emperors, for example, and the deification of Oriental monarchs.

But do you not see the stupendous difference, my friends? Those who deified the Roman emperors were polytheists; they believed in many gods. There was nothing extraordinary, therefore, in their believing that one more god was to be added to the great host of gods with which earth and heaven were already peopled. Paul, on the other hand, was a monotheist. He believed that there was one God and one God only, the Maker of heaven and earth. He was a Jew, and the Jews were nothing if not monotheists. Both before and after his conversion, the belief in one God was the very breath of his life. With all his soul he hated the very thought that any other could be called God save that One.

Yet it was such a monotheist sprung of a race of monotheists who paid to one of his contemporaries, Jesus, honors that belong only to God, who reposed in him a truly religious faith, who applied to him Old Testament passages that spoke of Jehovah the covenant God of Israel, the one living and true God, the God who in the beginning created the heavens and the earth.

No, there is nothing like that in the whole history of mankind, nothing like that ascription of deity to the man Christ Jesus by the apostle Paul. It is no wonder that H. J. Holtzmann, a blessed representative, perhaps, of the unbelief of the nineteenth and beginning of the twentieth century, admitted that for the deification of the man Jesus as it appears in the epistles of Paul he was able to cite no parallel in the religious history of the race.[2]

I tell you, my friends, only ignorance can trip along lightly over this amazing phenomenon. Real scholars are at least immensely intrigued by it.

But so far I have not mentioned what is the most surprising thing of all about it. The truly amazing thing is not merely that Paul believed in the deity of Christ, but that he does not argue about it; the truly amazing thing is that he seems to treat it as a matter of course. About other things there was bitter debate. There was debate, for example, about the place of the law in the attainment of salvation. About that, opponents of Paul appealed to Peter and the original apostles of Jesus against Paul. Even about that, indeed, their appeal was a false appeal. The original apostles were really with Paul and against those Judaizers. But about the deity of Christ the Judaizers evidently did not make any appeal at all. Paul just assumes that everyone in the church, including his opponents, will agree with his stupendous view of Jesus Christ. Still more clearly does he assume that the original friends of Jesus will agree with it. That is the truly extraordinary thing. The intimate friends of Jesus—think of it—those who had walked and talked with him when he was on earth, those who had seen him subject to all the petty

---

2. H. J. Holtzmann, in *Protestantische Monatshefte*, iv, 1900, 465f. And in *Christliche Welt*, xxiv, 1910, column 153.

limitations of human life—these intimate friends of Jesus stood, so far as we can see from the epistles of Paul, in the most complete agreement in their view of Jesus with one who regarded Jesus as very God.

Who was this Jesus who was exalted to the throne of God not by later generations but by his own intimate friends? The Gospels give the only believable answer to that question. Their picture of Jesus is independent of Paul; it is certainly not just spun out of what the Pauline epistles say about Christ. Yet it presents just the Christ whom the epistles presuppose.

Deny the truthfulness of the gospel picture of Jesus and you can never explain the origin of the religion of Paul. Take the picture as it stands, and all is clear. The two great testimonies to Christ—the Gospels and Paul—lead to the same end. And at the end of the testimony, we find the Savior of our souls.

18

The Holy Spirit

In bringing this little series of addresses now to a close, I want to say what a great pleasure it has been to me to become acquainted with you. Our conversations might, indeed, seem at first sight to have been just a little bit one-sided; in them I have done most of the talking. I hope you will not be unkind enough to say that that is the reason why I have enjoyed the conversations so much. I will confess that I do love to talk about these themes with which we have been dealing; but then, you see, I have also enjoyed the companionship I have had with you. These are rather trying days to a man who sorrows when a visible church that professes to believe the Word of God turns from it so often into the pathways of unbelief and sin; and in such days it is doubly comforting to converse with those who truly love the gospel of Christ and believe that it alone is the message that is forever new. I do rejoice with all my heart in the Christian fellowship which we have had together, and I trust that God will richly bless you, both in joy and sorrow, and may, by his Holy Spirit, cause you always to be grounded upon the rock of his holy Word.

One thing is clear, my friends—the Word of God will never fail. Many, indeed, have turned from it in our day. Religious persecution is going on apace in Russia, Germany, and Mexico; in those countries unbelief is blatant and unashamed and is endeavoring to stamp out the Christian religion by force. In our country the same tendency, though in less extreme form, is already mightily at work; and the visible church is often unfaithful to its great trust and, in some cases, is engaged in driving out real Christian testimony from its communion.

But this is not the first time of discouragement in the history of the Christian church; sometimes the darkest hour has just preceded the dawn. So it may be in our day. Let us never forget that the Spirit of God, who inspired the writers of the Bible, is all-powerful, and that he can make even dead churches live.

Then I want to say a word of farewell also to any of you who have disagreed with what I have been trying to say. I appreciate your being broadminded enough to listen to that with which you do not agree; and I do trust that, if I have not been able to convince you of the truth of what I have been saying, God may send you a messenger of his own choosing who is better fitted than I to proclaim to you that truth which I have so imperfectly proclaimed.

It must be admitted, as we come to the last talk of this little series, that the title of the series is something of a fraud. It is not an intentional fraud, to be sure; but still an unkind person might say that it is a fraud. I have certainly not succeeded in treating "The Christian Faith in the Modern World" in any comprehensive way. Indeed, I have made only a bare beginning of treating it. I have spoken of the Bible, from which the Christian faith is derived, and I have spoken of the biblical doctrine of God. But I have not treated all the divisions even of that latter topic. I have spoken a little of the Trinity and can only—in the present talk—touch slightly upon the last part of that great subject; and I have not been able to speak, for example, of the decrees of God at all.

As for the other parts of the system of doctrine that the Bible contains, I have not been able even to make a beginning of treating them. I have not spoken of the biblical doctrine of man and of sin; I have not spoken of the biblical doctrine of salvation. I hope to be able to deal with those themes at some future time. Meanwhile, I can just bid you turn to God's Word and read it for yourselves. Doing that, after all, is far more worthwhile than listening to expositions even though they were far better than mine. May the Holy Spirit increasingly unfold to you the boundless treasures of truth that the Bible contains!

As I utter that prayer, I am brought to the theme that is next in order for me to deal with in our little series of talks. That theme would be the teaching of the Bible concerning the Holy Spirit. I have talked to you just a little about the Father, and I have tried to present to you just a little of what the Bible says about the Son, but so far I have not spoken to you specifically about the third person of the Trinity, the Holy Spirit. Please do not understand by that neglect that I do not think the subject is important.

If only I had time, I might naturally treat that subject much more fully than it can be treated now.

Even if I did have more time, I should not, indeed, give as much time to that subject as I should give, for example, to the subject of the deity of

Christ. Devout persons sometimes seem to think that there is something derogatory to the third person of the Trinity, the Holy Spirit, in the fact that theologians and preachers do not devote so much time or space to the doctrine of the Holy Spirit as they do to the doctrine of the deity of Christ. These persons are prone, I think, to be particularly severe on the so-called "Apostles' Creed," for example, because, after it has set forth a number of facts about Christ, the only thing that it says about the third person of the Trinity is just the bare clause, "I believe in the Holy Ghost." Surely that extreme brevity, they will be inclined to say, is derogatory to the third person of the Trinity, who is equal in power and glory to the Father and the Son.

Well, I do not know whether we ought to be so very hard on the Apostles' Creed at this point. No doubt it *is* defective—at this point as at a good many other points. No doubt it ought to say something more about the Holy Spirit than just "I believe in the Holy Ghost." But, after all, the work of the Holy Spirit is to bear witness to the Son and to the Father. So, although the Bible has a great deal to say about the work of the Holy Spirit, the plain fact is that it does not devote so much space to the doctrine that sets forth the truth about the Holy Spirit himself as it does to certain other doctrines.

So, we, in this little series of talks, have already said a good deal about the *work* of the Holy Spirit—at least *one* work of the Holy Spirit—when we spoke of the inspiration of the Bible, and if we do not say more about the Holy Spirit himself that may perhaps be partially excused by the fact that the doctrine of the Holy Spirit, important though it is, could be set forth more briefly than, for example, the doctrine of the Son.

The teaching of the Bible about the Holy Spirit is found not only in the New Testament but also in the Old Testament. The second verse of the Bible speaks of the Spirit of God as active at the beginning. "The Spirit of God," that verse says, "was hovering over the face of the waters" (Gen 1:2). We think also, of course, of the work of the Spirit in empowering the prophets when they came forward with a message from God. In some places, the Spirit appears as the giver of some special qualification; but the Spirit also appears as determining a holy life. "Take not your Holy Spirit from me," says the psalmist (Ps 51:11). There is a tendency in some quarters to underestimate the richness of the Old Testament teaching regarding the Spirit of God.

But it must be admitted that in the Old Testament we have no clear presentation of the personal distinctness of the Spirit of God. We may have intimations of it, as we have intimations of the doctrine of the Trinity, but for clear teaching regarding it we must turn to the New Testament books.

In the New Testament books, this clear teaching is certainly present. At first sight, indeed, it might not seem to be so abundant as we might expect it to be. The deity of the Holy Spirit is everywhere perfectly plain, but the distinct personality of the Holy Spirit does not seem to lie so clearly on the surface. Hence, it is not surprising that in discussions of the doctrine of the Holy Spirit the question that is chiefly discussed is different from the question that is discussed with regard to Christ.

With regard to Christ, the distinct personality of the One who is presented is everywhere perfectly clear, and therefore argument is quite unnecessary about that. The question that needs discussion about Christ is the deity of the One spoken of. Christ appears to a superficial observer not as God but as a man. What needs to be done, therefore, is to show that superficial observer that this man, Jesus Christ, is both God and man.

But with regard to the Holy Spirit, it is just the other way around. The deity of the Holy Spirit is everywhere perfectly clear; but what seems at first sight paradoxical, what seems to require discussion, is the true personality of the Spirit. It is clear, without any discussion, that the Spirit of God is God; but it might seem at first sight very strange that the Spirit of God should be a distinct person within the Godhead.

However, strange though that is, the Bible makes perfectly clear that it is true. A careful reading of the Bible shows that the true personality of the Holy Spirit, though not often made the subject of direct exposition, really underlies and gives meaning to everything that the Bible says about the Spirit of God.

For one thing, the great Trinitarian passages in the Bible really imply the personality of the Spirit. When, for example, our Lord in the Great Commission at the end of the Gospel according to Matthew commands the apostles to make disciples of all the nations, "baptizing them in the name of the Father and of the Son and of the Holy Spirit" (Matt 28:19), can he possibly mean that although the Father and the Son are persons, the Holy Ghost is a mere impersonal aspect of the being of the Father or of the Son? The perfect coordination of the three—Father, Son, and Holy Ghost—would seem to make such an interpretation extremely unnatural. So it is with the apostolic benediction at the end of the Second Epistle to the Corinthians: "The grace of the Lord Jesus Christ and the love of God and the fellowship of the Holy Spirit be with you all" (2 Cor 13:14). Here also to deny the distinct personality of the Spirit would seem almost to involve denying the distinct personality of the other two members of Paul's triad; and since that would be out of accord with the apostle's whole teaching, it seems perfectly clear that he regards the Holy Ghost as a person just as he regards each of the other two.

But the passage where the personality of the Holy Spirit is most clearly and gloriously set forth is found in the intimate discourses of our Lord with his apostles, as those discourses are recorded in the Gospel according to John. Here our Lord speaks of the Holy Spirit as "another Helper" (John 14:16), or rather (by what is probably a better translation of the word) "another advocate." The Holy Spirit, then, is in one sense "another" as over against Jesus. Indeed, in John 16:7, Jesus says that his, Jesus's, departure means the Spirit's coming: "It is to your advantage that I go away, for if I do not go away, the Helper will not come to you. But if I go, I will send him to you."

It would hardly be possible to set forth more clearly than is done in these words the distinct personality of the Holy Spirit. He is not just an aspect of the person of Jesus; indeed, it is said that if Jesus departs, he will come.

In another sense, indeed, even according to this very passage, the coming of the Spirit is the coming of Jesus. Human analogies break down in the presence of the mystery of the Trinity. One cannot separate what the Son does and what the Father does from what the Spirit does, as would be the case with three finite persons.

But, all the same, it remains true that the Holy Spirit does appear very clearly in this precious passage as a true person. He proceeds from the Father and the Son, not as a mere emanation or a mere force, but as a person who stands in a truly personal relationship with the two other persons in the Godhead. Again and again in this wonderful passage, the personal relationship between all three persons of the Trinity is set forth. In one verse at least, our Lord uses the first-person plural in speaking of himself and God the Father. "If anyone loves me," he says, "he will keep my word, and my Father will love him, and we will come to him and make our home with him" (John 14:23). Here, Jesus of Nazareth, a man who walked upon this earth, joins himself with God the Father in a fellowship in which one person joins himself with another. "*We* will come," he says. The human mind is aghast in the presence of that stupendous "we." God has certainly revealed to us wondrous things in his holy Word.

In this personal fellowship between the Father and the Son, the Holy Spirit, who is to be sent as another Comforter, appears as a third member of the fellowship. He stands in personal relation both to the Father and to the Son. "And I will ask the Father," says Jesus, "and he will give you another Helper, to be with you forever" (John 14:16). Here the Spirit appears as being sent by the Father at the insistence of the Son. In another place, he appears as being sent by the Son, and yet as proceeding from the Father. "But when the Helper comes, whom I will send to you from the Father, the Spirit of truth, who proceeds from the Father, he will bear witness about me" (John 15:26). All through this passage, the relationship between all three appears as a warm relationship of love between persons.

In the light of what our Lord here says, all thought of regarding the Father, Son, and Holy Ghost as being merely three modes in which one person works, or merely three aspects in which one person may be regarded, is seen to be contrary to the very heart of what the Bible teaches. No, the Bible teaches us certainly that there are three persons in the Godhead.

But, in teaching us that, the Bible never allows us to forget the primary truth that there is but one God. That truth is pressed home in the Old Testament, but it is pressed home just as insistently in the New Testament. When the New Testament teaches that Father, Son, and Holy Ghost are three persons, it teaches with equal insistence that these three persons are one God. The New Testament writers never seem to be conscious that one of these two great truths could by any chance be regarded as in contradiction with the other. They are never for one moment conscious of any danger lest when they present the deity and the personality of the Son and of the Spirit they may lead men away from the unity of God. So, in the Gospel of John, Jesus says, "I and the Father are one" (John 10:30); yet in that same Gospel, he says, about the Father and himself, "*We* will come" (John 14:23); and still again in that same Gospel, he says, "And I will ask the Father, and he will give you another Helper" (John 14:16). One God, three persons, each person God—so the Bible presents, in majestic harmony, what God has graciously revealed to us of the mysteries of his being.

The three persons of the Godhead are, as the Shorter Catechism puts it, "the same in substance, equal in power and glory" (WSC Q&A 6). But is that so? Are the three persons of the Godhead really the same in substance and equal in power and glory?

One of the early heresies said, "No." The Son is of like substance with the Father, said the adherents of that heresy, but not of the same substance. But widely removed indeed was that heresy from the teaching of the Bible. I know that the difference between these two expressions—"of the same substance" and "of like substance"—has often been ridiculed as being the difference merely of an iota, the smallest letter in the Greek alphabet. The Greek word for "of like substance" has an iota in it, and the Greek word for "of the same substance" is that word with the iota left out. What a hair-splitting distinction, then, it is said, was that distinction which kept the church in a turmoil for so many years! The whole trouble was over one tiny little iota!

Well, my friends, the unbelief of our day uses a great many arguments, but I doubt whether any argument ever was used in any debate that was much more foolish than this.

Is the difference between the meanings of words really to be measured by the number or the size of the letters by which the words differ? In that case the difference between "just" and "unjust" for example, would be very slight. Just put the little syllable "un" in front of "just" and you get "unjust." What a very slight difference that is! So, I suppose you are not at all interested in the question whether a man says your decisions are just or whether he says they are unjust! It is merely a difference of that little syllable! Even the word "not" is not a very big word. So, I suppose it makes no difference to you whether somebody says you are a liar or whether he says you are not a liar! Why indulge in hair-splitting distinctions? Why quarrel over such a little word as "not"?

Well, we do quarrel over such little words and little letters. Little words and little letters sometimes make a vast deal of difference. So that little Greek letter, iota, made a whole world of difference in the great debate to which we have just referred. If Christ is said to be only of like substance with the Father, in the sense in which that early heresy meant it, then we have a miserable mythology that breaks down the gulf between the creature and the Creator, between the finite and the infinite. The Bible does no such thing. There is no such thing as "almost God" according to the Bible. The next thing less than the infinite, according to the Bible, is infinitely less.

So, the Bible certainly teaches that the Son is of the same substance with the Father and that he is equal to the Father in power and glory. Only so can he be very God. And it also teaches that with regard to the Holy Spirit. The three persons of the Godhead are, according to the Bible, the same in substance and equal in power and glory.

Do you know that triune God as your God, my friends? We pray that you may know him so. We pray that the Holy Spirit may enable you to believe in the Son, and that, redeemed by his precious blood, you may stand in the Father's presence forevermore.

Part 2

The Christian View of Man

Preface to *The Christian View of Man*

This book constitutes the second part of a series of radio addresses that the author has been delivering over station WIP under the auspices of Westminster Theological Seminary, Philadelphia. The first part, which was published in February 1936 under the title *The Christian Faith in the Modern World*, dealt with the authority of the Bible and with the biblical doctrine of God. The present volume deals with the biblical doctrine of man, including the related subjects of the decrees of God and predestination. A considerable part of the discussion is concerned with what the Bible says about sin.

The book does not pretend in the slightest to be original. It is dependent throughout upon the masters of Reformed theology—particularly upon Charles Hodge, A. A. Hodge, B. B. Warfield, and Geerhardus Vos—and grateful acknowledgment is due to Caspar Wistar Hodge, of whom, as of Warfield and Vos, the author was formerly a pupil. The author believes that the Reformed faith should be preached as well as taught in the classroom, and that the need for the preaching of it is particularly apparent at the present time. The author is trying to preach it in this little book, and preach it very specifically to the people of our generation.

The book is not, indeed, a collection of sermons. Its several chapters proceed in logical sequence and seek to develop one central theme. But it does seek to show that the Reformed doctrine of man, and particularly the Reformed doctrine of sin and grace, is not something useful merely to the theologian but a matter of the most vital concern to every man.

Grateful acknowledgment is again made to the Rev. Edwin H. Rian, of the Board of Trustees of Westminster Seminary, to whom the initiation and continuance of the radio addresses is due. The author is grateful also to his colleagues in the Faculty of Westminster Theological Seminary whose wise counsel and generous assistance have been of great value at a number of points.

      J. Gresham Machen

Note: This volume, including the above preface, was completed and sent to the publisher by the author before his death. It has been a slight labor of love on the part of his undersigned colleagues in the Faculty of Westminster Theological Seminary to see the book through the press.

      John Murray and Paul Woolley

19

The Living and True God

As we begin to consider the Christian view of man, with the decrees of God which underlie man's existence, we certainly find ourselves in the midst of a troubled world. We are certainly living in a time of rapid changes. Less than twenty years after a war that was supposed to have been fought to make the world safe for democracy, democracy almost everywhere is lying prostrate and liberty is rapidly being destroyed. Who would have thought, twenty years ago, that within so short a period of time all freedom of speech and of the press would have been destroyed in large sections of Western Europe? Who would have thought that Europe would sink back into a worse-than-medieval darkness?

America has been no exception to this decadence. Liberty is being threatened, and there is coming up before us in the near future the specter of the hopeless treadmill of a collectivistic state.

Certainly, when we take the world as a whole, we are obliged to see that the foundations of liberty and honesty are being destroyed and the slow achievements of centuries are being thrown recklessly away.

In such a time of kaleidoscopic changes, is there anything that remains unchanged? When so many things have proved to be untrustworthy, is there anything that we can trust?

One point, at least, is clear—we cannot trust the church. The visible church, the church as it now exists upon this earth, has fallen too often into error and sin.

No, we cannot appeal from the world to the church.

Well, then, is there anything at all to which we can appeal? Is there anything at all that remains constant when so many things change?

I have a very definite answer to give to that question. It is contained in a verse taken from the prophecy of Isaiah: "The grass withers, the flower fades, but the word of our God will stand forever" (Isa 40:8). There are many things that change, but there is one thing that does not change. It is the Word of the living and true God. The world is in decadence, the visible church is, to a considerable extent, apostate; but when God speaks we can trust him, and his Word stands forever sure.

Where has God spoken? Where shall we find that Word of God? I tried to give the answer in the first part of this series of talks. We can find the Word of God in the Bible. We do not say merely that the Bible *contains* the Word of God; we say that the Bible *is* the Word of God. In a time of turmoil and distress, and in the perplexity and weakness of our own lives, we can turn with perfect confidence to that blessed book.

When we say that the Bible is the Word of God, we mean something very definite indeed. We mean that the Bible is true. We mean that the writers of the Bible, in addition to all their providential qualifications for their task, received an immediate and supernatural guidance and impulsion of the Spirit of God which kept them from the errors that are found in other books and made the resulting book, the Bible, to be completely true in what it says regarding matters of fact and completely authoritative in its commands. That is the great doctrine of the full or plenary inspiration of Holy Scripture.

That doctrine does not, as is so often charged, do violence to the individuality of the biblical writers; and it does not mean that they became mere automata without knowledge of what they were doing. But it does mean that the work of the Holy Spirit in inspiration was a supernatural work. It was not a mere work of God's providence; it was not a mere employment by God of the resources of the universe that he had made, but it was a gracious interposition into the course of nature by the immediate power of God.

That doctrine means that the Bible is God's book, not man's book. Other books give advice that is good and advice that is bad; this book gives only advice that is good, or rather it issues commands that come with the full authority of the sovereign God.

It is upon that high view of the Bible that the present series of talks is based. I am going to seek to explore the Bible with you in order to see what God, and not merely man, has said.

In that presentation of what God has told us in the Bible, I hope indeed not to be without sympathy for the man who does not believe as I believe; I hope not to be without sympathy for the man who has doubts. I hope to be able to show such a man, as I go along, that some of the objections to the teaching of the Bible which are current among men today are based upon a misunderstanding of what the Bible means or upon a failure to consider important confirmatory evidence of the Bible's truth. But all that should not obscure what I am trying to do. I am not trying to present to you things that I have discovered for myself, and I am not trying to help you to discover things for yourselves; but I am asking you to listen with me to what God has told us in his Word.

In the series of which the present series is the continuation, I made a beginning of talking to you about what God has told us in his Word.

The revelation of God that is contained in the Bible, we observed, is not the only revelation that God has given. God has revealed himself through the universe that he has made. "The heavens declare the glory of God, and the sky above proclaims his handiwork" (Ps 19:1). He has also revealed himself through his voice within us: the voice of conscience. "For when Gentiles, who do not have the law, by nature do what the law requires, they are a law to themselves, even though they do not have the law" (Rom 2:14). The Bible puts the stamp of its approval upon what may be called "natural religion."

But the revelation of God through nature is not the only revelation that God has given. In addition to it, he has given a revelation that is called "supernatural" because it is above nature.

Such supernatural revelation was needed for two reasons.

In the first place, the revelation of God through nature had become hidden from men's eyes through sin. The wonders of God's world ought to have made men worship and glorify the Creator, but "their foolish hearts were darkened" (Rom 1:21). The voice of conscience ought to have told plainly what is right and what is wrong, but man's conscience had become "seared" (1 Tim 4:2). So, a new and plain confirmation of what nature and conscience said was needed by sinful man.

In the second place—and even more important to observe—a sinner needed to have revealed to him about God certain things of which nature and conscience provided no slightest hint. He needed to have revealed to him the grace of God. He was not only blinded by sin, but he was lost in sin. He was under its guilt and curse. He was under its power. He needed to be told the way in which God had saved him. Nature said nothing whatever about that. Knowledge of that could come to sinful man only in a way which was in the strictest sense supernatural.

How wonderfully rich is that supernatural revelation as it is found in the Bible! How far it transcends the revelation of God through nature! The whole doctrine of the Trinity, the whole appearance and work of the Lord Jesus Christ, the entire application of the work of Christ to the believer through the Holy Spirit, the whole glorious promise of a world to come—these things are not told to us through nature; they are told to us in the Bible and in the Bible alone. They are told to us by a revelation that is not natural but supernatural.

In the previous series, I made a beginning of talking to you about that revelation. I talked to you about the great biblical doctrine of the triune God. There is but one God, but God is in three persons—Father, Son, and Holy Ghost.

At the heart of that establishment in the Bible of the doctrine of the Trinity, we saw, is the teaching of the Bible regarding the deity of Jesus Christ.

Some nineteen hundred years ago, there lived in Palestine a certain person named Jesus.

There are two opinions about him.

Some regard him simply as a great religious genius, the founder of one of the world's great religions, a man who kept his own person out of his gospel, did not ask that men should have any particular opinion about him but simply proclaimed to them the Father God, asked not that men should have faith in him but only that they should have faith in God like the faith which he had in God. According to those who hold that view, Jesus was simply a teacher and example, the pathfinder for mankind on the way to God. That view is the view of unbelievers.

But there is another view of Jesus. According to that other view, the person known to history as Jesus of Nazareth existed from all eternity. He was the infinite, eternal, and unchangeable God. It was through him that this vast universe was made. He came into this world by his own voluntary act. He took upon himself our nature, being born as a man in order that he might redeem his people on the cross. When he was on earth, he offered himself to men as the object of their faith, not asking them merely to have faith in God like the faith which he had in God, but asking them to have faith in him. Upon faith in him he made salvation to depend. He died on the cross as a sacrifice to satisfy divine justice and reconcile us to God. He rose from the dead. He is "God and man in two distinct natures, and one person, forever" (WSC Q&A 21). He will come again and we shall see him with our very eyes. This view of Jesus is the view of Christians.

We saw that this Christian view of Jesus is the view that is taught in the Bible, and that it is the view that Jesus taught regarding himself.

Did Jesus really present himself when he was on earth merely as an example for men's faith? Did he say merely, "Have faith in God like the faith which I have in God"? Was he indifferent to what men thought of him?

These questions are easy to answer if we take the Bible record of Jesus as a whole. The Jesus who is presented in the Bible as a whole clearly offered himself to men as the object of their faith, and made faith in him essential to the attaining of eternal life.

But unbelievers will not accept the Bible record of Jesus as a whole. I will say to an unbelieving friend, "Here is a New Testament. Take it and choose any passage in it that you will in order to prove that your view of Jesus is right. You do not like my passages. Well, let us see what your passages say."

We observed in our last series of talks that there is one passage which an unbeliever is more likely to choose than any other when so challenged. It is the passage called the Sermon on the Mount. There, it is said by unbelievers, we have a nontheological Jesus, a Jesus who issued lofty commands and supposed that those commands could be obeyed no matter what men thought of him. We are constantly told that. Theology, we are told, is not the important thing, even the theology that deals with Jesus Christ. If, we are told, men would just get up and do what Jesus says in the Sermon on the Mount, that would be far better than coming to any particular opinion about him or about the meaning of his death.

"Well," I will just say to such an unbelieving friend, "let us just take that passage which you have chosen, let us just take that Sermon on the Mount, to see whether it really bears out your view of Jesus, whether it really presents to us a Jesus who was merely a teacher and example and did not ask men to have any particularly high view of him."

We did that in our last series. We took the Sermon on the Mount and examined it that way. And what did we find? Did we find a Jesus who kept his own person out of his gospel and did not care what men thought of him?

Most emphatically we did not. Instead, we found in the Sermon on the Mount a Jesus who, in the most amazing way, dispensed the rewards in the kingdom of God; a Jesus who placed his commands fully on equality with the commands of God in the Old Testament Scriptures; a Jesus who did not say as the prophets said, "Thus says the Lord," but who said, "*I say to you*" (Matt 5:21); a Jesus who pronounced blessedness upon the men who stood in a certain relation to him: "Blessed are you when others revile you and persecute you and utter all kinds of evil against you falsely on my account" (Matt 5:11); a Jesus who claimed that he would one day sit on the judgment seat of God and determine the final destinies of men, sending some into everlasting punishment and others into eternal life.

No, we cannot in the Sermon on the Mount find any escape from the Christ of the rest of the New Testament. We cannot find in that passage—favorite passage of unbelievers though it be—any merely human Jesus who was indifferent to what men thought of him and merely asked them to take him as their example and to follow his leading on the pathway to God. We find in that passage, as in every other passage, one Christ and one Christ only—the Christ who was truly man and truly God.

If, moreover, we did find in the New Testament the Christ that some men are seeking, a mere leader and example, a mere explorer of the pathway which leads men to God, what possible good could such a Christ be to our souls? What possible good could a mere example and guide be to those who, like us, are dead in trespasses and sins and are under the just wrath and curse of God?

I remember that several years ago I addressed a meeting in Philadelphia that was devoted to a consideration of the topic "The Responsibility of the Church in Our New Age."[1] One of the speakers, who was not a Christian—I mean, not even a professing Christian at all—had some very kind things to say about Jesus. But the climax of his address came when he quoted Jesus's words from the New Testament regarding love of God and of one's neighbor: "You shall love the Lord your God with all your heart and with all your soul and with all your strength and with all your mind, and your neighbor as yourself" (Luke 10:27).

"Is that not dogma enough for anybody?" said the speaker.

Well, of course, it is not dogma at all, or doctrine, but a command. But was the speaker right in holding that it is large enough for anybody? And if he was right in holding that it is large enough for anybody, why do we Christians insist on adding to it extensive doctrines including the doctrine of the deity of Christ? Why do we not just content ourselves with saying, "You shall love the Lord your God and you shall love your neighbor as yourself?" Is that not indeed large enough for anybody?

What is the answer from the Christian point of view? The answer from

---

1. See Hart, D.G, *J. Gresham Machen: Selected Shorter Writings* (Phillipsburg: P&R, 2004)

the Christian point of view is very simple. Yes, certainly that great double command of Jesus, "You shall love the Lord your God with all your heart and with all your soul and with all your strength and with all your mind, and your neighbor as yourself," is plenty large enough for anybody. Ah, but do you not see, my friends? It is far too large, and therein is the whole trouble. That is the whole reason why we are Christians. That stupendous command of Jesus is too large; it is so large that we have not succeeded in keeping it. If we had loved God and our neighbor, in the high sense in which Jesus meant that command, all would have been well with us; we should then have needed nothing more; we should not have needed any doctrine of the cross of Christ because we should not have needed any cross of Christ; we should not have needed any doctrine of the person of Christ—"God and man in two distinct natures, and one person, forever" (WSC Q&A 21)—because there would have been no necessity for Christ to become man at all. We should have been righteous, and we should have needed no Savior.

But as it is, we are sinners. That is the reason why we need more than a teacher and example and lawgiver; that is the reason why we need what unbelievers despise as being merely doctrine and what we prefer to call the gospel; that is why we cling with all our souls to the great Bible doctrines of the person and work of Jesus Christ.

Suppose I had listened to Jesus merely as a great example and lawgiver. Suppose I had heard him say, "You shall love the Lord your God . . . and your neighbor as yourself" (Luke 10:27); suppose I had heard him say, in the Sermon on the Mount, "Blessed are the pure in heart, for they shall see God" (Matt 5:8). What should I say to him then? Should I say, "I thank you, Jesus; that is all I needed to know; I am so glad to know that if I love God and my neighbor and am pure in heart, all will be well and I shall enter into the kingdom of God."

Well, my friends, I do not know what you would say. But I know that I could say nothing of the kind. I could only say, after listening to those commands of Jesus, "Alas, I am undone; I have not loved God and my neighbor; I am not pure in heart; I am a sinner; Jesus, have you anything, despite your high commands, to say to me?"

When I come thus to Jesus as a sinner, confessing that I have not obeyed his commands, confessing that I have nothing to offer to him but am utterly unworthy and utterly helpless, has he anything to say to me? Does he say merely, "You have heard my high commands; that is all that

I have to say; that is all the gospel that I have to give you; that is all the doctrine you can have"?

No, thank God, that is not all that he has to give me—that cold comfort of a command that I have not kept and cannot keep. He gives me something more than that. He gives me himself. He offers himself to me in the Bible as my Savior who died for me on the cross and who now lives as the one whom I can trust. He offers himself to me in the great doctrines of his person and his work. If he were some other, he could not save me and I could not trust him to save me. But because he is very God, he could save me and did save me, and I have been united to him by the Holy Spirit through faith.

Do you not see, my friends? That is the reason why the Christian clings to the doctrine of the deity of Christ. He does not approach it as a cold academic matter, but he comes to it as a drowning man lays hold of a plank that may save him from the abyss. No lesser Christ could save us; this Christ alone could save us from eternal death.

It is in that way that we are going to approach the things that we hope to deal with in the talks that follow. The doctrine presented in the Bible is not to us just a matter of curious interest; it is not a thing to be relegated to schools or classrooms. It is a matter of tragic import; it is a matter of life or death. Here we stand on the brink of eternity. We are sinners. We deserve God's wrath and curse. There is hope for us only in what God has told us in his Word. Let us listen to it while there is yet time.

20

The Decrees of God

In a former series of talks, I spoke to you about who God is. Now I want to begin to talk to you about what God does.

But before we speak about *what* God does, the first question to ask is whether God can really do anything at all. There are many ways of thinking about God that deny him the power to act altogether. If, for example, God is just a blind force or just another name for the universe as a whole, or if he is merely a name for one aspect of the universe or a mere symbol to express the highest aspirations of humanity, then it is only by a very loose use of language that he can be said to act. Strictly speaking, only people act, and when we come to talk about God as acting, we do so only because we reject all impersonal conceptions of him and regard him, as the Bible does, as a person.

Because God is a person, he is free. Freedom is a characteristic of personality. A machine is not free; a current flowing downward in a groove fixed for it is not free; a plant is not free. But a person is free to act or not to act, and he is free to act in this way or in that. Because God is a person he also is free. Indeed, he is free to an extent to which no finite person is free.

But when we say that God is free, it is very important that we should understand exactly what we mean and what we do not mean.

Do we mean that his actions are quite uncertain, so that it is always impossible to be sure beforehand whether he will act or how he will not act? Do we mean that his will is a sort of balance which may swing this way or that way without any rhyme or reason? Do we mean that there is nothing at all to which his actions conform or by which they are bound?

I think a little reflection will show that we cannot possibly mean that. If we did mean that, we should be obliged to say that God might break his covenant with his people or do any other base deed. But if one thing is certain above all else, it is that God will never do anything of that kind. I think it is not wrong to say that he *cannot* do anything of that kind.

Why can he not do such things? Because there is an external compulsion upon him not to do them? Because if he does them his actions will anywhere be called in question? Most assuredly not. There is no compulsion of any kind resting upon God; he is absolutely sovereign; he can do just exactly as he wills; there is none who can say to him, "What are you doing?"

Yet it is entirely certain, where a good action is being contemplated in comparison with a bad one, that he will choose the good and reject the bad. In fact, there is nothing at all that is more certain than that. It is upon that certainty that all other certainties depend. It is absolutely impossible that God should do wrong.

Why is it impossible? Surely the answer is plain. It is impossible for him to do wrong because for him to do wrong would be contrary to his own nature. "God is a Spirit, infinite, eternal, and unchangeable, in his being, wisdom, power, holiness, justice, goodness, and truth" (WSC Q&A 4). Those are his attributes; without those attributes, he would not be God; those attributes determine all his actions. Never in the very smallest of all his works will he depart by one hair's breadth from that perfect standard that the perfection of his own nature sets up.

I think that is what one of my old teachers meant when he said, if I remember rightly, that God is the most obligated being that there is. He is obligated by his own nature. He is infinite in his wisdom; therefore, he can never do anything that is unwise. He is infinite in his justice; therefore, he can never do anything that is unjust. He is infinite in his goodness; therefore, he can never do anything that is not good. He is infinite in his truth; therefore, it is impossible that he should lie.

Even a man's actions are somewhat similarly determined. They spring from the nature of the man. Experience surely teaches that. But the Bible teaches it most clearly of all. "A healthy tree cannot bear bad fruit, nor can a diseased tree bear good fruit" (Matt 7:18). A man's choices are free in the sense that they are not just determined by external compulsion. But they are not free if by freedom is meant freedom from determination by the man's own character.

So it is in the case of the supreme person, God. His actions are free in the sense that they are not determined by anything external to him. But they certainly are determined by his own nature. They will always be holy and they will always be just and good because he is holy and just and good.

Indeed, the actions of God are even more completely determined by his own nature than a man's actions are determined by *his* own nature. A man's actions spring from his nature. Yes, but the man's nature may be changed; God can change it. But in the case of God, no such possibility of change exists; God is infinite, eternal, *and unchangeable*. Never, never, never, therefore—never by the remotest possibility—can he perform an action which is not holy and wise and powerful, just and good and true.

His actions, therefore, are freer than the actions of finite persons, and at the same time more directly determined than the actions of finite persons. They are far more free than the actions of finite persons because never, either directly or indirectly, can they be determined by anything external to God himself, as is possible in the case of finite persons; his actions are more directly determined than the actions of finite persons because never by any possibility can there be any change in the nature of God himself.

Thus, it is very important for us to observe that the freedom of God's actions does not mean that they can, by any possibility, be out of accord with God's nature.

But there is another thing that it is very important to observe that the freedom of God's actions does not mean. It does not mean that they are purposeless actions; it does not mean that they are undetermined by ends which God has in view.

At this point also, there is a real analogy between the freedom of God and the freedom of finite persons. Take the finite person with whom we are most familiar—namely, man. Does the freedom of a man's will mean that a man acts independently of motives? Does it mean that when a man chooses to do one thing rather than to do another thing his choice is determined by nothing at all except just that it is his choice? Well, some people have apparently thought that that is the case. But surely these people are wrong. Surely the actions of a person, just because they are free actions and not mere meaningless vagaries of blind chance, are determined by motives. When a man is placed before some important turning point in his life, he sets before himself the considerations on one side and then the considerations on the other side, and then in light of those considerations—of the preponderance on the one side or on the other—he acts. It is just that operation of motives in determining the man's action that makes the action a truly personal action and so makes it, in the right sense of the word, a "free" action.

If then a finite person, man, in his truly personal actions, is determined by motives, something like that is also true of the infinite person, God.

God also has ends in view when he acts. His will must not be thought of as though it were swinging blindly in a sort of vacuum, without relation to this infinite knowledge and wisdom. No, the choices of God's will are always—not sometimes, but always—determined by the ends which his infinite knowledge and his infinite wisdom place before him.

A denial of that view of the will—a denial that is of the view that truly personal actions are not the actions of an undetermined will but of a will determined by motives or ends—is sometimes represented as though it were in the interests of freedom. How can a person really be free, it is said, if his actions are fixed by something other than his will itself at the moment when he makes his choice? How can a person be free if he cannot act irrespectively of the ends that he has in view?

But a little reflection will show that the exact opposite is the case. If a man's choices are not determined by the ends that he has in view, but simply by meaningless oscillations of his will, then they are determined by nothing but chance, and the man becomes the mere plaything of something external to himself.

That is particularly clear in the case of the supreme person, God. If God's choices were not determined at all times by the holy ends that he has in view, if his will swung this way or that without reference to anything save his will itself—considered as though it were separate from his knowledge and wisdom—then his actions could only be regarded as dependent upon a blind, meaningless chance; and in that case, they would cease to be really personal actions and God would cease to be God.

No, we must really hold to a sound determinism when we think of the will. The will of man is not free in the sense that it operates independently of the feelings and the intellect. Indeed, if we regard the will as a sort of separate something inside of a man—going about its business in its own way, capable of taking advice from other parts of man's nature but also capable of acting quite independently of such advice when the mood strikes it—if we think of the will thus, we are getting very far away from reality indeed. We are really making of something that we call the will a little separate personality; we are doing away with the unity of the man's personality. As a matter of fact, there is really no such thing as the will out of relation to the other aspects of the person. What we call the will is just the whole person making choices.

With regard to the infinite person of God, we have to speak differently in important respects from the way in which we speak of finite persons. Yet of him, as of the finite persons whom he has created, it does remain true that when he wills to do something, he wills to do it because of ends that he has in view. His actions are not the chance hither and yon swinging of something within him that can be called his will, but they are the actions of the majestic unity of his being, and they are determined by high and holy ends.

I do not mean that when God wills to do something *we* can always see what the end is. On the contrary, in countless cases, we can only see that it is his will, and that should be enough for us. We are sure that whatever he does is done with a holy purpose. The purpose is often hidden in the mystery of the divine wisdom. For us to refuse to bow to God's will just because we do not know what his purpose is—that is the very height of irreligion. It is the sin of all sins; it is to pit our ignorance against his infinite wisdom and knowledge; it is rebellion and pride and madness. May God save us all from such a sin as that!

Yet although we have no *right* to know what God's purposes are, he has, in his wonderful goodness, been pleased to lift here and there the veil that hides his counsels from our eyes. With what reverence ought we to look into the mysteries within the veil! With what reverence ought we to approach the holy book in which those mysteries are revealed!

We have spoken of the purposes of God. The theologians when they speak of them call them his decrees.

How many are there of such decrees? An infinite number, we might be tempted to say. How manifold are the manifestations of God's goodness in our own lives! And when we think of the vastness of the universe and the countless ages, we naturally say that the decrees of God are beyond anything that by any possibility can be numbered.

If we say that, we are saying something that is profoundly true; and yet when we look at the matter a little more closely and more deeply, there is a true sense in which we can say that the purposes of God, infinite in number though they may seem to be, are all just one purpose, are all just portions or aspects of one great plan.

That is what the Shorter Catechism means when it says that "the decrees of God are his eternal purpose" (WSC Q&A 7). It is not by chance that the singular number of the word "purpose" is there used. The many decrees all constitute just one purpose or one plan. They are not without relation to one another, but form a mighty unity as God himself is one.

You will notice that the Shorter Catechism speaks of that purpose as an *eternal* purpose. "The decrees of God," it says, "are his eternal purpose" (WSC Q&A 7). What does it mean by that? Well, it means something that it is very important indeed for us to observe, and it means something which is close to the heart of what the Bible teaches.

The Bible does often speak of the decrees of God as though they came one after another, in an order of time. Indeed, the Bible sometimes uses some very bold language about these matters. It speaks even of God's repenting of what he has done. For instance, it says that "it repented the LORD that he had made man" (Gen 6:6; KJV); and that "the LORD repented that he had made Saul king over Israel" (1 Sam 15:35; KJV). These passages might seem, to a superficial reader, if they were taken by themselves, to mean that God makes many decrees at many different times, and as though the decrees were widely different from one another.

But that would be a very superficial interpretation of those passages. When we look a little more closely we see plainly what the Bible means. When it speaks of God as repenting of something that he has done, it is looking at the thing from the point of view of men who are living in a succession of time upon this earth. God does one thing at one time, and one thing at another. He made man, and then, when man had sinned, he destroyed man, with the exception of the few whom he preserved. He made Saul king, and then removed him from being king. Looked at from the point of view of the execution of God's decrees, it is as though God's decrees or purposes had changed, and the Bible makes that clear in simple language drawn from the ordinary lives of men. But it is also perfectly clear that the Bible does not mean such language to be taken literally as though it meant that God was surprised in the way in which a man would be surprised, or as though it meant that the plans of God are shifted as a man's plans are shifted to meet developments over which he has no control.

At this point, it is possible that I may be met with an objection. "There you are," the objector may say, "you miserable believers in the inspiration of the Bible are up to your old tricks. When you find anything in the Bible that you like, you insist on taking it with a most distressing literalness; but when you find anything that you do not like, you crawl out of it, as in the present case, by saying that figurative language is being used."

Such is the objection. But, do you know, my friends, I am not so very much dismayed by it. I think I have a perfectly good answer to it. "Yes," I would say to an objector, "I do take some things in the Bible literally and some things figuratively. But I have a perfectly good reason for doing so. I have a perfectly good way of deciding which things in the Bible I shall take literally and which things I shall take figuratively. It is not that I take those things literally which I like and explain away those things as figurative which I do not like; but I take those things literally which the Bible intends literally and those things figuratively which the Bible intends figuratively."

You see, I hold that the Bible is essentially a plain book. Common sense is a wonderful help in reading it. I am not forgetting that the enlightening of the eyes which the Holy Spirit gives in the new birth is necessary in order that sinful man may really lay hold upon the central message in the Bible; but sometimes I am tempted to say that one of the most obvious effects of the new birth should be the restoration of plain common sense in the understanding of the perfectly plain utterances of Holy Scripture. So, I submit that if a man really reads with ordinary good sense and good will those utterances of the Bible where the Bible speaks of God as repenting of the things that he has done and the like, he will have no difficulty whatever in seeing that those passages are most emphatically not to be interpreted literally, and that a literal interpretation of them is a very heinous exhibition of misunderstanding and bad taste.

Such anthropomorphic language—if you will permit me to use a long word—sets forth an important truth. It teaches us that God deals with us as a living person deals with us. He follows our actions and the changing circumstances of our lives, and his actions are related to changes in our actions and in our circumstances. The Bible sets that forth by using the language that we have been speaking.

But the Bible also very plainly teaches us that when we look at the depth of this matter we must see that the purpose of God, which is executed in his infinitely varied dealing with mankind and with the universe in an order of time, is itself quite out of anything like temporal succession. There is no before and no after to God. He created time, indeed, when he created finite beings, and time, like the rest of the universe which God created, is not a mere appearance, but has a real existence. But to God all things are eternally present.

So, the Shorter Catechism is right when it says that "the decrees of God are his eternal purpose" (WSC Q&A 7). I think that really runs throughout the Bible. It is not obscured one bit by the simple, anthropomorphic language about which we have spoken this afternoon. At times it comes into particularly plain view, as when the Bible says in the first chapter of Ephesians that God chose us in Christ before the creation of the world

(Eph 1:4). But what ought to be emphasized above all else is that the doctrine of an eternal purpose of God is the foundation upon which all the teachings of the Bible are really based. Back of all the events of human history, back of all the changes in the inconceivable vastness of the universe, back of space itself and time there lies one mysterious purpose of him to whom there is no before or after, no here or yonder, to whom all things are present and before whom all things are naked and open—the living and holy God.

21

God's Decrees and Man's Freedom

The decrees of God, we have observed, may be thought of as many, if we look at them from the point of view of their execution in the infinitely varied course of God's dealings with the world that he has made; but it is a still profounder truth to say that they are all really one decree, one eternal purpose or plan.

How much is embraced in that eternal purpose of God?

The true answer to that question is very simple. The true answer is, "Everything." Everything that happens is embraced in the eternal purpose of God; nothing at all happens outside of his eternal plan.

It is obvious that nothing is too great for God. The stupendous spaces of the universe, which astronomers talk of in terms of light-years but of which neither they nor any of the rest of us can really form any conception at all, contain no mysteries for God. He made all and he rules all, and all is embraced in his eternal purpose.

It is equally clear that nothing is too small for God. Jesus expressed that truth with a vividness that can never be surpassed. "Are not two sparrows," he said, "sold for a penny? And not one of them will fall to the ground apart from your Father. But even the hairs of your head are all numbered" (Matt 10:29–30). No, nothing is too trivial to form a part of God's eternal plan. That plan embraces the small as well as the great.

Modern science has disclosed new wonders in the starry heavens, and it has also told us of the infinitesimal universe that the atom contains. Well, it is all naked and open before God, and it all is the product of his infinite wisdom and power.

But wait a moment. We said that everything that happens is embraced in God's eternal plan, being determined from all eternity in one majestic purpose. Did we really mean that? When we said "everything," did we really mean "everything"? Did we allow no exceptions? Is everything fixed and determined in God's plan? Is there nothing at all that is free?

How about, then, the free actions of personal beings such as man? Is not man's freedom of choice a delusion if all is fixed in God's eternal plan?

There are those who have been impressed by this objection and have actually regarded the personal choices of persons, especially man, as lying outside the range of the things that are fixed in God's eternal purpose. When God created persons, they have said, he left the persons free; otherwise they would not have been persons at all. So, they have said, God voluntarily refrains from using his omnipotence so far as the actions of his personal creatures are concerned. He was powerful enough as Creator even to create beings with the mysterious gift of free will. He then stands aside and lets those beings exercise that mysterious gift. Their actions in detail, therefore—so the argument runs—are not fixed in God's eternal plan but are dependent upon that mysterious power of choice which God gave them once for all.

This view may be held in two forms. In the first place, those who hold it may say that God does not even know beforehand what choices the persons whom he has created will make; and in the second place, they may say that God knows beforehand what choices the persons whom he has created will make but simply does not determine those choices; he foreknows those choices but does not foreordain them; he knows what things his creatures will do but does not secure their doing of them.

The former of these two forms of the theory seems to do away with the omniscience of God. Whatever may or may not be said of the possibility that God should voluntarily refrain from using his omnipotence, it is quite clear that to say that he refrains from possessing his omniscience is simply to indulge in a contradiction in terms. If God really knows all things, then he knows what his creatures, including man, will do. I really do not see how we can get away from that.

If God does not know what his creatures, including man, will do, then a wild, unaccountable factor is introduced into the universe. Can that unaccountable factor be isolated? Can we hold that although God does not know what the persons whom he has created will do, yet he can go on governing the rest of the universe in an orderly fashion? Surely we cannot hold that at all. No, there is a marvelous concatenation in the course of the world; one part cannot possibly be isolated from the rest in that fashion.

If God does not know what the personal beings in the universe will do, then the whole course of the world is thrown into confusion. The order of nature then ceases to be an order at all.

Moreover, on that view, God ceases to be God. He becomes a being who has to wait to see what his creatures will do; he becomes a God who has to change his plans to meet changing circumstances. In other words, he becomes a God who stands in a temporal series, to whom there is such a thing as before and after, then and now; he ceases to be the eternal God. In other words, he becomes a finite being; he becomes not God but *a god*—even if we could become acquainted with him we should still have to search for the God who is God indeed.

It would be difficult to imagine a view that is more utterly unphilosophical than this view that God stepped voluntarily aside and was dependent for the rest of his plans upon what his creatures would deign to do. But it is just as unscriptural as it is unphilosophical. If one thing lies at the basis of the whole biblical teaching about God it is that God knows all things. But he does not know all things if he does not know what his creatures will do. Such a God with limited knowledge is very different from the God of the Bible, the God before whom no secrets are hidden.

Also very unsatisfactory, however, is the other form in which the theory with which we are dealing has been held. According to that other form of the theory, while God does not determine or foreordain the actions of the personal beings whom he has created, he does leave their actions to the operation of their free will, and yet knows beforehand what their actions will be.

A little reflection, I think, will show that this form of the theory does not really overcome the difficulty that it was intended to overcome. The difficulty that it was intended to overcome was that if the actions of personal beings, including man, are to be free—if, in other words, they are to be really personal actions—they cannot be fixed beforehand. Therefore, the theory holds, they cannot have been fixed beforehand by God; therefore, God must with respect to them have voluntarily limited the exercise of his power.

Well, but the trouble is that if God really created these personal beings knowing beforehand what, if created, they would do, he did really determine their actions. Their actions were certain before they did them. But if the certainty of an action before it is accomplished means that the action is not a free or truly personal action, then those actions, being foreknown with absolute certainty by God, were not free; and the theory is open to all the objections that are urged against *our* doctrine.

It is open to all those objections. Yes, and it is faced by other objections of a much more serious kind.

What sort of God is it who merely knows beforehand that his creatures will perform certain actions and yet does not purpose that they shall perform those actions? Is it not a God who is aware of some necessity outside his own will? It does look as though that certainty of the future actions of those created persons, which enables God to predict their actions, must be due either to the purpose of God or to some blind fate, which God knows about but which is independent of God. The latter alternative dethrones God. Logically, it involves the abandonment of that high view which attributes the existence of all things to the mysterious will of an all-powerful person. It really involves the abandonment of a theistic view of the world, little though its advocates may be aware of such an implication.

No, we must discard all such compromises. They are exceedingly dangerous. But what settles the matter for us is that they are quite opposed to the Bible. The Bible makes no exceptions when it speaks of God's government of the world. According to the Bible, God governs all, and the Bible is particularly clear in teaching that he determines the voluntary acts of his creatures. Nothing, according to the Bible, lies outside of God's eternal plan.

But at that point a further objection is often raised: "Are not you Calvinists forgetting one thing?" the objector says. "If God foreordains even the free actions of the persons, including man, whom he has created, how about sinful actions? Has he foreordained them? And if he has foreordained them, what becomes of his holiness? Must we not attribute sinful actions, at least, solely to the free choice of the sinners who commit them and not at all to the plan or purpose of a holy God?"

In answer to the objection, it is easy to point to words of Scripture which teach the exact opposite of the view that the objector holds. The crucifixion of Jesus was certainly a sinful act; no one can possibly have any doubt about that. Yet the Bible says repeatedly that it was part of the plan of God. "This Jesus, delivered up according to the definite plan and foreknowledge of God, you crucified and killed by the hands of lawless men" (Acts 2:23). The word here translated "plan" is a very plain word; it means "wish" or "purpose." But what was it that, according to this verse, was done thus by the purpose of God? It was the delivering over of Christ. I think that means the delivering over of Christ by Judas, rather than the delivering over of Christ to his enemies by God. If so, then the wicked act of Judas, his betrayal of his Lord, is designated as something which was a part of God's plan. But even if the delivering over that is meant was the delivering over of Christ to his enemies by God, we can hardly escape the plain implications of the passage. It seems very clear, when the verse is taken as a whole, that the entire crime by which Jesus was brought to his death was accomplished, according to this verse, by the "definite plan and foreknowledge of God."

That is, if anything, even clearer in another passage in the book of Acts. In the fourth chapter of Acts it is said: "for truly in this city there were gathered together against your holy servant Jesus, whom you anointed, both Herod and Pontius Pilate, along with the Gentiles and the peoples of Israel, to do whatever your hand and your plan had predestined to take place" (Acts 4:27–28). Those wicked men, by their wicked act, were not defeating, or doing anything outside of, the plan of God. No, they did only what God's hand and God's plan determined before to be done. Even the wicked acts of men are, therefore, no exceptions to the all-inclusiveness of God's eternal purpose. The Shorter Catechism is quite in accordance with the Bible when it says that by that eternal purpose God "hath foreordained whatsoever comes to pass" (WSC Q&A 7)—not whatsoever comes to pass except the free or at least the wicked acts of created persons, but whatsoever comes to pass without any exception at all.

I remember a sermon that I heard last summer. I was at Zermatt in the Swiss Alps. On weekdays, I climbed the mountains—the Matterhorn, the Weisshorn, and others of those great peaks. On Sundays, I went to church.

The particular sermon that I now have in mind was one on the text: "If he is cursing because the Lord has said to him, 'Curse David,' who then shall say, 'Why have you done so?'" (2 Sam 16:10) Those words were spoken by David when he was fleeing from Absalom. As the king was passing along with his melancholy little company, Shimei cast stones at him and cursed him, and said: "And Shimei said as he cursed, 'Get out, get out, you man of blood, you worthless man! The Lord has avenged on you all the blood of the house of Saul, in whose place you have reigned, and the Lord has given the kingdom into the hand of your son Absalom. See, your evil is on you, for you are a man of blood'" (2 Sam 16:7–8).

Such was the cursing of Shimei. It is no wonder that Abishai the son of Zeruiah said to the king: "Why should this dead dog curse my lord the king? Let me go over and take off his head" (2 Sam 16:9).

But David said: "What have I to do with you, you sons of Zeruiah? If he is cursing because the Lord has said to him, 'Curse David,' who then shall say, 'Why have you done so?'" (2 Sam 16:10)

The preacher in that little Protestant chapel in Catholic Switzerland took the incident as an example of the way in which God uses the actions of wicked men. David recognized a great truth. Even the cursing of Shimei, said David, had a place in God's plan. "The Lord bade him curse me," said David.

Of course, said the preacher at Zermatt, David did deserve cursing. He did not, indeed, at all deserve the particular cursing which Shimei heaped upon him. He was not a bloody man in his dealings with the house of Saul, as Shimei said he was. But for other things that he had done—for his murder of Uriah the Hittite, for his inordinate lust—he deserved cursing only too well.

There was One, however, said the preacher, of whom that could not possibly be said, and upon whom nevertheless curses were heaped. There was One who hung upon a shameful cross and endured the cursing and mocking of his enemies. They wagged their heads as they passed by and cursed and mocked him as he hung there upon the cross.

Those curses, at least, were entirely undeserved. They were directed against the one truly innocent man among all those who have ever lived upon this earth; they were black, horrible sin on the part of those who uttered them.

Yet they surely did not stand outside of God's plan. Nay, they were at the very heart of that plan. By those curses heaped upon the holy and just One, and by the death which went with them, we all, if we belong to God's people, are saved.

Yes, surely the wicked actions of men have a place in God's eternal purpose. The Bible makes that abundantly clear. Wicked men may not think they are serving God's purposes, but they are serving his purposes all the same, even by the most wicked of their acts.

At that point, however, serious questions might seem to arise. If wicked actions of wicked men have a place in God's plan, if they are foreordained of God, then is man responsible for them, and is not God the author of sin?

To each of these questions the Bible returns a very unequivocal answer. Yes, man is responsible for his wicked actions; and no, God is not the author of sin.

That man is responsible for his wicked actions is made so plain from the beginning of the Bible to the end that it is quite useless to cite individual proof texts. But it is equally clear in the Bible that God is not the author of sin. That is clear from the very nature of sin, as rebellion against God's holy law. It is also expressly taught. "Let no one say when he is tempted, 'I am being tempted by God,'" says the Epistle of James, "for God cannot be tempted with evil, and he himself tempts no one. But each person is tempted when he is lured and enticed by his own desire" (James 1:13–14).

How, then, can we meet the difficulty? We have said that God has foreordained whatsoever comes to pass. The sinful actions of sinful men are things that come to pass. Yet we deny that God is the author of them and we put the responsibility for them upon man.

How can we possibly do that? Are we not involving ourselves in hopeless contradiction?

The answer is found in the fact that although God foreordains whatsoever comes to pass, he causes the bringing of those things to pass in widely different ways.

He does not cause the bringing to pass of the actions of personal beings in the same way as the way in which he causes the bringing to pass of events in the physical world. That is true even of the good actions of men who are his children. Even when God causes those men to do certain things by the gracious influence of his Holy Spirit, he does not deal with them as with sticks or stones, but he deals with them as with men. He does not cause them to do those things against their will, but he determines their will, and their freedom as persons is fully preserved when they perform those acts. The acts remain their acts, even though they are led to do them by the Spirit of God.

When God causes the bringing to pass of the *evil* actions of men, he does that in still a different way. He does not tempt the men to sin; he does not influence them to sin. But he causes the bringing to pass of those deeds by the free and responsible choices of personal beings. He has created those beings with the awful gift of freedom of choice. The things that they do in exercise of that gift are their acts. They do not, indeed, surprise God by the doing of them; their doing of them is part of his eternal plan; yet in the doing of them they, and not the holy God, are responsible.

What is the real difficulty here? Is it the difficulty of harmonizing the free will of the creature with the certainty of the creature's actions as part of God's eternal purpose? No, I do not think that is the real difficulty. The real difficulty is the difficulty of seeing how a good and all-powerful God ever could have allowed sin to enter the world that he had created. That difficulty faces not only the consistent and truly biblical view of the divine decree which we have tried to summarize this afternoon, but it also faces the inconsistent views that we have rejected. It can never be used, therefore, as an argument in favor of any one of those inconsistent views and against the consistent view.

For both, the problem remains. How could a holy God, if he is all-powerful, have permitted the existence of sin?

What shall we do with the problem? I am afraid we shall have to do with it something that is not very pleasing to our pride; I am afraid we shall just have to say that it is insoluble.

Is it so surprising that there are some things that we do not know? God has told us much. He has told us much even about sin. He has told us how at infinite cost, by the gift of his Son, he has provided a way of escape from it. Yes, God has told us much. Is it surprising that he has not told us all? I do not think so, my friends. After all, we are but finite creatures. Is it surprising that there are some mysteries which God in his infinite goodness and wisdom has hidden from our eyes? Is it surprising that there are some things in his counsels about which he has bidden us be content not to know but instead just to trust him who knows all?

22

What Is Predestination?

In the last talk, I may be charged with having spent all my time talking about one word—one word in the definition of the decrees of God that is found in the Shorter Catechism. It was only one word, but it was a tremendous word that might well have occupied all our Sunday afternoons for many years. "The decrees of God," says the Shorter Catechism, "are his eternal purpose, according to the counsel of his will, whereby, for his own glory, he hath foreordained whatsoever comes to pass" (WSC Q&A 7). The word that I was talking to you about was that word "whatsoever." Has God foreordained *whatsoever* comes to pass, or has he foreordained only some of the things that come to pass, leaving other things—the things due to the choices of personal beings—outside of his eternal plan? I defended the former view, showing how that view alone is in accordance with the Bible. I maintained, in accordance with the Bible, that not some things that happen but all things—all things including the free choices of personal beings, all things including even the wicked actions of wicked men and devils—are brought to pass in accordance with God's eternal purpose.

Those things are not all brought to pass by God in the same way. God does not bring to pass the actions of personal beings in the same way as the way in which he brings to pass events in the physical world. He brings the actions of personal beings to pass in a way that preserves to the full their freedom of choice, and that does not at all destroy their responsibility. He brings to pass the wicked actions of personal beings in a way that does not at all make him the author of sin. But that should not obscure in the slightest the fact that God does bring all things to pass. They are brought to pass in execution of God's purpose.

Wicked men may not think that they are serving God's purpose, but they *are* serving his purpose all the same, even by the wickedest of their acts. The crucifixion of Jesus Christ our Lord, the most terrible sin that has ever been committed upon this earth, was accomplished, "according to the definite plan and foreknowledge of God" (Acts 2:23). Nothing whatever surprises God; all things that happen are absolutely certain from all eternity because they are all embraced in God's eternal plan.

People sometimes call that fatalism. It would be more correct to say that it is the diametrical opposite of fatalism. The difference between it and fatalism is the difference between fate and God, and surely there could be no greater difference than that. Fatalism grounds the certainty of all things in a blind, impersonal something that it calls fate; the view that we have presented grounds the certainty of all things in the holy purpose of a living God.

But the difference concerns far more than the ultimate grounding of all things. It would be utterly incorrect to say that we agree with the fatalist in holding that human freedom is a delusion and mechanism rules all, and differ from him merely in holding that back of the mechanism there lies the purpose of a personal God. Oh, no. We differ from the fatalist in a far more comprehensive way than that. We hold that just because the God that stands back of all things is a personal God, therefore there is a wonderful discrimination in the way in which he executes his decrees. We hold that when he deals with persons he deals with them as with persons, and that the certainty with which through them he accomplishes what he has purposed does not destroy their freedom or their responsibility but preserves it to the full.

In the presence of that certainty with which God accomplishes his purpose, we stand, indeed, in awe. "It is a fearful thing," says the Bible, "to fall into the hands of the living God" (Heb 10:31). Yes, it is a fearful thing indeed. But it is a very different thing from being in the clutches of a blind and impersonal fate. Biblical theism and fatalism are really at opposite poles.

Moreover, if the view that we have presented is the diametrical opposite of fatalism, it is also the only formidable opponent of fatalism. Patchwork theologies, crazy-quilt views of the world that regard God's plan as being broken in upon here and there by the incalculable actions of personal beings, are not formidable opponents of fatalism at all. They bear too plainly upon their surface the marks of being nothing but compromises and makeshifts.

I suppose that is what a certain eminent scientist meant if he really did say, as he was once reported to me to have said, that from the point of view of science, Calvinism is "the only respectable theology." Calvinism alone does justice to the unity of the world, as it certainly alone does justice to the teaching of the Bible.

If, then, we hold to that high biblical view, if we hold that whatsoever comes to pass comes to pass in accordance with the eternal purpose of God, can we know anything at all about what that eternal purpose is?

Yes, we can certainly know something about it. We cannot know all about it; what we know about it is very small compared with what we do not know: but still we do know something about it, and that something is very important indeed.

We do not know that something about it because we have discovered it by any searching of our own, but we know it because God has been graciously pleased to reveal it to us in his Word.

What then do we know about the purpose of God? Why did God create the universe? Why did he order it just thus and so?

Did he create and order the universe because of some purpose found in the universe itself? Surely not. That would make the world an end in itself; it would elevate it to a position that belongs only to God. No, the creation of the world must have had as its purpose something that existed before the world was. But God himself is all that existed before the world was. Therefore, the purpose of the world must be found in God.

So we might reason, and if we so reasoned I think our reasoning would be good reasoning; it would be based upon what God has truly revealed to us regarding himself. But we are not compelled to rely only upon such reasoning, good though the reasoning is. God has also directly told us what his purpose is. He has told us in the Bible that all things are brought to pass by him for his own glory.

That truth is so pervasive in the Bible that I do not know whether I need to cite individual passages. I might cite such a glorious passage, for example, as the first chapter of Ephesians. There we are given as comprehensive an insight, perhaps, into the counsels of God as in any other one passage in the Bible. We are carried through the whole sweep of the divine plan, beginning with God's choice of his people before the foundation of the world. But if that is where the majestic drama begins, where does it end? Does it end merely with the blessedness of the redeemed people? Does it end merely with any blessedness of God's creatures? No indeed. Such blessedness is glorious. But it is not the end of all. There is something higher still, something to which that blessedness of God's creatures is merely a means. Why are the creatures blessed? The passage makes that perfectly plain: "so that we who were the first to hope in Christ might be to the praise of his glory" (Eph 1:12). That is the ultimate end. The ultimate end of all things that come to pass including the ultimate end of the great drama of redemption is found in the glory of the eternal God.

Again and again that comes out in the Bible. The Bible differs from human books on religion not merely in this point or that but in the center about which everything moves. Human books are prone to find that center in man; the Bible finds it in God.

Men do not like that fundamental characteristic of the Bible. They prefer to think of the happiness of the creature as the goal; they wrongly interpret the text "God is love" to mean that God is only love and that God exists for the benefit of his creatures; reversing the Shorter Catechism, they hold that God's chief end is to glorify man. But the Bible plainly agrees with the Shorter Catechism; the Bible plainly teaches that "man's chief end"—and the chief end of all things—"is to glorify God" (WSC Q&A 1).

People have a sort of vague notion that that attributes selfishness to God. It would be selfish and abominable for one of us to make his own glory the goal of his activities, and people jump to the conclusion that what is selfish in us is also selfish in God, and so they try to find some goal of God's activities outside of God himself.

Such reasoning, however, ignores the infinite gulf between the Creator and the creature. God is infinitely exalted above all finite creatures. If he made finite creatures the supreme end of his working, that would be to put a lower end in the place that belongs only to the higher. There is nothing higher than the glory of God. That, therefore, must be the supreme end of all things.

But what do we mean by the glory of God? I think it is very important for us to be clear about the answer to that question. We do not mean anything that is like the glory of a man. No, we mean something that is infinitely comprehensive. In the glory of God is comprehended the whole majesty of the divine perfections—infinite wisdom, infinite power, infinite goodness, infinite love. That it is—that full splendor of the being of God and the working of it and the recognition of it in ceaseless praise—the supreme end of all things. There can be no higher end; the substitution of any other end for it would be an abomination.

We hold, therefore, with all our souls to the great definition of the decrees of God in the Shorter Catechism of our church. "The decrees of

God are his eternal purpose, according to the counsel of his will, whereby, for his own glory, he hath foreordained whatsoever comes to pass" (WSC Q&A 7).

We have treated in general the great truth set forth in that definition. It now remains to touch upon one particular sphere in which the truth is to be applied. I refer to the sphere of salvation. The doctrine of the divine decrees, when it is applied especially in that sphere of salvation, is called "predestination."

As I utter that word, some of my hearers may experience a shiver. "Predestination" is thought to be such a very thorny doctrine; at least it is thought to be an idiosyncrasy of one particularly straight sect. It is often thought, even by those who profess belief in it, to be a doctrine which is better left aside in ordinary preaching—something to be relegated to the theological classrooms, but not something which will ever be acceptable to the rank and file of the church.

Such is the way in which men are prone to look upon the matter. But just take up your Bible, my friends, and read it without prejudice. If you do so, you will be obliged to confess that the Bible looks upon the matter in an entirely different way. Far from relegating the doctrine of predestination to some secondary place, the Bible puts it right at the heart of all its teaching.

What, then, is the doctrine of predestination? Before I answer that question very briefly, I want to refer you to one or two things on the subject which I think, if you are interested, would be useful for you to read.

In the first place, there is a splendid article by one of the very greatest of modern theologians, B. B. Warfield. It is entitled "Predestination," and it is found in Hastings's *Dictionary of the Bible* and also in Warfield's collected works, in the volume called *Biblical Doctrines*.

In the second place, there is a popular treatment of the subject by Loraine Boettner in a book called *The Reformed Doctrine of Predestination*, which appeared just a few years ago and has been received in such a way as to show that interest in these great things of God's Word has by no means died out even in our unbelieving age.

Today I have time only to say a very few words about this great doctrine. I hope to come back to it; but just now I shall be able only to indicate briefly what the doctrine is, as the Bible sets it forth.

I think I can make clear to you what the doctrine of predestination is by putting it in connection with what I have been saying in the last two talks.

I have been speaking of the eternal purpose of God, whereby for his own glory he has foreordained whatsoever comes to pass. Well, among the things that come to pass, according to the Bible, are the salvation of some men and the loss of others. If all things are foreordained by God's eternal purpose, then those two things are foreordained by it. The setting forth of the fact that they are foreordained by it is called the doctrine of predestination. That doctrine is just one particularly important application, therefore, of the doctrine of the divine decrees.

If that doctrine of the divine decrees is true, then this special application of it is true. That is clear.

But the Bible does not leave us to any such mere logic as that, good and inescapable though the logic is. It does not just let us get the doctrine of predestination by a mere inference from the general doctrine of the universality of the divine decree. No, it expressly teaches that doctrine of predestination and teaches it in the clearest possible way. The Bible clearly teaches that when some men are saved and others are lost, neither of these two things comes as a surprise to God, but both come to pass because they both stand in God's eternal plan.

The Bible lays the chief stress upon the former of these two things; it lays more stress upon the fact that the saved are predestinated to their salvation than it does upon the fact that the lost are predestinated to their eternal retribution. Why does it do that? Does it do it because it seeks to obscure in any way the predestination of the lost? Certainly not. On the contrary, it teaches that latter doctrine in certain passages in the clearest possible way. Why, then, does it lay the chief stress upon the predestination of the saved to salvation?

I think I can tell you at least one reason why it does so. It does so because it regards the salvation of the saved and not the eternal loss of the unsaved as the really surprising thing. *We* are prone to look at the matter in exactly the opposite way. The thing that *we* regard as surprising is that any members of the human race, any of those excellent creatures known as men, who are supposed to be doing the best they can and to be guilty, at the most, of merely trifling and thoroughly forgivable faults, should ever fall under the divine displeasure. But the thing that the Bible regards as surprising is that any of those fallen creatures known as men, all of whom, without exception, deserve God's wrath and curse, should be received into eternal life. We regard it as surprising that any are lost; the Bible regards it as surprising that any are saved. Naturally it is the surprising or unexpected thing upon which the chief stress is laid. It is for that reason, or at least partly for that reason, that the biblical doctrine of predestination is concerned chiefly with the predestination of the saved to their salvation rather than with the predestination of the unsaved to their eternal loss. The latter side of the matter is less extensively expounded simply because it is everywhere presupposed. It forms the dark background upon which the wonder of God's purpose for those whom he has chosen for salvation is thrown into glorious relief.

Why is it that some men are saved? Is it because of anything that they have done? Is it because they are less guilty in the sight of God than others? The whole Bible is concerned with denying that. God chose Israel, according to the Bible, from among all the peoples of the earth. Why? Was it because Israel was more deserving of the divine favor, or because it possessed excellent qualities which God saw that he could use? A man who thinks so, a man who thinks that that is the meaning of the Old Testament, just shows thereby that he has never understood at all the heart of what the Old Testament teaches. Underlying everything else in the consciousness of the Old Testament people of God, as that consciousness was formed by the divine revelation given through lawgiver and prophets, was the profound sense of wonder in that God had chosen such an insignificant people, a people not stronger or better than others, to be his peculiar people. Whatever else there may be in the Old Testament, that is the heart of it. But that is predestination. Israel was God's people not because of anything that it had done or could do or might do but simply because of God's sovereign choice.

When we come to the New Testament, the same thing appears. There is, in the New Testament, clearer revelation of what the divine choice involves. New glories are revealed as being kept in store for the people of God. There is clearer revelation as to the persons who compose that people of God. It is a people chosen from among all the nations of the earth. But there is no change whatever in the basic revelation as to the sovereignty of the divine choice. According to the New Testament, as according to the Old Testament, those who form God's people, those who are destined to salvation, are chosen to form God's people not because of anything that they have done or would do but simply because of the sovereignty of God's good pleasure.

That sovereignty of God's good pleasure is the basic thing; everything else follows from it. Those whom God has chosen believe in Christ. But

God did not choose them because he foresaw that they would believe. It is exactly the other way around. They were not chosen by God because they believed, but they were enabled to believe because they were chosen by God. A man who misses that has missed something that lies very close to the heart of the Bible; he has missed the true meaning of the grace of God.

23

Does the Bible Teach Predestination?

In the last talk, I began to speak to you about the great Scripture doctrine of predestination. That doctrine, I observed, is only one particular application of the doctrine of the divine decrees. If God foreordains by his eternal purpose all things that come to pass, and if among the things that come to pass are the salvation of some men and the loss of others, then it follows with inevitable logic that he foreordains both of these two things. God's foreordination of these two things has come to be called by the special term "predestination." The doctrine of predestination is just the doctrine of the divine decrees applied to the special sphere of salvation.

But the doctrine of predestination does not come to us merely as an inference from the general doctrine of the divine decrees; it is also expressly taught in the Bible in the clearest possible way.

Why is it, according to the Bible, that some men are saved and enter into eternal life, while other men receive the just punishment for their sin?

Is it simply because some men believe in Jesus Christ while others do not?

Well, certainly all those who believe in Jesus Christ are saved and all those who do not believe in Jesus Christ are lost. That is clear.

But why is it that some men believe in Jesus Christ, while others do not believe in him?

Is it simply because some men, of their own free will, choose to believe in Christ, while others, equally of their own free will, choose not to believe? Is the human will thus the ultimate factor in this decision between believing and not believing?

Or do some men believe and others not believe because they are foreordained to one or the other of these courses in the eternal purpose of God?

If the former alternative is right, the doctrine of predestination is wrong. If the human will is the ultimate factor in his choice between believing and not believing, between being saved and not being saved, then it is rather absurd to go on talking about predestination.

Some people do, indeed, indulge in that absurdity. Predestination, they say, means merely that those who believe are predestined to receive salvation. Whether they believe depends upon themselves, but once they have believed by their own choice, then they are predestinated to receive eternal life.

Surely that is a misuse of language. You can hardly speak of a thing as being "predestined"—as being fixed beforehand—if, as a matter of fact, it is not fixed at all but is uncertain until it is set in motion by an act of the human will.

The reason for such a misuse of language on the part of these people is plain. You see, they believe in the Bible. The Bible uses the word "predestinate"; therefore, they have to use that word, although they reject what that word, on any commonsense view of its meaning, would certainly seem to denote.

Let us not, however, lay the chief stress upon the word, but let us rather get back to the thing that underlies the word. Let us try just to get to the heart of the real question.

What is the real question at issue? I think I can tell you very plainly. It is the question whether a man is predestinated—if for the moment we concede to our adversaries in the debate their loose use of that term—it is the question whether a man is predestinated by God to salvation because he believes in Christ or is enabled to believe in Christ because he is predestinated.

That question is no mere unimportant or purely academic question. It is no mere theological subtlety. On the contrary, it is a matter of profound concern to the souls of men.

I know, indeed, that some truly Christian people decide the question wrongly; they are in error regarding this point and yet hold on to enough of the rest of what the Bible teaches in order that they may be really Christians. Yet it would be a great mistake to draw from that fact the conclusion that the question is unimportant. On the contrary, the more I have looked out upon the state of the church at the present time and the more I have contemplated recent church history, the more firmly I am convinced that error regarding the question that we are now dealing with leads inevitably to more and more error, and often constitutes the entering wedge by which the entire Christian testimony of individuals and of churches is undermined.

Very well. If the question is so important, how shall it be decided? Shall it be decided merely by our likes and dislikes or by mere reasoning on our part as to what we would think right and proper? Shall one party to the debate merely say: "I do not like this notion of an absolute predestination; I do not like this notion that the exact number and identity of the saved and the exact number and identity of the lost are fixed from all eternity in the purpose of God; I much prefer the notion that whether I am saved or lost depends on my own choice." And shall the other party to the debate merely say, in reply to all that: "I, for my part, like just the things that you do not like; I like the notion of an absolute predestination; I like to believe that when a man is saved that depends altogether upon God and not at all upon man; I prefer just to fall back, when I contemplate what is mysterious in this matter, upon the unsearchable counsel of God's will."

Is that the way in which the debate shall be carried on? Shall it be carried on merely as a matter of likes and dislikes? I think not, my friends. Indeed, if it were to be carried on merely in that way, it would hardly need to be carried on at all. If this question is merely a question of our likes and dislikes, then it would seem to fall under the condemnation of the ancient adage that there should be no disputing about tastes. The whole dispute in that case had perhaps better stop. No, my friends. There is just one way to settle this question. It is to see what the Bible says about it. We shall never settle it by saying we like one answer better than another; but we shall settle it only if we listen to what God has said about it in his holy Word.

Very well, then; let us see what the Bible says about this matter of predestination.

But before we seek the Bible answer to the question, it is important for us to be perfectly clear about just what the question is.

We have already stated the question briefly. Are some men predestinated by God to salvation because they believe in Christ, or are some men enabled to believe in Christ in the first place because they are predestinated? In other words, is predestination to salvation dependent upon that act of the human will known as faith, or is that act of the human will known as faith itself the result of predestination?

That is the question briefly put. But it is important to observe that the former of the two answers to the question has been held in two different forms.

If predestination to salvation is held to be dependent upon a decision of the human will between faith and unbelief, then the further question arises whether God knows beforehand what that decision of the human will is going to be.

Some have said, "No. God does not know beforehand what the decision of the human will is going to be; he simply waits to see what man will do, and then, when man has finally acted, God acts accordingly, bestowing salvation upon those who have chosen to believe and sending into eternal death those who have chosen not to believe."

According to this view, the only predestination that we may speak of at all is a conditional predestination. It is predestination with a large "if" attached to it. God does not predestinate any individuals to life or any others to eternal death but simply pre-establishes the general arrangement that *if* anyone believes in Christ he will enter into life and *if* anyone does not believe in Christ he will enter into eternal death. The decision as to which category any individual man will enter rests upon the individual man, and God does not even know how the decision will come out.

The other form in which the theory that we are dealing with is held attributes foreknowledge to God but not really foreordination. God knows beforehand, it holds, what the choice of any man will be as to believing or not believing in Christ, but he does not determine that choice.

This form of the theory, as we pointed out when we were dealing with the divine decrees in general, is a miserable hybrid. It is a halfway measure; it retains all the difficulties, real or supposed, which face the doctrine of a straight out-and-out foreordination by God of all things that come to pass, and it is also faced by overwhelming difficulties of its own.

But it is time to turn to the Bible. Fortunately, the Bible is perfectly clear about this whole question. It is dead against both forms of the theory of which we have just spoken. It is utterly opposed to the view that God does not know what man will decide, and it is equally opposed to the view that what God foreknows he does not foreordain. Over against all such views, it tells us in the clearest possible way, not only in general, that God has foreordained all things according to the counsel of his will but also in particular that he has foreordained the salvation of some men and the loss of others.

That appears really even in the Old Testament. Nothing could be more utterly abhorrent to the Old Testament revelation about God than this notion that the choices of man constitute a sort of exception to the sovereignty of God. If there is any one thing more than another about which the Old Testament is completely clear it is that God is absolute master of the heart of man. He can change the heart; he can take the old heart out and put a new heart in its place. These are just ways of saying that man's actions springing from man's heart do not lie outside the plan of God but form an integral part of it. God, according to the Old Testament, is King, and he is King with an absolute sovereignty which admits no qualifications or exceptions whatsoever.

It is in exercise of that absolute sovereignty, according to the Bible, that God chose Israel. His choice of Israel was not due to any greatness or virtue which Israel could show. The Old Testament rings the changes upon that great thought. No, it was due to God's mysterious grace. Israel was God's people not because it had chosen to be God's people but because it was predestinated to be God's people. A man who misses that has missed the heart and core of Old Testament revelation.

But when we come to the New Testament, what was really clear in the Old Testament becomes even more wonderfully clear and explicit. When men are saved, according to the New Testament, they are saved because of the mysterious foreordination of God.

I can only mention a few of the great passages in which that is taught.

It is taught in the teaching of our Lord reported in the Synoptic Gospels. When Jesus offered salvation, some accepted it and some turned away. Why? Simply because of the choice of men independent of the decree of God? Jesus himself gives the answer. "I thank you, Father, Lord of heaven and earth, that you have hidden these things from the wise and understanding and revealed them to little children; yes, Father, for such was your gracious will" (Matt 11:25–26). "It seemed good in thy sight"—there, according to Jesus, lies the ultimate reason why some received a saving knowledge of God and some did not.

It is taught with special clearness in the teaching of our Lord that is reported in the Gospel according to John. "I am not praying for the world," says Jesus, "but for those whom you have given me" (John 17:9). "Yours they were," says Jesus in a verse a little before, "and you gave them to me" (John 17:6). I do not see how predestination could possibly be taught more clearly than it is in the whole of this high-priestly answer of Jesus in the seventeenth chapter of John. A master thought—I think I might almost say *the* master thought in it—is that predestination precedes faith. The disciples belonged to God—that was in his eternal plan—before they believed; they did not come to belong to God because they believed, but they were enabled to believe because they already belonged to God and because, in execution of his plan, he drew them.

The same doctrine is taught in the book of Acts. That is the book, be it remembered, that contains the famous answer to the question of the jailer at Philippi. "What must I do to be saved?" said the jailer. "Believe in the Lord Jesus, and you will be saved," said Paul (Acts 16:30–31). Salvation is here offered on the sole condition of faith in Jesus Christ. But how comes it, according to the book of Acts, that some believe while others do not? The book gives the answer in the clearest possible way. Speaking of the preaching of Paul and Barnabas at Pisidian Antioch, it says that some of the Gentiles who heard them believed. Well, which of the Gentiles who heard them believed? Did those believe who simply chose of their own motion to believe? Not a bit of it. No, we are expressly told something entirely different. What does the book say about the matter? I will quote its exact words. "As many as were appointed to eternal life believed" (Acts 13:48). I do not see how it would be possible to put the doctrine of predestination more plainly or in fewer words than it is here put. Only those men believe in Christ who are foreordained thereto in the counsels of God. They are not predestinated because they believe, but they are enabled to believe because they are predestinated.

In the epistles of Paul, the great doctrine of predestination is taught again and again. In fact, it would hardly be too much to say that it forms the basis of everything else that Paul teaches. The apostle is concerned, moreover, to clear away any inconsistencies in the minds of his readers regarding this great doctrine; with an utterly fearless logic he pursues our human pride into its last fastnesses and brings us face-to-face with the ultimate fact of God's mysterious will.

"Though they were not yet born," he says of Jacob and Esau, "and had done nothing either good or bad—in order that God's purpose of election might continue, not because of works but because of him who calls—she was told, 'The older will serve the younger.' As it is written, 'Jacob I loved, but Esau I hated'" (Rom 9:11–13). How could it possibly be said more plainly than in this passage that the predestination of Jacob to salvation and of Esau to rejection was not due to anything that they did or may have been foreseen as doing—even to the foreseen faith of one and the foreseen unbelief and disobedience of the other—but to the mysterious choice of God?

Then the apostle takes up an objection. It is an objection that is still urged in the twentieth century against this great doctrine of predestination. Does not the doctrine attribute injustice or partiality to God?

Well, how does the apostle deal with the objection? Does he deal with it in the customary modern fashion of receding from the position against which the objection constitutes an attack? Does he explain away the doctrine of predestination by saying that all he meant was a predestination conditional upon a man's future choices or the like?

Not at all. He does nothing of the kind; he does not recede from his position a single inch and he does not explain the doctrine away. On the contrary, he appeals again in support of the doctrine to the sheer mystery of the sovereign will of God.

"Is there unrighteousness with God?"—so the objection runs—"By no means!" says Paul in answer to it:

> For he says to Moses, "I will have mercy on whom I have mercy, and I will have compassion on whom I have compassion." So then it depends not on human will or exertion, but on God, who has mercy. For the Scripture says to Pharaoh, "For this very purpose I have raised you up, that I might show my power in you, and that my name might be proclaimed in all the earth." So then he has mercy on whomever he wills, and he hardens whomever he wills.
>
> You will say to me then, "Why does he still find fault? For who can resist his will?" But who are you, O man, to answer back to God? Will what is molded say to its molder, "Why have you made me like this?" Has the potter no right over the clay, to make out of the same lump one vessel for honorable use and another for dishonorable use? What if God, desiring to show his wrath and to make known his power, has endured with much patience vessels of wrath prepared for destruction, in order to make known the riches of his glory for vessels of mercy, which he has prepared beforehand for glory—even us whom he has called, not from the Jews only but also from the Gentiles? (Rom 9:15–24)

I do not see how the doctrine of predestination could be set forth more clearly than it is set forth here. But what is particularly to be observed is that this passage does not stand alone in the epistles of Paul and does not stand alone in the Bible. On the contrary, it only makes a little more explicit than usual what is everywhere presupposed. It really stands very close to the heart of what God has revealed to us in his Word.

All men deserving of God's wrath and curse, some men, and these not more deserving of God's favor than others, saved by his mysterious grace—these things are indeed at the heart of the Bible. Obscure them in the interests of human merit or human pride and you have substituted man's wisdom for the Word of God.

In the next talk, I want to clear away certain misconceptions of the great doctrine of predestination. I want to say a few words to you about certain things that the doctrine of predestination does not mean. It does not mean that God's choice of some men for salvation is arbitrary or without good and sufficient reason, as mysterious though the reason may be to us. It does not mean that God takes pleasure in the death of a sinner; it does not mean that the door of salvation is closed to anyone who will enter in; it does not mean that anyone in this life is reduced to the despair of knowing that God's grace will not be extended to him. Some of the horror with which this great doctrine of the Bible is often regarded is due to sad misconceptions regarding what it means.

But what I want to ask you to do just now is to take down your Bible and read what it says for yourselves. If you do that, I think you will be convinced that the doctrine of predestination, so distasteful to human pride, is really the only solid ground of hope for this world and for the next. Little hope have we, my friends, if our salvation depends upon ourselves; but the salvation of which the Bible speaks is rooted in the eternal counsel of God. There is no break and no possibility of break in the mighty working out of God's eternal plan. "And those whom he predestined," says the Bible, "he also called, and those whom he called he also justified, and those whom he justified he also glorified" (Rom 8:30). "For those who love God all things work together for good" (Rom 8:28)—how little comfort there would be in those words if the verse stopped there—if we had been told merely that all things work together for good for those who love God, and then we had been left to kindle that love of God in our cold, dead hearts. But, thank God, the verse does *not* end there. The verse does not just say: "For those who love God all things work together for good." No, it says: "And we know that for those who love God all things work together for good, for those who are called according to his purpose" (Rom 8:28). There, my friends, is the true ground of all our comfort—not in our love, not in our faith, not in anything that is in us, but in that mysterious and eternal counsel of God from which comes all faith, all love, all that we have and are and can be in this world and in the world to come.

24

Objections to Predestination

Before we pass on to the next topic in this little series of talks, I think I ought to say just a few words more in explanation of the great biblical doctrine of predestination, about which I have been speaking in the last two talks.

That doctrine, we observed, applies the doctrine of the decrees of God to the special sphere of salvation. As God brings all things to pass by his eternal purpose in accordance with the counsel of his will, so he brings to pass thus in accordance with the counsel of his will the eternal salvation of some men and the just punishment of other men for their sins. Salvation, therefore, does not depend ultimately upon any act of the human will, even the act of faith in Jesus Christ. Faith itself is induced, in those who are saved in accordance with the eternal purpose of God. They are not predestinated to salvation because they believe, but they are enabled to believe because they are predestinated.

We saw how very pervasive that doctrine is throughout the Bible. It is really taught by implication in the Old Testament, and it becomes fully explicit in the New Testament.

But clearly and fully though this great doctrine is taught in the Bible, a good many people—even a good many Christian people—have special difficulty with it.

Why have they such difficulty?

Well, partly, no doubt because the doctrine runs so directly counter to many of our preconceived ideas. It writes God entirely too large and man entirely too small to suit our human pride. We are so prone to make man's salvation depend on something that is in man.

Yet I think it would be a mistake to let our treatment of people's difficulties stop when we have said that. Some, even though not all, of the difficulties which people have with the doctrine of predestination are due to the fact that people do not understand the doctrine. They think the doctrine means what it does not mean, and so they turn aside from it with a horror which the true doctrine does not at all deserve.

I want therefore, just now, in the present little talk, to tell you one or two things which the doctrine of predestination does *not* mean.

It does not mean, in the first place, that God's choice of some men for salvation while others are passed by is due to mere chance or that there is anything arbitrary about it.

We do not, indeed, know what the reason for God's choice is. We only know that whatever the reason for it may be, the reason is not to be found in any superior receptivity to the gospel on the part of those who are chosen; it is not to be found in any recognition by God of any superior capacity in them for faith in Jesus Christ. On the contrary, those who are saved deserve eternal death just as much as do those who are lost, and they, exactly like those who are lost, are utterly unable to believe in Christ until they are born again by an act which is an act of God alone. Even their faith is worked in them by the Holy Spirit in accordance with God's choice of them from all eternity. Thus, their salvation is not due to anything that is in them. It is a matter of pure grace.

But because *we* do not know what the reason is for God's choice of some and his passing by of others, that does not mean that there is no reason. As a matter of fact, there is without doubt an altogether good and sufficient reason. We can be perfectly sure of that. God never acts in arbitrary fashion; he acts always in accordance with infinite wisdom; all his acts are directed to infinitely high and worthy ends. We must just trust him for that. We do not know why God has acted thus and not otherwise, but we know the One who knows and we rest in his infinite justice and goodness and wisdom.

I think the Christian man glories in his ignorance of God's counsels at this point. He rejoices that he does not know. The hymns of the evangelical church are full of celebrations of the *wonder* of God's grace. It is such a strange, such an utterly mysterious thing that God should extend his mercy to such sinners as we are. We deserved nothing but his wrath and curse. It would have been completely just if we had been lost as others are lost; it is a supreme wonder that we are saved. We cannot see why it is; we could not possibly believe it unless it were written so plainly in God's Word. We can only rest in it as a supreme mystery of grace.

In the second place, the doctrine of predestination does not mean that God rejoices in the death of a sinner. The Bible distinctly says the contrary.

Hear that great verse in the thirty-third chapter of Ezekiel: "As I live, declares the Lord GOD, I have no pleasure in the death of the wicked, but that the wicked turn from his way and live" (Ezek 33:11).

It may be the same thing that is taught in the First Epistle to Timothy, where it is said: God desires "all men to be saved, and to come unto the knowledge of the truth" (1 Tim 2:4; KJV). This latter verse cannot possibly mean that God has determined by an act of his will that all men should be saved. As a matter of fact, not all men are saved. The Bible makes that abundantly clear; without that, all its solemn warnings become a mockery. But if, when as a matter of fact not all men are saved, God had determined that all men should be saved, then that would mean that God's decree has been defeated and his will overthrown. In that case, God would simply cease to be God.

The verse must mean something quite different from that blasphemous thing. That is clear. But what does it mean? I am inclined to think it means very much what that great Ezekiel passage means; I am inclined to think it means simply that God takes pleasure in the salvation of sinners and that he does not take pleasure in the punishment of the unsaved.

Another view has, indeed, been held by some. It has been suggested that the phrase "all men" in this verse in First Timothy means "all sorts of men," and that the verse is directed against those who limited salvation to the Jews as distinguished from the Gentiles or to the wise as distinguished from the unwise. There is perhaps something to be said for such a view because of the context in which the verse occurs. But I am rather inclined to think that the phrase "all men" is to be taken more strictly and that the verse means that God takes pleasure in the salvation of the saved and does not take pleasure in the punishment of those who are lost, so that so far as his pleasure in the thing directly accomplished is concerned he wishes that all men shall be saved.

At any rate, that is clearly the meaning of the Ezekiel passage, whatever may be true of the First Timothy passage; and a very precious truth it is indeed. The punishment of sinners—their just punishment for their sins—does, as we have seen, have a place in the plan of God. But the Bible makes perfectly plain that God does not take pleasure in it for its own sake. It is necessary for high and worthy ends, mysterious though those ends are to us; it has its place in God's plan. But in itself it is not a thing in which he delights. He is good. He delights not in the death of the wicked but in the salvation of those who are saved by his grace.

In the third place, the doctrine of predestination does not mean that men are saved against their will or that they are condemned to eternal punishment when they want to believe in Christ and be saved.

I think that it is in this misconception that the really central objection to the great doctrine with which we have been dealing arises in the minds of so many people.

They have a sort of notion that the doctrine of predestination means that some people, before they decide whether to believe in Christ or not, can know beforehand whether they are predestined to salvation or predestined to destruction.

They imagine someone saying—on the assumption that the doctrine of predestination is true—"I have listened to the gospel; it touches my heart a little; I might possibly accept it: but what is the use? Whether I shall be saved or lost is all fixed beforehand anyway; what difference, therefore, does it make what I decide?"

Or—what seems even more horrible—they imagine someone saying, again on the assumption that the doctrine of predestination is true: "I have listened to the gospel; I wish I were one of those who could accept it. But, you see, they are predestinated to salvation, they are among the elect of God, whereas I have been predestinated to destruction, so that, struggle as I may, there is for me no hope."

Or—to take another example—they imagine someone saying, again on the assumption that the doctrine of predestination is true: "I am among the elect of God; I can look down upon those who are not among the elect; and since I am among the elect I can live as I please, being assured that ultimately the plan of God for me will be worked out and I shall enter into eternal blessedness when I die."

All three of these horrible examples, and many others similar to them, are based upon a totally wrong notion of what the doctrine of predestination means.

That doctrine does not mean that those who are predestinated to eternal life are saved against their will. On the contrary, only those who willingly embrace Jesus Christ as he is offered to us in the gospel are saved. Suppose a man says, "I have decided not to have faith in Christ." Can such a man comfort himself with the thought that perhaps he is predestinated to eternal life after all? Certainly not, provided that the decision not to have faith in Jesus Christ is the man's final decision. No man who does not willingly have faith in Jesus Christ is saved. That is perfectly clear.

But when a man does willingly put his trust in Jesus Christ, does that act of the man's will lie outside the purpose of God? That is what the Bible most emphatically denies. No, it does not lie outside the purpose of God. No man is saved against his will. That is clear. But his will itself is determined in accordance with God's eternal plan.

I think I can make clear exactly what I mean if I take a very simple example from the Bible itself.

When Paul was in that ship of Alexandria being taken as a prisoner to Rome, he said to the frightened sailors and passengers: "there will be no loss of life among you, but only of the ship" (Acts 27:22). He said that as a prophet, having received, as he expressly told the company, supernatural guidance. He had had revealed to him part of God's eternal plan. It was predestined in the purpose of God that no one on that ship was to lose his life. The preservation of everyone in that ship's company was absolutely certain before it was accomplished.

Very well, then. So far, so good. But what do we read a little farther down? What did Paul say to that ship's company a little later? Here is what he said: "Unless these men stay in the ship, you cannot be saved" (Acts 27:31). The sailors, namely, had been about to flee from the ship in the boat. To stop them, Paul said to the centurion and to the soldiers: "Unless these men stay in the ship, you cannot be saved."

He had previously told the ship's company that they would all be preserved alive. That came on the authority of God; it was absolutely certain; it was predestinated. Yet now he tells them that that thing which was absolutely certain to take place would not take place unless a certain condition were fulfilled. It would not take place unless the sailors stayed in the ship.

Did that condition at all destroy the certainty of the working out of God's plan in accordance with the previous prophecy? Not a bit. Why not? Simply because God provided for the fulfilling of the condition when he provided for the accomplishment of the final result for which the fulfilling of the condition was necessary.

Yes, it was certainly true that that ship's company would not be saved unless the sailors remained in the ship. But that did not involve any risk lest the plan of God might be defeated. You see, the sailors did remain in the ship, and so the original prophecy went straight on to its fulfillment.

Those sailors did not remain in the ship by chance. No, they were, although they did not know it, under the guiding hand of God. The centurion and the soldiers who kept them in the ship were God's instruments in seeing to the final accomplishment of God's plan.

We learn by this simple example a very great truth. It is simply this—that when the final result is foreordained by God all the steps to it are also foreordained. Straight through all the apparently tangled course of human history runs the accomplishment of God's eternal plan.

Apply that to the matter of faith and salvation, and I think some of your difficulty with the doctrine of predestination will disappear. God has predestinated some men to final salvation, just as he predestinated to the preservation of their earthly lives those men who were on that ship. Yet in both cases the fulfillment of a condition was necessary to the accomplishment of the final result. The men on that ship were all predestinated to get safely ashore; yet they would not have finally got safely ashore unless the centurion had kept those sailors in the ship. So, God's elect are all predestinated to eternal salvation; yet they will not attain eternal salvation unless they believe in the Lord Jesus Christ.

Does the interposition of a necessary condition introduce any uncertainty in the final accomplishment of God's plan? Not a bit of it. Not in either case. Not in the simple case of the preservation of that ship's company on that ship of Alexandria, and not in the case of the salvation of God's elect. In both cases God has provided for the fulfillment of all the conditions just as truly as he has provided for the accomplishment of the ultimate end.

But is our sense of the freedom of our will at all incompatible with the complete certainty of God's ordering of our lives? Well, I am just going to appeal at this point to any man within the sound of my voice who is aware of the moment when he was born again. Not all Christians are aware of the moment when they were born again. All have been born again, but not all know when they were born again. But some can give the very moment when they were saved. I am appealing now to any one of these.

You were born again at that blessed moment, were you not, my brother? Now was that your act or God's act? The Bible tells you it was God's act— "who were born, not of blood nor of the will of the flesh nor of the will of man, but of God" (John 1:13). And your experience confirms the Bible, does it not? You know in your inmost soul that it was God's act. You were blind and God made you to see. God did it, not you. You are as sure of that as you are sure of anything in this world.

Now at the moment when you were born again you believed in Christ.

That was the immediate sign of your being born again, and it was due solely to the wonderful regenerating power of the Spirit of God. Well, my brother, did that wonderful act of God do violence to your freedom as a person? Did you feel that the newfound faith that you had in the Lord Jesus Christ was any the less your act—a free choice of your will—because it was due to the resistless regenerating act of the Spirit of God? I think not, my friend. I think rather that you will be inclined to say you never were so free as you were at that blessed moment when, in absolutely resistless fashion, the Holy Spirit of God worked faith in you and you turned to the Lord Jesus Christ as your Savior and Lord.

No, indeed, the eternal plan of God and even the execution of that plan at the supernatural act of regeneration or the new birth are not in the slightest incompatible with our freedom and our responsibility as personal beings.

What a great mistake it is, then, to think that the doctrine of predestination is contrary to the free offer of salvation to all. Of course, that offer is given to all. Of course, it remains true in the fullest and richest sense that whosoever will may come. None who will trust in Christ is excluded. None, I say—none without any exception whatever.

Never have we any right to assume that any man or group of men that we can name is outside of God's plan for salvation; never have we any right to assume that any man upon this earth is beyond the reach of the grace of God; never have we the right to withhold the gospel from any man wherever he may be.

But when we thus proclaim the gospel, what a comfort the doctrine of predestination is! What a comfort it is to know that salvation depends solely upon God's mysterious grace! We all deserved to perish in our sins, and so did all those to whom we preach. But God's grace is wonderful. He has in his eternal plan a people chosen for his name. Happy are we if we are God's instruments in gathering into his kingdom any of those who from all eternity belong to him.

25

God's Works of Creation and Providence

Having spoken of the decrees of God, I come now to speak of the way in which God executes his decrees.

But is God's execution of his decrees to be distinguished from his decrees themselves? There have, I believe, been those who have said, "No." With God, they say, to plan is the same thing as to act; finite creatures, they say, may plan first and act afterward, but God's plan and God's action are the same thing. Indeed, some of those who engage in this way of thinking go, I believe, still further. They say that not only is action the same as purpose with God, but purpose is the same as thought. We, they say, can think a thing and not do it, but for God to think a thing is to purpose that it shall come into being, and for him to purpose that it shall come into being is the same as bringing it into being. The vastness of the universe, they say, is simply the unfolding of the thoughts of God. But these persons are mistaken; they have fallen into a very serious error.

It is certainly true that to God there is no external obstacle to making realities of all of his thoughts. He has infinite power, and anything that he thinks, he can do.

But, because he can do everything that he thinks, it does not follow that everything that he thinks, he does do. The things that he does actually do are chosen with perfect wisdom out of an infinity of things that he chooses not to do. Never ought we to confuse God's thoughts with his purposes.

Indeed, if we did fall into that confusion we should be in danger of obscuring the true nature of the personality of God. If God purposes everything that he thinks, if there is no selection in his purposes among the things that he contemplates, then it might almost be said that the purposes of God are only falsely called purposes and become rather the involuntary unfolding of some impersonal dialectic process.

But if God's purposes are to be distinguished from his thoughts, a further distinction must also be made. As God's purposes must be distinguished from his thoughts, so also his actions must be distinguished from his purposes. There is a true distinction between the decrees of God and the execution of his decrees.

To obliterate that distinction is again to engage in a perversion of a truth.

It is perfectly true that everything that God purposes comes inevitably to accomplishment. *We* purpose many things that we do not bring to pass, but it is not so with God. What he purposes he always does.

It is perfectly true also that there is no before and after to God. He is beyond time; he is infinite and eternal; he does not have to wait, as we do, for any stream of time, independent of him, to bear him on to the point where he can engage in the execution of his decrees. All things to him are eternally present. It might seem, therefore, as though in his case there were no interval and indeed no distinction between a decree and the execution of the decree, no distinction between purpose and act.

Such reasoning, however, is fallacious and dangerous. Even if we cannot apply temporal notions to the life of God, even if therefore there is to him no interval, in the ordinary sense, between purpose and act, still there is an important distinction between the two. It is still important to remember not only that God is all-wise in his plans, but also that he is all-powerful in his acts.

But is it true to say even that there is no interval of time between God's purposes and his actions, between his decrees and the carrying out of his decrees? I think it is but a half-truth.

It is true that God, being eternal, is beyond time. But that is not to say that time has no real existence; it is not to say that time, as we know it, is a mere semblance. No, what we ought to say, as I think I heard one of my teachers say years ago, is that God created time when he created finite things. He *really* created time, and we really stand in a temporal sequence.

Therefore, we are not uttering an untruth when we say that he purposed long ago what he brings to pass now. All things that come to pass were in his purpose from all eternity, but he brings them severally to pass at those points in the order of time which he in his infinite wisdom has fixed. We who stand, as finite creatures, in the order of time observe the gradual unfolding of the execution of God's eternal plan; and as we observe its gradual unfolding, as we observe the way in which, without haste yet with perfect sureness, God's purposes are worked out, we join in praise of him to whom a thousand years are but as yesterday when it is past and as a watch in the night, in praise of him whose ways are not as our ways and whose thoughts are not as our thoughts, who, in infinite wisdom, has planned all things from the beginning and brings all things to pass according to his eternal purpose and in his own good time. Thus do all finite creatures and the very order of time in which they stand serve the eternal purpose for which they were created: the glory of God.

Holding, therefore, that there is a true distinction between God's decrees and the execution of his decrees, we are prepared to ask how God executes his decrees. The Shorter Catechism says, in answer to that question, "God executeth his decrees in the works of creation and providence" (WSC Q&A 8).

I want to say a few words in turn about God's work of creation and God's works of providence.

With regard to the work of creation, the Shorter Catechism says it is "God's making all things of nothing" (WSC Q&A 9).

I think we ought to pause a few moments to ask what that means.

The answer is in the main surely not difficult. Look out upon the vast universe in which we are living. How did it come into being? Various answers have been given, but the answer of the Bible is plain. The universe came into being, the Bible says, by the act of a personal God; it came into being because God made it. That has at least the merit of being easy to understand.

But what is meant by the words "of nothing" in that definition? What is meant when it is said that God made all things "of nothing"? Two things at least are meant.

In the first place, it is meant that God did not make all things of something; he did not make the universe out of some already existing material.

A great many people have held that when God made the universe he found some material ready to his hand. He molded that material, they say; he gave it its form and he reduced it from chaos to order: but the material was already there.

Then the question arises: "From where did that already existing material come?"

When we look at the world as it is, we ask naturally how it came into being. We can trace its processes back a certain distance. Everything has a cause. This thing happened because that thing previously happened; and that thing in turn happened because some still earlier thing happened. So we can reason from effect to cause through a prolonged series. But unless the series is really infinite, we come at length to the beginning of the series. All the causes that we see in the world about us were in turn caused by other causes; but at the beginning of the series must stand a First Cause, a cause that is not caused by anything else.

What is that First Cause? The simple Christian, with his Bible open before him, has a ready answer. The First Cause is God. The universe came into being, he says, by the voluntary act of an infinite and eternal person.

That answer has the merit of simplicity. There is something wonderfully satisfying about it. It does not make the mistake that so many philosophies do of giving to what is lower an honor that would seem rightfully to belong to what is higher.

I do make bold to say that when a man has once had the veil taken from his eyes—so that he can think of God as the personal God, the living God, the sole and all-sufficient First Cause of all things—he wonders at his former blindness and pities with all his soul those who still do not understand.

How sadly this simple answer to the riddle of the universe is marred or rather destroyed by those who say that when God made the universe he made it out of something! If God made the universe out of something, then that something was already in existence, and in existence independent of God, when the universe was made.

In that case, what do we arrive at when we start out in our search for a First Cause? What do we arrive at when we trace back the things that now are to their causes, and then those causes back to still earlier causes of which they in turn are effects, until we get to a cause which was not produced by any previous cause, which, in other words, was the First Cause? Why, on the theory about which we are now speaking, we get to not one First Cause but two first causes—God and the material which he used when he made the world. But two first causes are one too many. A doctrine like that will never be a satisfactory view of the world. It gives us a blind, inert material which is quite unfitted to be regarded as a First Cause, and it gives us a God who is no God at all. It gives us a God who is not really infinite but is limited in his working by a world-stuff which does not owe its being to him.

For such dualism—if you will pardon me for using a somewhat technical word—we turn with relief to the high theism of the Bible. Our God, the God of the Bible, is no mere artificer using as best he may the material put into his hands, but he is the great originator of all things that are. There are not two first causes—God and the material that God used—but one First Cause: God and God alone.

That is the first thing that we mean when we say that God made all things of nothing. We mean that he did not make all things of something; we mean that he did not make all things out of some previously existing material.

But there is another thing that we mean when we say that God made all things of nothing. We mean that he did not make all things of the substance of his own being.

If he made all things out of the substance of his own being, then all things are a part of God, and we have an error akin to the deadly error of pantheism.

There are many who have fallen into that error. The world, they hold, is an emanation in the life of God; it is an unfolding of his being; its stuff is the stuff of which he himself is composed.

That error, like so many other errors of which we have spoken, is the perversion of a great truth. It is certainly true that the universe proceeded from God as its cause. When the Bible teaches us that all things were made of nothing, it does not mean that all things came into being without a cause. On the contrary, all things came into being with a thoroughly adequate cause—namely, God.

It is perfectly true, moreover, that when God brought the universe into being he did not do so without reference to his own nature. On the contrary, he acted in accordance with his own infinite wisdom. The creation of the world was not an arbitrary act but served high and worthy ends, and those ends were in accordance with the Creator's infinite goodness and wisdom.

But, in saying all that, we are not at all saying that the universe proceeded by some process of emanation from the being of God. On the contrary, it was created by an act of God's will. God did not owe it to anyone to create the world, and the creation of the world was not necessary to the completion of his own life. God is absolutely self-sufficient; he was fully God before the world ever was created, and the present existence of the world is not necessary to his divine life. "Before the mountains were brought forth, or ever you had formed the earth and the world, from everlasting to everlasting you are God" (Ps 90:2). Being God from all eternity, he determined for his own high and worthy ends to bring this universe into being. We can only stand in awe before the Creator's infinite wisdom and power.

Thus, it is highly important for us to stress those words "of nothing," in that definition of the Shorter Catechism. God did not make all things of something already existing, and he did not draw forth all things out of the substance of his being; but he made all things of nothing.

But if those words "of nothing" are to be stressed in that definition, we should also not forget the words "all things." We should not forget the fact that, in God's work of creation, "things" were created.

There have been many who have denied that. There is no such thing, they say, as an external world. When I contemplate a tree, they say, all I really have knowledge of is the idea of the tree in my own mind. I cannot really go beyond what is in my mind. But are there other minds? I have never been able to see that people of this way of thinking really have any right to hold that there are. A consistent idealist, I am inclined to think, ought to hold that even other minds have no existence except as an idea in his own mind. But consistently or not many idealists do hold that there are other minds, and many of them hold that there is a supreme mind, and that the universe exists only in that supreme mind: the mind of God.

Against such a philosophy, the Christian, with his Bible open before him, ought to believe in the existence of an external world. I think he ought to quote with approval what I remember hearing B. B. Warfield quote years ago: "What is mind? No matter. What is matter? Never mind." Mind and matter ought not to be confused. And certainly, the Christian ought to hold that our minds, and the matter of which our bodies are composed, and this whole universe to which our bodies and our minds belong were truly created by an act of the all-wise and all-powerful God.

What sort of universe is this which thus came into being by the act of the all-powerful God? Is it a good universe or is it a bad universe? Pessimists have said that it is a bad universe. Indeed, some of them have said that it is the worst universe that could possibly have been created. What does the Christian say?

The Bible gives the answer very simply, in words of one syllable: "And God saw everything that he had made, and behold, it was very good" (Gen 1:31). No, this universe is not a bad universe. Nothing that God makes is a failure. It is not a bad universe but a good universe.

Indeed, it is the very best universe that could possibly have been created. God is never content with the second best; there are no limitations either to his wisdom or to his power; nothing that he does varies by a hair's breadth from that which is absolutely best.

When we say that the universe is the best that could possibly have been created, we do not, of course, mean that it is the best for our ends, and we do not necessarily mean that it is the universe that conduces the most to our pleasure. On the contrary, we are obliged, sooner or later, to learn the hard lesson that the universe was not made for our enjoyment alone. We have to learn to take the universe as it is.

Accepting the universe is the root idea of a book by a brilliant and thoughtful skeptic of the present day—Walter Lippmann's *Preface to Morals*, which was a best seller a few years ago. A baby, says Walter Lippmann, thinks that the universe is run just for its peculiar benefit; all that it has to do is to reach out its little hand and those things will be given to it that satisfy its wants. But then, as it grows older, it learns that very often the reached-out hand has to be drawn back empty; it learns that there is a vast world outside quite indifferent to its desires. When it really learns that, it is becoming mature.

Many men, says Walter Lippmann, never do become thoroughly mature, never do really grow up, never do really get rid of the notion that the universe either is or ought to be run for their benefit. In order to get rid of that notion, says he, it is not sufficient that a man should have mere knowledge of details about the universe. A boy can take you out into the night and rehearse to you a great many facts about the stars, but unless he "feels the vast indifference of the universe to his own fate, and has placed himself in the perspective of cold and illimitable space, he has not looked maturely at the heavens."[1]

Well, we can go with Walter Lippmann part way. We can go with him in what he says on the negative side. We can go with him in holding that the universe does not exist for our particularly benefit, and that we are worse than petulant children if we complain because of that fact.

Only, we differ from him profoundly in what he seeks to substitute for this petulance of babyhood. He seeks to substitute for it what he calls "disinterestedness"—the recognition of and acquiescence in the fact that the universe is indifferent to our fate. We substitute for it the conviction that the universe was created for the glory of God.

---

1. Walter Lippman, *A Preface to Morals*, 1929.

For that end, the glory of God, though not for the ends that we might have cherished, this universe is the best universe that could possibly have been created. To that end, those starry heavens of which Walter Lippmann speaks contribute their part. When we contemplate their vastness, we are impressed indeed with our own insignificance. We can go with Walter Lippmann so far. But, unlike Mr. Lippmann, we do not stop there. To us the stars have no merely negative message; they do not merely tell us what we are not; rather, they also tell us what God is: "The spacious firmament on high, With all the blue ethereal sky, And spangled heavens, a shining frame, Their great Original proclaim."[2]

Or, in the words of Holy Scripture, of which that hymn of Joseph Addison is after all but a feeble exposition, "the heavens declare the glory of God, and the sky above proclaims his handiwork" (Ps 19:1). The end for which the universe was made is not, indeed, our enjoyment. But that does not mean that we know nothing about what the end is. The end, the Bible tells us, is the glory of God. And that end the universe attains in God's own way.

But are those starry heavens, is that vast fabric of nature, really indifferent to our fate? The Bible has something to say about that also. "And we know that for those who love God all things work together for good, for those who are called according to his purpose" (Rom 8:28). But those who can take to themselves the comfort of that text are not those who regard themselves, in childish fashion, as the end for which the creation exists; but they are those who have been enabled to find their true blessedness and the true purpose of all the world in singing the Creator's praise.

---

2. Joseph Addison, "The Spacious Firmament on High," 1712.

26

God's Works of Providence

In the last talk, I spoke to you about God's work of creation. It is a mysterious subject, yet the teaching of the Bible about it is, in its great outlines, plain. How did this vast universe come into being? The answer of the Bible is very simple. God made it. He did not make it out of some already existing material, and he did not draw it from his own being; he made it of nothing. By his act of creation, that came to be which before was not.

When God had thus created the universe, what was his relation to the universe that he had created? No relation at all, said the deists of 150 years ago. The universe, they said, was allowed by its creator to run of itself like a vast machine, and it is vain to seek any interference or governance from the great artificer.

That deistic view is now out of date. I do not think that it is widely held today—at least not among educated people. But other errors equally serious have taken its place.

Some have said that there is no such thing as a continued existence of the universe at all, but that God creates it anew every instant. All God's governance of the world is thus regarded as a work of creation; the work of creation is regarded as the only work in which God executes his decrees.

That view, at first sight, might seem to do honor to God. It denies to the world any continuity of existence and finds in the creative activity of God the only continuity that there is. But, in point of fact, that view does not really do honor to God but endangers very seriously our sense of the distinction between God and the world. If the world has no continuous existence, then it is hard to see exactly how God can be regarded as distinct from the world. But the distinction between God and the world that he has created is at the heart of what the Bible teaches us about God.

There are other ways also in which this theory of continuous creation can be shown to be contrary to God's Word. The Bible plainly teaches the real existence of the world; the continuity of the universe is not, according to the Bible, a mere semblance. When God created the universe, he created a true order of nature operating under laws established for it by its Creator. The Bible distinguishes sharply God's creation of the universe from God's government of the universe already created.

The truth lies, then, neither with those who say that the universe once created continued thereafter to exist without any activity of God, nor, on the other hand, with those who say that all the continuity which the world seems to possess is simply the continuity of a constantly repeated act of creation. Where, then, does the truth lie?

The truth lies in the biblical doctrine of providence. That doctrine is summed up in the following answer of the Shorter Catechism: "God's works of providence are his most holy, wise and powerful preserving and governing all his creatures, and all their actions" (WSC Q&A 11).

Notice in the first place that in this definition God is said to *preserve* all his creatures. What does that mean? It means that according to the Bible nothing in the whole universe would continue to exist for one slightest fraction of a second without God. We have said that the universe has real existence; its continuity is not a mere semblance. But that does not mean that it exists independently of the continued activity of God. On the contrary, it would cease to exist the very moment God should withdraw his preserving hand.

In the second place, the Shorter Catechism says that God's works of providence are his *governing* of all his creatures and all their actions. God's activity in the universe that he has made is not limited to his keeping it from destruction. He also works in it and through it in a positive fashion, bringing to pass through it those things that are in accordance with his eternal plan.

We noticed that fact when we were dealing with the decrees of God. All things that happen in the whole universe are included, we observed, in God's purpose; nothing that happens surprises God. But now we are speaking of the ways in which God accomplishes his purpose, the ways in which he carries out his plan. One of those ways in which he accomplishes his purpose is to be found in his works of providence.

When God accomplishes his purposes by his works of providence, is it God that works or is it the forces and the persons created by him?

Some have said that it is only the forces and the persons created by him. The people who have said that are the deists of whom we have already spoken. They hold that the activity of God in the universe is limited to the initial work of creation, and that once created the universe runs itself like a machine, without interference from God. It is perfectly clear that this deistic view is quite contrary to the Bible.

Others have said that it is God only who works, and that the forces and persons created by God do not really work at all. Everything that happens, they say, is an immediate work of God. God, they say, is the only cause, and it is only in appearance that, within the course of the world, one thing can be said to cause another.

Thus, according to this view, when we see a bullet hole in a pane of glass and ask what caused it and come to the conclusion that it was due to the firing of a gun across the street, we have no real right to talk in any such way; we have no real right to say that the hole in the glass was caused by the passage of the bullet through the glass, and the passage of the bullet through the glass was caused by the firing of the gun, and the firing of the gun was caused by the pulling of the trigger, and the pulling of the trigger was caused by the action of the man who had the gun in his hand. Not at all, say the persons of the way of thinking with which we are now dealing; this whole idea of cause within the course of this world is merely an illusion. What we call cause is really only observed sequence. The making of the hole in the pane of glass came after the firing of the gun, but we cannot say that it was caused by it; the emergence of the bullet from the gun came after the explosion of the powder in the cartridge, but we cannot say that it was caused by it. No, what we commonly think of as a relationship of cause and effect between different things in the course of the world, they say, is really only the observed manner of God's working. God, they say, is the only cause.

Is such a way of looking at the matter correct? Where can we get the answer to that question?

Well, we cannot get the answer from the scientists. They have usually no help to give us at this point. It is their business, they tell us, to observe what happens, not to explain how it comes to happen. They are content—at least many of them are—to leave the whole question as to what is meant when we say that one thing causes another to the philosophers and theologians.

Now I am expressing no opinion as to whether this modesty on the part of the scientists is wise or unwise. It may turn out that it is unwise, and it may turn out that, in being indifferent to the question whether the so-called forces of nature have real existence or are a mere semblance, the scientists have deprived science of its true dignity and its true basis, and that in the long run science even in detail may feel the ill effects of such degradation. Possibly, in other words, it may be important for science, as for every other branch of human endeavor, to be based upon a sound philosophy. No doubt it is better for the scientists to refrain from any philosophical opinion whatever than to do what they have so often done—namely, dish out to us a very crude philosophy as though that crude philosophy itself were science. But the best thing of all would be for them to have a true philosophy. It is better to have no philosophy at all than a bad philosophy, but it would be still better to have a good philosophy.

However that may be, whatever the effects in the field of what in the narrow sense of the word is called science, it is quite clear that to hold that God is the only cause and that nothing in the universe can be said to be the cause of anything else is quite disastrous to the moral life of man, and quite disastrous to man's view of God.

This opinion involves logically the complete denial of human responsibility. If the firing of that gun across the street is not the cause of the passage of the bullet through the pane, then the man who fired the gun cannot be said to be responsible for what damage the bullet may have done or for the death of anyone whom it may have killed.

This view involves also a real denial of the holiness of God. If God alone acts and the forces apparently operating in the world are merely ways of his working and are not really themselves working at all, then what we call the universe is merely a phase of the life of God, and the distinction between God and the world is broken down. But that distinction between God and the world is quite fundamental in any high view of God. It involves what the Bible calls the holiness of God. To break it down is disastrous indeed.

The Bible gives no warrant whatever for any such view, but plainly teaches that there are forces truly operating in the world. The theologians speak of those forces truly operating in the world as "second causes." God is the First Cause, but the forces of nature and the free actions of personal beings whom God has created are second causes; and it is extremely important, if we would be true to the Bible, that the existence of second causes should not be denied.

Thus, when it is asked whether, when anything happens in the course of nature, it is some force of nature or God that causes that event, the true answer is, "Both." That event is caused by a force operating in the world and it is caused by God.

Only, it is very important to observe that the two causes are not on the same plane. They are not coordinate, but one is completely subordinate to the other. In every event in the natural world God has completely accomplished what he willed to accomplish. He is not limited in any way by the forces of nature or by the free actions of his creatures. They truly act; but they truly act only as he has determined that they shall act. The correct way, therefore, of expressing the relationship between second causes and God, the great First Cause, is to say that God makes use of second causes to accomplish what is in accordance with his eternal purpose. Second causes are not independent forces whose cooperation he needs, but they are means that he employs exactly as he wills.

That is what the Shorter Catechism means when it says that "God's works of providence are his most holy, wise and powerful preserving and governing all his creatures, and all their actions" (WSC Q&A 11).

Stress should be laid also upon that word "all." No actions of created things lie outside the field of God's works of providence. By them all he brings to pass what he has determined in his eternal plan.

How pervasive is God's government of the world! It includes, in the first place, the ordinary operations of nature—rain, snow, hail, sunshine, the sprouting of the seed, the ripening of the grain. With what matchless beauty is this part of God's care for his creatures set forth in the 104th Psalm:

You make springs gush forth in the valleys;
    they flow between the hills;
they give drink to every beast of the field;
    the wild donkeys quench their thirst.
Beside them the birds of the heavens dwell;
    they sing among the branches.
From your lofty abode you water the mountains;
    the earth is satisfied with the fruit of your work.

You cause the grass to grow for the livestock
    and plants for man to cultivate,
that he may bring forth food from the earth

and wine to gladden the heart of man,
oil to make his face shine
    and bread to strengthen man's heart.

The trees of the LORD are watered abundantly,
    the cedars of Lebanon that he planted.
In them the birds build their nests;
    the stork has her home in the fir trees.
The high mountains are for the wild goats;
    the rocks are a refuge for the rock badgers.

He made the moon to mark the seasons;
    the sun knows its time for setting.
You make darkness, and it is night,
    when all the beasts of the forest creep about.
The young lions roar for their prey,
    seeking their food from God.
When the sun rises, they steal away
    and lie down in their dens.
Man goes out to his work
    and to his labor until the evening.

O LORD, how manifold are your works!
    In wisdom have you made them all;
    the earth is full of your creatures.
Here is the sea, great and wide,
    which teems with creatures innumerable,
    living things both small and great.
There go the ships,
    and Leviathan, which you formed to play in it.

These all look to you,
    to give them their food in due season.
When you give it to them, they gather it up;
    when you open your hand, they are filled with good things.
When you hide your face, they are dismayed;
    when you take away their breath, they die
    and return to their dust.

> When you send forth your Spirit, they are created,
> and you renew the face of the ground. (Ps 104:10–30)

Have we outgrown that wonderful passage? Have we outgrown the conviction that God feeds the lions that roar after their prey in the night, that he provides a habitation for the birds of heaven, that all his creatures, small and great, wait upon him that he may give them their meat in due season? Have we outgrown the words of the Lord Jesus when he said that God has so clothed the lilies of the field as that "even Solomon in all his glory was not arrayed like one of these" (Luke 12:27)? Have we outgrown his conviction that not a sparrow falls to the ground without God (Matt 10:29), and that God feeds them from day to day (Luke 12:24)?

Has scientific agriculture or the scientific study of botany or biology made these things to be out-of-date? Have we with our overmuch knowledge outgrown that simple conviction of Jesus and of the psalmist that every living creature receives its meat from God (Luke 12:24; Ps 104:21)?

Well, my friends, if that is so, if these things have really come to be out of date, then we have lost far more than we have gained. We have gained knowledge in some directions, but we have lost a knowledge that is vastly more important than all the knowledge that we have acquired.

Let us not blame science for that loss. There is nothing in modern science that invalidates the teaching of the Bible regarding God's care for his creatures; nay, there is much that wonderfully confirms it, if only we had eyes to see. Something quite other than true science has put the mist and darkness over men's eyes.

When will the lost simplicity and the lost profundity be regained? Only when God in his supernatural grace shall have removed the blindness of sin in order that again men may see. When that blessed day comes, men will look out again upon the wonders of the world with the profound simplicity of the psalmist, and will detect in all the processes of nature no mere cold, unguided working of some mechanical force but the mysterious and infinitely discriminating hand of the living God.

Are, then, God's works of providence limited to his use of the impersonal forces of nature? Is there a little island of resistance to his will here in the midst of his world—a little island of resistance in the form of the free actions of personal beings? Are those actions beyond his governance? Has he, so far as they are concerned, abdicated the throne of his power?

We saw in dealing with the decrees of God that there are some who say yes. But we saw also that the Bible says no. The Bible plainly teaches that God works his will just as surely through the free actions of personal beings, including man, as he does through the courses of the heavenly bodies or the silent ripening of the grain.

I need not now repeat the proof of that fact. It is writ large in the Bible from Genesis to Revelation. God, according to the Bible, is master of the heart of man just as much as he is master of the impersonal forces of nature, and from man's heart man's actions come.

Even the wicked actions of men serve God's purposes and it is by his works of providence that he permits those wicked actions to be done.

Just pass in review, my friends, the history of Bible times. Nation after nation rises on the scene—Egypt, Assyria, Babylon, Persia, Rome. Wicked nations are these—cruel, hard, and proud. Yet how does the Bible represent them? How does the Bible represent even the cruel devastations that they carried on amid the people of God? As defeating God's eternal purpose, as contravening his governance of the world? No, my friends, the Bible represents those wicked nations as unwitting instruments in God's almighty hand.

Take also the wicked acts not of nations but of individual men. Were *they* accomplished without the providence of God; did *they* defeat his governance of the world? The Bible tells us no. Joseph said to his wicked brethren, "You meant evil against me, but God meant it for good, to bring it about that many people should be kept alive" (Gen 50:20). Even the supreme crime of all the ages, the crucifixion of Jesus our Lord, was not brought about apart from the providence of God. "For truly," says the book of Acts, "in this city there were gathered together against your holy servant Jesus, whom you anointed, both Herod and Pontius Pilate, along with the Gentiles and the peoples of Israel, to do whatever your hand and your plan had predestined to take place" (Acts 4:27–28).

No, my friends, there are no exceptions here. Everything that is done in the whole course of the world—by forces of nature or by the free actions of men good and bad—everything has God as its great First Cause.

But though God brings all these things to pass, he brings them to pass in widely different ways. He does not bring to pass the free actions of personal beings in the same way as the way in which he brings to pass the ripening of the grain. He brings to pass the actions of personal beings in a way that preserves their freedom and their responsibility to the full.

Shall that be accounted a thing inconceivable? We persuade our fellow men, yet their freedom is preserved when they do what we persuade them to do. Shall not then God be able to do with certainty what we with our little power do with uncertainty? Does not God, who made the soul of man, know how to move it in accordance with its own nature so that its freedom shall not be destroyed?

Shall he not be able even to use the evil actions of men for his own holy purposes? The Bible tells us plainly that he does so use those evil actions. Even they do not lie beyond his governance as the great First Cause. Yet the Bible tells us with equal plainness that he is not the author of sin but that sin is ever hateful in his eyes. Why he allowed sin to enter is the mystery of mysteries, but that he did so we are plainly told, and that he did so for some high and holy end.

Thus all nature, including the nature of man, is a wondrous instrument of many strings, delicately tuned to work God's will and upon which he plays with a master hand. But all such figures of speech go only a little way; there is a point at which they break down. The relationship of God to the course of nature is vastly more intimate than the relationship of a musician to the instrument upon which he plays. The musician is outside of his instrument as the engineer is outside of the machine that he controls and guides. But God pervades the course of nature. No recess of it is apart from him; he pervades it through and through. Infinitely separate, yet everywhere near—such is the great mystery of the immanence and transcendence of God.

And is that all? Does God, now that the course of nature has been made, operate only in and through that course of nature? Or does he operate and has he operated in a way that is above nature? Are his works of providence now his only works, or does he work—or has he at any time worked—in such creative fashion amid the course of the world as he did when he first called the world into being from the abyss of nothingness by his initial creative word?

With that question—the question of the supernatural—we shall deal in the next of these talks.

27

Miracles

In the last two talks I spoke to you, first, about God's work of creation and, second, about God's works of providence. The distinction between the two is important because upon it depends our belief in the real existence of the world. If God's work of preserving and governing the universe is the same thing as his work of creating the universe, if creation has to go on constantly every instant, then it follows with inevitable logic that the thing created at any one instant does not remain in existence.

Such a view is quite contrary, we observed, to the Bible. The Bible plainly teaches the real existence of the created universe.

God created the universe by his work of creation; and then he preserves and governs the created universe by his works of providence.

But did God's work of creation take place all in one act at the very beginning, so that after that initial act all of God's works in the universe are works of providence and none of them are works of creation? When God had once created the world, did he thereafter work only through the course of nature that he had made? Or did he also, from time to time, act directly, without the use of means, as when he first called the world into being by his creative fiat?

I can see no reason whatever why we should assume, before investigation, that the former of these alternatives must be correct. I can see nothing antecedently improbable in the second alternative. Why should it be thought incredible that God who once created the world of nothing should again put forth his creative power? Why should it be thought incredible that he who once acted without the use of means should again choose so to act? Why should it be thought necessary that God, when once he had created the course of nature, should ever thereafter limit himself to the use of that course of nature and should never act in a way that is above nature and independent of it?

Those questions, I think, are unanswerable. There is no reason whatever why anyone who really believes in creation should regard as impossible an entrance into the world already created of God's creative power. What God has done once, he obviously can do again. He acted independently of the course of nature when he created the course of nature in the first place. He may, therefore, act in equal independence of the course of nature at any time when he will.

Such an act of God, independent of the course of nature, would properly be called "supernatural." It would not be contrary to nature for one of God's actions is never contrary to another: but it would certainly be "above nature." The possibility of supernatural acts of God entering into the course of nature cannot be denied by anyone who really believes in God's initial act of creation.

But if supernatural acts of God entering into the course of the world are perfectly possible, are they also actual? God might conceivably perform them, but has he actually done so?

That question can be answered only by an examination of the record of God's actions which is found in the Bible. And when the record is examined, the answer that it gives is found to be perfectly clear. The Bible plainly records the occurrence of acts of God which are not natural but supernatural.

Those supernatural acts of God, those supernatural events recorded in the Bible, are of two kinds. Some of them are in the external world. These are events witnessed by the bodily eye or at least events which might conceivably be witnessed by the bodily eye. Others of them are events within the hidden realm of the soul.

I cannot think that this distinction goes to the very depth of things. We must guard ourselves against thinking that a supernatural event in the soul of man is less supernatural than a supernatural event in the external world. On the contrary, we ought to think of it as just as supernatural and just as wonderful. We must also guard ourselves against thinking that a supernatural event in the soul of man is without effects in the external world. On the contrary, it has very obvious effects in the external world. When a supernatural change is wrought in a man's soul, the man's actions become different. The effects of the supernatural change in the man's soul are quite visible and quite tangible. They appear to all observers; they are very decidedly in the external world.

Nevertheless, the distinction about which we are speaking, though the importance of it ought not to be exaggerated, is still important. We ought not to ignore it. We ought not to ignore the fact that the supernatural events recorded in the Bible are of two classes. Some of those events are in the external world and some of them are not.

Those that are in the former class, those that are events in the external world, are properly called miracles.

The Bible contains a great many accounts of miracles, both in the Old Testament and in the New Testament. Among the New Testament miracles are, for example, the feeding of the five thousand, the walking of our Lord upon the water, the raising of Lazarus from the dead, and the resurrection of our Lord himself.

But just what is a miracle? How is the word "miracle" to be defined? The answer has already been given in what we have just said. A miracle is an event in the external world that is wrought by the immediate power of God. I have never seen any reason to abandon that definition, which I learned from one of my teachers a great many years ago.

In saying that a miracle is an event that is wrought by the immediate power of God, we do not mean that while miracles are acts of God, other events are not acts of God. On the contrary, ordinary events are just as much acts of God as miracles are. Only, in the case of ordinary events, God uses means, the order of nature that he has created, in order to bring those events to pass; whereas in the case of miracles he uses no means but puts forth his creative power as he put it forth when he first made all things of nothing.

Various other definitions of miracles have been proposed. Thus, it has sometimes been said that miracles are just extraordinary events of which we in our ignorance do not know the cause. They have some natural explanation, it is said, but we do not know what it is. If we ever do learn what the natural explanation of any of these events is, the event will cease to be to us a miracle. So, it is said, many events formerly regarded as miracles are now not regarded as miracles at all. The progress of science, it is said, has put them out of the miracle category.

It is perfectly evident that that definition of miracle really destroys any true distinction between miracles and other events. The only distinction that remains according to that definition is found in our ignorance. A miracle is defined as an event about the cause of which we happen just now to be ignorant. Well, in that case, it does not in itself differ from any other event. Such a definition really denies the distinctness of that which is being defined. Those who favor it really deny, by implication, that there are any events outside of the course of nature. All events, they hold, have a natural explanation, even though in the case of some events we do not happen to know what the natural explanation is.

Very similar is the definition, favored by some rather devout people, to the effect that a miracle is an event brought about by the operation of some higher law of nature than the laws which we know. Take a miracle like the feeding of the five thousand, for example. It seems at first sight to be entirely incapable of explanation under the laws of nature. According to all the laws of nature that we know, five loaves and two small fishes could not have been multiplied suddenly so as to feed five thousand men. Well, then, are we to say that in bringing that event to pass God disregarded the laws of nature that he himself had established? Not at all, say the advocates of the definition that we are now considering. God did not disregard his own laws. No, he merely used some law of nature higher than the laws which he has been pleased to reveal to us.

I have said that this definition of a miracle is similar to the definition that I considered a moment ago. I should have said that it is not only similar to that definition, but actually identical with it, except for the fact that the people who put the definition in this latter form often seek to preserve a certain special prerogative of God in the case of the events called miracles. I think they are usually inclined to say not only that we do not now know the laws that were operative in the events that we call miracles but that we never shall know them. They are mysterious laws which God has chosen to hide from us.

But even so, this definition denies anything really distinctive in a miracle. Like every other event, a miracle, according to this definition, is an event that takes place in the course of nature and in accordance with nature's laws.

Why should a definition like that be advocated? Why do some people—even some rather devout people—seem to dread so much the simple admission that God has chosen, from time to time, to enter in creative fashion into the course of the world, not acting in accordance with the laws of nature that he has established but acting as he acted when he first made the world of nothing by the word of his power?

Well, I think these people have a sort of notion that unless God acts always in accordance with the laws of nature that he has established, he is introducing an element of disorder and arbitrariness into the course of the world. Would God break his own laws? they might indignantly ask. They reason that if he did do so, would that not be a sort of confession that his own laws are imperfect or unrighteous? Would it not almost mean that God had broken faith with us, his creatures? He has placed us here in this course of nature. He has led us to depend upon the regular operation of its laws; he has led us to have confidence that the sun will rise in the morning and set at night, that spring will follow winter and summer will follow spring. How can he then, without something like bad faith, enter arbitrarily into the orderly course of this universe that he has made? If he did so, would it not destroy the security that he led us to expect when he placed us here under a reign of natural law?

In answer to that objection, I just ask you to consider whether the mere fact that we are under a reign of natural law is the thing that gives us security. Is this universe such a very safe place to live in after all? There are some exceedingly destructive forces in nature; and man, who is himself part of nature, bids fair to use those forces for the destruction of the race. Every now and then we read something about lethal rays or wings over Europe or the like. These things are fiction, but there is a large measure of scientific basis for them. Great progress in bombing planes and poison gases undoubtedly was made during the World War. Without doubt, far greater progress still has been made since the war was over. Scientists tell us that the atom, infinitesimal though it is, contains a boundless store of energy. Who can tell us when man may discover the secret of releasing that energy? And when man discovers the secret of releasing it, what possible security for any of us will be left?

There are also astronomical possibilities of destruction beyond number. Great stars are destroyed, and our earth is a mere speck of a satellite revolving around one of the smaller of the stars, which we call the sun. The destruction of such a tiny fragment would not cause very much of a jolt in the vast machinery of the universe.

There are, moreover, possibilities in the course of nature far more appalling than the sudden destruction of the whole human race and of the earth on which it lives. They are the possibilities that arise from man's tyranny over man. Before us today there rises with ever-increasing menace the specter of a tyranny of the experts—a tyranny compared with which all the tyrannies of the past are as nothing—a tyranny which would bring the details of life under expert regulation and make mankind's dreams of freedom and glory to be a thing of the past. Such a tyranny has made great strides in Germany and Russia in our day. It menaces us here in America. It menaces all men everywhere. If it gains control of the race, better would it have been by far that mankind should never have appeared upon the earth.

Sometimes I feel tempted to be appalled when I think of these things. I look out upon all that is sweet and beautiful in the world, and then think with what a very precarious tenure that is all held. If we consider what we know of nature and of that part of nature that is called man, we can almost say that the very existence of humanity hangs by a thread.

Where then is security to be found, if indeed it can be found at all? Well, I will tell you. It is not to be found in nature; least of all is it to be found in that part of nature that we call man. I will tell you where it can be found. It is to be found only in God.

What guarantee have I that someone will not invent a poison gas that will be capable of wiping out the population of whole cities by the dropping of a single bomb? What guarantee have I that the secret of atomic energy may not be discovered, to the destruction of the human race? What guarantee have I that all the high aspirations of humanity will not come to an utterly brutal and meaningless end?

I have no guarantee in nature; and I have no guarantee in man. There is nothing whatever in the composition of the universe, so far as we know it, to put these things outside the bounds of possibility.

How then do I retain my equanimity in view of the appalling possibilities revealed by modern science? How do I know that whatever may be the end of the human race upon this earth, it will not be a brutal and meaningless end, but will be an end that will accomplish some high and holy purpose?

In one way and in one way only—through my faith in God. There are destructive forces in nature. We may well be in terror if we think of those forces as being turned loose upon us. We shall be still more in terror if we think of those forces as getting into the control of scientific experts; for the tyranny of experts is the most soul-crushing tyranny that could possibly be set up.

There is one way and one way only to overcome such terror. It is to remember that all the destructive forces of nature, and even the scientific and pseudo-scientific experts that are such a menace to freedom, are instruments in the hands of an all-wise God. We can contemplate lethal rays and the boundless stores of dangerous energy said to be contained in the atom, and the menace of tyrannical power placed in the hands of psychiatrists and other experts who often stand on very low moral ground, without losing all hope—we can contemplate such things for one reason and one reason only—because we have faith in God. Very terrible things may come upon the human race, but not the brutal and meaningless destruction which might seem to be so imminent today. We can trust God, you see, for that. God has his purposes; he has revealed something of them in the Bible; and we can trust him to carry them out. Our trust is not in nature; it is in God.

But if our trust is in God, it does not make any essential difference how God chooses to bring his counsels to pass. He does so partly through the course of nature; he rules all things in nature by his providence. But if he chooses to do so in part in a way that is independent of nature, that does not in the slightest destroy our confidence in his wisdom and in his goodness and in his power.

Miracles, in other words, are not arbitrary events. They do not introduce the slightest disorder into the course of nature. They are, indeed, above nature, but they proceed from the source of all the order that nature contains—namely, from the all-wise and all-holy decree of the living God.

To some extent we can detect the reason for miracles. The miracles of the Bible are due—for the most part, let us say, to be very cautious—to the fact of sin. When God created the world, it was all very good. But then sin was introduced. Why God permitted it we do not know. That is the mystery of mysteries. But that he did so for high and holy ends we are sure. Sin introduced a terrible rend into the course of nature. To heal that rend, God put forth his creative power in the miracles of the Bible, especially the great miracles of the incarnation and the resurrection of Jesus Christ our Lord. Do those blessed miracles destroy our confidence in the regularity of nature's laws? Certainly not. But why not? The answer is plain. Simply because they are acts of the same God as the God to whom nature's laws are due. God does not contradict himself.

Miracles today have ceased. I think there is some confusion on that point among Christian people. "Have not some of us witnessed miracles?" they say. A loved one has lain upon a bed of sickness. The physicians have given up the case; they have warned us that there is no hope. But then Christians have prayed; they have brought their dear one before God in prayer. God has graciously heard the prayer, and the loved one has been raised up. Is not that a miracle?

We answer, "No." It is a very wonderful work of God, but it is not a miracle. When we prayed to God for the recovery of that beloved person we were not asking God to work a miracle like the healing of blind Bartimaeus or the raising of Lazarus from the dead. No, we were just asking him to use the resources of nature for the recovery of our loved one.

Often, we ask a human physician to do that same thing. Someone is stricken down. If the physician is not called in promptly the person dies. But the physician is called in and the person lives. How does the physician attain that end? Well, not by a miracle, but by a skillful use of the remedies which nature affords.

But why should not God be asked to do what a mere finite person is asked to do? His power is vastly greater than that of the physician. Why may he not be asked to use those vast resources of nature, which he, unlike the human physician, holds in the hollow of his hand?

Or take this matter of praying for rain. "Ought we to pray for rain?" we are often asked. If we say yes, the modern skeptics hold up their hands in horror. Could such obscurantism, they say, possibly be imagined as surviving in the twentieth century? Rain and sunshine are governed, they say, by meteorological laws. Do you mean to tell us, they ask, that those laws can be set aside by your prayers?

Well, my friends, I cannot for the life of me see that to pray for rain involves asking God to set aside meteorological laws. It is not at all beyond the bounds of possibility that even man may learn to use those laws for the production of rain and sunshine as he wills. We hear about that possibility every now and then. If it becomes actuality, we may think of ourselves very soon as applying to Washington to the FWCA—Federal Weather Control Administration—asking them please to send us the kind of weather that we desire.

I hope for my part, indeed, that we shall never arrive at that point. I hope—despite the droughts and sandstorms in the West—that we shall never learn how to control the weather; for if we do there will be very serious disputes as to the kind of weather that we shall have, so that what I know as the only really safe topic of casual conversation may become a cause of civil war. But at least human control of the weather is not by any means outside the bounds of possibility. Why then, may we not ask God to do what we might conceivably ask even man to do? Why may we not ask God to use the resources of nature in order to send gentle rain and refreshing streams? God governs the course of nature. It may well prove to be his will to use that course of nature and use even our humble prayers to send refreshment to a thirsty land.

There is one advantage in asking God for rain, as compared with asking some bureaucrat in Washington. We can be perfectly sure in the case of God, as we cannot be sure in the case of a bureaucrat in Washington, that he will not grant our request if to do so is unwise or would work injustice to someone else.

Such an ordering of the resources of nature by God is not a miracle; and I repeat what I have already said: in our day miracles have ceased.

They have not ceased forever; but for the present they have ceased. There is a good reason why they have ceased.[1] But though miracles have ceased, certain other supernatural acts of God are wrought every day, when men and women are born again by the mysterious creative work of the Holy Spirit that the Bible calls the new birth. We hope to have something to say about those supernatural acts of God before we have finished this little series of talks.

---

1. B.B. Warfield, *Counterfeit Miracles*, 3–31.

28

Did God Create Man?

We have been speaking about the ways in which God works, the ways in which he executes his decrees. He executes his decrees, we observed, first, by his work of creation and, second, by his works of providence.

Then, in the last talk, we discussed the question of whether God's work of creation ceased altogether after his works of providence began. Did God perform his work of creation all in one act, and ever thereafter limit himself in his working to a use of the order of nature that he had already created; or did he, from time to time, enter into the course of nature in supernatural fashion, not using means but acting immediately by his creative power?

We saw that the latter answer is correct. The Bible contains a record not only of God's works of providence, but also of certain events which were produced by God without the use of means but by an immediate exercise of his power. Those events, when they took place in the external world, as distinguished from events like the new birth which take place in the hidden realm of the soul, are called miracles.

The miracles recorded in the Bible are—for the most part at least, if we may be very cautious—events that took place in connection with God's work of the saving of his people from sin. That is true, I think, of the miracles of the Old Testament as well as of the miracles of the New Testament. By certain miracles of the Old Testament, God defended his chosen people and authenticated the true commission of his servants, the prophets. But the choice of one people from among the peoples of the earth and the necessity for sending the prophets with their particular messages were due to the entrance of sin into the world.

Then, however, the question arises whether there were not other supernatural acts of God, coming after God's first work of creation and yet so basic in the very constitution of the world as we know it, that we think of them rather as acts of creation producing the course of nature than as miracles entering into a course of nature already produced.

In other words, did creation take place all at once, or did it take place in several successive acts of God?

I suppose the first impulse of most Christians, as they read the first chapter of Genesis, is to give the second answer to this question. The book of Genesis seems to divide the work of creation into six successive steps or stages. It is certainly not necessary to think that the six days spoken of in that first chapter of the Bible are intended to be six days of twenty-four hours each. We may think of them rather as very long periods of time. But do they not at least mark six distinct acts or stages of creation, rather than merely six periods in which God molded by works of providence an already-created world?

It is not so easy to answer that question as might at first thought be supposed. Mr. John Murray, who is in charge of the department of systematic theology in Westminster Theological Seminary and to whom I am indebted in a great many ways this autumn and last spring in my preparation for this little series of talks, has called my attention, for example, to an interesting article by B. B. Warfield, which is published now in his collected works on "Calvin's Doctrine of the Creation."[1] In it, Warfield points out that John Calvin was inclined to reserve the term "creation" to God's initial act by which he made things strictly of nothing and to avoid using that word to designate the subsequent acts of God mentioned in connection with the six days of the first chapter of Genesis. Those subsequent acts would thus appear to have been regarded by Calvin as a molding by God of what he had already created rather than as additional acts of creation in the strict sense.

I think we had better not stop to consider this somewhat difficult question, but had better proceed at once to speak of the origin of man.

At that point, at least—that is, in connection with the origin of man—Calvin, as Warfield points out, found a work of creation in the very strictest sense of the word; and I think every careful reader of the Bible who accepts the biblical account as true must agree with him. The origin of man, according to the Bible, was not due solely to God's work of providence, to God's governing of the course of nature that he had already created, but it was due to an act of God that was truly supernatural. God did not merely

---

1. B. B. Warfield, "Calvin's Doctrine of the Creation," in *Calvin and Calvinism*, 1931, 287–349.

order the course of nature in such fashion that man should be produced, but he created man.

When I say that, some of my listeners may turn away in disgust. "Do you mean to tell us," they may say, "that you hold to that antiquated theory of special creation? Why, everybody knows today that man was evolved from lower animals; even an elementary study of the bodily structure of man as compared with that of other animals shows that beyond peradventure; the theory of evolution has established itself firmly, and a person who rejects it is an ignoramus who is not worth listening to for a moment."

Well, before I am finally dismissed in this summary fashion, I wonder whether I might just be permitted to say a word or two with regard to the way in which this question seems to me to present itself. I do not feel in the slightest compelled to discuss the question with any fullness. There are colleagues of mine in our faculty to whom I should be obliged to refer you. But I do want to tell you very briefly what I think the question at bottom is.

The real question at issue here is whether at the origin of the race of mankind there was or was not a supernatural act of God.

We have seen that there really is an existing course of nature. The things that this course of nature brings forth have God, indeed, as their First Cause, but they have secondary causes within the course of nature itself. They are brought forth by God, but they are brought forth by him by a use of the course of nature that he has made.

We have also seen that from time to time God has entered into the course of nature in direct fashion, not using the course of nature already made, but acting in a way essentially similar to the way in which he acted when he first made all things of nothing by the word of his power.

When such supernatural acts of God are in the external world as distinguished, for example, from the hidden realm of the soul, they are called, as we have seen, miracles.

Now the miracles of the Bible are often closely interwoven with events which are not miracles but natural events. So, our Lord placed his fingers in a man's ears on one occasion and healed the man of his deafness. Placing his fingers in that man's ears was certainly not a miracle. But in connection with that perfectly natural event a miracle was wrought. We do not know just exactly where the natural event ended and the miracle began, but we do know that a miracle was wrought. God did use natural means there; but the natural means were not sufficient to produce the result. There was also, in addition to the use of natural means, a miracle.

So it is also, according to the Bible, with the creation of man. There was a use of the course of nature already made. The Bible expresses that in simple language when it says that "God formed the man of dust from the ground" (Gen 2:7). But there was also something more than the use of the course of nature already made. The Bible expresses that in various ways. It expresses it, for example, when it says that God created man in his own image. It seems clear that the word "created" is there to be taken in its strictest and loftiest sense.

But is the Bible right when it says that? Is the Bible right in teaching that a supernatural act of God took place at the beginning of the life of the human race?

A great many people say no. Modern science, they say, has shown clearly that man is the product of evolution.

Well then, I ask how it has shown that. In reply to that question, I am told that the most minute similarity exists between the structure of man and the structure of the lower animals. The real state of the case is, then, that an unbroken line of generations unites man with other forms of animal life.

Now I am not going to argue at all about the facts to which appeal is made in this connection. I am not competent to do so, and fortunately I do not think that I am obliged to do so. The question that I am raising just now is concerned not so much with the facts as with the relevance of the facts to the real question at issue.

Let us see whether we can bring the question right out into the open where we can look at it a little better.

At first sight, it does not seem to be very much out in the open. It seems to be hidden away in a region of great mystery. The origin of the first man took place a long time ago. We do not know exactly when it took place; even the Bible does not really tell us that. We do not even know exactly where it took place. It seems, therefore, to be very remote from us. We are somewhat confused by our sense of that remoteness.

Very well, then, let us take something that lies a good deal nearer at hand. The origin of the first man, which believers of the Bible declare to be a supernatural event, lies very far off; but the origin of the human life of another man, which believers in the Bible declare to be also a supernatural event, lies in the full light of historical times and in a country that is perfectly well known.

If you go down to a steamship ticket office today you can buy a ticket to a little country called Palestine, which lies on the eastern shore of the Mediterranean Sea. The history of that country is fairly well known. There have been obscure periods in its history—for example, during parts of the Middle Ages—but there was one period in its history about which we have rather abundant information. That was the highly literate and civilized period during which Palestine was under the Roman Empire.

In order to learn something of the men and the animals that lived in that period, you do not have to draw inferences from any scanty fossil remains; you do not have to learn of the succession of events from the way in which the strata in the earth's crust are superimposed one upon another.

No, we have glorious sculptures coming from that period and still more glorious ones coming from a slightly earlier period in Greece. We have, moreover, historical records, and many kinds of vivid descriptions of the kind of life men lived in that age. In Egypt there have even been discovered a great many private letters which people wrote to each other in those days. From all these sources of information we get the rather clear impression that the people of those days were not so very different from the people who live now. They were very much the same kind of beings that are now called men.

In that age which is so well known to us, there lived in a country that we can still visit any day, and at a time which can be approximately fixed, a man who was known as Jesus of Nazareth. It is not denied by any serious historians that this man did live. He lived not at a period of remote antiquity but in historical times, and we can today look out upon the very scenes upon which he looked out, when he walked along the shores of the Lake of Galilee.

What was the origin of the human life of this man, Jesus? Was he descended from previous men by ordinary generation? Was he a product of evolution?

Well, if we had only the kind of evidence that is relied upon to establish the doctrine of evolution with regard to the origin of the first man, we should certainly answer that question in the affirmative; we should certainly say that Jesus of Nazareth most assuredly was descended from previous men by ordinary generation. He did not make upon anyone the impression of being at all abnormal in his appearance. He was amazingly different, indeed, from other men in his character and in his powers, but I really do not think that there is much doubt but that, if his body as it was when he lived on earth were still somewhere upon earth—which, as a matter of fact, it is not—and if some archaeologist or geologist should discover remains of it in the rocks or in the soil, those remains would show the most thoroughgoing similarity to the bodily structure of previous men.

What inference would be drawn from that if the same kind of reasoning were used as the reasoning which is used when evolutionists argue for the descent of the first man from other forms of animal life? Why, the inference would be drawn that of course Jesus was descended by ordinary generation from the men who lived before him on the earth. The evidence of continuity of bodily descent—which in the case of the first man is, after all, very far indeed from being complete, since, to say the least, there are enormous gaps between the remains of man and the remains of other forms of animal life—would, in the case of the man Jesus, seem to be absolutely complete. The proof would seem to be overwhelming.

Yet, despite all that evidence, we hold, on the testimony of the first chapter of Matthew and the first chapter of Luke, that Jesus was not as a matter of fact descended from previous men by ordinary generation, but that at the beginning of his life upon this earth there was a creative act of God, the supernatural conception in the womb of the virgin Mary. Not even the body of Jesus, to say nothing of his human soul, was produced, then, according to our belief, merely by evolution, merely by ordinary generation in the ordinary course of nature, but it was produced also by a supernatural act of God. There you have an instance of special creation right in the full light of historical times.

Of course, a great many people deny that that biblical narrative of the virgin birth is true. You are wrong, they tell us, in holding that Jesus was conceived by the Holy Ghost in the womb of the virgin Mary. As a matter of fact, he was just the child of Joseph; he was a product of ordinary generation after all.

All right, I know that people say that. I know perfectly well that many people deny the virgin birth of Christ. But my point is that when they deny it, and when in denying it they reject the view about it that I hold, they cannot rule me out of court on the ground that I lack some vast fund of expert knowledge that they possess. They cannot say to me, as evolutionists say to me regarding the origin of the first man: "You have not a sufficient knowledge of biology and of geology to give you a right to have an opinion; we are the experts in this field, and as experts we tell you that Jesus was the son of Joseph by ordinary generation." If they said that, they would only make themselves ridiculous. Obviously, the question is one about which the biological expert is not one tiny little bit more competent to judge than is the plain man. Similarity of bodily structure between Jesus and the men who lived before him on the earth is admitted by everyone. Yet despite that similarity of bodily structure, we hold, on the basis of what we regard as adequate testimony, that Jesus was not descended from previous mankind by ordinary generation, but that at the origin of his human life there was an entrance, into the course of the world, of the immediate power of God.

But if there was an entrance of the immediate power of God in connection with the origin of the human life of Jesus, why may there not have been also an entrance of the immediate power of God in the case of the first man who ever appeared upon the earth? If similarity of bodily structure does not disprove the occurrence of the miracle in the one case, why should it do so in the other?

I am indeed perfectly well aware of the fact that there is a great difference between the two cases—not only a difference between the men who appeared in each case as a result of the supernatural act of God (Adam being man and man only, and Jesus being God and man), but also a difference in the supernatural act of God itself. I do not for a minute admit that the beings who lived before the first man upon this earth were as much like that first man in external appearance as the men who lived before our Lord were like our Lord in external appearance. I hold that the immense gaps which admittedly exist in the evidence for continuity between the lower animals and man are highly significant and I do not believe that they will ever be filled up.

But the point I am making is that the real decision as to what view is to be held about the origin of the first man is not reached by a consideration of the evidence adduced by biologists or by geologists. If it were reached by a consideration of such evidence, possibly the plain man might be held not to have a right to an opinion about it. It might then seem to be a question to be fought out by experts, with the plain man meekly accepting whatever verdict the experts might bring forth. But, as a matter of fact, the decision is reached on the basis of other kinds of evidence, which are just as much within the competence of the plain man as they are within the competence of experts.

Is there a God, Creator and Ruler of the world? Is he free to enter in creative fashion into the world that he has made? Has he actually so entered in creative fashion in the person of Jesus Christ and in the miracles recorded in the Bible?

If a negative answer is given to these questions, then no doubt the evolutionary view will be held regarding the origin of man. The biological and geological evidence obviously does not of itself justify such a view. There are, to say the least, stupendous gaps in the evidence and the relevance of the evidence may be seriously questioned. Obviously, a leap must be taken before the evolutionary hypothesis is accepted. But that leap will seem to be almost a matter of course to the man who does not believe in a transcendent, personal God, eternally free as over against the world that he has made, or to the man who does not believe that, in the person of Jesus Christ, God has actually entered by an immediate, supernatural action into the course of the world.

On the other hand, to the person who does not share those naturalistic presuppositions, that leap from the actual evidence to the evolutionary hypothesis will seem to be a reckless leap indeed. To the person who does not believe that Jesus Christ was a product of evolution, but who believes that he came into this world by a stupendous miracle, the testimony to an equally supernatural origin of the first man will seem to be overwhelming. Such a person will say with great confidence not that man is a product of evolution but that God created man.

29

How Did God Create Man?

In the last of these little talks I spoke to you about the question, "Did God create man?" Today I want to speak to you about the question, "How did God create man?"

The answer to that question that is given in the Shorter Catechism of the Presbyterian churches is as follows: "God created man male and female, after his own image, in knowledge, righteousness and holiness, with dominion over the creatures" (WSC Q&A 10). The Westminster Confession of Faith, making a little more explicit one thing that is implied in the Shorter Catechism, says that God created man "with reasonable and immortal souls" (WCF 4.2). I want to speak to you first about that very important thing.

Unquestionably the Bible recognizes the presence of two distinct principles or substances in man—his body and his soul.

That is made plain in the first book of the Bible, where, in the account of the creation of man, it is said: "the LORD God formed the man of dust from the ground and breathed into his nostrils the breath of life, and the man became a living creature" (Gen 2:7). But it is so pervasive throughout the Bible that any citation of individual passages in support of it would seem to be almost superfluous. When Jesus makes the distinction between soul and body in his solemn words: "And do not fear those who kill the body but cannot kill the soul. Rather fear him who can destroy both soul and body in hell" (Matt 10:28), he is only making explicit what really underlies all the teaching of the Word of God.

The Bible does not, indeed, teach that it is desirable for the soul to be separated from the body; it does not encourage at all the Greek notion that the body is the prison-house of the soul, and that a disembodied state is a state of freedom for which we ought to long. On the contrary, it teaches very plainly that the connection between soul and body is the normal and desirable thing and that a disembodied state is a state of nakedness from which the Christian desires to be delivered. Thus, the Christian doctrine of the resurrection of the body is very different from the Greek doctrine of the immortality of the soul.

Nevertheless, the Bible does teach that the soul is a substance distinct from the body and that it may exist, and in the case of those who die before the return of Christ and the last judgment, actually does exist, separate from the body.

In thus affirming the existence of the soul, the Bible is in direct conflict with many powerful tendencies in modern unbelief. Great hosts of unbelievers deny not only the existence of a personal God but also the existence of the human soul. Indeed, the two denials are very closely related. It is a true saying which declares that if one does not believe that there is a soul in the little world of man's life, neither is he likely to believe that there is any God in the great world of the universe.

The most thoroughgoing way of denying the existence of the soul is found in the doctrine of materialism, which has been expressed picturesquely in the dictum that the brain secretes thought as the liver secretes bile.

I wonder whether you ever felt the depressing pull of that doctrine, as I did in one period of my life.

There is something rather uncanny, is there not, in the close connection between the mind and the brain? Certain mental functions have been shown to be connected with certain areas of the brain. Injure those brain areas, and those mental functions cease. Does not that show, then, that all mental functions are just forms of physical reaction—particularly intricate forms of physical reaction, no doubt, but still forms of physical reaction all the same?

Touch a sensitive plant, and the plant curls up. No mental activity on the part of the plant is involved. Now certain reactions on the part of animals and of men seem to be not essentially different. There is some sense stimulus that is transmitted to the brain by the sensory nerves; an impulse is immediately transmitted from the brain to the muscles, and an action immediately follows. It looks as though it were all just a particularly delicate piece of machinery.

In the case of some sense stimuli, the action does not so immediately follow. Light rays coming from a printed page impinge on the retina of the eye; the optic nerve transmits the impression to the brain; nothing then seems to happen. We say the man is reading. He goes on sitting quietly in his chair; he does not seem to react in any immediate way to those sense impressions.

Sometimes I confess I have difficulty in avoiding an immediate reaction. There are some forms of tommyrot so outrageous that when I come across such tommyrot on the printed page I feel as though I ought to do something about it at once. But I restrain myself. I go on sitting quietly in my chair; I do not curl up like a sensitive plant; I do not kick as I do when a doctor hits me on my crossed knee to see whether my nerves are in the proper condition. I just seem to do nothing about it.

But, says the materialist, an impression has been made on my brain nevertheless. That tommyrot on the printed page has left its mark in my brain. After reading it I shall never be the same again. The physical impression in the brain is too minute to be detected by the most powerful microscope; but it is there, and at some time—perhaps years afterward—it may have its effect upon my conduct. The brain, in other words, has the faculty of recording impressions in a physical way, like impressions made upon a phonograph record, and at some future time the record thus made may be run off.

All right, that is beautifully simple, is it not? All disconcerting factors have been removed. The whole universe has been brought under the unified reign of a law of conservation of physical energy.

Of course, some questions may conceivably be asked by us ignorant folk. All the physical actions of many have been beautifully explained by the materialistic theory; they have all been explained as being due ultimately to physical impressions made upon the brain. But then is not one thing forgotten? How about thought; how about consciousness? Is not this rather a curious piece of mechanism after all? Is a machine, no matter how intricate, aware of itself and aware of the world about it? Must not this therefore be something more than a machine? Must not the mind be something rather different from the brain?

Well, the materialist does not give any serious attention to such ignorant questions as that. Of course, he admits that there is this curious concomitant of certain brain phenomena which we call consciousness or thought. We do not know exactly what to do with it. We cannot look at it through the microscope; we cannot weigh it in a chemical balance. But we ought not to bother much about it. A thing that cannot be looked at through the microscope and cannot be weighed in a chemical balance is certainly not scientifically respectable. It has no effect on the mighty process of nature. That goes smoothly on under the law of the conservation of energy quite regardless of this strange will-of-the-wisp of consciousness that plays meaninglessly around some of its operations. No, we ought not to trouble our heads about such a very intangible something-or-other as that. "Bane and blessing, pain and pleasure"[1]—these things may be all very well for poets and children; but they ought to be quite beneath the attention of scientific men.

Such is the attitude of the materialist. There is a certain strange fascination about it; it possesses the fascination of simplicity. I remember, as I say, that there was a time in my life when I was troubled by it. But then I read Ward's *Naturalism and Agnosticism* and other books, and succeeded in getting out of it. Or, rather, God graciously delivered me from the abyss.

The truth is, the simplicity of materialism is a baneful simplicity. It is the simplicity which is arrived at by ignoring some of the facts. Every problem becomes simple if you treat it in that way—if, that is, you ignore those elements in it that will not fit into some preconceived view regarding the solution.

Chess problems are somewhat similar. You think you have the solution of the problem: "White to play and mate in three moves!" You make what you think is the best move for White; then you try over what you think are all the moves that Black might make; then you meet them all by devastating moves on the part of White. And so poor Black goes straight on to his doom. At White's third move Black seems inevitably to be checkmated, and you think you have solved the problem; you think that as a solver of chess problems you are really pretty good. But then you look at the problem a little closer, and you discover that Black had a perfectly good answer to that first move of White. He had a knight or castle or bishop which could be moved so as to ward off the threatened attack.

Well, what do you do when you discover that possible move of Black? Do you stick to your solution of the problem all the same? Do you say: "It was a mighty good solution, and I am just going to stick to it by ignoring that disconcerting move of Black that broke it up." Not at all! You cannot do that at all. There is no such thing as "nearly right" in a chess problem. That one disconcerting move of Black broke up your solution just as

---

1. John Bowring, "In the Cross of Christ I Glory," 1825.

completely as if there had been a dozen moves like that. Just because of the possibility of that one move for Black, you have to make an entirely different first move for White. You have to begin all over again.

So it is with the materialist and his easy solution of the problem of the universe. He has his solution all nicely worked out. It is a very neat little solution. It seems to be quite beautiful in its simplicity. It seems to be quite worthy of being listed among the successful solutions in tomorrow's newspaper column.

But then I come along and point out to him the fact that his solution ignores the presence, as one of the factors in the problem, of mind or consciousness or thought.

What does he say when I point that out to him? Well, perhaps he says he does not like the thing that I have pointed out to him. He is a scientist, he says, and it is beneath his dignity to deal with such an imponderable thing as consciousness or mind.

What do I then say to him? Well, I am afraid I am rather hard-boiled about the matter. I say to him: "Yes, I know that you do not like this imponderable thing that is called consciousness. I do not wonder that you do not like it, because it demolishes your whole solution of the problem of the universe. I am really awfully sorry for you, old man. It must be very disappointing to have to start out in the solution of the problem all over again. But then you see, I really cannot help it. After all, we have to take the facts as we find them. We cannot get rid of any of them because we do not like them. As a scientific man, you surely ought to recognize that."

Such might be the answer that I might render to the materialist. I hope you may not think that in making that answer I am falling into that same undue simplicity with which I charged my opponent in the debate. I do not for a moment claim that with my solution of the problem of the universe, which I am seeking to substitute for the solution of the materialist, I have answered all possible questions and removed all mysteries. But still I do make bold to say rather confidently that, whatever my solution of the problem may be, no solution is satisfactory which does not take account of the reality of consciousness or mind.

Indeed, when you come to think of it, is not the reality of consciousness or mind even more certain than the existence of the material world? After all, is not consciousness or mind the thing that we are aware of most clearly of all?

I confess that I have a certain sympathy for the position of the idealist at this point. The materialist says that matter is the only reality. Then comes along the idealist and says: "No, the only reality is mind." I say I have a certain sympathy for him when he says that. I do not say that I agree with him. But I have a certain sympathy for him. I can see that he is under a delusion; but at least I can understand how he got that way.

You see, the thing that we know most immediately of all is our own mind. I may say, indeed, that I perceive other things beside what is in my own mind; I say I perceive a microphone there in front of me in this broadcasting station. To adapt the words of Mark Twain, "It looks like a microphone, it's located like a microphone and blamed if I don't believe it *is* a microphone."[2] So I reason if I reason like Mark Twain's blue jay in investigating his hole in the roof, and so I reason also if I reason like the ordinary American citizen.

But then along comes the idealistic philosopher, and *he* reasons very differently. "You say you see a microphone there in front of your eyes," he says to me. "Well, you don't mean to tell me that you think that microphone really exists." I am a little alarmed at this point. Is there anything wrong with me? Am I "seeing things"? I am almost afraid to answer. But finally I pluck up courage. "Yes, sir," I say, "I did think it was a real microphone." "How do you know it is a real microphone?" says he. "Because I see it," I say. "There it is; it is a perfectly good brown-colored microphone." At this point, my idealist philosopher friend gives a chuckle. He evidently thinks he has me where he wants me. "What is that you said?" he asks. "Did you say that the microphone is brown? Well, what do you mean by 'brown'? Suppose that microphone had always been in a perfectly dark place, and never could by any possibility be anywhere except in a perfectly dark place; and suppose, furthermore, that there were not and never could be anybody to look at the microphone, would there be any meaning in saying that the microphone was brown or black or white? Is not the color of the microphone, then, really something in the observer's mind and not something that belongs to the microphone itself?"

Well, I begin to think it over, and perhaps come to the conclusion that there may be something in what my philosopher friend is saying. The color of the microphone does perhaps seem to be something that is in the mind of the observer rather than something that belongs to the microphone itself. But then a bright thought strikes me. Am I not aware of the existence

---

2. This quote was attributed to Mark Twain, though no direct citation exists.

of that microphone in other ways than through the sense of sight? "Why," I say to my idealist friend, "I know that microphone exists because I can reach out and touch it. There! I have touched it. It is hard, and it has a certain size because it takes me a certain time to move my finger over it from side to side. Now, my philosopher friend, what are you going to do with that? You cannot possibly reduce anything as hard and as big as that microphone to a mere idea in my mind. A person cannot stump his toe on an idea. If I stump my toe on a thing or feel it with my hand I know that it is not an idea in my mind but something that does sure enough exist."

But those philosophers are mighty hard to silence in an argument. You may stump your toe, but you cannot stump a philosopher. They have an answer to everything. And so, my idealist philosopher friend is not a bit impressed by my appeal from the sense of sight to the sense of touch. "After all," he says, "the senses from the philosopher's point of view are all essentially alike, and they are all equally untrustworthy. When I say that I touch that microphone, all that I am really aware of is a certain sensation in my mind. As a philosopher, I really cannot go beyond that. So if there *were* an external world independent of my mind, I could never know what it is in itself. How then do I know such an external world exists? I do not really know it at all. Mind, therefore, is the only reality."

So says the idealist philosopher about the problem of mind and matter. What do you say about the idealist philosopher? Well, I am afraid some of you may be unkind enough to say plenty about him. I am afraid some of you may be unkind enough to say that he is completely "nutty." Why should we devote our attention to "nuts" like him?

Now possibly you are nearly right about the idealist philosopher. I am not saying you are not. But then, you see, when a form of insanity becomes as prevalent as this idealistic philosophy, with its attendant skepticism about the existence of an external world, has become in the course of human history, and when it dominates whole ages and percolates down from the philosophers and the poets until it touches the plain man's life at a thousand points, why then I think some attention ought to be given to it by everyone who loves his fellow men.

Of course I am bound to say that in its consistent form—the form in which alone anything very plausible can be said for it—it can easily be shown to involve consequences that are quite absurd. The solid consideration with which it starts is the difficulty of seeing how I can really be sure of any reality that exists independently of my own mind. But to say that there is no reality except what is in my own mind is quite absurd. It would mean that China, Japan, and India never had any existence until those countries came within my consciousness. But, say many idealistic philosophers, there are other minds, and so China, Japan, and India existed before they came into my consciousness because they existed in those other minds. Indeed, they existed, and all things exist, and I exist, and you exist, in the mind of God.

Thus is idealism pushed straight on from the absurd but consistent view that things exist only in my mind to the depressing but less obviously absurd pantheism which holds that things exist only in the divine mind.

The trouble is, however, that in taking that step, idealistic philosophy has sacrificed everything that makes its view at all plausible. The minute I admit that there are minds other than my own, I have admitted that there is a reality outside of my own mind; and when I have admitted that, I have taken the really difficult step, and there is not the slightest reason why I should not go on and admit the existence of the whole external world just as the plain man does.

I am afraid, however, that some of you may be impatient with this whole discussion. "Is it not high time," you may say, "that we should return to common sense?" Others of you may want to return to the Bible. "Is it not time that we should return to our Bible?" you may say. Was not this hour supposed to be devoted to an exposition of what the Bible teaches? And here we are wasting our time on a lot of philosophical subtleties.

I am inclined to have a good deal of sympathy with both of these suggestions. I am perfectly ready to return to common sense, and I am perfectly ready to return to the Bible. And the best of it is that if we do one of these two things, with regard to the subject that we are now dealing with, we shall also do the other.

The Bible is a wonderfully commonsense book. Amid the excesses of philosophers on the right hand and on the left, the Bible goes straight on along the pathway of common sense; and it does not seem to be at all ashamed of doing so. With a certain majestic assurance, it confirms the common judgment of mankind that mind is one thing and matter another, and that both truly exist.

But, you may say, how about our initial difficulty? How about the connection between the facts of consciousness and physical changes in the brain? Do you deny that there is some connection?

No, I say, I do not deny that there is some connection. When I engage in the unwonted mental exercise of thinking, I sometimes get a headache from it. I daresay some physical change in my brain always accompanies all my thinking and all my feeling.

But what of it? The materialist explains that connection between physical processes in the brain and thought processes in the mind by saying that only physical processes exist and that what we call the mind is only a very intricate form of physical process. The explanation is quite absurd, when you come to think of it. But why is there not another perfectly good explanation? Why cannot the connection between brain processes and mind processes be explained equally well just by saying that the mind makes use of the brain as its instrument? That thesis was defended with great force in Thomson's *Brain and Personality* that appeared some years ago. There is really nothing whatever against it.

No doubt the relation between the mind and the brain is a great mystery. Mental processes and physical processes seem to be so utterly disparate. But there are many mysterious things which yet must be accepted as facts. So, with great confidence we can accept the teaching of the Bible to the effect that man has a body and also has a soul, and that neither soul nor body is a mere semblance but that both do most truly exist.

30

God's Image in Man

We spoke in the last talk about the soul of man. God created man with a body, we say, but he also created man with a soul.

I think we ought to hold not only that man has a soul, but that it is important that he should know that he has a soul.

A good many people seem to think it is not particularly important. Just study the behavior of people, they say, classify your observations; and then seek to get people to form such habits as that behavior will result of a kind to promote the wellbeing of the race. That, say these men, is the proper scientific method. In it all introspection, all interrogation by a man of the facts of his own inner life, all talk about the existence of a soul and the like should be rigorously avoided. Just take human behavior, study it as it is, and leave metaphysical or philosophical questions about the soul or about God rigidly alone!

Such is the method. The strange thing is that some people who do, I suppose, believe in the existence of the soul and of God seem to think that this method can safely be followed as far as it goes. Why may we not accept the psychological studies of those psychologists who do not believe in the soul and in God, and then use them in the propagation of a philosophy and a theology very different from the skepticism of these men? Why may not the research of these psychologists be regarded by the Christian as being all right in their own limited sphere?

Such reasoning is very precarious. As a matter of fact, you cannot well keep one department of knowledge separate from another in such a watertight compartment as that. No, the views that a man has about the soul and about God will color his interpretation of the phenomena of human behavior; and, on the other hand, a false or limited observation of the phenomena of human behavior will color what a man thinks about the existence of the soul and the existence of God.

I think, then, that it is not only important that I have a soul, but also important for me to know that I have a soul.

What, then, does it mean when I hold that I have a soul? What does the Bible mean when it tells me that I have one?

For one thing, it means what I spoke to you about in the preceding talk. It means that the materialists are wrong, and that, contrary to their view, the mind or consciousness is something different from the brain.

But it means also something more than that. It means not only that man has mind or consciousness, but also that his mind or consciousness is a unity. It is not a mere stream of consciousness, but the consciousness of a person. Not merely does thinking go on within me, but it is *I* that think. It was I many years ago, and it is the same I today, and it will be the same I to all eternity. That is what the Bible means when it tells me that I have a soul.

It is rather an appalling thing—this terrible isolation of the individual soul. That isolation is expressed by theologians and philosophers in many learned works; but it is also expressed by the cry of the human heart. It is expressed, for example, in words of one syllable in a Negro song that I dearly love. Did you ever listen to it in a lighter mood as though it were an amusing thing? Well, I think if you listened to it in any such mood, you will say that though you went to laugh you came away to pray. I remember how much my mother used to speak of the solemnity with which that song sets forth the loneliness of the soul in the presence of God. "It's not my father," the song says in words that I cannot exactly remember, "it's not my mother, it's not my brother; it's me, O Lord, standin' in the need of prayer."[1]

There we have the cry of the human soul, in its awful separation from all else, in the awful loneliness of its existence as an indivisible and immortal soul.

That loneliness and indivisibleness of the soul belongs to all sorts and conditions of men. It is one of the things that most clearly constitute us men; it was stamped upon us by the creation once and for all. Even sin does not destroy it, though sin makes it no longer a blessing but an unspeakable horror and curse.

Such, at least in bare outline, is what the Bible means when it says that man has a soul.

---

1. "Standing in the Need," in *The Book of American Negro Spirituals*, ed. James Weldon Johnson and J. Rosamond Johnson, 1925.

At this point, it becomes necessary for us to deal in passing with one subsidiary question, just in order that the teaching of the Bible regarding the nature of man may stand out in its true simplicity.

We have been saying that according to the Bible man has a body and a soul. But a great many readers of the Bible—some of them not only very learned but also very devout readers—have told us that is not a complete statement of what the Bible teaches. No, they say, man is composed, according to the Bible, not just of body and soul, but of body, soul, and spirit. Thus they favor not a twofold but a threefold division of the nature of man.

People who hold this view differ, no doubt, somewhat as to what constitutes the difference between what they call the soul and what they call the spirit. Some of them have, no doubt, thought of the "soul" as simply the principle of animal life—the principle of life which man shares with the lower animals. But I am inclined to think that, in the form in which the theory is most prominent today, the "soul" is thought of as comprising faculties of man including some of the faculties of intellect, feeling, and will, which are distinctly human faculties, but do not include some still higher part of man's nature by which he enters into communion with God.

But is this theory correct or is it incorrect? Does the Bible really teach that the spirit of man is to be distinguished from his soul, or does it teach that the soul of man and the spirit of man are exactly the same thing, called by two different names?

I think the answer to this question is given with particular clearness in one great passage in the Bible, the passage which is found in the second chapter of the First Epistle to the Corinthians running into the beginning of the third chapter.

In that passage Paul repeatedly distinguishes the soul from the spirit, and speaks of the man characterized by "soul" as distinguished from the man characterized by "spirit." "But a soul-man," he says, "receiveth not the things of the Spirit of God: for they are foolishness unto him: neither can he know them, because they are spiritually discerned. But the 'Spirit-man' judgeth all things, yet he himself is judged of no man." I have just quoted First Corinthians 2:14–15. Probably many of you will say that the quotation is not just exactly right. What the English Bible says is: "The natural man receiveth not the things of the Spirit of God: for they are foolishness unto him: neither can he know them, because they are spiritually discerned. But he that is spiritual judgeth all things, yet he himself is judged of no man" (1 Cor 2:14–15; KJV). I think we shall see in a moment that that is really a splendid translation, a translation that comes just about as near to the meaning of the original as any translation into the English language possibly could come. But what the Greek really says instead of "the natural man" is "the soulish man"—only we have no such word as "soulish" in the English language, and so we come as near to the meaning as we possibly can when we translate as the Authorized Version of the Bible does at this point.

But if the Bible contrasts the "soulish man" or the "soul-man" with the "spirit-man" in this passage, have we not here a very clear example of the threefold division of man's nature— the division not just into body and soul but into body, soul, and spirit? Does not this passage clearly distinguish the spirit of man from the soul of man?

The answer is most emphatically, "No." On the contrary, this passage distinctly discourages the threefold division of man's nature into body, soul, and spirit, and encourages the twofold division into body and soul. The plain fact is that the word "spirit" in the adjective "spiritual" used in the phrase "the spiritual man" does not refer to the spirit of man at all, but refers to the Spirit of God. I do not see how it would be possible to make that much clearer than this passage makes it. "For who knows a person's thoughts," says the passage in the eleventh verse, "except the spirit of that person, which is in him? So also no one comprehends the thoughts of God except the Spirit of God" (1 Cor 2:11). Then the passage goes on to speak about the man who knows the things of God because the Spirit of God is in him.

What then is meant by the "spirit-man" or the "spiritual man" as over against the "soul-man"? Why, the thing is as plain as day. The "soul man" is a man who has only a human soul, and the "spiritual man" is the man who, in addition to this human soul, has the Holy Spirit, the Spirit of God.

How utterly wrong is it then to say that the "spiritual" man is the man who has developed a higher aspect or part of his own nature, called the "spirit" as over against the "soul"! No, the "spiritual" man is the man who has been transformed by the Holy Spirit, the Spirit of God, the third person of the Trinity; and the "soul-man" is the man who has merely his human soul not so transformed. The key to this passage, as to other passages in the epistles of Paul, is given if we think of the word "Spirit" in the adjective "spiritual" as being spelled with a capital letter because it refers not to the spirit of man but to the Spirit of God.

Very different is the use of the word "spiritual" in modern religious parlance. I have come almost to hate that word, so terribly is it being misused.

It is constantly being used to designate a religious man, a man who has developed some supposedly peculiar religious faculty of his nature as over against other faculties. So it is sometimes said of some unbeliever in the pulpit, if objection is made to the opposition between his preaching and the Word of God: "Oh, but he is so spiritual!" The meaning is, I suppose, that he is not interested in dollars and cents or in things to eat, but is interested in the things of the human spirit. That is certainly very far indeed from the biblical sense of the word. In the biblical sense, the spiritual man is the man who has been begotten again, and has had not a part of his nature but all of his nature transformed by the supernatural act of the Spirit of God.

I think, then, that the threefold division of man's nature into body, soul, and spirit is out of accord with the true meaning of that great passage in the second and third chapters of the First Epistle to the Corinthians. But are there not other passages in the Bible which seem to favor that threefold division?

It seems to me that the only passage which can be appealed to with any plausibility as doing so is found in First Thessalonians 5:23, where Paul prays that his readers' spirit, soul, and body may be kept whole and without blame at the appearance of our Lord Jesus Christ. But certainly that passage cannot rightly be used to overthrow the clear teaching of the rest of the epistles of Paul and the rest of the Bible. It seems clear that Paul is just using a fullness of expression there to express his hope that the whole beings of the Thessalonian readers may be kept so as to stand blameless at the second coming of Christ. He is just heaping up words to express that idea. I think we may say that if there had been other words, in addition to the two words "soul" and "spirit," to express the idea he would have used those other words too.

We ought to reject very firmly, therefore, the view that the nature of man is divided by the Bible into body, soul, and spirit. The more I reflect about the matter, the more I am convinced that the view of the threefold nature of man is rather a serious error. It is an error that has been held by a great many devout Christian people, and it has been learnedly and reverently defended; and yet it is a serious error all the same.

It encourages what may be called an "empty room" view of the presence of God in the redeemed man—the notion that before a man becomes a Christian he is pretty much all right except that there is one room in him that is vacant, the room that ought to be a temple of God. It encourages, in other words, the notion that what happens when a man becomes a Christian is merely that one part of the man's nature, the "spiritual" part, a part previously neglected, is developed and given the place which it ought to have in human life.

Such a notion fails to do justice to the teachings of the Bible. The real state of human nature after the fall of man is not that one part of it has been cut off or can attain only a stunted growth, but that all of it is corrupt. The real thing that happens when a man becomes a Christian is not that God is set up and enthroned in a part of man's nature which before was like an empty room, but that the whole man, corrupt before because of sin, is transformed by the regenerating power of the Spirit of God.

I think we ought to be very clear, then, that the Bible does not distinguish the human spirit from the human soul. No doubt these two words designate the same thing in two different ways, and it would be interesting to study the difference between them; but the important thing to observe now is that they do designate the same thing. They are just two different words to designate what we can call in English either man's soul or man's spirit, and which, in order to avoid confusion, we shall now speak of as man's soul.

What have we been doing in this discussion? Have we been engaging in undue subtleties that have taken us away from the simplicity of the Bible? On the contrary, I think we have been rubbing away the subtleties with which the interpretation of the Bible at this point has sometimes been overloaded, in order to recover the true simplicity of the Word of God. The Bible presents a view of the nature of man which is very simple. Man, according to the Bible, has a body and he has a soul. I think we ought to return to that simple biblical teaching.

When we do return to it, we are in a position to consider its implications. No longer distracted by any attempt to distinguish man's soul from man's spirit, we can go on to envisage the great mystery that the Bible designates by both of these words.

That mystery is set forth by the Bible when it tells us that God made man in his own image. "So God created man," says the Bible, "in his own image, in the image of God he created him; male and female he created them" (Gen 1:27).

The "image of God" cannot well refer to man's body, because God is a spirit; it must therefore refer to man's soul. It is man's soul that is made in the image or likeness of God.

But what was there in man's soul, as he was created, which was like God? Well, one important element in that likeness has already been set forth. God is a person, or, rather, three persons in one God, and man is a person. In that man is like God.

What a stupendous mystery that is! Here is man, a finite creature, product of God's creative hand, walking here upon this earth in a body made of the dust of the ground. Yet this being, so contemptible as he might at first sight seem, possesses the strange and terrible gift of personal freedom, and is capable of personal companionship with the infinite and eternal God. That the Bible certainly means when it says that God created man in his own image.

But is that all that it means?

Some have said so. Some have said that the image of God in man means not that man as created was in any respect the same kind of person as God is, but simply and solely that he was a person. It does not, say these men, involve any moral likeness between man as created and God.

Those who have said that may be divided into two classes.

In the first place, there are those who have said that man, before he fell into sin, was simply neutral with respect to good and evil. He was free, and that was all. He was neither good nor bad, and it was for him to determine whether he would become good or bad. He had not made any choices between good and evil. If he made good choices he would become good; if he made bad choices he would become bad: but as created by God he was neither one nor the other. He was like God simply because he had personal freedom: and personal freedom, not goodness, is what the Bible means by the image of God.

That view involves a very deadly error. It involves the deadly error in which the will of a free person is represented as swinging in a sort of vacuum undetermined by any character of the person as either good or bad. The Bible holds no such view. The Bible says: "out of the abundance of the heart the mouth speaks" (Matt 12:34), and: "A healthy tree cannot bear bad fruit, nor can a diseased tree bear good fruit" (Matt 7:18). According to the Bible, good actions come from a good person and evil actions come from an evil person; according to the Bible, goodness and badness do not inhere simply in individual conscious actions but inhere also in something that lies far deeper than individual actions. If we are true to the Bible, we cannot possibly speak of a person who is neither good nor bad; we cannot speak of a person who is morally neutral, whose moral quality is left to be determined by his own future choices, being good only as each individual action is good and bad only as each individual action is bad. We ought to get rid of that whole notion in a very radical way.

Other theologians have held a view similar to the one of which we have just spoken, but have endeavored to avoid some of its most obviously wrong implications.

Man as created, they have held, was morally neutral. In saying that they say something that is like the view of which we have just spoken. The image of God in which the Bible says man was created means, say these theologians, simply personal freedom, not goodness. But then, these theologians say, God at once gave to man—distinct from his creation—a supernatural gift of goodness, which was necessary in order that harmony in his appetites should be secured. When man fell by sinning against God, what happened was simply that that supernatural and additional gift of goodness was lost, but the image of God, which consisted simply in the nature of man as a free person, remained intact.

That view also is very wrong. It involves a shallow view of sin, and it is quite contrary to the teaching of the Word of God.

No, when the Bible tells us that man was created in the image of God, it means more than that man had personal freedom. That, indeed, is a necessary element in what the Bible means by the image of God; but that is not all that the Bible means by the image of God. The Bible means also that man as created was like God in that he was good. He was not, as created, morally neutral—indeed the whole notion of a morally neutral person is a monstrosity—but his nature was positively directed to the right and opposed to the wrong. Goodness was not something accidental, something that came in after man was created, but it was something that was stamped upon him in the very act of creation by the Creator's hand. About man as about all the rest of the creation the Bible says: "And God saw everything that he had made, and behold, it was very good" (Gen 1:31).

Yet man fell. How great a fall was that! It was not merely the loss of a gift not part of man's original being, but it was the loss of something that belonged from the beginning to the very image of God in man. How sadly was God's image marred! We must speak of that in the next of these talks.

31

The Covenant of Life

We observed in the last talk that when the Bible says God created man in his own image, that means something more than that man as created was a person as God is a person. The image of God in man does mean that, but it means far more than that. It also means that there was a moral likeness between man and God. Man as created, in other words, was like God not only in that he was a person but also in that he was good.

We saw that that view of the image of God in man, denied though it is by erroneous ways of thinking of various kinds, is supported by certain very powerful considerations drawn from the entire way in which the Bible speaks of the creation of man. But it is also supported by two New Testament passages to which particular attention ought now to be paid. These passages are found in the third chapter of the Epistle to the Colossians and in the fourth chapter of the Epistle to the Ephesians.

In Colossians 3:10, Paul speaks of his readers as having put off the old man and as having "put on the new self, which is being renewed in knowledge after the image of its creator." Here we have a mention of the image of God. What light does the passage shed upon the question of what the image of God means?

No doubt the direct reference here is not to the first creation of man, which we are studying just now, but to the new creation which takes place when a man becomes a Christian—that new creation which is essentially the same thing as that which is spoken of elsewhere in the Bible as the new birth.

But although the direct reference is to the new creation, there is the plainest possible allusion to the first creation, the very words of Genesis 1:27 being in part used; and in particular, we learn from this passage something very important about what the image of God in that Genesis passage means. The image of God, which is mentioned here in Colossians, is plainly intended to be essentially the same as the image of God which is spoken of in the Genesis passage.

Very well, then. By examining what Paul here says about the image of God we can learn something about what is meant by that phrase in Genesis 1:27.

What, then, does our examination of the Pauline passage show? Why, it shows that the image of God, as the Bible means it, includes knowledge. Having "put on the new self," says Paul, "which is being renewed *in knowledge* after the image of its creator."

But that word knowledge is unquestionably a very rich term. The knowledge of which Paul is speaking, and which he here says to be part of the image of God in man, is not merely intellectual knowledge like that which the demons have when they tremble before God, but it includes also a true apprehension of God such as only they possess who stand in communion with him. Such knowledge therefore must have been part also of the image of God in which man was first created according to the book of Genesis.

I do not mean that the redeemed people of God, the people who have passed through the new creation or the new birth, have not more knowledge of God than Adam had when he was first created; indeed, they certainly do have much more. But all the same, we do obtain from this passage in Colossians very clear information to the effect that the scriptural idea of the image of God, in which the book of Genesis says that man was originally created, includes a knowledge that is a truly moral as well as an intellectual possession.

The other New Testament passage to which I call your attention is Ephesians 4:24. In that passage, Paul speaks of his readers as having so learned Christ that they have put on the new man, "created after the likeness of God in true righteousness and holiness." Here, as in the Colossians passage, Paul is speaking of the new creation by which men become Christians, and not directly of the first creation of man narrated in the book of Genesis. But here, as in the Colossians passage, there is a clear allusion to that first creation of man and clear light is shed upon it. The words which the English Bible translates "after the likeness of God" clearly mean "according to God," "with God as a model." Thus the passage clearly teaches that a man who is created "with God as a model," or—to express exactly the same idea with other words—who is created after the image of God, necessarily possesses righteousness and holiness. Thus when the book of

Genesis says that God created man in his own image that is shown to mean—if we may interpret Scripture by the aid of Scripture—that God created man in righteousness and holiness.

How utterly the plainly intended parallel between the new creation and the first creation would break down if the image of God were to be interpreted in entirely different senses in the two cases—as involving righteousness and holiness in the case of the new creation, and as involving the mere gift of personal freedom without moral quality in the case of the first creation! No, nothing so inconsequential as that is meant. When the Bible speaks of being like God as the high ideal for man—as Jesus, for example, said, "You therefore must be perfect, as your heavenly Father is perfect" (Matt 5:48)—it is thinking primarily of moral likeness. So moral likeness is certainly not excluded when the first book of the Bible tells us that God created man in his own image.

The Shorter Catechism, then, in answer to the question, "How did God create man?" is entirely right when it says, "God created man male and female, after his own image, in knowledge, righteousness and holiness, with dominion over the creatures" (WSC Q&A 10).

Well, we have got that far anyway, in our account of God's dealings with man. Man was created in knowledge, righteousness, and holiness.

But did God leave man alone after he had thus created him? No, he did not leave him alone; he entered into a covenant with him.

That was, of course, only one thing that he did with man. By his works of providence, he preserved and governed man and all his actions as he preserved and governed all his creatures. But the Shorter Catechism is right in singling out that formation of a covenant with man as a "special act of providence" that God exercised "toward man in the estate wherein he was created" (WSC Q&A 12).

Now the Bible does not actually use the word "covenant" at this particular point. Yet the arrangement which it does describe is so similar to other arrangements where it actually uses that term that we can hardly deny to the theologians the right to use the term here. Plainly God did, according to the book of Genesis, enter into what, according to scriptural language elsewhere used, was a covenant.

Now when the Bible speaks of a "covenant" in a connection like this, where God was one of the parties, it does not mean exactly what we often in ordinary parlance mean by that term. We mean by a "covenant," or in more modern language a "contract," an arrangement which either party is free to enter into or not as it pleases. The Bible does not mean such an ordinary covenant or contract when it uses the term to designate an arrangement between God and man. The reason is that man, though one of the parties, has no choice whatever as to whether he will enter into the arrangement or not. At least, he certainly has no freedom of proposing any other arrangement to put into its place. He has no power to say to God: "No, I refuse to enter into such an arrangement with you; here is what I propose instead; you can take the contract that I offer you or else we shall just make no contract at all." He might say that to some human contracting party, but he cannot say that to God.

No, God remains absolutely sovereign, in his covenants as in everything else that he does. Man does not contract with him on anything in the remotest degree resembling equality. The covenant is an expression of God's will, not man's, and man must listen to its terms, trust God that they are holy and just and good, and order his life accordingly.

What is there, then, about these biblical covenants that causes the Bible to use the term "covenant" with regard to them? I think the answer is rather plain. It is that these covenants involve a promise on the part of God—a promise with a condition. God does engage to fulfill his part of the arrangement. He was not obliged so to engage; he was perfectly free not to do so: but when he has once done so, when he has once established the covenant, his honor is involved in the fulfillment of his part of it.

So it was in the case of the covenant into which God entered with man in the estate wherein he had created him. God entered into it freely: he was not under obligation to enter into it, except in the sense in which all God's actions are determined by the infinite goodness of his own being. But although he entered into it freely and not under any sort of pressure from or obligation to the other party, man, yet when he had once entered into it, man could be quite sure that he would fulfill his part of it to the full.

What, then, were the terms of that covenant into which God entered with man? The terms of it were very simple indeed. If man kept perfectly the commands of God, God would give him life. That was the covenant.

It is true, the Bible does not describe the covenant in just exactly that way. It does not describe it in positive terms but only in negative terms, and it does not describe it in general terms but only by the presentation of a concrete example of the kind of conduct on the part of man that would deprive man of the benefits of the covenant. Here is what the Bible says: "And the Lord God commanded the man, saying, 'You may surely eat of every tree of the garden, but of the tree of the knowledge of good and evil you shall not eat, for in the day that you eat of it you shall surely die'" (Gen 2:16–17).

But although the covenant is directly put only in a negative form, the positive implications are perfectly clear. When God established death as the penalty of disobedience, that plainly meant that if man did not disobey he would have life. Underlying the establishment of the penalty there is clearly a promise.

Moreover, the one prohibition which God expressly mentioned—the prohibition against eating of the tree of the knowledge of good and evil—is plainly put as a test of man's obedience in general.

The Shorter Catechism, therefore, is fully justified in speaking of this covenant as "a covenant of life" into which God entered with man, "forbidding him to eat of the tree of the knowledge of good and evil, upon the pain of death" (WSC Q&A 12).

The question then arises what is meant by "life," which God promised to man in this "covenant of life" into which he entered with him, and what is meant by the "death" which was to be the punishment of disobedience?

In answer to that question, I think we ought decidedly to say that the life and the death here spoken of include physical life and physical death. The Bible does seem rather clearly to teach that if man had not disobeyed the command of God, his body would not have died, he would not have passed through that dissolution between soul and body which is brought by the death of a man who has lived upon this earth. I think the fifth chapter of Romans as well as the book of Genesis teach that rather plainly.

It is another question to ask in just what way that preservation of life would have been accomplished. Would it have been accomplished because man's body, as created, was not at all subject to death—was not at all subject to that process of decay which now runs through all nature? I am not quite sure that the Bible requires us to say that. It is true, there are in the Bible, in the eighth chapter of the Epistle to the Romans, some very mysterious words regarding what may be called the cosmic effects of sin. They may fairly be held to mean that if sin had not entered, the whole course of the world and not merely of human life would have been very different from what it now is. Paul speaks of the creation as being now subject to the bondage of corruption and as groaning and travailing in pain together until now and as being destined to be delivered from this bondage of corruption into the freedom of the glory of the children of God (Rom 8:19–22). What is particularly noteworthy about this passage for our present purpose is not that it promises a glorious transformation of the created world in the future. That is promised elsewhere in Scripture. Isaiah, for example, speaks of the time when there shall be a new heaven and a new earth (Isa 65:17). But the thing that is especially noteworthy is that Paul seems so clearly to connect the present imperfect condition of the world with sin. That is in accord with what the book of Genesis says to the effect that the ground was cursed for Adam's sake and that it should bring forth thorns and thistles to him, the sinner (Gen 3:17–18). These passages do seem to indicate that the course of nature would have been different if sin had not entered into the world.

Yet I think we might perhaps be going beyond what is written if we said that except for sin the body of man as originally created, and as it would have been found in Adam's posterity, would have had the natural faculty, without further change, of being free from death. There are no doubt certain difficulties in the way of such a view as that. I will not say whether they are insuperable or not. At any rate, it seems to me that we are not necessarily running counter to the teaching of Scripture if we hold that the prevention of death, if Adam had not sinned, would have taken place in some way other than by the operation of the course of nature. Would Adam perhaps have passed through some kind of transformation or translation before his body would have become immortal? We simply do not know.

Yet even if we think of the matter in some such way as that which I have just suggested as possible, we still, I suppose, feel rather keenly the clash between this biblical teaching and the ideas to which we have become accustomed at the present time. We have become accustomed to a view of nature which practically, though not necessarily in theory, ignores God, which universalizes our observations of the course of nature as we now know it and ignores the fact that the Creator of nature still lives and can do what he will with the work of his hands. On the basis of that view into which we have fallen, it seems to some people incredible that man as created should not pass through those processes of decay and death which we now see operative everywhere in the world where life, whether vegetable or animal, is to be found.

But let us look at the thing for the moment from the Christian point of view. We Christians expect, do we not, the resurrection of the body; we look for a life of man, in the body, that shall have no end. Why, then, should we regard as impossible for Adam, had he not sinned, that which we firmly expect for ourselves, as redeemed? Perhaps, indeed, you may object that even Christians will die; their bodies are not exempt, then, from the processes of decay which run all through the natural world. Yes, we reply, but not all Christians will die; those Christians will not die who are alive at the second coming of our Lord. They will be transformed without passing through any dissolution of soul and body in death. We return, then, to our analogy. Why should it be thought a thing incredible that God should have preserved Adam from physical death had he not sinned, if in accordance with his promise he will preserve from physical death some, at least, of those whom he has redeemed from sin by the blood of Christ? There is really no reason why he should not have done so.

I think, then, that we can with great confidence say that if Adam had not sinned he would not have passed through the experience of physical death. There are many things that are mysterious about the way in which that preservation from death might have been accomplished, but about the fact of it I think the Bible allows little doubt. The Bible seems rather clearly to teach that death, even physical death, was the penalty of sin, and that life, even physical life, would have been the result of obedience.

It should be observed, however, very clearly at this point that although physical death was included in the death that was the penalty of sin, and although physical life was included in the life that was to follow upon obedience, yet physical life and physical death do not by any means exhaust the meaning of the life and the death that are here in view. Life, according to the Bible, is not just existence, but it is existence in the presence and with the favor of God; and death is not just the death of the body but it is separation from God and a doom that should fill the heart of man with a nameless dread. Great vistas of blessedness and of woe are here opened out before us. Very tremendous, according to the Bible, is the issue between life and death.

That issue was placed before man in accordance with what the Shorter Catechism calls the "covenant of life" into which God entered with Adam (WSC Q&A 12). That same covenant is also sometimes called the "covenant of works." It is rightly so called because by the terms of it man was to have life or death in accordance with what he did. By the terms of the covenant, man was placed on probation. No absolute promise of life was given him; but he was to have life only if he obeyed perfectly the commandments of God.

Do you think that probation was to last forever, or do you think that if man had not sinned there would have come a time when his period of probation would have been over?

Well, unquestionably it would remain true to all eternity that *if* man sinned he would die. That is quite clear. But the question is whether there would have come a time when that "if" would have lost all practical importance because the possibility of man's sinning would have been done away.

That is what I mean when I ask whether man's probation, as described in the second chapter of Genesis, was permanent or temporary.

I think that question can be very clearly answered. The answer is not, indeed, given by the Bible in so many words; but I think the theologians are right in holding that it is clearly implied.

When God had created man, he permitted him to be tested. He permitted temptation to come to him. If man had stood the test successfully, if he had resisted the temptation, do you think that he would have been brought again and again into jeopardy to all eternity? Do you think, in other words, that if he had resisted the temptation he would have been essentially no better off than he was before? In other words, would there have been for man always a possibility of a fall, but never a possibility of attaining a state of final security?

The former alternative seems to be contrary not only to the implications of the narrative in Genesis, but also to the analogy of certain other dealings of God with men.

We do know, if we believe the Bible, that there are men in whose case the possibility of sinning is gone. Those are the company of the redeemed in heaven.

In what does the Christian hope consist? Does it consist merely in the hope of being given a new chance to obey the commands of God, to have sin removed, and to have set before us all over again in another world the alternative of life and death as it was set before Adam in Paradise?

No Christian who has any inkling of the true richness of the great and precious promises of God will say that; on the contrary, the Christian hope is the hope of a time when even the possibility of our sinning will be over. It is not the hope then of a return to the condition of Adam before the fall but the hope of an entrance into a far higher condition.

Now do you think that if Adam had not sinned, the entrance to that higher condition would have been closed to him? Do you think that he would have been left to an eternal jeopardy in which the dread possibility of his sinning would ever have been before his eyes?

I do not believe you will think that if you read your Bible with care. No, the probation into which Adam was put was not an eternal probation. It was a temporary probation, and if it had been passed through without sin it would have been followed by an assured blessedness.

Thus that covenant of works into which God entered with man was a gracious thing. It contained, indeed, a possibility of death, but it contained also the promise of assured and eternal life. If the temptation was yielded to, there would be death but if the temptation was resisted, even the possibility of death would be removed.

32

The Fall of Man

In the last of these talks, I spoke to you about the covenant into which God entered with man in the estate wherein he was created. The terms of the covenant were very simple. If man obeyed perfectly the commands of God, he was to have life; if he disobeyed, he was to die. That covenant amounted to a probation in which man was put by God.

Just at the close of the talk, we were observing that the probation was not intended to last forever but was to be replaced, if man passed successfully through it, by a condition of assured blessedness. If that is not said in so many words in Scripture, I do maintain that the theologians are right in holding it to be very clearly implied.

If they are right, then we must supplement in rather an important way what we have said about the original state of man.

In the last two talks, we insisted, against erroneous views of various kinds, that man as created was positively good. The image of God, in which the Bible tells us man was created, did not consist merely in personal freedom, but it included knowledge, righteousness, and holiness. Man, as created, was like God not merely in being a person, but also in being good.

Now, however, we must observe that although man as created was righteous he was not created in the highest state to which he was capable of attaining. He was righteous, but there was in him a possibility of becoming unrighteous. A still higher state remained for him to attain. It was a state in which the very possibility of his sinning would be removed.

The means used by God to place that higher state before man as a goal to be attained was the issuance to him of a definite command. "But of the tree of the knowledge of good and evil you shall not eat," said God (Gen 2:17). That was the test of man's obedience; that was man's probation.

If the probation had been successfully passed through, then man would have been received at once into eternal life. He possessed life before, but then life would have been assured. The "if" would all have been removed from the promise of life; the victory would have been won; nothing further could ever by any possibility have separated God from his child.

Very different, however, was the result. Man was left, as the Shorter Catechism puts it, to the freedom of his own will, and he made sad use of his freedom (WSC Q&A 13). He might have chosen the way of life, but as a matter of fact he chose the way of death; he fell from the estate wherein he was created by sinning against God. It was a sad choice indeed.

When we say that man had free will and that he chose the way of death, we do not mean that his choice was outside of the eternal plan of God. We do not mean that he surprised God when he sinned. On the contrary, the eternal plan of God, as we saw when we dealt with God's decrees, embraces all things that come to pass. Even the sin of man was brought to pass in accordance with the counsel of God's will.

But as we observed when we dealt with that subject, God brings to pass different things in widely different ways. So he brought to pass the fall of man in a way that preserved to the full man's personal freedom and man's responsibility. God is not the author of sin. The tempter and man himself were the authors of man's sin. God's righteousness is forever pure. Yet God used even that terrible evil for his own holy purpose; he permitted man to fall.

Do not ask me why he did so. I cannot tell you. That is the eternal mystery of evil; it is to us an insoluble riddle. We must trust God alone for the solution of it.

One thing, however, is clear. Man had no excuse when he fell. He was guilty in the sight of God. Being left to the freedom of his own will, he fell from the estate wherein he was created by sinning against God.

That brings us to an exceedingly important question—the question, "What is sin?" It is a question that we cannot ignore. From false answers to it have come untold disaster to mankind and to the church, and in the right answer to it is to be found the beginning of the pathway of salvation.

How shall we obtain the answer to that momentous question? I want to try to tell you something about that in the next talk. But I think we can make a very good beginning by just examining the biblical account of the way in which sin entered into the world.

That account is given in the book of Genesis in a very wonderful manner. The language is very simple; the story is told almost in words of one syllable. Yet how profound is the insight which it affords into the depths of the human soul!

"And the LORD God," says the Bible, "commanded the man, saying, 'You may surely eat of every tree of the garden, but of the tree of the knowledge of good and evil you shall not eat, for in the day that you eat of it you shall surely die'" (Gen 2:16–17).

It has been observed that no reason is said to have been given to Adam to tell him why he should not eat of that tree, and it has been said that that fact is perhaps significant. Eating of the tree was not in itself obviously wrong; the command not to eat of it was not reinforced by any instinct in man's nature. It appeared therefore all the more clearly as a sheer test of obedience. Would man obey God's commands only when he could detect the reason for them, or would he obey them knowing simply that they were God's commands, knowing that because he gave them they had some quite sufficient reason and were holy and just and good? How clearly and simply that is brought out in the narrative in the book of Genesis!

An equal simplicity and an equal profundity characterize the following narrative—the narrative of the temptation and the fall.

Adam and Eve were in the garden. The serpent said to the woman, "Did God actually say, 'You shall not eat of any tree in the garden'?" (Gen 3:1)

I think we can detect even there the beginnings of the temptation. The woman is asked to eye the things that God has forbidden as though they were desirable things. It is hinted that the commands are hard commands; it is hinted that possibly they might even have involved the prohibition to eat of any of the trees of the garden.

Or else perhaps an attempt is made to cast doubt upon the very fact of the command. "*Hath* God said?" says the tempter. The woman is asked to envisage God's commands as a barrier which it would be desirable to surmount. Is there no loophole? Has God really commanded this and that? Did he really mean to prohibit the eating of the trees of the garden?

The woman's reply states the fact—certainly in the main. God's command did not prohibit the eating of all the trees in the garden but only of one tree. "And the woman said to the serpent, 'We may eat of the fruit of the trees in the garden, but God said, "You shall not eat of the fruit of the tree that is in the midst of the garden, neither shall you touch it, lest you die"'" (Gen 3:2–3).

There at last there comes a direct attack upon the truthfulness of God. "You will not surely die," said the tempter (Gen 3:4). "You will surely die," said God; "You will not surely die," said the tempter. At last the battle is directly joined; God, said the tempter, has lied, and he has lied for the purpose of keeping something good from man. "You will not surely die," said the tempter. "For God knows that when you eat of it your eyes will be opened, and you will be like God, knowing good and evil" (Gen 3:4–5).

At that point, the question arises in our minds what the element of truth was in those words of the tempter. Those words were a lie, but the truly devilish lies are those that contain an element of truth, or, rather, they are those lies that twist the truth so that the resulting lie looks as though it itself were true.

Certainly, it was true that by eating the forbidden fruit Adam attained a knowledge that he did not possess before. That seems to be indicated in verse 22 of the same chapter of the book of Genesis, where we read: "Then the Lord God said, 'Behold, the man has become like one of us in knowing good and evil.'" Yes, it does seem to have been true that when he ate of the forbidden fruit man came to know something that he had not known before.

He had not known sin before; now he knew it. He had known only good before; now he knew good and evil. But what a curse that new knowledge was, and what an immense loss of knowledge as well as loss of everything else that new knowledge brought in its train!

He now knew good and evil; but, alas, he knew good now only in memory, so far as his own experience was concerned; and the evil that he knew he knew to his eternal loss. Innocence, in other words, was gone.

At this point, the question naturally arises in our minds whether innocence was the highest state for man. Is a goodness that is good merely because there has never been any knowledge of evil the highest form of goodness? Or is that goodness still higher which has maintained itself in the very face of evil?

Well, I think we ought to be very cautious about answering that question and I do not think we ought to adopt any answer which will involve making evil a necessary means to the production of good. That would be a very deadly error indeed; for if evil is necessary that there should be good, if good could never exist unless evil were also present, then evil would in some sort cease to be evil and would become itself a kind of good. Indeed, in that case—if evil is necessary to good—evil must be thought of as having a place in the life of God himself before the creation of the world; and that is the abyss of blasphemy.

But I think we may say that for man as he was actually created, and with evil already present in the world of created beings, resistance to temptation was a pathway to a higher level of perfection than was that innocence in which he was created.

I do not mean that it is ever right to seek temptation in order that we may show how finely we can resist it. The thought of doing that is one of the most often used snares of the devil. A man who is dissatisfied with what Satan calls childish innocence and deliberately seeks temptation has already yielded to temptation, and in the effort to transcend childish ignorance has shown himself to be in the worst sense of the word a child and a dupe. "Lead us not into temptation"—that petition in the prayer that our Lord taught his disciples ought to be the prayer of every strong Christian man, and I think it is correct to say that the stronger and the more mature a Christian man is, so much the more fervently will he pray that prayer.

It is very different, however, when temptation comes through no volition of our own—when we hate it and yet it comes. In those cases, it may be the occasion for the attainment of new heights of victory. "Count it all joy, my brothers, when you meet trials of various kinds" says the Epistle of James (James 1:2); and if it be preferred to translate the word that is used there "trials" instead of "temptations" and to interpret it of persecutions which came to the Christians in that early age, still the meaning of the verse is not essentially different. If "trials" are in view, rather than what we customarily call temptations, still those trials are here distinctly envisaged as involving temptations—temptations to discouragement, temptations to disloyalty to Christ, or the like. At any rate, James here uses exactly the same Greek word to designate trials or temptations as that which is used in the petition in the Lord's Prayer as reported in the Gospel according to Matthew.

So our Lord taught us to pray, "Lead us not into temptation" (Matt 6:13); yet the inspired writer of the Epistle of James bids us count it all joy when we fall into temptations. Is there any contradiction? No, there is not a bit of contradiction. It is very wicked to seek temptation; yet when it comes it may be a means of blessing, if God gives us strength to resist. It would be very wicked, for example, to pray for that kind of temptation which comes to a Christian through persecution from the adversaries of the faith; it would be very wicked to pray to God: "Oh Lord, put it into the heart of this tyrannical ruler or that to persecute the church, withdraw from him the restraints of thy common grace, in order that the church may receive the blessing which persecution might bring." It would be very wrong to pray that prayer, and it would be very wrong to provoke a wicked ruler in any way whatever to persecuting zeal. Yet when persecution does come—does come, despite the prayers of God's people and despite their peaceable lives—it does remain true very often that "the blood of the martyrs is the seed of the church."[1] God overrules evil for good.

So it is also with temptations in our own individual lives. It is very wrong to seek them; if we seek them we have already yielded to them in part. We ought resolutely to turn our eyes from things that are evil, and obey rather the apostle's injunction: "Finally, brothers, whatever is true, whatever is honorable, whatever is just, whatever is pure, whatever is lovely, whatever is commendable, if there is any excellence, if there is anything worthy of praise, think about these things" (Phil 4:8). Yet if temptations do come, and if we can honestly say in the secret of our own souls and in the presence of God who searches the heart that we have not sought them out but have prayed earnestly that they may be kept from us, then, if God gives us grace to resist, the temptations may be to us the means for the attainment of new strength and new power.

No, there is no contradiction whatever between the Lord's Prayer and the Epistle of James. The man who prays with all his soul, "Lead us not into temptation," will be just the man who will count it all joy when he falls into diverse temptations and when he has the privilege of suffering dishonor and pain at the hands of wicked men for the sake of his Lord.

Much that I have just said can be applied to the temptation that is narrated in the third chapter of Genesis. There are, it is true, important differences. The situation of Adam in the garden of Eden was different in important respects from the situation of the men who have lived after the fall. It was obviously different from the situation of those who have not believed in Jesus Christ for the salvation of their souls; for whereas Adam, before the fall, was good, those men are the slaves of sin. But it was also different from the situation of those who have been begotten anew by the power of the Holy Spirit and have been redeemed by the precious blood of Christ. No, never again will there be a return to the situation in which Adam found himself before the fall. That situation came once and once only in the whole history of mankind.

Yet there are certain fundamental principles of temptation which show themselves both in the Christian's present battle against sin and in the probation in which Adam stood according to the early chapters of the book of

---

1. Tertullian, *Apologeticus*, AD 197.

Genesis. In both cases it does remain true, in accordance with the teaching of the Word of God, that temptation resisted brings advance for the soul of man.

What would have been the advance which resistance to that first temptation would have brought to Adam and Eve? We have already pointed out the central feature of that advance. It would have meant, we have observed, that the possibility of sinning would have been over. The probation would successfully have been sustained; man would have entered into a blessedness from which all jeopardy would have been removed.

But the advance which a successful resistance to the temptation would have brought would also have been an advance in knowledge. That tree was called the tree of the knowledge of good and evil. Well, there is perhaps a real sense in which it would have been to man a tree of the knowledge of good and evil even if he had not eaten of the fruit of it. If he had resisted the temptation to eat of the fruit of that tree, he would have come to know evil in addition to the knowledge that he already had of good. He would not have known it because he had fallen into it in his own life, but he would have known it because in his resistance to it he would have put it sharply in contrast with good and would deliberately have rejected it. A state of innocence, in other words, where good was practiced without any conflict with evil, would have given place to a state of assured goodness which evil would have been shown to have no power to disturb.

Such was the blessed state into which God was asking man to come when he entered into that covenant of life with him about which we spoke in the last of these talks. It was a state which included what I think we can call a knowledge of good and evil. Certainly, it was a state in which the difference between good and evil would have been clearly discerned.

Such discernment was promised by the tempter: "You will be like God, knowing good and evil," he said (Gen 3:5). But there was a right way and a wrong way of seeking to attain that discernment. The right way was the way of resistance to evil; the wrong way was the way of yielding to it and seeking to know it by experience.

How often that wrong way is suggested to men in the temptations that come to them now! Innocence being despised, the ancient lie is put into men's hearts again and again and again that the only way to attain a state higher than innocence is to have experience of sin in order to see what sin is like. Sowing wild oats is thought to be rather a good way of transcending childish innocence and of attaining strong and mature manhood.

Do you know how that lie can best be shown to be the lie that it is? Well, my friends, I think it is by the example of Jesus Christ. Do you despise innocence? Do you think that it is weak and childish not to have personal experience of evil? Do you think that if you do not obtain such experience of evil you must forever be a child?

If you have any such feeling, I just bid you contemplate Jesus of Nazareth. Does he make upon you any impression of immaturity or childishness? Was he lacking in some experience that is necessary to the highest manhood? Can you patronize him as though he were but a child, whereas you with your boasted experience of evil are a full-grown man?

If that is the way you think of Jesus, even unbelievers, if they are at all thoughtful, will correct you. No, Jesus makes upon all thoughtful persons the impression of complete maturity and of tremendous strength. With unblinking eyes, he contemplates the evil of the human heart. "He himself knew what was in man," says the Gospel according to John (2:25). Yet he never had those experiences of sin which fools think to be necessary if innocence is to be transcended and the highest manhood is to be attained. From his spotless purity and his all-conquering strength that ancient lie that experience of evil is necessary if man is to attain the highest good recoils naked and ashamed.

That was the lie that the tempter brought to Adam and Eve in the garden of Eden. Man was told to seek discernment in Satan's way and not in God's.

Had man resisted the temptation, what heights of knowledge and strength would have been his! Satan would have fled from him like a cringing slave and he would have entered forever into a state of kingship in company with God.

But he yielded, and what was the result? A sad result indeed! He sought to attain knowledge, and lost the knowledge of good; he sought to attain power, and lost his own soul; he sought to become as God, and when God came to him in the garden he hid himself in shameful fear.

It is a sad story indeed. But it is the beginning and not the end of the Bible. The first chapters of the Bible tell us of the sin of man. The guilt of that sin has rested upon every single one of us, its guilt and its terrible results; but that is not the last word of the Bible. The Bible tells us not only of man's sin; it also tells us of something greater still: it tells us of the grace of the offended God.

33

What Is Sin?

We come now to a very momentous question—the question, "What is sin?" We have spoken about the first sin of man. Now we ask what sin at bottom is.

Widely different answers have been given to this question, and with these different answers have gone different views of the world and of God and of human life.

The true answer is to be obtained, as we shall see, very clearly in the Bible; but before I present that true answer to you, I want to speak to you about one or two wrong answers, in order that by contrast with them the true answer may be the more clearly understood.

In the first place, many men have notions of sin which really deprive sin of all its distinctiveness, or, rather, many men simply deny the existence of anything that can properly be called sin at all.

According to a very widespread way of thinking in the unbelief of the present day, what we popularly call morality is simply the accumulated experience of the race as to the kind of conduct that leads to racial preservation and well-being. Tribes in which every man sought his own pleasure without regard to the welfare of his neighbors failed, it is said, in the struggle for existence, whereas those tribes that restrained the impulses of their members for the good of the whole prospered and multiplied. By a process of natural selection, therefore, according to this theory, it came more and more to be true that among the races of mankind those that cultivated solidarity were the ones that survived.

In the course of time—so the theory runs—the lowly origin of these social restraints was altogether lost from view, and they were felt to be rooted in something distinctive that came to be called morality or virtue. It is only in modern times that we have got behind the scenes and have discovered the ultimate identity between what we call "morality" and the self-interest of society.

Such is a very widespread theory. According to that theory, "sin" is only another name—and a very unsatisfactory name too—for antisocial conduct.

What shall we say of that notion of sin from the Christian point of view? The answer is surely quite plain. We must reject it very emphatically. "Against you, you only, have I sinned," says the psalmist (Ps 51:4). That is at the very heart of the Bible from beginning to end. Sin, according to the Bible, is not just conduct that is contrary to the accumulated experience of the race; it is not just antisocial conduct: but it is an offense primarily against God.

Equally destructive of any true idea of sin is the error of those who say that the end of all human conduct is, or (as some of them say) ought to be, pleasure.

Sometimes the pleasure which is regarded as the goal to be set before man is the pleasure of the individual—refined and thoroughly respectable pleasure no doubt, but still pleasure. Such a view has sometimes produced lives superficially decent. But even such superficial decency is not apt to be very lasting, and the degrading character of the philosophy underlying it is certain to make itself felt even on the surface sooner or later. Certainly, that philosophy can never have a place for any notion that with any propriety at all could be called a true notion of sin.

Sometimes, it is true, the pleasure which is made the goal of human conduct is thought of as the pleasure, or (to use a more high-sounding word) the happiness, not of the individual but of the race. According to that view, altruism—namely, regard for the greatest happiness of the greatest number—is thought to be the sum total of morality.

A little reflection will show how widespread and how influential this doctrine is. Examine, for example, some of the schemes of character education which are being proposed for use in public schools or elsewhere. What do they amount to? Well, I am afraid they amount to an appeal to human experience as the basis of morality. This is the kind of conduct, they say in effect, which is found to work well; this is the kind of conduct, therefore, which good citizens ought to practice.

What should the Christian say of such schemes of so-called character education? Well, I think he ought to oppose them with all his might. Far from building character they undermine character in the long run, because they substitute human experience as the basis of morality for the law of God.

The things that they advocate in detail are, indeed, in many cases things that the Christian man also can advocate. Certainly the notion that the greatest happiness of the greatest number is the thing that should be put before us as the goal does produce in detail many maxims of conduct that coincide with what the Christian, on his very different basis, advocates. It is obvious that murder and theft and robbery are not conducive to the greatest happiness of the greatest number, and it is also obvious that they are contrary to the Christian's standard. Therefore, the Christian and the non-Christian, though for very different reasons, can unite in telling people not to enter upon a life of crime.

Nevertheless, the difference between Christian morality and the morality of the world is a very important difference indeed.

For one thing, it is a difference even in details. Although there is a large area where the conduct advocated by modern utilitarians, on the basis of their principle that the standard of morality is to be found in the experience of the race, is exactly the same, in detail, as the conduct which is advocated by Christians, yet there are cases where the underlying difference of principle comes to the surface even in differences in detail.

Thus we have seen in the newspapers recently a good deal of discussion about "mercy killing" or "euthanasia." Certain physicians say very frankly that they think hopeless invalids, who never by any chance can be of use either to themselves or to anyone else, ought to be put painlessly out of the way. Are they right?

Well, I daresay a fairly plausible case might be made out for them on the basis of utilitarian ethics.

I am not quite sure—let me say in passing—that even on that basis it is a good case. This is a very dangerous business—this business of letting experts determine exactly what people "never will be missed." For my part, I do not believe in the infallibility of experts, and I think the tyranny of experts is the worst and most dangerous tyranny that ever was devised.

But, you see, that does not touch the real point. The real point is that the modern advocates of euthanasia are arguing the thing out on an entirely different basis from the basis on which the Christian argues it. They are arguing the question on the basis of what is useful—what produces happiness and avoids pain for the human race. The Christian argues it on the basis of definite divine commands. "You shall not murder" (Exod 20:13) settles the matter for the Christian. From the Christian point of view, the physician who engages in a mercy killing is just a murderer. It may also turn out that his mercy killing is not really merciful in the long run.

But that is not the point. The real point is that be it ever so merciful, it is murder, and murder is sin.

The views of sin that we have considered so far are obviously opposed to Christianity. No Christian can hold that morality is just the accumulated self-interest of the race, and that sin is merely conduct opposed to such self-interest. The Christian obviously must hold that righteousness is something quite distinct from happiness and that sin is something quite distinct from folly.

Other erroneous views of sin, however, are not so obviously erroneous, and not so obviously, even though just as truly, anti-Christian.

There is, for example, the notion that sin is the triumph of the lower part of man's nature over the higher part, that it is the triumph of the appetites of the body over the human spirit—the human spirit which ought to be that in man which rules.

This definition appeals—falsely, it is true—to certain biblical expressions, and it is a very ancient notion in the visible Christian church.

In its extreme form, it represents matter as being in itself evil. The human soul or spirit is enclosed, it holds, in the prison house of the material world, and the goal of the soul's efforts should be to get free. Sin is everything that prevents that liberation of the soul from the material world.

Obviously such a doctrine is quite contrary to the Bible. It is a pagan notion, not a Christian notion. For one thing it really does away with the Christian idea of God altogether. If matter is essentially evil, and if God is good, then God could not have created matter, but matter must have existed always independently of him. So, it is not surprising to find that in the days of the ancient church those who regarded matter as being essentially evil were dualists, not theists. That is, they did not believe in one God, Creator of all things that exist, but they believed that there are two ultimately independent principles—a good principle, God; and an evil principle, matter.

In marked contrast with all such views, the Bible teaches from beginning to end that the material world, like the world of spirits, was created by God, and that none of God's works is to be regarded as evil.

Moreover, the Bible not only combats that view as a theory of the universe, but it also combats very earnestly the effects of it in human conduct. Those who regard matter as being essentially evil tend always to asceticism. They tend, always, that is, to abstention from enjoyment of the good things of this world as though such abstention were in itself a virtue—not a means to an end, but an end in itself; not a thing necessary on occasion, but a thing always necessary if real sainthood is to be attained.

To such asceticism the Bible is everywhere opposed. "Do not handle, do not taste, do not touch," said the ascetics who were impairing the supremacy of Christ in the Colossian church (Col 2:21). Very vigorously does the apostle Paul combat their teaching. "The earth is the Lord's, and the fullness thereof," he says also in another epistle (1 Cor 10:26). So teaches the Bible from beginning to end. There is not a bit of support in Holy Scripture for the notion that the material world is essentially evil and that the enjoyment of it is sin.

At this point, however, there may possibly be an objection. Does not the Bible repeatedly designate "the flesh" as an evil thing, and in doing so does it not teach that sin consists after all in the triumph of man's lower or bodily nature over his higher nature?

To that objection we answer that certainly the Bible does repeatedly designate "the flesh" as an evil thing, but that the whole question is what it means in those passages by "the flesh."

Some people think that the word refers, in those passages, to the bodily nature of man, a lower part of his nature as over against a higher part. That view is presented in several of the recent translations of the Bible—better called mistranslations—which are leading so many people astray at the present time. One of those translations renders the word meaning "the flesh" in the eighth chapter of Romans as "the physical nature"; another translates it as "the animal nature."

Do you see exactly where those translations lead? They lead to the view that the conflict between the flesh and the Spirit according to the epistles of Paul is a conflict between the physical and the spiritual part of man's nature, and that the triumph of the physical or animal nature in the conflict is what the Bible calls sin.

Is that view right? No, my friends, it is not right. On the contrary, it is a very deadly and far-reaching error. A man who holds that notion of sin has not the slightest inkling of what the Bible holds sin to be, and he is not apt, alas, to have the slightest inkling of what the Bible says about salvation from sin.

It is perfectly true, of course, that in many places the Bible means by "flesh" simply a certain part of the bodily structure of man or animals. It speaks of "flesh and blood" or the like. That is the simply physical sense of the word. Undoubtedly it does occur in the Bible.

But we are speaking now about those passages where "the flesh" is presented in the Bible as an evil thing. Does the word have its simply physical meaning in those passages?

The answer is emphatically, "No." In those passages the word is used in a very special sense indeed—a sense far removed from the original, purely physical sense. In those passages, it designates not the physical nature of man or the animal nature of man but the whole nature of man, as that nature is now, in its fallen condition, separate from God.

The principal stages by which the word "flesh" comes to have that meaning in the Bible seem to be fairly clear. First, the simple physical meaning. Then "flesh" designating man in his weakness, all of him being designated by a word that properly designates the part of him in which his weakness is most clearly shown, as when the Bible says: "All flesh is grass, and all its beauty is like the flower of the field" (Isa 40:6). Then "flesh" designating man as he now is, lost in sin—as he now is until he is transformed by the Spirit of God. It is this third meaning of the word which is found in those great passages where "the flesh" is represented in the Bible as being an evil thing.

As thus used, the word does not designate a lower part of man's nature as over against a higher part. It designates all of man's nature, in its present sinful state, as over against the divine holiness. It does not designate the body of man as over against the spirit of man, but it designates the whole of man as over against the Spirit of God.

That appears with particular clearness in such a passage such as First Corinthians 3:3, where Paul says, according to the King James Version: "For ye are yet carnal: for whereas there is among you envying, and strife, and divisions, are ye not carnal, and walk as men?" The word translated "carnal" here comes from the word for flesh; it might just as well be translated "fleshly." Well, what does it mean? The apostle tells us himself. "Are ye not carnal, and walk as men?" he says. Evidently being carnal or fleshly and walking as men are intended here to be taken as the same thing. One of these expressions explains the other. How ought the Corinthian Christians to walk? According to God. How do they actually walk? According to men. But walking according to men as distinguished from walking according to God is, Paul says, the same as being fleshly. Thus the flesh does not mean, as those sadly mistaken translations of the Bible make it mean, the animal nature of man as distinguished from some higher part of his nature; it means simply all of human nature—that is, human nature as it now is, under the control of sin, as distinguished from the Spirit of God.

Paul makes the thing even clearer in the following verse: "For when one says, 'I follow Paul,' and another, 'I follow Apollos,' are you not being merely human?" (1 Cor 3:4) Here the apostle treats being men—that is, being merely men, and not transformed by the Spirit of God—actually as a thing worthy of blame and as just the same thing as being fleshly. "Are ye not carnal?" he says in verse 3. "Are you not being merely human?" he says in verse 4. The two mean the same thing, and they both mean being controlled or acting as though one were controlled simply by one's fallen human nature as distinguished from being controlled by the Spirit of God.

What a gulf there is between this biblical way of regarding fallen human nature and the modern paganism, proclaimed by so many preachers of the present day, which actually takes as a leading article in its creed the words, "I believe in man." What a gulf there is between the modern pagan confidence in human resources and the teaching of the Bible which makes the question, "Are ye not men?" the same thing as "Are ye not carnal?" and treats both questions as bringing a terrible reproach to Christian people!

Thus sin, according to the Bible, is not just "the brute in us." No, it is very much more serious than that. Alas, sin is not the brute in us; it is, rather, the man in us. It is the man in us, because the whole man—spirit or soul just as much as body—is sold under sin until transformed by the regenerating power of the Spirit of God.

Certainly the Bible does teach that sin sits in our bodies, that it makes our bodies its instruments, and that uncontrolled bodily appetites constitute a very large part of the occasion for our falling. All that is perfectly true. But that is very different indeed from saying that bodily appetites constitute the essence of sin. No, when the Bible gives us one of those terrible lists of sins that occur, for example, here and there in the epistles of Paul, when it catalogues, as in the fifth chapter of Galatians, "the works of the flesh" (Gal 5:19–21), it includes not only what we are accustomed to speak of as fleshly sins but also, and very prominently, sins such as pride and hatred, which are not, in our sense, sins of the flesh at all. Indeed, those sins of pride and the like, and not what we call fleshly sins, are just the sins that Paul is speaking of in that passage in First Corinthians when he charges his readers with being fleshly.

The Bible finds sin, moreover, in a world of spirits—it speaks of spiritual hosts of wickedness "in the heavenly places" (Eph 6:12)—as it finds sin, alas, in the spirit of fallen man. If we want to be true to the Bible, we must get rid of this whole notion that the essence of sin is found in the rebellion of a lower part of our nature against a higher part.

What, then, is sin? We have said what it is not. Now we ought to say what it is.

Fortunately, we do not have to search very long in the Bible to find the answer to that question. The Bible gives the answer right at the beginning in the account that it gives of the very first sin of man—that account which we studied together in the previous one of these little talks.

What was that first sin of man, according to the Bible? Was it the gratification of a bodily appetite? Yes, it was that. The woman saw that the tree was good for food and that it was pleasant to the eyes, we are told. But was the sin merely the gratification of a bodily appetite? Most certainly not. No, it was a highly intellectual, spiritual thing. The serpent said that the eating of the fruit of that tree would make man wise. That part of it was not a bodily appetite at all.

What, then, was that first sin of man? Is not the answer perfectly clear? Why, it was disobedience to a command of God. God said, "You shall not eat of the fruit of the tree" (Gen 3:3); man ate of the fruit of the tree, and that was sin. There we have our definition of sin at last.

"Sin is any want of conformity unto, or transgression of, the law of God" (WSC Q&A 14). Those are the words of the Shorter Catechism, not of the Bible; but they are true to what the Bible teaches from Genesis to Revelation.

34

The Majesty of the Law of God

In the last of these talks we considered the momentous question, "What is sin?" Various answers to that question have been given, but the true answer, we observed, is the one that is contained in the Shorter Catechism. "Sin," the Shorter Catechism says, "is any want of conformity unto, or transgression of, the law of God" (WSC Q&A 14).

The full meaning of that definition will become clearer, I hope, as we go on to speak of the consequences of Adam's sin for the human race.

Just now, however, we are taking the thing only in its simplest and most obvious form. The most elementary thing about sin is that it is that which is contrary to God's law. You cannot believe in the existence of sin unless you believe in the existence of the law of God. The idea of sin and the idea of law go together. Think of sin, in the biblical sense of the word, and you think of law; think of law, and—at least as humanity now is—you think of sin.

That being so, I ask you just to run through the Bible in your mind and consider how very pervasive in the Bible is the Bible's teaching about the law of God.

We have already observed how clear that teaching is in the account which the Bible gives of the first sin of man. God said, "You shall not eat of the fruit of the tree" (Gen 3:3). That was God's law; it was a definite command. Man disobeyed that command; man did what God told him not to do, and that was sin.

But the law of God runs all through the Bible. It is not found just in this passage or that, but it is the background of everything that the Bible says regarding the relations between God and man.

Consider for a moment how large a part of the Old Testament is occupied with the law of God—the law as it was given through Moses. Do you think that came by chance? Not at all. It came because the law is truly fundamental in what the Bible has to say.

All through the Old Testament there is held up a great central thought: God the lawgiver, man owing obedience to him.

How is it, then, with the New Testament? Does the New Testament obscure that thought? Does the New Testament depreciate in any way the law of God?

There have been those who have thought so. The error called "antinomianism" has held that the dispensation of grace which was ushered in by Christ abrogated the law of God for Christian people.

What a truly horrible error that is! It is certainly true, in one sense, that Christians are, as Paul says, not under the law but under grace. They are not subject to the curse which the law pronounces against sin; Christ has set them free from that curse by bearing the curse in their stead on the cross. They are not under any dispensation where their acceptance with God depends upon their own obedience to God's law; instead, their acceptance with God depends upon the obedience which Christ accomplished for them. All that is perfectly true. But does that mean that for Christian people the law of God is no longer the expression of God's will which they are solemnly obligated to obey; does it mean that they are now free to do as they please and are no longer bound by God's commands?

Let the whole Bible, let the whole New Testament, in particular, give the answer.

"Do not think," said Jesus, "that I have come to abolish the Law or the Prophets; I have not come to abolish them but to fulfill them" (Matt 5:17). Then he goes on to place his righteousness in contrast with the righteousness of the scribes and Pharisees. Is it easier than theirs? No, he himself tells us that it is harder. "For I tell you," he says, "unless your righteousness exceeds that of the scribes and Pharisees, you will never enter the kingdom of heaven" (Matt 5:20). Does his righteousness partake less of the nature of law than the rules which the scribes and Pharisees set up? Is his righteousness something that a man can take with a grain of salt? Is it something that he can suit himself about heeding? Well, I can only say, my friends, that if that is the way you read the words of Jesus as they are recorded in the Gospels, you have not even got barely to the threshold of understanding them. "If your right eye causes you to sin," says Jesus, "tear it out and throw it away. For it is better that you lose one of your members than that your whole body be thrown into hell" (Matt 5:29). "I tell you," he says in another place, "on the day of judgment people will give account for every careless word they speak" (Matt 12:36). Are these the words of one who substitutes some other reign for the reign of the law of God? Are these the words of one who believed that men could trifle with God's law?

I know that some people hold—by veritable delirium of folly, as it seems to me—that the words of Jesus belong to a dispensation of law that was brought to a close by his death and resurrection and that therefore the teaching of the Sermon on the Mount, for example, is not intended for the dispensation of grace in which we are now living.

Well, let them turn to the apostle Paul, the apostle who has told us that we are not under the law but under grace. What does he say about the matter? Does he represent the law of God as a thing without validity in this dispensation of divine grace?

Not at all. In the second chapter of Romans, as well as (by implication) everywhere else in his epistles, he insists upon the universality of the law of God. Even the Gentiles, though they do not know that clear manifestation of God's law which was found in the Old Testament, have God's law written upon their hearts and are without excuse when they disobey. Christians, in particular, Paul insists, are far indeed from being emancipated from the duty of obedience to God's commands. The apostle regards any such notion as the deadliest of errors.

"Now the works of the flesh," says Paul, "are evident: sexual immorality, impurity, sensuality, idolatry, sorcery, enmity, strife, jealousy, fits of anger, rivalries, dissensions, divisions, envy, drunkenness, orgies, and things like these. I warn you, as I warned you before, that those who do such things will not inherit the kingdom of God" (Gal 5:19–21).

Great, indeed, according to Paul, is the advantage of the Christian, as of those who even before Christ came were saved by the merit of the sacrifice that he was to make upon the cross (being saved, as Christians are now, by the grace of God through faith). Christians are not under the curse of the law; in that tremendous sense, they are not under the law but under grace. Christ has borne the just penalty of the law for them. They have moreover within them a new power, the power of the Holy Spirit, which the law of itself could never give.

But that new power does not emancipate them from obedience to God's holy commands. Nay, it enables them to obey those commands as they could never obey them before.

Consider for a moment, my friends, the majesty of the law of God as the Bible sets it forth. One law over all—valid for Christians and valid for non-Christians, valid now and valid to all eternity. How grandly that law is promulgated amid the thundering of Sinai! How much more grandly still, and much more terribly, it is set forth in the teaching of Jesus—in his teaching and in his example! With what terror, we are fain to say, with Peter, in the presence of that dazzling purity: "Depart from me, for I am a sinful man, O Lord" (Luke 5:8). Nowhere in the Bible, in the teaching of Jesus our Savior, do we escape from the awful majesty of the law of God—written in the constitution of the universe, searching the innermost recesses of the soul, embracing every idle word and every action and every secret thought of the heart, inescapable, all-inclusive, holy, terrible. God the lawgiver, man the subject; God the ruler, man the ruled! The service of God is a service that is perfect freedom, a duty that is the highest of all joys; yet it is a service still. Let us never forget that. God was always and is forever the sovereign King; the whole universe is beneath his holy law.

That is the atmosphere in which the Bible moves; that is the rock upon which it is founded. God's law embracing all! And what sort of law is that? Is it an arbitrary enactment of some cruel tyrant, a meaningless sport of one whose power exceeds his wisdom or his goodness? No, this law is grounded in the infinite perfection of the being of God himself. "You therefore must be perfect," said Jesus, "as your heavenly Father is perfect" (Matt 5:48). That is the standard. God's law is no arbitrary or meaningless law; it is a holy law, as God himself is holy.

If that be the law of God, how awful a thing is sin! What tongue can tell the horror of it? Not an offense against some temporary or arbitrary rule proceeding from temporal authority or enforced by temporal penalties, but an offense against the infinite and eternal God! What nameless terror steals over us when we really contemplate such guilt as that!

But do we really contemplate it? That question must certainly be asked. I know that some of my hearers regard what I have been saying as being no more worthy of consideration than the hobgoblins and bogies with which nurses used to frighten naughty children. An outstanding characteristic of the age in which we are living is a disbelief in anything that can be called a law of God and, in particular, a disbelief in anything that can properly be called sin. The plain fact is that the men of our day are living for the most part in an entirely different world of thought, feeling, and life from the world in which the Christian lives. The difference does not just concern this detail or that: it concerns the entire basis of life; it concerns the entire atmosphere in which men live, move, and have their being. At the heart of everything that the Bible says are two great truths, which belong inseparably together: the majesty of the law of God, and sin as an offense against that law. Both these basic truths are denied in modern society, and in the denial of them is found the central characteristic of the age in which we are living.

Well, what sort of age is that? What sort of age is this in which the law of God is regarded as obsolete and in which there is no consciousness of sin?

I will tell you. It is an age in which the disintegration of society is proceeding on a gigantic scale. Look about you, and what do you see? Everywhere the throwing off of restraint, the abandonment of standards, the return to barbarism.

But, you say, has not liberty at least been attained? Now that morality has been abandoned—Victorian convention and all that—surely liberty must have free course. Ah, but does it, my friends? A man has to be completely blind to say that it does. On the contrary, liberty lies prostrate in Russia, in Germany, in Italy, and in many other countries of the earth. How slow was the progress of Europe up from tyranny to democracy and freedom! And now that hard-won liberty is rapidly being thrown away.

There are indeed islands of resistance to the tyrant's march. We read the other day how the people of Great Britain stood silent when they received the news that their king—symbol of liberty—just died. A hush seemed to fall upon the nation, and selfish strife for the moment ceased. It was an eloquent silence indeed—eloquent of the love of a great people for things that treasure can never buy, eloquent of centuries of glorious history:

> This happy breed of men, this little world,
> This precious stone set in the silver sea,
> Which serves it in the office of a wall
> Or as a moat defensive to a house,
> Against the envy of less happy lands,—
> This blessed plot, this earth, this realm, this England.[1]

But do you think that even Great Britain is safe—safe, I mean, not from the battleships and the airplanes and the armies of her enemies, but safe from the far more dangerous foes within?

---

1. William Shakespeare, "Richard II," act 2, scene 1.

I do not think so, my friends. Safe, no doubt, if any country of the earth is safe; but still not safe. Look back upon the history of Great Britain, and I think you will see that always before she had one possession that she is now in danger of losing. She had the conviction that there is a transcendent principle of right to which all the peoples of the world are subject. I know that there were times when that eternal principle of right was lost very largely from view. There were times of widespread debauchery. There have been times in the history of the British Empire when some very terrible national crimes were committed. But always there was a large remnant in the British people that had a firm and well-grounded belief in their obligation to the law of God. That was the precious salt that preserved the nation from decay, and gave it that marvelous stability which ought to be an object of emulation to the whole civilized world. Liberty under the law of God—that and not far-flung battle lines or an Empire upon which the sun never sets—is the thing that has made Great Britain great.

Today that is seriously endangered in Great Britain as well as everywhere else. There are hosts of people who do not believe that there is a law of God, and the number of those who do believe is smaller today and is less influential in the heart of the national life than it has ever been in recent centuries. I do not know whether you agree with me, my friends, but I am bound to say that I am afraid for Great Britain today, and being afraid even for Great Britain I am still more afraid for all the rest of the world. Everywhere tyranny is stalking through the earth, and decadence disguised under a hundred newfangled and high-sounding names.

Well, what shall be done about it? Many people who are not Christians at all agree with us in holding that something ought to be done. Even materialists and other atheists can see that. Something obviously has to be done even to keep the animal, man, in some kind of healthy condition upon the earth—to prevent him from destroying himself, for example, by another world war.

So all sorts of things are being proposed to check the ravages of crime. One proposes that we shall all be fingerprinted and be treated like paroled criminals required to show identification cards as we walk the streets, whenever required to do so according to the whims of the police—no longer allowed to go about our business unhindered until there is some sort of legitimate suspicion that we are guilty of crime. Another proposes that teachers even in private schools and Christian schools shall be regarded as government officials, being required to take an oath of allegiance as is done in Hitlerized Germany. A thousand nostrums are being brought to our attention, different in many particulars but all alike in being destructive of that civil and religious liberty which our fathers won at such cost.

Such measures will never accomplish even the end that they have in view. Patriotism can never be implanted in people's hearts by force. The attempt to do that serves only to crush out patriotism when it is already there. The march of communism or other forms of slavery can never be checked by the suppression of freedom of speech. Such suppression serves only to render more dangerous the progress of the destructive ideas. What then is the remedy for the threatened disruption of society and for the rapidly progressing decay of liberty?

There is really only one remedy. It is the rediscovery of the law of God.

If we want to restore respect for human laws, we shall have to get rid of this notion that judges and juries exist only for the utilitarian purpose of the protection of society and restore the notion that they exist for the purposes of justice. They are only very imperfect exponents of justice, it is true. There are vast departments of life with which they should have nothing whatever to do. They are exceeding their God-given function when they seek to enforce inward purity or purity of the individual life, since theirs is the business only of enforcing—and that in necessarily imperfect fashion—that part of righteousness which concerns the relations between man and man. But they are instruments of righteousness all the same, and when that is not recognized, disaster follows for the state. Society will never be preserved by attaching savage penalties to trifling offenses because the utilitarian interests of society demand it; it will never be preserved by the vicious practice (followed by some judges) of making "example" of people in spasmodic and unjust fashion because such examples are thought to have a salutary effect as a deterrent from future crime. No, we say, let justice never be lost from view—abstract, holy, transcendent justice—no matter what the immediate consequences may be thought to be. Only so will the ermine of the judge again be respected and the ravages of decadence be checked.

Ah, but all that does not touch the really important matter. Underlying all these considerations of nations and of society is the great question of the relation of the soul to God. Unless men are right with God, they will never be right in their relations with one another.

How, then, shall they be right with God? Oh, you say, there is the gospel; there is the sweet and comforting teaching of Jesus Christ.

Yes, but do men come to Jesus Christ? Do they come to him for the salvation of their souls? No, they patronize him as a fine religious teacher, and then they pass him by.

How, then, shall they be brought to him? The Bible gives the answer. "So then," it says, "the law was our guardian until Christ came, in order that we might be justified by faith" (Gal 3:24). That was true of the Hebrews in Old Testament and post-Old Testament times, about whom Paul is speaking in that passage; but it is also true of everyone who really and truly comes to Jesus Christ as his Savior from sin. The consciousness of sin alone leads men to turn to the Savior from sin, and the consciousness of sin comes only when men are brought face-to-face with the law of God.

But men have no consciousness of sin today, and what are we going to do? I remember that this problem was presented very poignantly in my hearing some time ago by a preacher who was sadly puzzled.

> Here we are living in the twentieth century. We have to take things as we find them; and as a matter of fact, whether we like it or not, if we talk to the young people of the present day about sin and guilt they will not know what we are talking about; they will simply turn away from us in utter boredom, and they will turn from the Christ whom we preach. Is not that really too bad? Is it not really too bad for them to miss the blessing that Christ has for them if only they would come to him? If, therefore, they will not come to Christ in our way, ought we not to invite them to come in their way? If they will not come to Christ through the consciousness of sin induced by the terror of the law of God, may we not get them to come through the attraction of the amiable ethics of Jesus and the usefulness of his teaching in solving the problems of society?[2]

I am afraid that in response to such questions we shall just have to say no. I am afraid we shall just have to say that being a Christian is a much more tragic thing than these people suppose. I am afraid we shall just have to tell them that they cannot clamber over the wall into the Christian way. I am afraid we shall just have to point them to the little wicket gate, and tell them to seek their Savior while yet he may be found in order that he may rescue them from the day of wrath.

---

2. The name of the preacher Machen references here is unknown.

But is not that utterly hopeless? Is it not utterly hopeless to try to get the people of the twentieth century to take the law of God with any seriousness or to be the slightest bit frightened about their sins?

I answer, certainly it is hopeless. Absolutely hopeless. As hopeless as it is for a camel to try to pass through the eye of a needle.

But, you see, there is One who can do hopeless things; that is the Spirit of the living God.

Do not fear, you Christians. The Spirit of God has not lost his power. In his own good time, he will send his messengers even to a wicked and adulterous and careless generation. He will cause Mount Sinai to overhang and shoot forth flames; he will convict men of sin; he will break down men's pride; he will melt their stony hearts. Then he will lead them to the Savior of their souls.

35

Is Mankind Lost in Sin?

We have spoken of the first sin of man, and we have spoken of the question, "What is sin?" The question now arises what consequences that first sin of man has had for us and for all men.

Some people think it had very slight consequences—if indeed these people think that there ever was a first sin of man at all, in the sense in which it is described in the third chapter of Genesis.

I remember that some years ago, when I was driving home in my car after a summer vacation, I stayed over Sunday in a certain city without any particular reason except that I do not like to travel on that day. Being without any acquaintance with the city, I dropped into what seemed perhaps to be the leading church in the central part of the town.

What I heard in that church was typical of what one hears in a great many churches today. There was nothing particularly remarkable about it. I really do not know just why it has lingered so long in my memory, since I have heard essentially the same thing said in many places and in many ways.

It was the Sunday on which the new Sunday school teachers were being inducted into office. The pastor preached a sermon appropriate to the occasion. There are two notions about the teaching of children in the church, he said. According to one notion, the children are to be told that they are sinners and need a Savior. That is the old notion, he said, and it has been abandoned in the modern church. According to the other notion, he said, which is of course the notion that we moderns hold, the business of the teacher is to nurture the tender plant of the religious nature of the child in order that it may bear fruit in a normal and healthy religious life.

Was that preacher right, or was what he designated as the old notion right? Are children born good, or are they born bad? Do they need, in order that they may grow up into Christian manhood, merely the use of the resources planted in them at birth, or do they need a new birth and a divine Savior?

That is certainly a momentous question. We may answer the question in this way or in that, but about the importance of the question I do not see how there can well be any doubt. That preacher, in the church of which I have spoken, recognized the importance of the question. That was why I was interested in his sermon. He answered the question that he raised quite wrongly, but at least he was right in looking the question fairly in the face.

In the present talk and the next one, I propose that we should imitate that preacher in facing the question fairly, even though our conclusion may turn out to be different from his. Are children born good or are they born bad? Is each man the captain of his own soul, and a pretty capable captain too, or is all mankind lost in sin?

When we approach the Bible with that question in our minds, one thing is at once perfectly clear. It is that the Bible from Genesis to Revelation teaches that all men (with the one exception of Jesus Christ) are as a matter of fact sinners in the sight of God. How they all came to be sinners is another question of which we shall speak in the following talk, but what we are now concerned to observe is that according to the Bible they are as a matter of fact all sinners.

In one great passage, particularly, that truth, that all men are sinners, is made the subject of definite exposition and proof. That passage is found in Romans 1:18–3:20. There the apostle Paul, before he goes on to set forth the gospel, sets forth the universal need of the gospel. All have need of the gospel, he says, because all, without exception, are sinners. The Gentiles are sinners. They have disobeyed God's law, even though they have not that law in the particularly clear form in which it was presented to God's chosen people through Moses. Because they have disobeyed God's law, and as a punishment for their disobedience of it, they have sunk deeper and deeper into the mire of sin. The Jews, alas, says Paul, are sinners. They have great advantages in that they have a special revelation from God; in particular, they have a supernatural revelation of God's law. But it is not the hearing of the law that causes a man to be righteous but the doing of it; and the Jews, alas, though they have heard it, have not done it. They too are transgressors.

So all have sinned, according to Paul. He drives that truth home by a series of Old Testament Scripture quotations beginning with the words: "None is righteous, no, not one; no one understands; no one seeks for

God. All have turned aside; together they have become worthless; no one does good, not even one" (Rom 3:10–12).

I think it is hardly too much to say that if this Pauline teaching about the universal sinfulness of mankind is untrue, the whole of the rest of that glorious epistle, the Epistle to the Romans, falls to the ground. Imagine Paul as admitting that a single mere man since the fall ever was righteous in the sight of God, not needing, therefore, redemption through the precious blood of Christ; and you see at once that such a Paul would be a totally different Paul from the one who speaks in every page of the Epistle to the Romans and in every one of the other Pauline epistles that the New Testament contains. The light of the gospel in the teaching of Paul stands out always against the dark background of a race universally lost in sin.

Is the case any different in the rest of the Bible? Well, we have not time here to pass all the sixty-six books of the Bible in review; but if you will just try to think of them as a whole as well as you can at this moment, you will see, I feel sure, that the universality of sin is at the very heart and core of the message that they contain. I care not at this point whether you turn to the Old Testament or to the New Testament. Everywhere there is the same terrible diagnosis of the ill of mankind. Brushing aside all excuses, the Bible teaches us everywhere to look at ourselves as God looks at us, and that doing so bids us beat upon our breasts and cry to God: "Unclean, unclean!"

I know that some people hold that an exception is to be found in this gloomy chorus of the biblical books. Paul, they admit, believed that all are sinners and need to have their sins washed away in a holy victim's blood, but Jesus, they say, appealed with confidence to the good that men's hearts contained.

Do you know, my friends, I am amazed when I hear people talk in that way? I am not amazed because they show thereby that they themselves have no consciousness of sin. Alas, the lack of a consciousness of sin is only too common among those whose hearts have never been touched by the Holy Spirit in saving grace. But what does amaze me is that educated men, living in the supposedly enlightened twentieth century, should show so little historical sense as to attribute their own pagan confidence in humanity to Jesus of Nazareth. I am not surprised that *they* have confidence in man, but I am considerably surprised that they should think that Jesus had.

Of course, if they think so they must put the four Gospels aside, as those Gospels stand, in the New Testament. That is clear at the start; for in the Fourth Gospel it is said in so many words that Jesus did not have confidence in man. "Now when he was in Jerusalem," the Fourth Gospel says, "at the Passover Feast, many believed in his name when they saw the signs that he was doing. But Jesus on his part did not entrust himself to them, because he knew all people and needed no one to bear witness about man, for he himself knew what was in man" (John 2:23–25). Alas, Jesus knew what was in man only too well. Others, who looked merely upon the outward appearance, might have confidence in human goodness; but he knew the depths of the heart, and, knowing those depths, he was slow to trust those who seemed at least superficially to trust him.

No doubt this passage does not mean that Jesus's estimate of all men was like his estimate of those who came to him at that first Passover time in Jerusalem. The meaning is rather that because of his profound insight into the human heart he could discriminate between those who were relatively trustworthy and those who were not; he did not need that anyone should tell him, "Beware of this man or that," but could himself tell which men were not to be trusted.

All the same, the passage does give a picture of Jesus which is far removed indeed from the picture given by those who make him an adherent of the modern creed "I believe in man." This Jesus of the Fourth Gospel is no advocate of that incorrigible optimism regarding human nature which is thought to be a virtue by so many preachers of the present day.

Indeed, according to the Fourth Gospel, Jesus said to Nicodemus, "You must be born again" (John 3:7) and "Unless one is born again he cannot see the kingdom of God" (John 3:3). All that men call goodness, in other words, is useless if a man would come into God's presence. He must receive a new birth if he would be received. The universal sinfulness of mankind is there taught with a plainness that could hardly be surpassed.

Of course, the Fourth Gospel will not be accepted by the preachers of whom I am now speaking. Most of them will not admit that it was written by John the apostle or that it gives a truthful account of what Jesus really taught.

How is it, then, with the other three Gospels? Do they give any other account of Jesus's attitude toward human claims to goodness than that which is given in the Gospel according to John?

No, they give exactly the same account. Let us look at this thing carefully and fairly.

Before Jesus began his public ministry, according to the three Synoptic Gospels, there had appeared a prophet called John the Baptist.

Well, what did this great prophet do? He called on the people to be baptized unto the remission of sins and the people came to him confessing that they were sinners.

Did he call on *some* of the people to confess their sins and be baptized, or did he call upon *all* of them? This question needs only to be put in order that it may be answered. Without a doubt, he called on all of them—all save the one sinless man, Jesus of Nazareth. Surely that indicates, then, that he held them all, save that one, to be sinners.

Indeed, in this universal call to repentance, John the Baptist did not even make exception of himself. "I need to be baptized by you," he said as Jesus came to him to be baptized, "and do you come to me?" (Matt 3:14) What a clear testimony that is to the universal sinfulness of mankind! Even John the Baptist was not exempt. He was a stern preacher of righteousness; he called the people to repentance. But before he called the people to repentance, he repented himself. In the presence of the holiness of the Son of God, John the Baptist, greatest of the prophets, confessed himself a sinner like the rest.

Did Jesus differ from the teaching of John the Baptist at this point? John the Baptist taught the universal sinfulness of mankind. Did Jesus repudiate such teaching?

Surely that question, again, needs only to be asked in order that it may be answered. Far from repudiating John the Baptist's ministry, Jesus put the unmistakable stamp of his approval upon it. "What did you go out into the wilderness to see?" he said. "A reed shaken by the wind? . . . What then did you go out to see? A prophet? Yes, I tell you, and more than a prophet. . . . Truly, I say to you, among those born of women there has arisen no one greater than John the Baptist" (Matt 11:7,9,11). Evidently, Jesus regarded that stern preacher of righteousness as his true forerunner. The necessary preparation for Jesus's ministry was, according to Jesus himself, the recognition of that universal sinfulness which John the Baptist so powerfully proclaimed.

We cannot, however, stop there. Jesus did not teach the universal sinfulness of mankind (and the consequent universal need of repentance) merely by endorsing the Baptist who taught these things. No, he also taught these things himself. Do you remember how the Gospel according to Matthew reports the preaching with which Jesus came forward in Galilee after John the Baptist had been put into prison? Well, it reports it in exactly the same words as those in which it reports the Baptist's preaching. "Repent," said

Jesus, "for the kingdom of heaven is at hand" (Matt 4:17). That is word-for-word what John the Baptist had said (Matt 3:2).

Did Jesus address that call to all of the people or only to some? Did he say: "Repent, those of you who are sinners, but there are some of you who need no repentance"?

There is one saying of Jesus in the Gospels which, if we took it absolutely alone, and closed our eyes completely to the connection in which it was spoken, might lead us to say that Jesus did make exceptions in his call to repentance. "I came not," he said, "to call the righteous, but sinners" (Mark 2:17). Ah, but, my friends, when we take this verse in its context and in connection with all the rest of Jesus's teaching, we see that those among Jesus's hearers who placed themselves in the category of the righteous who need no repentance were regarded by Jesus as needing repentance most of all.

"Two men," said Jesus, "went up into the temple to pray, one a Pharisee and the other a tax collector. The Pharisee, standing by himself, prayed thus: 'God, I thank you that I am not like other men, extortioners, unjust, adulterers, or even like this tax collector. I fast twice a week; I give tithes of all that I get.' But the tax collector, standing far off, would not even lift up his eyes to heaven, but beat his breast, saying, 'God, be merciful to me, a sinner!'" (Luke 18:10–13)

Which of those two men received a blessing from God when he prayed there in the temple—the man who thought he was an exception to God's call to repentance or the one who beat upon his breast and confessed himself a sinner? Jesus tells us very plainly. The publican went down to his house justified rather than the other.

Ah, my friends, how terrible is the rebuke of Jesus again and again and again for those who think that they form exceptions to the universal sinfulness of mankind!

A rich young ruler came running to Jesus one day, and asked him, "Good Teacher, what must I do to inherit eternal life?" Jesus repeated to him a number of the commandments. The man said, "All these I have kept from my youth." Jesus said: "You lack one thing: go, sell all that you have and give to the poor." The young man went away sorrowful. (Mark 10:17–22)

Do you think that was a bad young man? No, he was a good young man—that is, if any man is good. We are expressly told that when Jesus looked at him he loved him. Yet he lacked something; he was not good as God regards goodness.

I do not think the point of the narrative is found in the particular thing that he lacked. The point is rather that every man always lacks something. No man comes up to God's standard; no man can inherit the kingdom of God if he stands upon his own obedience to God's law.

Did you ever observe what incident comes just before this incident of the rich young ruler in all three of the Synoptic Gospels—in Matthew and in Mark and in Luke? It is the incident of the bringing of little children to Jesus, when Jesus said to the disciples, as reported in Mark and similarly in Luke: "whoever does not receive the kingdom of God like a child shall not enter it." (Mark 10:15; Luke 18:17) There is a profound connection between these two incidents, as there is also a connection of both of them with the parable of the Pharisee and the publican which in Luke immediately precedes.

Some years ago, I heard a sermon on the incident of the rich young ruler. I suppose that in the course of my life I have heard other sermons on that incident, but they have all gone completely from my memory. What are the sermons that we are apt to remember? I think they are the sermons where the preacher does not preach himself but where he truly unfolds the meaning of some great passage of the Word of God. After we have heard such a sermon, then when we come to that passage ever and again in our reading of the Bible, we think of the way in which God's messenger made the meaning of it clear to us; and we thank God anew.

The sermon of which I am now thinking is one which was preached some time ago in a Philadelphia church by my colleague, Professor R. B. Kuiper. He took the incident of the rich young ruler together with the incident of the bringing of the little children to Jesus and he showed how both incidents teach the same great lesson—the lesson of the utter helplessness of man the sinner and the absolute necessity of the free grace of God. You cannot depend for your entrance into the kingdom of God upon anything that you have or anything that you are. You must be poor, and you must be a child. You must be utterly poor in order that you may enter in, and you must be as helpless as a little child. Your reliance cannot be on your own goodness, for you have none. It can only be upon the mysterious grace of God.

I tell you, my friends, that teaching does not lie merely somewhere upon the surface of Jesus's teaching; it lies at the very heart of it. The great central message of Jesus Christ—nay, also his great central work in the gift of himself for sinners upon the cross—is altogether without meaning unless all men without exception are sinners deserving only God's wrath and curse.

No, the teaching of Jesus most emphatically does not form an exception to the teaching of the Bible regarding the universal sinfulness of mankind. According to the whole of the Bible, and particularly according to Jesus, mankind is lost in sin.

The Bible does not say that just in some far-off, general terms. It brings it right home to every man. It brings it right home to you. According to the Bible, you are lost in sin today—unless you have been saved by God's grace.

How do you know that you are lost in sin? How do we all know that we are sinners?

Well, our own hearts condemn us. We know it in that way except when our consciences have become seared as with a hot iron. But there is also Another that tells us we are sinners. Our own heart condemns us, but "God is greater than our heart" (1 John 3:20). God has told us we are sinners; he has told us in his own holy Word from beginning to end. Well may the apostle John say, in view of the whole of the Bible: "If we say we have not sinned, we make him a liar" (1 John 1:10).

God is not a liar, my friends. The whole Bible is right. This world is lost in sin, and you too are lost in sin unless the Holy Spirit has led you or is leading you at this hour to have recourse to God's grace which has been extended you freely and wonderfully in Jesus Christ our Lord.

36

The Consequences of the Fall of Man

We observed in the preceding talks that according to the Bible all men are sinners. We observed particularly that the teaching of Jesus forms no exception whatever to this biblical condemnation of mankind. In his teaching, just as in the rest of the Bible, we are told that mankind is lost in sin.

Yet according to Jesus that universal sinfulness of mankind is not something that belongs to man just because he is man. It is by no means a necessary part of human nature as such.

There are two ways at least in which we can show from the teaching of Jesus that it is not.

In the first place, Jesus commands his disciples to be perfect as their heavenly Father is perfect. He could not have commanded them to be something which it was never the intention of God that they should be. Therefore, sin is not a necessary part of human nature.

In the second place, Jesus himself presents one example of a man without sin—a person truly having a human nature and yet having no sin. That also shows plainly that sin does not necessarily belong to human nature as such.

The example of a sinless man which Jesus presents is the example of himself. In the words of Jesus as recorded in the Gospels there is no trace of any consciousness of sin. Jesus taught his disciples to pray, "Forgive us our debts" (Matt 6:12), but he did not pray that prayer himself. He says to his disciples, "If you then, who are evil" (Matt 7:11), but he did not say, "If *we* then, being evil." He did not include himself in that sinfulness which he attributes to other men. We have here only one instance of a very strange thing that runs throughout the words of Jesus as they are recorded in the Gospels—namely, the strange separation which Jesus always preserves between himself and his hearers in the matter of the relationship to God and in particular in the matter of sin. Jesus never says, "our Father" to God, joining himself with his disciples in that word "our," and certainly he never joins himself with his disciples in any confession of sin. I think we have sometimes failed to give sufficient attention to that stupendous fact. Imagine any other teacher saying to his hearers, "If you then, being evil!" How abominable that would be on the lips of any other than Jesus! Any other religious teacher would say, "If we all—you and I—then, being evil, know how to give good gifts unto our children." But Jesus says, "If *you* then, being evil."

Here, as always, Jesus separates himself with the utmost clearness from sinful humanity. All mankind, he teaches, is lost in sin, but he himself is without sin. Surely that is a strange fact.

Is it because Jesus was not a man? No, that explanation will not do at all. The Gospels throughout represent Jesus as being truly a man, and Jesus so represents himself. Well, then, in Jesus we have a man who was without sin. That shows very clearly that sin is no necessary part of human nature; it is not something constitutive of man's nature as man.

A very serious problem, then, arises. If sin is no necessary part of human nature, how comes it that all mankind, save one, are sinners? How are we to explain this strangely uniform reign of sin?

The same problem is also presented by what we have said in previous lectures in this little series. We have observed that man, as created, was good. God created man in his own image—in knowledge, righteousness, and holiness. Well, then, if God created man good, how comes it that all men now are bad? How did sin pass into all mankind?

That question is no mere theoretical matter; it is no matter of merely curious interest. On the contrary, it is a matter of the greatest practical importance. From wrong answers to the question of how all men came to be sinners have come wrong answers to the question of what sin is, and from wrong answers to the question what sin is have come continuance in sin and a turning away from the grace of God. I think that it is of very great moment for our souls that we should get this matter straight once and for all in our minds.

Here is the question then. Man was created good. How comes it then that all men upon this earth are now bad? What caused this stupendous change from good to bad?

It does seem as though we ought to have at least a hint of the right answer in what we have said in previous talks in this series. We have seen how sin came into the world; it came in through the sin of Adam. If then the Bible tells us that all men, descended from Adam by ordinary generation, are sinners, surely it is natural for us to say that the universal sinfulness of Adam's descendants was due to Adam's sin. Surely it is natural for us to say that Adam's descendants do not begin life sinless as he began it, but that they begin it tainted in some way or other with the sin that Adam committed. A uniform effect seems to demand that unitary cause.

As to the exact way in which all mankind is involved in Adam's sin, there have been differences of opinion in the church. Some have held that mankind forms so much of a unity that what Adam did all men actually did. Mankind, these persons have held, was all concentrated in Adam, so that his act was the act of every single one of us.

It is perfectly clear that this view is contradictory both to common sense and to the Bible. Mankind, both according to common sense and according to the Bible, is a plurality of persons, not one person; therefore, it cannot be said that what Adam did was actually done by every one of his descendants. I have done many wrong things in my life, but I did not eat the forbidden fruit in the garden of Eden. That was not done by me; it was done by another person, Adam.

How comes it, then, that all mankind and not merely Adam is involved in Adam's first sin?

I am going to quote to you what the Shorter Catechism says on that point, and then I am going to ask you whether what the Shorter Catechism says is or is not in accordance with the Bible.

"Did all mankind fall in Adam's first transgression?" so the question reads. Here is the answer. "The covenant being made with Adam, not only for himself, but for his posterity; all mankind, descending from him by ordinary generation, sinned in him, and fell with him, in his first transgression" (WSC Q&A 16).

You will remember what is here meant by the covenant. It is the covenant of works or the covenant of life, which we observed to be so very simple in its terms. If Adam kept perfectly the commandments of God—so the covenant ran—he would have life; if he disobeyed, he would have death.

But now the Shorter Catechism says that that covenant was made with Adam not only for himself but for his posterity. Has it biblical warrant for saying so?

I think that even the book of Genesis, in which the fall of Adam is narrated, indicates rather clearly that the Shorter Catechism has perfectly good biblical warrant. If Adam transgressed, he was to die. Death was to be the punishment of disobedience. Well, he did transgress. What then happened? Was Adam the only one who died? Did his descendants begin where he began? Did they have placed before them all over again that same alternative between death and life that was placed before Adam? Not at all. The book of Genesis indicates the contrary very clearly. No, the descendants of Adam already, before they individually made any choices at all, had that penalty of death resting upon them. The book of Genesis just seems to take that as a matter of course.

What, then, does that mean? It means that when that covenant of life was made with Adam it was made with him as the divinely appointed representative of the race. If he obeyed the commandments of God, the whole race of his descendants would have life; if he disobeyed, the whole race would have death. I do not see how the narrative, when you take it as a whole, can mean anything else.

That view of the matter, presupposed in the book of Genesis, becomes more explicit in certain important passages of the New Testament. In the latter part of the fifth chapter of Romans, the apostle Paul makes it plain. "Therefore, as one trespass led to condemnation for all men," he says, "so one act of righteousness leads to justification and life for all men" (Rom 5:18). "For . . . by the one man's disobedience," he says in the next verse, "the many were made sinners" (Rom 5:19). In these words, and all through this passage, we have the great doctrine that when Adam sinned he sinned as the representative of the race, so that it is quite correct to say that all mankind sinned in him and fell with him in his first transgression.

All mankind did not actually sin when Adam sinned because all mankind did not yet exist. We cannot say that Adam's descendants by any act of their own wills ate the forbidden fruit, because when the forbidden fruit was eaten their own wills and their own personalities were not yet in existence. There is no such thing, strictly speaking, as a collective will of humanity, and therefore it is not correct to say that the collective will of humanity performed that sinful act.

But how comparatively slight is the error of those who say that there is a collective will of humanity and that the collective will of humanity performed that sinful act compared with the error of those who say that humanity was not involved in Adam's sin at all! How slight is the error of those who say that all mankind *actually* sinned when Adam sinned compared to the error of those who say that all mankind did not sin at all, did not sin in any sense, when Adam sinned! The Bible plainly teaches that Adam sinned as the representative of all mankind, and that the consequences which his first sin had for him it had also for all his posterity.

Adam was the representative of all mankind by appointment of God. We cannot fathom the divine counsels sufficiently to say exactly why God made such an appointment, but we can see that there was something very fitting about it. There is a profound and mysterious connection between the parent and the child. So, there is a profound and mysterious connection between Adam and the whole race of his descendants. If he had been made the representative of angels or of some equally diverse order of beings, then indeed we should find it difficult to detect anything fitting in such an arrangement; but when he was made the representative of his own descendants, that is surely in analogy with other things that God does, and we can in contemplating it detect something of the perfect wisdom and harmony to be found in all God's dealings with his creatures.

When Adam sinned, then, all mankind sinned in him and fell with him. All the consequences which his first transgression had for him it had also for his posterity.

It is quite right, therefore, when the next question in the Shorter Catechism reads not "Into what estate did the fall bring Adam?" but "Into what estate did the fall bring mankind?" We must study now the consequences of Adam's first sin for all humanity.

The Shorter Catechism says in its answer to the question just quoted that those consequences of Adam's first sin may be summed up if we say that the fall brought mankind into an estate of sin and misery (WSC Q&A 17).

Wherein, then, consists the sinfulness of that estate whereinto the fall brought mankind?

The answer of the Shorter Catechism to that question is one of the weightiest in the whole of that wonderful summary of Bible teaching. I trust you will attend to it very carefully with me now; and then, if you have questions in your mind about it and difficulties regarding it, I trust you will let me try in the following talk to show you how, despite those questions and despite those difficulties, the teaching of the Bible on this great subject stands triumphantly and majestically against the assaults of opposing views. Particularly do I want you to see that these matters are not just theological subtleties, but are of profound moment for every man and every woman and every child.

Let us then take as the basis of our discussion that weighty answer in the Shorter Catechism to the question regarding the sinfulness of the estate into which the fall brought mankind. "The sinfulness of that estate whereinto man fell," says the Shorter Catechism, "consists in the guilt of Adam's first sin, the want of original righteousness, and the corruption of his whole nature, which is commonly called original sin; together with all actual transgressions which proceed from it" (WSC Q&A 18).

The first thing that this answer says is that the *guilt* of Adam's first sin rested upon all his descendants. Every man descended from Adam by ordinary generation comes into the world bearing the awful penalty which God pronounced upon disobedience.

At this point, some of you may hold up your hands in horror. How, you may say, can one person bear the guilt of another person's sin? How can we possibly suppose that before infants have done anything either good or bad they yet are punished because of what Adam did so long ago?

Well, I should just like to point out to you that if it is impossible in the nature of things for one person to bear the guilt of another person's sins, then we have none of us the slightest hope of being saved and the gospel is all a delusion and a snare. At the heart of the gospel is the teaching of the Bible to the effect that Jesus Christ, quite without sin himself, bore the guilt of our sins upon the cross. If that be true then we cannot pronounce it impossible that one person should bear the guilt of another person's sins.

The apostle Paul insists upon this analogy in the latter part of the fifth chapter of Romans. In that part of that chapter, we find set forth the great Scripture doctrine that is called the doctrine of imputation.

That doctrine, if you take it as the Bible sets it forth as a whole, involves three great acts of imputation. First, Adam's first sin is imputed to his descendants. Second, the sins of saved people are imputed to Christ. Third, Christ's righteousness is imputed to saved people.

When the Bible teaches that the sins of saved people are imputed to Christ, that means that Christ on the cross bore the penalty rightly resting on saved people. He was not deserving of death; he had not sinned at all. Yet he suffered as though he had sinned. God treated him as though he had sinned, although he was not a sinner. The sin for which he died was not a sin that he had committed; it was our sin that was imputed to him.

So, when the Bible teaches that Christ's righteousness is imputed to saved people, that does not mean that the saved people are then actually righteous. On the contrary, they are sinners. But they receive the blessed reward of life which Christ's righteousness deserved. Christ's righteousness is not actually theirs, but it is imputed to them.

So, finally, when the Bible teaches that Adam's first transgression was imputed to his descendants, that does not mean that those descendants had actually committed that first transgression. But the penalty which God pronounced upon that sin of Adam rested upon them. Adam committed that first transgression as their representative. They, as well as he, bore the penalty.

Listen to the wonderfully clear way in which this is taught in the fifth chapter of Romans:

"Therefore, as one trespass led to condemnation for all men, so one act of righteousness leads to justification and life for all men. For as by the one man's disobedience the many were made sinners, so by the one man's obedience the many will be made righteous" (Rom 5:18–19).

"One trespass led to condemnation for all men . . . By one man's disobedience the many were made sinners"—there we have, expressed with a clearness that could scarcely be surpassed, the doctrine of the imputation of Adam's sin to his posterity. All mankind, descended from Adam by ordinary generation, bore the penalty which God pronounced upon Adam's first transgression.

Does, then, that doctrine of the imputation of Adam's sin to his posterity mean that the descendants of Adam, though themselves good, yet suffer the penalty of Adam's sin? Does it mean that good people, because of what Adam did so long ago, are treated by God as though they were bad—suffering, although they are good, many miseries in this life and the pains of hell forever?

No, indeed, it does not mean that at all. On the contrary, every person who suffers the penalty of Adam's sin is also himself bad. Indeed, badness is necessarily involved in that penalty itself.

God said to Adam that if he disobeyed he would die. What is the meaning of that death? Well, it includes physical death; there is no question about that. But, alas, it also includes far more than physical death. It includes spiritual death; it includes the death of the soul unto things that are good; it includes the death of the soul unto God. The dreadful penalty of that sin of Adam was that Adam and his descendants became dead in trespasses and sins.

When I say that, I do not mean that God is the author of sin, either the sin that comes because of prior sin or any other kind of sin. But I do mean that as a just penalty of Adam's sin, God withdrew his favor and the souls of all mankind became spiritually dead.

That spiritual deadness is described in the Shorter Catechism in the words that follow, "the guilt of Adam's first sin," which we have been trying to expound. "The sinfulness of that estate whereinto man fell," says the Shorter Catechism, "consists in the guilt of Adam's first sin, the want of original righteousness, and the corruption of his whole nature, which is commonly called original sin; together with all actual transgressions which proceed from it" (WSC Q&A 18). The want of original righteousness and the corruption of man's whole nature, into which the fall brought mankind, constitute spiritual death.

That want of original righteousness, that corruption of man's whole nature, that spiritual death, is itself sin. It is not just the basis for sin, the substratum of sin, the root out of which sin comes. It is, indeed, all that. All actual transgressions proceed from it. But it is more than the basis or the substratum of sin. It is itself sin. The soul that is spiritually dead, the soul that is corrupt with that dreadful corruption, is no longer sinful merely with the imputed guilt of Adam's first transgression. No, it is sinful with its own sinfulness. It is guilty not only because of Adam's guilt but also because of its own sin. It deserves eternal punishment because it itself is now sinful.

Many questions arise in many persons' minds regarding that Scripture doctrine of original sin. "Is a man really responsible," they ask, "for a corruption of his nature that he cannot help, a corruption of his nature with which he was born? Can he really be commanded to do something that he has no ability to do? Can he really be commanded to be something that he cannot be?"

If such questions arise in your mind, I ask you to attend to what will be said in the following talk.

37

What Is Original Sin?

In the last talk, we spoke of the way in which all men came to be sinners. God made a covenant with Adam. If he obeyed perfectly the commandments of God, he was to have life. If he disobeyed, he was to die. The death with which he was to die was not only physical death. It was also spiritual death. It meant the death of the soul to things that were good and to God, a profound corruption of man's whole nature.

That covenant, we observed further, was made with Adam not only for himself but for his posterity. It was made with Adam as the representative of the whole human race, and whatever it meant for Adam, therefore, it meant for all mankind. If he had kept the covenant, not only he but all mankind would have had eternal life. There would have been no more probation; there would have been no more jeopardy. Mankind would not only have had righteousness as it had had when Adam was created, but it would now have had an assured righteousness; the very possibility of sinning would have been removed.

As a matter of fact, however, Adam did not keep the covenant; he sinned against God by eating the forbidden fruit. The result was that not only he but all mankind received the dreadful penalty pronounced against disobedience. The penalty was death—not only physical death but also the far more terrible spiritual death, the death of the soul to things that are good, the death of the soul to God.

Thus all mankind through the fall has become corrupt and utterly unable to please God. The individual sins that men commit are but manifestations of that profound corruption of man's nature. The fruit is corrupt because the tree is corrupt.

Such, according to the Shorter Catechism, and according to the Bible, is the sinfulness of that estate whereinto man fell.

But the Shorter Catechism, again in accordance with the Bible, says that the estate whereinto man fell was an estate not only of sin but also of misery.

What, then, is the misery of that estate whereinto man fell? The Shorter Catechism gives the answer with words which at least are perfectly easy to understand. "All mankind," it says, "by their fall lost communion with God, are under his wrath and curse, and so made liable to all miseries in this life, to death itself, and to the pains of hell forever" (WSC Q&A 19).

Do you think we need elaborate the discussion to prove that this answer is in accordance with the Bible? I am inclined to think not, my friends. Just run through the Bible in your mind, and you will see that the Shorter Catechism is perfectly right.

"All mankind by their fall lost communion with God" (WSC Q&A 19). What a vivid picture of that loss we have in the book of Genesis: "And they [Adam and Eve] heard the sound of the LORD God walking in the garden in the cool of the day, and the man and his wife hid themselves from the presence of the LORD God among the trees of the garden" (Gen 3:8). Gone were the days when God conversed with Adam freely as with his child; gone was the joy which Adam formerly had in the presence of God. He hid himself now from God, and soon a flaming sword separated him from the garden where he had had communion with his heavenly Father. The Bible certainly loses no time in making it clear that all mankind by their fall lost communion with God.

The Bible makes it equally clear that all mankind by their fall came under God's wrath and curse. The doctrine of the wrath of God is not a popular doctrine, but there is no doctrine that is more utterly pervasive in the Bible. Paul devotes to it a large part of three chapters out of the eight chapters in his great Epistle to the Romans which he devotes to the exposition of his message of salvation, and he is at particular pains to show that the wrath of God rests upon all men except those who have been saved by God's grace. But there is nothing peculiar within the Bible in that great passage in the first three chapters of Romans. That passage only puts in a comprehensive way what is presupposed from Genesis to Revelation and becomes explicit in passages almost beyond number.

Does the teaching of Jesus form any exception to the otherwise pervasive presentation of the wrath of God in the Bible? Well, you might think so if you listened only to what modern sentimentality says about Jesus of Nazareth. The men of the world, who have never been born again, who have never come under the conviction of sin, have reconstructed a Jesus to suit themselves, a feeble sentimentalist who preached only the love of God and had nothing to say about God's wrath. But very different was the real Jesus, the Jesus who is presented to us in our sources of historical information. The real Jesus certainly proclaimed a God who, as the Old Testament that he revered as God's Word says, is a "consuming fire" (Deut 4:24). Very terrible was Jesus's own anger as the Gospels describe it, a profound, burning indignation against sin; and very terrible is the anger of the God whom he proclaimed as the Ruler of heaven and earth. No, you certainly cannot escape from the teaching of the Bible about the wrath of God by appealing to Jesus of Nazareth. The most terrible even among the biblical presentations of God's wrath are those that are found in our blessed Savior's words.

Finally, the Shorter Catechism says that all mankind by their fall are "made liable to all miseries in this life, to death itself, and to the pains of hell forever" (WSC Q&A 19). Here again the biblical warrant is perfectly plain, and here again at the heart of the biblical warrant is to be found what was said by Jesus. Where do you find the most terrible descriptions of hell in the whole of the Bible? In the book of Revelation, perhaps you may say. Well, I am not sure. At least equally terrible are those that are found in the teaching of Jesus. It is Jesus who speaks of the sin that shall not be forgiven either in this world or that which is to come; it is Jesus who speaks of the worm that does not die and the fire that is not quenched (Mark 9:48); it is Jesus who has given us the story of the rich man and Lazarus (Luke 16:19–31) and of the great gulf between them; it is Jesus who says that it is profitable for a man to enter into life having one eye rather than, having two eyes, to be cast into hell fire (Matt 18:9). Just let your mind run through the teaching of Jesus, and I think you will really be surprised to find how pervasive in his teaching is the thought of hell. It appears in the Sermon on the Mount; it appears of course in the great judgment chapter, the twenty-fifth chapter of Matthew; it appears in passages too numerous to mention. It is not somewhere on the circumference of his teaching but at the very heart and core of it.

I do not believe we always understand quite clearly enough how great is the divergence at this point between the teaching of Jesus and current preaching both at home and on the mission field. Men are interested today in this world. They have lost the consciousness of sin, and having lost the consciousness of sin they have lost the fear of hell. They have tried to make of Christianity a religion of this world. They have excogitated the so-called social gospel. They have come to regard Christianity as just a program for setting up the conditions of the kingdom of God upon this earth, and they are tremendously impatient when anyone looks upon it as a means of entering into heaven and escaping hell.

The strange thing about this way of thinking is not that men engage in it. The thought of hell is of course not palatable to men who have never been born again; it is an offense to the natural man. But what is indeed strange is that in support of this this-worldly way of thinking men should appeal to Jesus of Nazareth.

As a matter of fact, the teaching of Jesus centers altogether on the thought of heaven and of hell: "Do not lay up for yourselves treasures on earth, where moth and rust destroy and where thieves break in and steal, but lay up for yourselves treasures in heaven, where neither moth nor rust destroys and where thieves do not break in and steal. For where your treasure is, there your heart will be also" (Matt 6:19–21). "Do not fear those who kill the body, and after that have nothing more that they can do. But I will warn you whom to fear: fear him who, after he has killed, has authority to cast into hell. Yes, I tell you, fear him!" (Luke 12:4–5) Those words are typical of all of Jesus's teaching. The teaching of Jesus is intensely other-worldly. A man who regards it as consisting essentially in a program for this world has not got the slightest inkling of its meaning. Let not anyone who thinks that fear of hell should be put out of the mind of unregenerate men ever suppose that he has the slightest understanding of what Jesus came into the world to say and do.

But please understand exactly why it is that I am alluding to this subject now. I am not doing so because it is my intention to set forth now what the Bible says about the future life. That would belong to another series of talks. My purpose now is somewhat different. I have mentioned the biblical teaching about hell simply because it is necessary in order that you may understand the biblical teaching about sin. The awfulness of the punishment of sin shows as nothing else could well do how heinous a thing sin really is in the sight of God.

I have tried to present to you in a bare outline something like the whole picture—man guilty with the imputed guilt of Adam's first sin, man suffering therefore the death that is the penalty of that sin—not only physical death but also that spiritual death that consists in the corruption of man's whole nature and in his total inability to please God—man bringing forth out of his corrupt heart individual acts of transgression without number, man facing eternal punishment in hell. That is the picture that runs throughout the Bible. Mankind, according to the Bible, is a lost race, lost in sin; and sin is not just a misfortune, but is something that calls forth the white heat of the divine indignation. Before the awful justice of God no unclean thing can stand; and man is unclean, transgressor against God's holy law, subject justly to its awful penalty.

As I try to present that picture to you, I think you as well as I are impressed with the fact that the men of the present day for the most part will have none of it. They will not admit at all that mankind is lost in sin. I remember a service that I attended some years ago in a little church in a pretty village. The preacher was distinctly above the average in culture and in moral fervor. I do not remember his sermon (except that it was a glorification of man); but I do remember something that he said in his prayer. He quoted that verse from Jeremiah to the effect that the heart of man is "deceitful above all things, and desperately sick" (Jer 17:9), and then he said in his prayer, as nearly as I can remember his words: "Oh Lord, thou knowest that we no longer accept this interpretation, but now think that man does what is right if only he knows the way." Well, that was at least being frank about the matter. We have a good opinion of ourselves these days, and if so, why should we not let the Lord in on the secret? Why should we go on quoting with a sanctimonious air confessions of sin from the Bible if we really do not believe a word of them? I think the prayer of that village preacher was bad—very bad—but I also think that perhaps it was not *so* bad as the prayers of those preachers who have really rejected the central message of the Bible just as completely as he had and yet conceal the fact by the use of traditional language. At least that prayer raised the issue clearly between the biblical view of sin and the paganism of the modern creed, "I believe in man."

At the very foundation of all that the Bible says is this sad truth—that mankind is lost in sin.

I want to say just a little more to you about that truth before I go on to speak of salvation from sin.

The Bible teaches, we have observed, that every man comes into the world a sinner, with a corruption of nature out of which all individual transgressions proceed. That is the doctrine of original sin. It is against that doctrine of original sin that the chief attack has been made; and I want to say a few words to you about the attack in order that the Bible doctrine which is attacked may become all the more clear.

The attack against the doctrine of original sin has come to be connected with the name of a British monk who lived in the latter part of the fourth and the early part of the fifth century after Christ. His name was Pelagius. From him the whole family of the Pelagians is named. It is a numerous family. There are millions of Pelagians living today, and most of them never knew that such a person as Pelagius ever lived.

Like many other people who have wrought untold harm to the souls of men, Pelagius seems to have been himself a very respectable gentleman. His great opponent was careful to say, I believe, that he recognized the attractiveness of Pelagius's life in many respects and certainly had no personal grudge against him.

The opponent of Pelagius was one of the greatest men in the whole history of the Christian church. His name was Augustine. The controversy between Augustine and Pelagius is one of the most famous controversies ever known in human history. Its fame is quite just. In that Pelagian controversy, an issue was fought out that is at the very vitals of the Christian church.

Fortunately, the story of the controversy has been told for us by one of the greatest masters in the field of the history of doctrine, the late B. B. Warfield, in an essay entitled "Augustine and the Pelagian Controversy" which he contributed originally to the *Library of the Nicene and Post-Nicene Fathers* and which is now reprinted in the volume entitled *Studies in Tertullian and Augustine* in his collected works. To Warfield I am indebted, to a very considerable extent, for what I am now saying regarding Pelagius. That brings me to confess in general with regard to this little series of talks that I am laying no claim to originality, and that before every talk I obtain great profit, for example, from reading over the relevant section in the great work *Systematic Theology* by Charles Hodge. It would be a fine thing if some of you would read over that great work with me. I think it a very great mistake indeed for us to suppose that nobody before our day ever understood anything of what the Bible teaches; and I for my part rejoice greatly in trying to stand in the great current of the Reformed faith. If I can show you a little bit of what that great system of doctrine is and a little bit of the basis for it in the Word of God, the purpose of these talks will have been fully attained.

But it is time for us to return to Pelagius and his attack on the biblical doctrine of original sin.

In contravention of that doctrine—though of course he supposed, however erroneously, that his teaching was in accordance with the Bible—

Pelagius said that every man, far from being born with a corrupt nature, begins life practically where Adam began it, being perfectly able to choose either good or evil. Indeed, said he, if a man has not that ability to choose either good or evil, he cannot be held responsible for his acts. He is not responsible for anything that he cannot help. Thus, if people were—as, said Pelagius, they are not—born with a corrupt nature, that corruption of nature would not be sin. Sin is just a matter of individual acts; it appears only in those cases where a man has ability to choose either good or evil and where as a matter of fact he chooses evil instead of good.

It seems evident that this doctrine of Pelagius involves at least two things. In the first place, it involves a certain view of what sin is; and in the second place, it involves a denial of any appreciable effects of Adam's sin upon his posterity.

Let us look at these two things for a minute or two in turn.

In the first place, let us look at this Pelagian notion that sin inheres only in sinful acts and that a man cannot be blamed for a corruption of nature that he cannot help.

When we do look at it, we observe that it is really quite absurd. Suppose a man has committed a murder or a robbery. Suppose we are old-fashioned enough to tell him that we think he ought not to have done it. What does he say to us if, in accordance with Pelagius's teaching, he supposes that a man cannot be blamed for that corruption of nature that underlies his individual acts?

Why, he says to us that we are quite wrong in blaming him. "Do you blame me," he says, "for committing that murder or that robbery? You ought not to blame me. I admit that murder and robbery do seem to be bad actions; but then, you see, I am a bad man and so I could not help committing those bad actions. Well, if I could not help it, I am not to be blamed for it. I simply acted in accordance with my nature. If a good man commits bad actions you can blame him, but if a bad man does so that is only to be expected; he is only acting in accordance with his nature, and no blame ought to be attached to him for doing what he does."

Well, perhaps I am impressed with what my murderer friend says to me; but still I cannot get rid of the feeling that murder and robbery are reprehensible, and that folks ought not to indulge in them to any great extent. So, I say to myself that surely I ought to be able to blame *somebody* for committing murders or for committing robberies. Now my murderer friend has told me that I can blame good people if they commit murders or robberies. So hopefully I go out in search of such people. But then I make a truly startling discovery—the discovery that good people do not commit murders or robberies. So, there is nobody at all whom I can blame for those acts. I cannot blame bad people for them because they cannot help committing them—they commit them merely in accordance with their nature—and I cannot blame good people for committing them, because good people do not commit them at all. Apparently I was wrong in thinking that any moral blame could be attached to such acts. Murder and robbery are apparently not deserving of blame after all.

Perhaps you say that that conclusion is absurd. Well, it may be absurd; but it is exactly the conclusion that is dominant, to an alarming extent, in the thought of the present day. Hosts of people deny the whole notion of moral obligation; they deny that anybody can really be blamed for murder or robbery or adultery or any other sin. Why do they do so? They do so for the simple reason that they cannot accept either the Pelagian notion or the biblical notion of sin; and so they just deny that there is any such thing as sin.

They cannot, in the first place, accept the Pelagian notion that bad actions are due simply to a bad choice of a will that had perfect ability to choose either bad or good. The facts are dead against that Pelagian notion. Even an elementary study of criminology shows that back of the bad action lies a bad nature of the criminal and, for that matter—though there we are anticipating another point—a bad nature with which the criminal was born.

But then these people about whom I am speaking also reject the biblical doctrine. They reject the doctrine that bad actions springing from a bad nature, and indeed the bad nature itself, are worthy of blame.

Well, then, if bad actions that spring from a bad nature of the criminal are not subject to moral reprobation, and if the bad nature itself is also not a thing for which the criminal can be blamed, and if people with a good nature do not commit bad actions, it follows that nothing at all and no one at all can be blamed, and we have simply the profoundly antimoral doctrine of modern criminology that there is no such thing as moral obligation and that therefore crime is a disease.

The only escape from the abyss of that doctrine—which means, if it is permanently dominant, the ruin of civilization, to say nothing of what may come in another world—is simply to fall back upon the biblical doctrine that a man most emphatically can be blamed for things that he cannot help and in particular that he most emphatically can be blamed, and is blamed by God, for the sinful nature with which he was born.

The Bible plainly teaches in the first place that sinful actions come from the corrupt nature of the man who commits them, and in the second place that that corruption of nature is itself sin. But I am going to ask you to look at this matter a little more fully at the beginning of the next talk, in order that then, having spoken of sin, we may go on to speak of salvation.

38

Sinners Saved by Grace

At the close of the last talk, we were speaking of a great attack which has been made upon the biblical doctrine of original sin.

The attack was first made in the early fifth century by Pelagius, the opponent of Augustine, but it has been made in one form or another in every age of the Christian church, and it is being made with particular insistence today.

Pelagianism, we observed, involves a certain view, first, as to what sin is, and, second, as to the effects of Adam's sin upon his posterity. I was speaking to you at the close of the last talk about the former of these two subjects—namely, the Pelagian view of the nature of sin.

According to the Pelagian view, certainly according to the logic of that way of thinking, sin is just a matter of individual acts; it is not a matter of the underlying state of the soul. The will, according to Pelagianists, has the power of self-determination at any moment, and it is the bad use of that power of self-determination that is to be called sin.

Upon that power of self-determination, Pelagians say, moral responsibility depends. A man, they say, cannot be held responsible for what he cannot help. Therefore, if his individual acts did come inevitably from the underlying state of his nature, he would not be responsible either for those individual acts or for the underlying state of his nature from which they came. As a matter of fact, Pelagians hold that no such state of affairs exists and that man is perfectly able at any time to choose either good or evil.

According to the Augustinian view of sin, on the other hand, individual wrong choices do most emphatically come from the underlying state of the person who engages in them. The will most emphatically is not free in the sense that it can choose this or that no matter what the nature of the person doing the choosing may be.

So far, the Augustinian view of sin is in accordance, I suppose, with what is said by most of the psychologists and criminologists of the present day. But it differs from what is said by those psychologists and criminologists in holding that a man most emphatically is morally responsible for wrong choices springing out of his evil nature, and that he is most emphatically responsible for the evil nature out of which those wrong choices spring. Augustinianism differs, in other words, both from Pelagianism and from modern psychology, in holding that a man is responsible for things that he cannot help. If he is a bad man, if he has a bad nature, he is responsible for that bad nature no matter how it came to be bad. Sin, according to Augustinianism, is not just a matter of individual actions; it also inheres in the state underlying the actions. A man who commits a bad action cannot, according to Augustinianism, be excused on the ground that he is and always has been a bad man; on the contrary, a bad man, even aside from any particular bad actions, is justly subject to reprobation and abhorrence by man and by God. Both the bad actions and also the bad state from which the bad actions come are, according to Augustine, sin.

Is that Augustinian view the correct view of the Bible? I think that question needs only to be raised in order to be answered. I am just going to quote one passage and then I am going to ask you whether that passage does not sum up the teaching of the whole Bible on this point. The passage which I am going to quote is not taken from what are sometimes supposed to be the more philosophical or theological parts of the Bible. It is taken from the teaching of Jesus as recorded in the Synoptic Gospels. Yet it refutes the whole Pelagian view of the freedom of the will, the whole Pelagian notion that sin is a matter only of individual actions; and it refutes that whole notion more effectively than could be done by entire volumes of philosophy. Here is the passage to which I refer: "Either make the tree good and its fruit good, or make the tree bad and its fruit bad, for the tree is known by its fruit. You brood of vipers! How can you speak good, when you are evil? For out of the abundance of the heart the mouth speaks. The good person out of his good treasure brings forth good, and the evil person out of his evil treasure brings forth evil" (Matt 12:33–35). In the light of these words of Jesus, so simple and so profound, how utterly shallow the whole Pelagian view of the will and of sin is seen to be! According to Jesus, evil actions come from an evil heart, and both the actions and the heart from which they come are sinful.

That view is the view of the whole Bible. There is in the Bible from beginning to end no shadow of comfort for the shallow notion that sin is a matter only of individual choices and that a bad man can, without being changed within, suddenly bring forth good actions. No, the Bible everywhere finds the root of evil in the heart, and by the heart it does not mean just the feelings but the whole inner life of man. The heart of man, it tells us, is deceitful above all things and desperately wicked, and, because of that, man is a sinner in the sight of God.

The question may perhaps arise at this point in the minds of some of you whether such a view does not do away with personal freedom and personal responsibility.

Well, what do we mean by personal freedom? Do we mean by it a freedom of the will as an unaccountable something-or-other that swings around loosely inside of a man without any reference to the rest of the man and in particular without any reference to the question whether the nature of the man is good or bad?

If we mean that, we mean something that not only is quite absurd but also destroys that personal freedom that it started out to defend. The thing that makes an action a personal action is just that it proceeds from the whole nature of the man that engages in it. If the will were really free in the sense that it were without roots in the underlying being of the man who wills, then its choices would not be personal choices at all but would be just the meaningless swinging hither and yon of a pendulum governed by blind chance. As a matter of fact, there is no such thing as the will, considered as a separate something-or-other inside of a man; but what we call the will is just the whole man willing, as what we call the intellect is the whole man thinking and what we call the feelings is the whole man feeling. What we really ought to mean, therefore, when we speak of the freedom of the will, is rather the freedom of the man. A man is free and therefore morally responsible when his actions spring from his own nature and when he is aware of the fact that they are his own actions. If, indeed, a man is compelled, by actual direct physical impulsion, to do something against his will, then that is not really his own personal act and he is not morally responsible for it; but if his will itself is determined by his own nature, then no matter how inevitable the thing that he does may be, it is most emphatically his own personal act and he most emphatically is morally responsible for it. An evil man inevitably performs evil actions; the thing is as certain as that a corrupt tree will bring forth corrupt fruit: but the evil man performs those evil actions because he wants to perform them; they are his own free personal acts and he is responsible for them in the sight of God.

Such is not only sound philosophy and sound common sense, but it is plainly the teaching of the Bible from Genesis to Revelation.

Still, however, an objection may perhaps remain. Can a man really be blamed for something that he cannot help? Can he be blamed for an evil nature which he never was without and with which, indeed, he was born?

With regard to that objection I should just like to point out this—that if a person cannot be blamed for an evil nature, then it follows with an inevitable logic that he cannot be praised for a good nature.

Do you say that a person cannot be blamed for a nature that he always had, a nature that underlies all his individual acts? Well, then, if that principle is true of blame it is also true of praise. Can a person be praised for a nature that he always had, a nature that he did not produce? Do you say, No? Well, then, how about God? His good actions spring inevitably from his infinitely good nature. Is he then not to be praised? Ask the heavenly hosts who delight ever to sing his praises before the throne; ask all the saints who bless him for his excellent name. How reads the last of the Psalms?

> Praise the Lord!
> Praise God in his sanctuary;
> > praise him in his mighty heavens!
> Praise him for his mighty deeds;
> > praise him according to his excellent greatness!
>
> Praise him with trumpet sound;
> > praise him with lute and harp!
> Praise him with tambourine and dance;
> > praise him with strings and pipe!
> Praise him with sounding cymbals;
> > praise him with loud clashing cymbals!
> Let everything that has breath praise the Lord!
> > Praise the Lord! (Ps 150)

On the Pelagian theory that chorus of praise would have to be silenced. God did not make himself good; he always was good. His good actions come, with unparalleled certainty, from his good nature: therefore, on the Pelagian theory, let him not be praised!

But perhaps you say that God's nature is so different from ours that we cannot reason from what is true about him to what is true about us.

Well, then, how about the good angels? Their good actions spring inevitably from the goodness of their nature, and they did not create their nature, but it was created for them by God. Are they then not to be praised? How about the saints also who have gone to their reward? Surely for them the possibility of sinning is over; they are as perfectly good as the good angels are; in their case, as in the case of the good angels, good actions spring from an underlying goodness of nature. And in their case also, unless the Bible is altogether wrong, the goodness of their nature is not a product of their own endeavors but a gift of God. It was given to them in the new birth. Yet surely they are to be pronounced blessed and gloriously free.

Do you not see, my friends, how absurd is this Pelagian notion that moral praise or blame is not to be applied to the underlying nature of persons but only to their individual acts? The true state of the case is that the individual acts obtain their moral quality largely because of their connection with the underlying nature of the person who engages in them. A person is good if his nature is good no matter how it came to be good, and a person is bad if his nature is bad, no matter how it came to be bad. So, bad men are sinners in the sight of God and are subject to his just wrath and curse even though they were born bad.

That brings us to the second part of the Pelagian contention. If Pelagianism holds a shallow view regarding the question what sin is, it also holds a shallow view regarding the sin of the human race. It denies that Adam's sin had any very appreciable effects for his posterity. Every man, it holds, begins life practically where Adam began it, with complete ability to choose either good or evil. Thus it rejects the whole doctrine of original sin; it rejects the whole doctrine that all men descended from Adam by ordinary generation come into the world with a corrupt nature which then leads inevitably to individual acts of sin.

Of course, an obvious objection faces any such Pelagian view. If all men descended from Adam by ordinary generation come into the world without a corrupt nature and with a full ability to choose good instead of evil, why is it that all men without exception choose evil? Why is it that all men are sinners? If the question whether men shall be righteous or sinners depends upon the choice of the individual men, and if every man has full ability to choose one way or the other, it does seem exceedingly strange that all men have happened to choose the same way. The chances according to any mathematical law of averages would be far more than ten billion times ten billion to one against any such result.

To this objection I am not sure whether Pelagius did or did not reply that as a matter of fact some men have chosen the right. I am not quite sure whether he did or did not deny the universal sinfulness of mankind. If he did deny it he certainly placed himself squarely against the whole of the Bible, as we have already seen. But at any rate Pelagianism can only explain the general reign of sin by the bad example which Adam set. Adam, according to Pelagianism, set a bad example to the race; Christ set a good example. Men are perfectly able to follow either Adam's example or Christ's example. That is just a matter for the choice of the individual human will.

Such are the limits to which both sin and salvation are reduced according to the Pelagian scheme. Do I need to say that this scheme is radically contrary to the Bible? The Bible from beginning to end plainly teaches that individual sins come from a sinful nature, and that the nature of all men is sinful from their birth, "Behold, I was brought forth in iniquity, and in sin did my mother conceive me" (Ps 51:5)—these words of the fifty-first Psalm summarize, in the cry of a penitent sinner, a doctrine of sin which runs through the Bible from Genesis to Revelation. Upon that biblical view of sin depends also the biblical view of salvation. Does the Bible teach that all Christ did for us is to set us a good example which we are perfectly able to follow without a change of our hearts? The man who thinks so is a man who has not come even to the threshold of the great central truth which the Scriptures contain. "You must be born again," said Jesus Christ (John 3:7). The man who believes that Jesus spoke the truth when he said that must make a clean break with Pelagianism in all its many forms. No, my friends, despite Pelagius and his millions of modern followers, there is no hope whatever for us until we are born again by an act that is not our own; there is no hope that we shall really choose the right until we are made alive from the dead by the blessed act of the Spirit of the living God. To the man who does not see that, the Bible is still a sealed book. At the very foundation of the teaching of the Bible is the great biblical doctrine of original sin. That doctrine means that all mankind, since the fall, are totally corrupt and totally unable to please God. I think we ought to pause just there for a minute or two.

The doctrine that is called the doctrine of "total depravity" is one of the so-called five points of Calvinism. But it is not only one of the five points of Calvinism. It is also one of the things upon which the Bible lays greatest stress. I think it is very important for us to observe exactly what it means.

It does not mean that all men not Christians are at every moment just as bad as they possibly can be. On the contrary it is perfectly consonant with what is also plainly taught in Scripture—that the Spirit of God, by his common grace, restrains even unregenerate men from the full manifestation of the power of evil that dominates them. What then does the doctrine of total depravity mean?

It means, in the first place, that the corruption of fallen man affects all parts of man's nature. His faculties remain, it is true; he is still a man, and as being still a man he is responsible. But all his faculties, all parts of his nature, are vitiated by the corruption into which he has fallen. Sin does not reside merely in the body; it does not reside merely in the feelings, or merely in the intellect, or merely in what is sometimes falsely set off from the rest of human nature under the name of the will. But it resides in all of these. The whole life of man, and not merely any one part of it, is corrupt.

In the second place, the biblical doctrine of total depravity means that nothing that fallen and unregenerate men can do is really well-pleasing to God. Many things that they do are able to please us, with our imperfect standards, but nothing that they do is able to please God; nothing that they do can stand in the white light of his judgment throne. Some of their actions may be relatively good, but none of them are really good. All of them are affected by the deep depravity of the fallen human nature from which they come.

That may seem to us to be a hard doctrine, but it is plainly taught in the Word of God. Moreover, it receives heartfelt recognition from the truest saints. Ask the men of really holy life in the history of the Christian church, and they will tell you as they look back upon their lives in the period before they became Christians—even in cases where those lives have seemed to other people to be fine, self-sacrificing lives—that all that supposed goodness was just filthy rags in the sight of God. No, my friends, mankind, until regenerated by the mysterious act of the Spirit of God, is unable even for an instant so to live as really to please God.

That brings us to another aspect of the great biblical doctrine of total depravity. It is found in the complete inability of fallen man to lift himself out of his fallen condition. Fallen man, according to the Bible, is unable to contribute the smallest part to the great change by which he is made to be alive from the dead. Every man in whom that great change takes place does indeed have faith in the Lord Jesus Christ; it is through that personal act of faith that he is united to the Lord Jesus. But the point is that that faith is worked in him by the Holy Spirit of God. Men who are dead in trespasses and sins are utterly unable to have saving faith, just as completely unable as a dead man lying in the tomb is unable to contribute the slightest bit to this resurrection. When a man is born again, the Holy Spirit works faith in him, and he contributes nothing whatever to that blessed result. After he has been born again, he does cooperate with the Spirit of God in the daily battle against sin; after he has been made alive by God, he proceeds to show that he is alive by bringing forth good works: but until he is made alive he can do nothing that is really good; and the act of the Spirit of God by which he is made alive is a resistless and sovereign act.

That is so fundamental in the Bible, the Bible lays such tremendous stress upon it, that it does seem strange that people who believe in the Bible should deny it. As a matter of fact, however, semi-Pelagianism, assigning some part to man in the attainment of salvation, has appeared in a great many different forms in the history of the church.

You will remember what pure Pelagianism is. According to the out-and-out Pelagian view, man needs no change of nature in order to lay hold upon the gospel and be saved; indeed, the gospel is really not strictly necessary for salvation at all; it merely brings to bear an additional persuasion upon a man in order to induce him to do what is right, and he is perfectly able to do what is right in accordance with the freedom of his own will.

The semi-Pelagian view is a sort of compromise between that out-and-out Pelagian view and the Augustinian view which is so plainly taught in the Bible. According to the semi-Pelagian view, man's nature is weakened by the fall; and although the weakening which every man derives from Adam is not in itself sin, it leads inevitably to sin unless the grace of God intervenes.

Then in addition to this semi-Pelagianism there has been a vast deal of 45-percent Pelagianism, 40-percent Pelagianism, and Pelagianism in almost every conceivable proportion. Some have held that although fallen man can do nothing positively to save himself, he can choose whether he will resist or accept the proffered grace of God. Thus man does have to do his part, even though it be only a negative part, in the work of salvation.

To all such compromises the Bible opposes its perfectly clear doctrine of the total inability of fallen man and the all-sufficiency of divine grace. Man, according to the Bible, is not merely sick in trespasses and sins; he is not merely in a weakened condition so that he needs divine help: but he is dead in trespasses and sins. He can do absolutely nothing to save himself, and God saves him by the gracious, sovereign act of the new birth. The

Bible is a tremendously uncompromising book in this matter of the sin of man and the grace of God.

The biblical doctrine of the grace of God does not mean, as caricatures of it sometimes represent it as meaning, that a man is saved against his will. No, it means that a man's will itself is renewed. His act of faith by which he is united to the Lord Jesus Christ is his own act. He performs that act gladly and is sure that he never was so free as when he performs it. Yet he is enabled to perform it simply by the gracious, sovereign act of the Spirit of God.

Ah, my friends, how precious is that doctrine of the grace of God! It is not in accordance with human pride. It is not a doctrine that we should ever have evolved. But when it is revealed in God's Word, the hearts of the redeemed cry, "Amen." Sinners saved by grace love to ascribe not some but all of the praise to God.

Part 3

The Final Broadcasts

39

The Progress of Christian Doctrine

In the beginning of this year's series of radio talks, I want to extend a word of welcome both to old friends whose interest has done so much to encourage us during the past two years and also to those who may be listening in this afternoon for the first time.

For the benefit of both classes of listeners, it may not be amiss for me to say just a word or two about the plan which has governed this Westminster Seminary Hour from the beginning.

What I have been trying to do is to present just as plainly as I can the great system of revealed truth which the Bible contains. When I say, "system of truth," I mean what I say. I mean by that that the Bible is not just a storehouse of inspiring sayings, thrown out in some haphazard or isolated fashion but that it presents one great logically concatenated system which ought to be considered, not just piecemeal, but as a whole.

I have been trying to present that system as a whole. Of course, in doing so I have been conscious not only of my own limitations, but also of the magnitude of the task. It is no easy thing to summarize what is taught in the Scriptures of the Old and New Testaments in such a way that the logical relations between the various parts of the teaching shall stand out clear, and in such a way that no great division of the teaching shall altogether be neglected.

Fortunately, I do not need to undertake this task as though no one has ever undertaken it before. The Bible has been in the world for nearly nineteen centuries and during all those centuries learned and truly devout men have been searching the Scriptures and have been endeavoring to summarize what the Scriptures teach. Errors in the understanding of the Bible have been detected and avoided. Omissions in the understanding of the

Bible have been filled up. There has been study, there has been meditation, there has been discussion, and there has been prayer. It would be a very great mistake for a man who desires to present what the Bible teaches to neglect what the church has thought and done during all these centuries.

That does not mean that we should ever be content to take the Bible at second hand. We must be ready always to compare what past generations of Christians and what the great councils of the Christian church have said in exposition of the Bible with what the Bible itself says. But, after all, the Holy Spirit who inspired the writers of the Bible in the first place has also been present in the church, and has graciously helped those whom he has united to Christ by faith in their understanding of the inspired Word.

He has not, indeed, been active in the church in the same way as that in which he was active when he inspired the biblical writers. He has never made the interpretation of the Bible in the church infallible as he made the Bible itself. The biblical writers were supernaturally preserved from all error, while even the very best expositors of the Bible have been liable to error, and so also have even the best of the ecclesiastical councils. That is a tremendous difference indeed.

Yet that difference in the manner of the Holy Spirit's working should not obscure the fact that it is the same Spirit who worked in both cases. The Holy Spirit has given us an infallible Bible, and the Holy Spirit has also been present in the church, enlightening the minds of sinners that they may understand God's Word for the saving of their souls, then graciously helping them in their study of the Word and guiding them when they have discussed it in the councils of the church.

It would be a sad mistake indeed if we should cut ourselves off from the past history of the Christian church in our interpretation of the Word of God.

I am trying not to make that mistake in this little course of talks. I am indeed trying to take you always to the fountainhead of truth, the Bible itself; but in my study of the Bible with you I have been dependent throughout upon what the collective wisdom of the church of all ages has been able to do, with the gracious indwelling of the Holy Spirit, toward the understanding of the truth that the Bible contains.

That collective wisdom of the church, under the guidance of the Holy Spirit, has found expression especially in the great Christian creeds. The earliest of them that we know anything very much about is the so-called Apostles' Creed. It contains only a very small portion of what the Bible teaches. Compared with the great creeds that were to follow, it seems very meager indeed. I am not one of those who believe that we ought to be content with it as the sole statement of our faith. To be content with it would be to cast despite upon great areas of biblical teaching; it would mean a woeful impoverishment of our Christian life. Yet the Apostles' Creed is entirely true as far as it goes, and it represents an important step in the ever-fuller presentation of Christian doctrine on the basis of the teaching of God's Word.

Then came the great ecumenical creeds, beginning with the Nicene Creed adopted in the year AD 325. In those creeds, the great biblical doctrines of the Trinity and of the person of Christ were set forth. They were not set forth without struggle; they were not set forth by indolent souls who shrank from controversy; but they were set forth after careful examination of plausible errors as they successively arose, and by way of refutation of those errors from the Scriptures.

Is Christ just the greatest of created beings? No, said the church, that is not what the Bible teaches. He is truly God, not a creature. Was he then only of like substance with the Father? No, said the church, that is not what the Bible teaches. He is of the same substance with the Father, and altogether equal to the Father in power and glory. So also the Holy Spirit is equal to the Father and to the Son.

Are then these three—Father, Son, and Holy Ghost—three gods? No, said the church, that is not at all what the Bible teaches. There is only one living and true God. Well, then, are Father, Son, and Holy Ghost merely three aspects of the one God? No, said the church, that is not what the Bible teaches. They are three persons. They stand in truly personal relations with one another. The Father loves the Son and the Son the Father. So they are three persons, yet one God. A great mystery, is it not? Yes, a great mystery, but not an absurdity, as unbelievers so glibly represent it as being. A great mystery, which we should never have been able to discover for ourselves, but which God has graciously revealed to us in his holy Word.

But if Christ was one of the persons of the Trinity, if he was very God, is he also man? Yes, said the church, he is also man. He truly became man. So now he is God and man. Well, then, what is the relation of the divine and the human in Christ? Is the humanity of Christ only a partial humanity? Does the divine in Jesus Christ take the place of the human spirit? No, said the church, that is not what the Bible teaches. Christ, according to the Bible, has a complete human nature. Well, then, are the divine and the human in Christ welded together so as to form a third something which is neither divine nor human, or is the human nature somehow caught up into the divine nature so as to be merged with it? No, said the church, that is not what the Bible teaches. The divine nature and the human nature in Christ are distinct the one from the other. Well, then, is the human nature in Christ a distinct person from the divine nature? Did a divine person, the eternal Son of God, merely enter into some sort of wonderfully intimate union with a human person, Jesus of Nazareth? No, indeed, said the church; that is a very great heresy indeed, that is not at all what the Bible teaches. There is only one person in Jesus, and that person is very God, the second person of the Trinity.

So there we have the great doctrine of the person of Christ—"God and man, in two distinct natures, and one person, forever" (WSC Q&A 21).

So far, the work of the church in the presentation of doctrine was carried on chiefly, though by no means exclusively, in the eastern part of the ancient Mediterranean world. But now we come to something that was accomplished especially in the West. That was the presentation of the biblical doctrine of sin and divine grace by Augustine, who was bishop in North Africa in the region where ancient Carthage had been.

Is man, after Adam's sin, still able to attain God's favor, still able to do right? Was all that Christ did for man, essentially, to set him a good example and so enable him to break the bad habits into which he had fallen? No, said Augustine, that is not at all what the Bible teaches. The guilt of Adam's first sin, according to the Bible, rests upon all mankind; mankind of itself, since the fall, is hopelessly corrupt. It is the grace of God alone which makes fallen men able to do what is right.

Augustine's view, rather than that of his opponent Pelagius, was accepted in principle by the church after a time; and yet it was not permanently accepted in its entirety. Practically, there was a compromise between Augustine's view and the view opposed to it. Complete consistency in the doctrines of sin and grace was not attained.

Then came the Middle Ages. We should be very narrow indeed if we represented that period as being a period of unrelieved darkness. Where in the modern world can we find an achievement like the nave of Amiens Cathedral or the choir of Beauvais? When the moderns begin to equal the splendor of such achievements as these, they may begin to bring a railing accusation against the ages that brought such achievements forth. There are just one or two things about the Middle Ages which cannot be learned from Mark Twain's *A Connecticut Yankee at King Arthur's Court*.

Yet in some respects it was a time of darkness, and at the close of it, its glories were on the wane.

Then came the Renaissance and the Protestant Reformation, and what a burst of freedom was that!

Yet many people who speak very kindly of the Reformation and are laboring under the impression that they are Protestants have not the slightest notion what the Reformation was. They have a sort of vague idea that at the Reformation authority in religion was rejected and every man became his own lawgiver and his own prophet.

Nothing could be further from the fact. As a matter of fact, the foundation of the Reformation was the Bible. Other authorities in religion were rejected, but they were rejected not in the interests of human autonomy, but in the interests of the authority of the Word of God.

In holding to the full truthfulness and absolute authority of the Bible, the Reformers were like the great church from which they broke away. They differed from that church in rejecting any infallible, living authority in the interpretation of the Bible, but to the authority of the Bible itself they held on with might and main. Their holding on to it was not a concession that they made reluctantly, as though to give tradition its due and not be too radical all at once. No, it was the thing to which they triumphantly appealed. They were opposed to certain other things just because in their judgment those other things prevented men from attending to and obeying God's Word.

It ought never to be forgotten that the belief in the full truthfulness of the Bible and the absolute authority of the Bible's commands is the foundational principle of the Protestant Reformation. A so-called Protestantism that rejects that principle is no Protestantism at all. It is far more remote from the view of the Reformers than is the great church from which the Reformers broke away.

Not only did the Reformers insist upon the authority of the Bible, but also, in their interpretation of the Bible, they agreed with much that had gone before. They maintained fully the truth of the great early creeds. They accepted the great doctrines of the Trinity and of the person of Christ that those creeds so clearly set forth. They built also upon the doctrine of sin and grace which Augustine had maintained against Pelagius so many centuries before. True Protestants should never admit, unless they will be untrue to their great heritage, that they are without organic connection with the previous history of the church universal.

I think there is an important lesson to be learned at that point from the example of the great Reformers. We also in our day believe that reform is necessary in the church. The larger Protestant churches have many of them drifted away from their moorings in the Bible; they have become, if the Bible be regarded as the standard, seriously corrupt. At such a time reform is obviously in place.

But how shall reform be accomplished? Some people seem to think that it ought to be accomplished by rejecting or ignoring all that has been done in the Christian church during all these centuries. Let us just return to the Bible, they say to themselves; we need to make a clean break with all the rubbish of the denominations. So they just sit down and try to summarize what the Bible teaches in some very hasty and brief little statement, and let the great creeds of the church sink, so far as they are concerned, into oblivion.

Now, do you know, I think it a very great pity when good people proceed in that way. It is splendid that they are returning to the Bible, but in returning to the Bible it is a pity that they reject the help of the historic Christian church in understanding what the Bible teaches.

I do not want to be misunderstood at this point. I do not think any one formulated human interpretation of the Bible, no matter how worthy it may be, is *essential* to the Christian church. If we could imagine all the creeds of Christendom as having been suddenly wiped out of men's memories, so that we should have to start all over again in our understanding of the Bible and in our summary setting forth of what the Bible teaches, I believe that in time the necessary creeds of the church would again be built up. It might take another nineteen centuries—if it be God's will that the present age shall remain that long; it might take twice that time. But sooner or later it would be done. The Bible is the really essential thing; it is the foundation. The creeds of the church are the superstructure. Take away the foundation, and all is lost. But take away the superstructure, and the superstructure can be built up again if the foundation remains.

How terrible, however, the loss would in that case be! How terrible it would be if we had to start all over again in our study of the Bible, without help from the great creeds, without help from Augustine, without help from the great theologians of the Reformation!

Thank God, we do not have to sustain that loss, and it is a very sad mistake to subject ourselves to it in needless fashion as so many are doing today. I think we ought to cherish the great heritage of Christian doctrine with all our mind and heart. I think we ought never to contemplate for one moment cutting loose from the history of the Christian church.

So in these talks I have been trying to stand in the full current of the church's life. I have been trying to present to you the purest line of progress in Christian doctrine, coming down to us through the great ancient creeds, through Augustine, and through the Reformation.

But where runs that purest line of Christian doctrine since the Reformation days? I will tell you very plainly what I think. I think it runs through Calvin and through that type of doctrine that is called the Reformed faith.

There were certain things about which the leading Reformers of the sixteenth century were agreed. All branches of the Reformation held to the sole authority of the Bible as over against all other authorities. All held, for example, also to the great biblical doctrine of justification by faith alone. But there are some things about which they differed, and with regard to those differences I stand with Calvin and his associates and followers over against certain other forms of Protestant doctrine. The system of doctrine which Calvin and his associates and followers maintained is sometimes called Calvinism. It is better called, I think, the "Reformed faith."

That system of doctrine, the "Reformed faith," spread over a considerable part of Europe. On the continent of Europe, the churches holding it came to be called the "Reformed" churches; in Scotland they came to be called the "Presbyterian" churches. Thus the "Reformed" doctrine, in the special sense of the word "Reformed," is the same thing as "Presbyterian" doctrine.

Members of various Reformed churches and various Presbyterian churches came to America, where there are now a considerable number of ecclesiastical bodies using each of these terms. Insofar as these bodies have remained true to their historic creeds, they hold to the system of doctrine called the Reformed faith.

It is that system of doctrine which I am trying to set forth in these Sunday afternoon talks. The reason why I am setting it forth is that I think that it is true, and the reason why I think that it is true is that I think it is taught in the Bible. At countless points it agrees with other systems of Christian doctrine, and I rejoice very greatly in that agreement. At the same time, I make no apologies for trying to set it forth in its entirety. It is, I hold, just consistent Christianity; and consistent Christianity in the long run is the Christianity that stands firmest against unbelief.

If some of my Christian hearers disagree with me at some points, I do not think they will be offended. Their very disagreement with some of the things that I say may lead them to turn again to their Bibles that they may consider anew the question of what the Bible means. When they do that, they will have great gain, and I shall rejoice. After all, what I am trying to do on these Sunday afternoons is to study the Bible with you. It should never be forgotten that all Christian doctrine is derived from and must ever be tested by the Word of God.

An objection may perhaps occur to some people at that point. If Christian doctrine consists simply in setting forth what the Bible teaches, and if the Bible is fixed once for all, is not Christian doctrine the enemy of progress?

In order to answer that objection, all that is necessary is just to do a tiny little bit of clear thinking. Suppose it be granted to the Christian that God has told us something once-for-all in the Bible. Does the acceptance of that thing as true prevent us from going on to the discovery of other things? Because we know one thing, are we prevented from making advances in learning other things? I cannot for the life of me see that we are.

Here we are in this world—sinners and subject to God's wrath and curse. God has saved us by the saving work of Jesus Christ. He has provided a record of that salvation in the Bible and has told us the things that we need to know in connection with it and in connection with its application in men's lives. He has graciously given us a revelation of himself in the Bible, a revelation of our lost condition, and a revelation of the way in which lost sinners are saved. That is his Word or his message to men.

Suppose we accept it as his Spirit enables us to, for the saving of our souls. Are we then prevented from going to an ever-fuller knowledge of things that his Word does not contain—things that are presented to us by God himself in the universe that he has made? Not a bit of it, my friends.

Quite the contrary. An acceptance of what God has told us in his Word once-for-all removes the shackles of sin and sets us free to enter into ever-wider avenues of knowledge. Far from being opposed to progress, an acceptance of the truth of the Bible makes real progress possible. When the Bible is rejected, as it has been so widely rejected, you find decadence like that which is so plainly manifest all over the world today. True progress for humanity, now so sadly arrested, will begin again when men return to the Word of God and build upon that solid foundation.

40

The Creeds and Doctrinal Advance

Last Sunday afternoon, in the first of our talks of this winter, I spoke to you in a summary sort of way about the progress of Christian doctrine in the church. I showed how the church advanced from the very meager statement which is commonly called the Apostles' Creed, on through the great early ecumenical creeds, setting forth the doctrines of the Trinity and the person of Christ, and through Augustine, with his presentation of the doctrine of sin and of divine grace, to the Reformation and to Calvin. I showed how that type of doctrine which follows on the path in which Calvin moved is called the Reformed faith.

The Reformed faith has found expression in a number of great creeds which all exhibit the same general type. One of these creeds is the Heidelberg Catechism. That is the official doctrinal standard of certain American churches whose members came originally from the continent of Europe. These churches are called "Reformed" churches. Another of the great creeds setting forth the Reformed faith is the one that consists of the Westminster Confession of Faith and the Larger and Shorter Catechisms. They are the official doctrinal standards of certain American churches whose members originally came chiefly from Scotland and Ireland. These are called "Presbyterian" churches. It is these doctrinal standards to which I have frequently referred in these little talks that I have been giving on Sunday afternoons during the past two winters.

Perhaps one question was in the minds of some of you as I reviewed the progress of Christian doctrine last Sunday afternoon: why should the progress be thought to have been brought to a close in the seventeenth century when the Westminster Confession of Faith and Catechisms were produced? Why should there not be still further doctrinal advance? If the church advanced in doctrine up to the time of the Westminster Standards, why should it now not proceed still further on its onward march?

Well, there is no essential reason why it should not do so. However, before it attempts to do so, it is very important for it to understand precisely what Christian doctrine is. It should understand very clearly that Christian doctrine is just a setting forth of what the Bible teaches. At the foundation of Christian doctrine is the acceptance of the full truthfulness of the Bible as the Word of God.

That is often forgotten by those who today undertake to write confessional statements. Let us give expression to our Christian experience, they say, in forms better suited to the times in which we are living than are the older creeds of the church. So they sit down and concoct various forms of words, which they represent as being on a plane with the great creeds of Christendom.

When they do that, they are simply forgetting what the creeds of Christendom are. The creeds of Christendom are not expressions of Christian experience. They are summary statements of what God has told us in his Word. Far from the subject matter of the creeds being derived from Christian experience, it is Christian experience which is based upon the truth contained in the creeds; and the truth contained in the creeds is derived from the Bible, which is the Word of God. Groups of people that undertake to write a creed without believing in the full truthfulness of the Bible, and without taking the subject matter of their creed from that inspired Word of God, are not at all taking an additional step on the pathway on which the great Christian creeds moved; rather, they are moving in an exactly opposite direction. What they are doing has nothing whatever to do with that grand progress of Christian doctrine of which I spoke last Sunday. Far from continuing the advance of Christian doctrine, they are starting something entirely different, and that something different, we may add, is doomed to failure from the start.

The first prerequisite, then, for any advance in Christian doctrine is that those who would engage in it should believe in the full truthfulness of the Bible and should endeavor to make their doctrine simply a presentation of what the Bible teaches.

There are other principles also that must be observed if there is to be real doctrinal advance. For one thing, all real doctrinal advance proceeds in the direction of greater precision and fullness of doctrinal statement. Just run over in your minds again the history of the great creeds of the church.

How meager was the so-called Apostles' Creed, first formulated in the second century! How far more precise and full were the creeds of the great early councils, beginning with the Nicene creed in AD 325! How much more precise and how vastly richer still were the Reformation creeds and especially our Westminster Confession of Faith!

This increasing precision and this increasing richness of doctrinal statement were arrived at particularly by way of refutation of errors as they successively arose. At first, the church's convictions about some point of doctrine were implicit rather than explicit. They were not carefully defined. They were assumed rather than expressly stated. Then some new teaching arose. The church reflected on the matter, comparing the new teaching with the Bible. It found the new teaching to be contrary to the Bible. As over against the new teaching, it set forth precisely the true biblical teaching on the point. So, a great doctrine was clearly stated in some great Christian creed.

That method of doctrinal advance is, of course, in accord with the fundamental laws of the mind. You cannot set forth clearly what a thing is without placing it in contrast with what it is not. All definition proceeds by way of exclusion. How utterly shallow, then, is the notion that the church ought to make its teaching positive and not negative—the notion that controversy should be avoided and truth should be maintained without attack upon error! The simple fact is that truth cannot possibly be maintained in any such way. Truth can be maintained only when it is sharply differentiated from error. It is no wonder, then, that the great creeds of the church, as also the great revivals of religion in the church, were born in theological controversy. The increasing richness and the increasing precision of Christian doctrine were brought about very largely by the necessity of excluding one alien element after another from the teaching of the church.

In recent years the church has often entered upon an exactly opposite course of procedure. It has constructed what purport to be doctrinal statements, but these supposed doctrinal statements are constructed for a purpose which is just the opposite of the purpose that governed the formation of the great historic creeds.

The historic creeds were exclusive of error; they were intended to exclude error; they were intended to set forth the biblical teaching in sharp contrast with what was opposed to the biblical teaching, in order that the purity of the church might be preserved. These modern statements, on the contrary, are inclusive of error. They are designed to make room in the church for just as many people and for just as many types of thought as possible.

There are entirely too many denominations in this country, says the modern ecclesiastical efficiency expert. Obviously, many of them must be merged. But the trouble is, they have different creeds. Here is one church, for example, that has a clearly Calvinistic creed; here is another whose creed is just as clearly Arminian, let us say, and anti-Calvinistic. How in the world are we going to get the two together? Why, obviously, says the ecclesiastical efficiency expert, the thing to do is to tone down that Calvinistic creed; just smooth off its sharp angles, until Arminians will be able to accept it. Or else we can do something better still. We can write an entirely new creed that will contain only what Arminianism and Calvinism have in common, so that it can serve as the basis for some proposed new united church.

Such are the methods of modern church unionism. Those methods are carried even to such greater lengths today than in the hypothetical example that I have just mentioned. Calvinism and Arminianism, which I have mentioned in this example, though they differ very widely, are both of them types of evangelical Christian belief. But many of these modern statements are so worded as to gain the assent not only of men who hold different varieties of Christian belief, like Calvinism and Arminianism, but also of men who hold to no really Christian belief at all.

Take some of the great world conferences on missions, for example. At those conferences are represented men who believe in the virgin birth of Christ, his substitutionary atonement, his bodily resurrection and other essential elements of the historic Christian faith, and also there are represented men who oppose these things or belittle them as entirely unimportant. There are many speeches—some of them from men generally thought to be evangelical Christians, some of them from distinguished Modernists. After days of such speechmaking, a common statement of belief is presented and is unanimously adopted.

What is that common statement like? Well, its outstanding characteristic is apt to be just what would be expected from the circumstances under which it was adopted. Its outstanding characteristic is apt to be a complete absence of character—a complete and unrelieved vagueness. Really, when I read some of these statements, I am amazed at the amount of printer's ink which it is possible to use up without saying anything at all. Words and phrases are indeed used which formerly had a meaning, and which ought to have a meaning now; but these words have been explained away so long that in themselves they now afford no evidence whatever as to what the person who uses them really believes.

When such a vague statement is issued there are always found people who rejoice. Was it not great cause for rejoicing, they say, that our differences were all ironed out? We had been afraid, they say, lest someone would have objected to an evangelical statement like the statement of that missionary council; but our fears were groundless, and even those at the council who were accounted most radical consented to the statement like all the rest. Was not that perfectly splendid?

No, I say when people talk to me in that fashion, I do not think it was splendid at all. I think it was very sad. I should not have thought it to be splendid even if the statement of the council had been really evangelical instead of only apparently so. Is it splendid when men who are plainly out of accord with an evangelical statement acquiesce in the issuance of it and then go on exactly as before in their opposition to the things that the statement contains? I am bound to think that that is the reverse of splendid. But, as a matter of fact, the statement in most cases is not really evangelical at all, but utterly vague. It is so worded as to offend no one. At least, it is so worded as to offend no one except those old-fashioned souls who are hungry for the bread of life and are not satisfied with a type of Christian doctrine that is afraid of its own shadow. The statement is usually so worded that the Modernists can interpret its traditional phrases in their own fashion; and, on the other hand, it is so worded that persons who are evangelical, or think they are evangelical, can bring it back to their constituency as a great diplomatic triumph of orthodoxy. Its great object is to avoid offense. The consequence is that it is just about as far removed as possible from the gospel of Christ. For the gospel of Christ is always offensive in the extreme.

When we pass from these modern statements to the great creeds, what a difference we discover! Instead of wordiness we find conciseness; instead of an unwillingness to offend, clear delimitation of truth from error; instead of obscurity, clearness; instead of vagueness, the utmost definition and precision.

All these differences are rooted in a fundamental difference of purpose. These modern statements are intended to show how little of truth we can get along with and still be Christians, whereas the great creeds of the church are intended to show how much of truth God has revealed to us in his Word. Let us sink our differences, say the authors of these modern statements, and get back to a few bare essentials; let us open our Bibles, say the authors of the great Christian creeds, and seek to unfold the full richness of truth that the Bible contains. Let us be careful, say the authors of these modern statements, not to discourage any of the various tendencies of thought that find a lodgment in the church; let us give all diligence, say the authors of the great Christian creeds, to exclude deadly error from the official teaching of the church, in order that thus the church may be a faithful steward of the mysteries of God.

That difference of purpose is a fundamental difference indeed. But, I am inclined to think that there is another difference that is more fundamental still. The most important difference of all is that the authors of these modern statements do not really believe firmly in the existence of truth at all. Because doctrine, they say, is merely the expression of Christian experience, doctrines change and yet the fundamental experience remains the same. One generation expresses its Christian experience in one doctrine, and then another generation may express the same Christian experience in an exactly opposite doctrine. And so the Modernism of today becomes the orthodoxy of tomorrow, which in turn gives place to a new Modernism, and so on in an infinite series. No doctrine, according to that theory, can remain valid forever; doctrine must change as the forms of thought change from age to age.

When you ask a person of this way of thinking whether he accepts the great historic creeds of the church, he says to you: "Oh yes, certainly I do. I accept them as expressions of the faith of the church. The Apostles' Creed expressed admirably the faith of the ancient church; the Westminster Confession was an admirable expression of the faith of men of the seventeenth century. But as for making these creeds the expression of my faith, of course I cannot possibly do that. I must express my faith in the terms that are suited to the people of the twentieth century. So I must construct a new and entirely different statement to be the creed of modern men."

"Well, then," I ask such a man, "do you think your statement is more true than those historic creeds?"

"Not at all," says he, if he really works out the logical conclusions of his conception of creeds. "Those creeds were true expressions of Christian experience. Mine also is a true expression of essentially the same experience in the forms of thought that are suited to the present age, but my statement is not a bit more true than those ancient creeds; it, not a bit more than they, can lay claim to permanency; it is true in the present age, but that does not mean at all that it will remain true in the generations to come."

What shall we say about this skeptical notion of what truth is—this skeptical notion with regard to the nature of Christian doctrine? Well, we can say at least this about it: that it is entirely different from the notion that was cherished by those who gave us the great creeds of the church. Those who gave us the great creeds of the church, unlike the authors of these modern statements, believed that the creeds that they produced were true—true in the plain man's sense of the word "truth." They believed that the truth they contained would remain true forever.

It is time now to get back to the question with which this talk began. Is it or is it not possible that there should be still further advance in Christian doctrine?

Yes, we answer, but only provided the necessary conditions for any real doctrinal advance be observed.

If there is to be any doctrinal advance, we must believe that doctrine is the setting forth of what is true, not a mere expression of religious experience in symbolic form; we must believe, in the second place, that doctrine is the setting forth of that particular truth that is contained in the Bible, which we must hold to be truly God's Word and altogether free from the errors found in other books; we must endeavor, in the third place, not to make doctrine as meager and vague as possible in order that it shall make room for error, but as full and precise as possible in order that it shall exclude error and set forth the wonderful richness of what God has revealed. Ignore these conditions and you have doctrinal retrogression or decadence; only if you observe them can you possibly have doctrinal advance.

Such doctrinal advance is certainly conceivable. It is perfectly conceivable that the church should examine the particular errors of the present day and should set forth over against them, even more clearly than is done in the existing creeds, the truth that is contained in God's Word. But I am bound to say that I think such doctrinal advance to be just now extremely unlikely. We are living in a time of widespread intellectual as well as moral decadence, and the visible church has unfortunately not kept free from this decadence. Christian education has been sadly neglected; learning has been despised; and real meditation has become almost a lost art. For these reasons, and other still more important reasons, I think it is clear that ours is not a creed-making age. Intellectual and moral indolence like ours do not constitute the soil out of which great Christian creeds may be expected to grow.

But even if ours were a creed-making age, I doubt very much that the doctrinal advance which it or any future age might produce would be comparable to the advance which found expression in the great historic creeds. I think it may well turn out that Christian doctrine in its great outlines, as set forth, for example, in the Westminster Confession of Faith, is now essentially complete. There may be improvements in a statement here and there, in the interests of greater precision, but hardly any such great advance as that which was made, for example, at the time of Augustine or at the Reformation. All the great central parts of the biblical system of doctrine have already been studied by the church and set forth in great creeds.

We need not be too much surprised to discover that this is the case. The subject matter of Christian doctrine, it must be remembered, is fixed. It is found in the Scriptures of the Old and New Testaments, to which nothing can be added.

Let no one say that the recognition of that fact brings with it a static condition of the human mind or is inimical to progress. On the contrary, it removes the shackles from the human mind and opens up untold avenues of progress.

The truth is, there can be no real progress unless there is something that is fixed. Archimedes said, "Give me a place to stand, and . . . I shall move the world."[1] Well, Christian doctrine provides that place to stand. Unless there be such a place to stand, all progress is an illusion. The very idea of progress implies something fixed. There is no progress in a kaleidoscope.

That is the trouble with the boasted progress of our modern age. The Bible at the start was given up. Nothing was to be regarded as fixed. All truth was regarded as relative. What has been the result? I will tell you. An unparalleled decadence—liberty prostrate, slavery stalking almost unchecked through the earth, the achievements of centuries crumbling in the dust, sweetness and decency despised, all meaning regarded as having been taken away from human life. What is the remedy? I will tell you that too. A return to God's Word! We had science for the sake of science, and got the World War; we had art for art's sake, and got ugliness gone mad; we had man for the sake of man and got a world of robots, men made into machines. Is it not time for us to come to ourselves, like the prodigal in a far country? Is it not time for us to seek real progress by a return to the living God?

---

1. A remark of Archimedes quoted by Pappus of Alexandria in *Collection*, Book VIII, c. AD 340.

41

God, Man, and Salvation

In the last two of these talks I have spoken to you about the progress of Christian doctrine in the church; and just at the close of the talk of last Sunday afternoon, I was saying that that progress may be said to have been brought to some sort of conclusion in that great creed which consists of the Westminster Confession of Faith and Catechisms. It is indeed perfectly conceivable that the Christian church in the future may be able to set forth, here and there, with even greater precision and fullness than is done in that creed, the teaching of the Word of God; but such future advance will hardly be comparable to that which came, for example, at the time of the great early creeds or of Augustine or of the Reformation. The general outlines of the whole biblical system of doctrine have already, in that great creed, been set forth.

Let no one say that recognition of that fact brings with it a static condition of the human mind or is inimical to human progress. On the contrary, it removes the shackles from the human mind and opens up untold avenues of progress.

The truth is that there can be no real progress unless there is something that is fixed. Archimedes said, "Give me a place to stand, and I will move the world." Well, Christian doctrine provides that place to stand. It sets forth what God has told us in his Word about God himself, about man, and about salvation. Grounding our lives upon the solid foundation of that knowledge, we can go forward to wonderful adventures both in the world of action and in the world of thought.

Indeed, it may fairly be said that the very idea of progress implies something that is fixed. There is no progress in a kaleidoscope.

For lack of taking something to be fixed, all the boasted progress of our modern age has turned out to be an illusion. The Bible, at the beginning of that modern age, or in the course of it, was very largely given up. Nothing, it was supposed, was to be regarded as settled. All truth was to be regarded as relative.

Well, what has been the result? I will tell you. An unparalleled decadence—liberty prostrate, slavery stalking almost unchecked through the earth, the achievements of centuries crumbling in the dust, sweetness and decency despised, dignity gone in the affairs of individuals and of nations, all meaning apparently taken away from human life!

If that is the result, what is the remedy? I will give you the answer to that question also. The remedy is a return to God's Word!

We had science for the sake of science and got the World War; we had art for art's sake and got ugliness gone mad; we had man for the sake of man and got a world of robots, men made into machines. Is it not time for us to come to ourselves, like the prodigal in the far country? Is it not time for us to seek real progress by a return to the living God?

Yes, my friends, I think it is; and to that end I am giving these talks. I am not presenting my own opinions. I am not giving you the benefit of my experience regarding the art of being religious. Anything more futile than either of those efforts on my part would be difficult to imagine. But I am just trying to study the Bible with you to see if we can fix in our minds and hearts, a little better than we have done before, an outline of what God has told us in his holy Word.

Let us now recall, in a word or two, that part of the outline of biblical teaching which has been covered, in some slight measure, in the talks which we gave during the past two winters. Then we shall proceed to the subjects that remain, with a better understanding of their place in the total system of doctrine that the Bible contains.

First, we spoke of the Bible itself, the book in which the subject matter of all Christian doctrine is found.

Is there a God, we asked, and if so, may he be truly known? Yes, we said, there is a God and we know something of him because he has been pleased to reveal himself to us.

He has revealed himself, in the first place, through nature and through his voice within us, the voice of conscience. These two constitute what is called general revelation. They afford real knowledge of God, and the man who does not receive that knowledge is without excuse. But men's eyes, alas, are blinded by sin. Therefore, they are prevented from seeing that which they ought to see.

In order that sinners who are thus blinded may see and be saved, God has revealed himself also in a way that is quite distinct from that general revelation. That general revelation is a revelation through nature. This other revelation, called "special revelation," is a revelation that is above nature; it is "supernatural."

There are two reasons why such supernatural revelation was necessary if sinners were to be saved. In the first place, as we have just said, though nature reveals God, man's eyes were blinded by sin. Therefore, they needed to have confirmed in supernatural revelation even those things about God which they ought already to have learned from nature.

In the second place, as sinners, they needed to know certain other things about God of which nature told nothing. They needed to know the way in which God was graciously pleased to show mercy to sinners and bring them again into communion with himself. Of that, nature contained no slightest hint. That was made known by supernatural revelation and supernatural revelation alone.

Together with that supernatural revelation went a supernatural act—the gracious act of God by which he redeemed sinners through the gift of his own Son, Jesus Christ our Lord. God wrought salvation not through the course of nature but in supernatural fashion, and he explained the meaning of his saving work in a revelation that was as supernatural as was the work which it explained.

The record of that supernatural work of salvation and of that supernatural revelation by which it is explained is found in the Bible. But it is a mistake to say merely that the Bible contains a record of supernatural revelation. No, it *is* supernatural revelation in all its parts. It does not merely contain the Word of God, but it *is* the Word of God.

It is the Word of God because of the inspiration of the biblical writers. In addition to all their providential preparation for their task of writing the books of the Bible, the biblical writers received a blessed, wonderful, and supernatural guidance and impulsion by the Spirit of God, so that they were preserved from the errors that appear in other books, and thus the resulting book, the Bible, is in all its parts completely true in what it says regarding matters of fact and completely authoritative in its commands. That is the great basic doctrine of the full or plenary inspiration of the Bible.

That doctrine does not mean that the biblical writers did not follow their own individual habits of style. On the contrary, it recognizes the individuality of the writers to the full.

It does not mean, in the second place, that the biblical writers did not use ordinary methods of obtaining information—their own memory, the reports of eyewitnesses, and the like. On the contrary, they certainly did use such ordinary methods of obtaining information, and it is very important to insist on that fact. Even before a man believes in the plenary inspiration of the Bible, he ought, if he is a good historian, to recognize the substantial trustworthiness of the history that the Bible contains.

But the point is that even when the biblical writers were recounting the simplest matters of fact, about which they obtained information in the most ordinary ways, they were supernaturally preserved from error. Therefore, even in those narrative parts of the Bible, although things are told there which could have been discovered and were discovered in natural and ordinary ways, yet the record of these things obtains in the Bible a supernatural certification that makes even such simple narrative parts of the Bible to be truly a part of God's Word.

Thus all the Bible is God's Word. Not only does the Bible contain a vast wealth of things that could never have been learned at all without supernatural revelation, but also even the things in it which could have been learned without supernatural revelation are certified to us by the supernatural work of the Holy Spirit in keeping the writers from error.

Having thus established the fact that the Bible as a whole is the Word of God, we opened the Bible to discover what God has told us in his holy book. If the Bible is the Word of God, we are supremely interested in the question of what the Bible says.

Theologians are accustomed to divide what the Bible says into three divisions—first, what the Bible says about God; second, what the Bible says about man; and third, what the Bible says about salvation. If you take up some great work on theology you are apt to find that it will be in three volumes. The first will be headed "Theology," meaning theology proper, as distinguished from theology in the broader sense. Theology means "the doctrine of God." The second volume will be headed "Anthropology." That is a long word to designate "the doctrine of man." The third volume will be headed "Soteriology." That is another long word for "the doctrine of salvation."

Of these three divisions we have covered—of course, only in a summary and inadequate kind of way—the first two, and we have made a beginning on the third.

Two years ago, I spoke about what the Bible says regarding God. I tried to present to you the biblical teaching about the Trinity, including of course the great doctrine of the deity of Christ. That part, together with the preceding treatment of the inspiration of the Bible, has appeared in book form under the title, *The Christian Faith in the Modern World*.

Then, during last winter, I spoke to you about what the Bible says regarding man. I tried to present to you especially the biblical doctrine of sin.

Finally, last spring, I made a beginning of presenting what the Bible says about the third of these three great subjects: the subject of salvation. That is the subject that I want to treat further in the part of our series of talks in which we are now engaged.

But before we can treat intelligently the subject of salvation, it is essential that we should recall to our minds what it is from which men are saved. The biblical doctrine of salvation is completely unintelligible unless we first understand the biblical doctrine of sin.

That is where so many treatments of salvation go wrong today. They present a gospel which would be splendid for good people, but which is utterly futile if sin is what the Bible says it is, and if all men are, as the Bible says to be the case, under sin's guilt and power. If sin is what the Bible says it is and if we are lost in sin, we need a very different doctrine of salvation—we need, in other words, a very different gospel from that which is commonly preached in the church today.

According to the Bible, Adam was created in knowledge, righteousness, and holiness. When he was created, God entered into a covenant of life with him upon condition of perfect obedience. In other words, he was placed on probation. If he had stood the probation successfully, if he had obeyed, the reward would have been eternal life. The possibility of his sinning would have been removed. He would have been not only righteous—as he was already from the beginning—but his righteousness would have become assured forever.

But he did not stand the test successfully. He transgressed the commandment of God. He fell, and by his fall he came into an estate of sin and misery.

Now that covenant of life had been made with Adam not only for himself but also for his posterity. He had been, by divine appointment, the representative of the whole human race. If he had obeyed God, all men without exception would have had eternal life. The very possibility of sinning would forever have been removed for the whole human race. What a glorious result! But, alas, he fell, and since he was, by divine appointment, representative of all, all men sinned in him and fell with him in his first transgression. All, therefore, came into that dreadful estate of sin and misery into which he came.

Thus all men became guilty; all men are under God's wrath and curse even before they individually have done anything either good or bad. All men, moreover, are utterly corrupt, for such corruption is part of the dreadful penalty of sin. All men are totally unable to do anything that can please God; and all men so soon as they come to years of discretion, show the inevitable fruits of this inborn corruption by individual acts of sin beyond number.

Such is the sinfulness of that estate into which all mankind fell through Adam's first transgression. But that estate is also an estate of misery. "All mankind, by that fall, lost communion with God, are under his wrath and curse, and so made liable to all the miseries of this life, to death itself, and to the pains of hell forever" (WSC Q&A 19).

How dreadful was the state of fallen man! But God did not leave all mankind to perish in the estate of sin and misery. From all eternity, in his eternal plan, he had chosen some for eternal life, and those whom he had thus chosen, he saved.

At that point men are prone to interpose a question. Why did not God predestine all to eternal life; why does he not save all? Why did he predestine only *some* to eternal life; why does he save only *some*?

Ah, what a difficult question that is, is it not? Whatever the right answer to it may be, one answer must plainly be rejected. The reason why God elected only some was certainly not that he foresaw any greater merit in those whom he elected than in those whom he did not elect. If the Bible makes anything clear at all, it makes that clear. His decree that some should be saved was not a matter of merit, either absolute or relative; it was a pure matter of grace.

The truth is that the question we are prone to raise about this matter is not the question that we really ought to raise. We ask why any men are lost; what we should ask, if we only looked at the matter from the Bible's point of view is, why any are saved? That is the real cause for wonder. All men, without any exception whatever, deserved to perish in their sins; justice demanded that all should die eternally. How marvelous it is, therefore, that a vast multitude are saved! We can never explain how that could be. As we contemplate it, we can only say that it is a manifestation of utterly mysterious grace.

When God had thus determined, in his mysterious grace, to save certain sinners deserving of his wrath and curse, he carried out his plan of salvation for them with sovereign power. What he did was not to make it possible for them to save themselves. No, he did far more than that. He saved them. He saved them with completely resistless power. Every step leading to the salvation of God's elect has been carried out in accordance with his eternal plan. That is the central thing that we want to make clear in our whole treatment of the biblical doctrine of salvation. Let me repeat it, and if by mere repetition I could impress it forever on your minds and hearts, I should love to repeat it a hundred times. God, I say, by his saving work *did not make it possible for sinners to save themselves; he saved them.*

That does not mean that God has ever saved anyone against his will. Far from it. What he has actually done is to change the will of those whom he saves. He has very sweetly and yet with sovereign power persuaded and enabled them to lay hold upon Jesus Christ in saving faith for the salvation of their souls. Never is a man so gloriously free as he is when the Holy Spirit, with resistless grace, works faith in him and unites him to Christ in a truly effectual calling.

There is another thing, also, which that great central doctrine of God's mysterious grace does not mean. It does not mean that any man who wants to receive Jesus Christ is rejected. It does not mean that any man in this life must look longingly into the warmth and joy of the household of God and say to himself, "That belongs to God's elect, but the door is shut for me, and I cannot enter in." No, indeed, thank God, it does not mean that.

The time will come, indeed, when the door will be shut, as our Lord taught in that solemn parable of the ten virgins; but that time has not yet come in this life. No, the door is yet open wide for all who will to come in. None is excluded. Whosoever will may come.

How broad is that gospel invitation, and what a privilege to let it ring out over all the earth! What a privilege it is for me to say this afternoon, to every man or woman or child within the sound of my voice—to say, moreover, not with any human authority, but as an ambassador of Jesus Christ—that if any one of you has not received Jesus as your Savior you may do so at this very moment and will be received into the household of faith amid the rejoicing of the angels above. If you do receive Jesus as your Savior, you show thereby that from all eternity you have been among the elect of God. No man comes to Jesus unless the Father draws him, and the Father draws those whom, in his eternal counsel, he has given to the Son.

As I give the gospel invitation, and give it to all without exception, I rejoice greatly in believing that acceptance of it on the part of any of you is in accordance with God's eternal plan. I rejoice greatly in believing that, despite the grip which unbelief and indifference have upon so many today, a grip that looks as though it could not be broken, God has many people in the world—many people who are to be saved in accordance with the counsel of his will. I rejoice greatly in believing that we preachers of the gospel are merely God's instruments in carrying out God's plan. I rejoice greatly that we have the inestimable privilege of seeking out God's scattered people and of bringing to them the gospel message through which it is God's will that they shall be saved. God grant that some of you within the sound of my voice today may receive the message and may show thereby that from all eternity you have been foreordained unto adoption as God's children through Jesus Christ our Lord.

42

Christ as Prophet, Priest, and King

Last Sunday afternoon I was reviewing with you the biblical doctrine of the plan of salvation. All mankind have come by the fall into an estate of sin and misery, being utterly lost in sin, deserving only of God's wrath and curse; yet God was pleased in strange and unaccountable mercy to elect some to everlasting life and enter into a covenant of grace with them to deliver them out of the estate of sin and misery and bring them into an estate of salvation.

That was God's plan. We shall be studying, during this winter, the way in which he carried it out. We shall be studying the wonderful unfolding of the covenant of grace.

We made a beginning of that study last spring, and this afternoon we must try to pick up the thread at the point where we there left off.

How has God carried out the covenant of grace? I observed last spring that he has done so through a redeemer. A redeemer is one who delivers someone else by the payment of a price. It was a redeemer in that full sense of the word that God provided for the salvation of those whom he had graciously chosen for eternal life.

Who, then, is the redeemer of God's elect? The answer of the Westminster Shorter Catechism to that question can hardly be improved: "The only redeemer of God's elect is the Lord Jesus Christ, who, being the eternal Son of God, became man, and so was, and continueth to be, God and man in two distinct natures, and one person, forever" (WSC Q&A 21). I observed last spring how every word and every phrase in that answer was arrived at by the Christian church only after long study of the Word of God, meditation, discussion, and prayer.

Notice, in the first place, that Jesus Christ is here called the *only*

Redeemer. That word "only" strikes against various errors that have arisen throughout the long history of the church; and it strikes particularly against the prevailing modern error which admits that the sufferings of Christ were redemptive but regards the sufferings of Christian people as being redemptive too. It strikes against the modern notion that the cross of Christ was just a particularly noble example of self-sacrifice. It safeguards the truth which is contained in that sweet Christian hymn: "There was no other good enough, To pay the price of sin, He only could unlock the gate, Of heaven and let us in."[1]

There was no other good enough, and there was no other great enough, to pay the price of sin. All through our study we must bear that truth in mind. We must keep steadily before us the fact that Jesus Christ is not *one* redeemer of God's elect among many, but the *only* Redeemer. Our only hope is in him.

Notice, in the second place, that this only Redeemer of God's elect is from all eternity God—"who, being the eternal Son of God," says the Shorter Catechism (WSC Q&A 21). That truth also finds a place, and a central place, in the hymns of the church:

> Who is this so weak and helpless,
> Child of lowly Hebrew maid,
> Rudely in a stable sheltered,
> Coldly in a manger laid?
> 'Tis the Lord of all creation,
> Who this wondrous path hath trod;
> He is God from everlasting,
> And to everlasting God.[2]

That great basic doctrine of the deity of Christ was not even postponed in our series so late as last year. It was treated two years ago, when we were dealing with the teaching of the Bible about God. The doctrine of the deity of Christ is an essential part of the great doctrine of the Trinity, the great doctrine which sets forth what the Bible tells us regarding Father, Son, and Holy Ghost, three persons in one God: "Holy, Holy, Holy! Merciful and mighty! God in three persons, blessed Trinity!"[3]

---

1. Cecil Frances Alexander, "There Is a Green Hill Far Away," in *Hymns for Little Children*, 1848.
2. William W. How, "Who Is This, So Weak and Helpless?" in *Psalms and Hymns*, 1867.
3. Reginald Heber, "Holy, Holy, Holy," 1826.

Notice in the third place that the answer in the Shorter Catechism says that the eternal Son of God *became man*. That is the doctrine of the incarnation, which is more fully set forth in the following answer: "Christ, the Son of God, became man, by taking to himself a true body and a reasonable soul, being conceived by the power of the Holy Ghost in the womb of the Virgin Mary, and born of her, yet without sin" (WSC Q&A 22).

That doctrine of the incarnation is treated by theologians—and rightly so—in an entirely different place from the doctrine of the deity of Christ. The doctrine of the deity of Christ is part of the biblical teaching about God. This person whom we now know as Jesus Christ would have been God even if no universe had been created and even if there had been no fallen man to save. He was God from everlasting. His deity is quite independent of any relation of his to a created world.

The doctrine of the incarnation, on the other hand, is a part of the doctrine of salvation. He *was* God from everlasting, but he *became* man—at a definite moment of the world's history, and in order that fallen man might be saved. That he became man was not at all necessary to the unfolding of his own being. He was infinite, eternal, and unchangeable God when he became man and after he became man. But he would have been infinite, eternal, and unchangeable God, even if he had never become man. His becoming man was a free act of his love. Ultimately its purpose, as the purpose of all things, was the glory of God; but that purpose does not conflict at all with the fact that it was a free act of mercy to undeserving sinners. He became man in order that he might die on the cross to redeem sinners from the guilt and power of sin.

The Bible not only tells us that the Son of God became man, but it tells us something of the way in which he became man. He "became man"—if we may quote the Shorter Catechism's summary of the Bible's teaching on this point—"by taking to himself a true body and a reasonable soul, being conceived by the power of the Holy Ghost in the womb of the Virgin Mary, and born of her, yet without sin" (WSC Q&A 22). According to the Bible, the Son of God became man not in some mere semblance, but actually. The body which he took to himself was not, as some early heretics said, a mere semblance of a body but it was a true body, a body of flesh and bones. Moreover, he took to himself "a reasonable soul." His human body was not just a human body indwelt by the divine Person, the eternal Son of God, but it was a human body that was indwelt, as other human bodies are, by a human soul—a human soul with all the faculties of reason which other human souls possess and which distinguish human souls from the lower creatures.

This stupendous act by which the eternal Son of God took upon himself a human body and a reasonable soul took place, according to the Bible, in the supernatural act of the virgin birth. He was conceived, according to the Bible, by the Holy Ghost and born of the virgin Mary. It is needless to say that the Bible does not narrate the virgin birth as one theory advanced among other possible theories to account for the incarnation. It simply narrates it as a fact. It does not say: "The Son of God became incarnate, and one explanation of the way in which he became incarnate is found in the story of the virgin birth." But it says simply, before it narrates the virgin birth: "Now the birth of Jesus Christ took place in this way" (Matt 1:18). That is not theory. It is history.

When the Son of God became man, he did not cease to be God. He certainly did not empty himself of any of his divine attributes, as an unfortunate translation, in the Revised Version, of a verse in the second chapter of Philippians tends to lead people to think. No, he remained all that he was before. He was infinite, eternal, and unchangeable before the incarnation; he remained infinite, eternal, and unchangeable after the incarnation. Indeed, to assert the contrary would be quite absurd. It would be quite absurd to say that an unchangeable being changed by becoming changeable. That would surely be a contradiction in terms. No, he was infinite, eternal, and unchangeable in all his divine attributes after the incarnation exactly as before. After the incarnation, exactly as before the incarnation, he was infinite, eternal, and unchangeable in his being, wisdom, power, holiness, justice, goodness, and truth.

So by the incarnation he did not cease to be what he was before. But he did become something that he was not before. He was God. He now became man. So after the incarnation he was God and man.

Does that mean that there was some kind of merger between the divine and the human Christ; does it mean that the human was somehow taken up into the divine and lost its identity in it? Or does it mean that divine and human entered, as it were, into some sort of chemical combination, so that a third something neither divine nor human but divine-human resulted? No, the Bible does not teach these things, and the church rightly rejected them as serious heresies. The Bible teaches that after the incarnation, the Son of God was God and man in two *distinct* natures. God is God, and man is man. There can be no confusion between the two, either in the person of Christ or anywhere else.

Well, then, does that mean that there are two persons in Christ—a divine person and a human person? Does it mean that what we have in Christ is a human person merely indwelt in some particularly intimate way by the Son of God? No, the Bible does not teach that at all. The church rightly rejected it as a terrible heresy. There are not two persons in Christ, but one person. The one person, the eternal Son of God, took unto himself a human nature—a complete human nature—at the incarnation, but he did not hereby become two persons. So, there we have the great biblical doctrine of the person of Christ: "God and man, in two distinct natures, and one person, forever" (WSC Q&A 21).

I ask you to consider for a moment how truly wonderful that doctrine is. I ask you to consider how wonderfully it satisfies the longings of our souls. Sinful men have been prone to seek a god who will be like them and near to them. They have fallen into the dreadful sin of worshipping and glorifying the creature more than the Creator; they have fallen into the sin of worshipping other men. Well, we Christians have a God who is truly near to us. We Christians can without sin worship one who is truly man. We Christians can without sin worship one who was tempted in all points like as we are; we can without sin worship one who is touched with the feeling of our infirmities. Yes, we can worship a God who is very close to us indeed—namely, Christ Jesus our Lord. We can worship him because he is God; he is wonderfully near to us because he is man. How marvelous was that act of love by which he became man!

But we never ought to forget that that act would never have been necessary except for our sin. It was our sin that caused him to die upon the cross; it was our sin that caused him to become man in order that he might thus die. That marvelous act of condescension by which the eternal Son of God became man was part of the glorious fulfillment of the covenant of grace. Man was estranged from God by the fact of sin. The Son of God became man that he might for God's people bring the estrangement to an end. Christ became man, in other words, that he might be the Mediator between God and man. He could not be the Mediator between God and man unless he were God; he could not be the Mediator unless he were man. It is as one who is both God and man that he has brought us to God. The doctrine of the person of Christ, in other words, is at the foundation of the doctrine of salvation. It is useless to try to set forth the meaning of Christ's death on the cross unless you first understand just who it was who there died.

We have seen who it was. It was not merely a righteous man, giving us an example of self-sacrifice. It was not merely a divine person taking on the semblance of a man. But it was one who was truly man and truly God; it was one who was God and man, in two distinct natures and one person forever. He it was of whom the First Epistle to Timothy speaks when it says: "For there is one God, and there is one mediator between God and men, the man Christ Jesus" (1 Tim 2:5). With that understanding, presupposing thus the great biblical doctrine of Christ's person, we now go on to study the great subject of Christ's mediatorial work. What has that Christ, who is "God and man in two distinct natures, and one person, forever" (WSC Q&A 21), done for us as our Redeemer?

The Shorter Catechism introduces the subject by distinguishing three offices that Christ executes. "What offices doth Christ execute as our Redeemer?" it asks. The answer is: "Christ, as our Redeemer, executeth the offices of a prophet, of a priest, and of a king, both in his estate of humiliation and exaltation" (WSC Q&A 23). In the talks that follow we shall speak of each one of these offices of Christ in turn. We shall speak of Christ as the Revealer of God and as the Revealer of the way of salvation which God has provided for man. That is his prophetic office. We shall then speak of the atonement which he has made for sin by dying in our stead upon the cross, and of his present intercession for us. That is his priestly office. Finally, we shall speak of the rule which he exercises over his church and of his defense of the church against all enemies. That is his kingly office.

But what ought to be observed very carefully is that Christ's execution of each of these offices is connected in the closest possible way with his execution of the others. Sad misunderstanding will result if we take any one of the offices of Christ in isolation. Thus, suppose we should concentrate our attention upon the prophetic office of Christ. Suppose we should say to ourselves: "Let us take Christ first of all as a revealer of God, and leave out of consideration the question whether he did or did not die as a sacrifice for sin upon the cross." Would we in that case obtain a right conception even of that part of the work of Christ which we started out to study? That is very far indeed from being the case. No, if you start out to consider Christ only as a revealer of God and leave his other offices out of account, you obtain an utterly distorted notion even of his work as a revealer. A very important part of what he revealed is found in his revelation of the meaning of his atoning work. A very important part of his work as a prophet—indeed, the very center and core and sum and substance of his work as a prophet—is found in his presentation of himself as priest and as king. So also even his work as a priest—his offering up of himself as a sacrifice to satisfy divine justice and reconcile us to God—would never have been applied to us except through his work as a prophet, his gracious revealing, through his Word and Spirit, of the meaning of his death upon the cross.

The point that I am now making is so important that I am not at all ashamed of lingering upon it. One of the root errors of much modern discussion about the Bible is found in the piecemeal method that is employed. Take some modern book about Jesus Christ. I am not thinking at all of any particular book, but am just trying to indicate the way in which any book ought and ought not to be evaluated. Well, this book presents itself for our consideration. Perhaps we have the job of reviewing it for *The Presbyterian Guardian* or for some other journal. Let us say that it is a book dealing with the teaching of Jesus Christ. Let us also say that as we read the book we observe at once that the writer does not believe in Jesus's atoning work; he certainly does not believe that on the cross Jesus died as a sacrifice to satisfy divine justice. He does not believe in the deity of Christ. He does not believe in the kingly office of Christ. He does not believe that Jesus is seated now upon the throne and that he will come again in glory. But he has some very favorable things to say about Jesus as a revealer of God.

What shall we say about that book in our review of it? Shall we say that it is a faulty book, but that it is true as far as it goes? Shall we say that it is certainly weak on the doctrine of the atonement and even weak on the doctrine of the deity of Christ but splendid in its presentation of Jesus as a revealer of God?

That is what we might say if we followed the method of reviewing books which is followed by many reviewers—even by many reviewers who can be called fairly orthodox. But as a matter of fact that method is radically wrong. It ignores the fact that the truth contained in the Bible does not consist in a series of isolated observations but constitutes a system of truth. You cannot reject any essential part of the system and still get the other parts of the system right. So a man who rejects the priestly work of Christ, and drags him from his kingly throne by denying his duty, cannot at the same time rightly present his prophetic work as a revealer of God. A man who presents Jesus only as a prophet has a false view even of his revealing work. You cannot rightly present Jesus as prophet unless you also present him as priest and king.

It is with that understanding that I am now beginning to consider with you the prophetic office of Christ. We shall go wrong at every point unless we understand that this One who, as prophet, reveals God to us is also the One who died for our sins upon the cross and is now seated upon the throne. Indeed, when he reveals God to us, the central part of that revelation is found in his revelation of himself as God—in his gracious presentation of himself as the eternal Son of God who became man to be our Savior. That revelation is what we rightly call the gospel. What I am trying to do in these talks is to be Christ's humble instrument in proclaiming that gospel to everyone within the sound of my voice. God grant that some of you who have not yet received it may receive it for the saving of your souls and that you who have received it may give thanks anew to him who is our prophet, priest, and king.

43

What Is a Prophet?

At the close of last week's talk, I was pointing out to you that the work of Christ as Mediator between God and fallen man may be summarized under three heads. In the words of the Shorter Catechism, "Christ, as our Redeemer, executeth the offices of a prophet, of a priest, and of a king" (WSC Q&A 23).

This afternoon we shall begin to consider the first of these—we shall consider Christ's office of a prophet.

Before we can do so—before we can consider Christ as a prophet—we must ask what the word "prophet" means. In answer to that question, our first impulse might be to say, on the basis of popular modern usage, that a prophet is a man who predicts future events. In that sense, we speak of all kinds of prophets. We speak, for instance, of weather prophets. A weather prophet is a man who tells, or tries to tell, what the weather is going to be. So also we have prophets in a great many other spheres. When I lived at Princeton, I used to hear a good deal about a man who was called a prophet because he predicted, or tried to predict, every year the score of the Yale-Princeton game. He was the world's worst prophet. His predictions were always wrong. But that does not affect the sense in which the word "prophet" was applied to him. He was called a prophet because he *tried*, at least, to predict the future.

This use of the word "prophet," however, is not the use that appears in the Bible. In the Bible the word "prophet" does not in itself designate a man who predicts future events. No doubt most prophets did, as a matter of fact, predict future events, but their power to predict future events was not the thing that caused them to be called prophets. Prediction of the future was usually part of the prophet's function, but it was not by any means all of his function. The word "prophet" in the Bible has a very much broader sense. It designates a man who speaks as a mouthpiece of God, a man who speaks what God, by supernatural revelation and by definite command, has commissioned him to speak. The things that the prophet says may, indeed, concern the future, and often they do concern the future; but they may also concern the present and even the past. They may consist in the imparting of information, but they may also consist in the issuance of commands. Whatever they consist in, they come with divine authority—not with the authority of the prophet, but with the authority of God who has commissioned the prophet and of whom he is the spokesman. A prophet, in other words, according to the Bible, is a man who can say, as he comes forward, "Thus says the Lord."

If that be so, the question arises how the prophet, in the biblical sense of the word, differs from the modern minister of the gospel. Does not the minister of the gospel today, like the prophet of biblical times, proclaim a message which God has given him to proclaim? Does he not preach the Word of God rather than his own word? Does he not, if he be a true minister, say, as he stands in his pulpit, "Thus says the Lord"? If that be so, how does he differ from the prophets of old?

The answer is not difficult. The minister of the gospel is like the prophet in that he proclaims the Word of the Lord, but he differs from the prophet in the way in which the Word of the Lord comes to him. The Word of the Lord comes to the minister of the gospel through the Bible, whereas it came to the prophets of old through no intermediary—through no book—but in direct, supernatural fashion. The minister of the gospel must always appeal to an authority which is outside of him and to which others have access equally with him, whereas the prophet appeals to no authority to which others can have access, but claims that God has spoken directly to him, so that his voice must be received as the voice of God.

I think great evil sometimes results today when this distinction is ignored—when modern persons claim to be prophets in the high biblical sense of the word. Some modern persons make that claim very definitely and clearly. They are the fanatics who occasionally arise and draw poor, deluded people away after them. Sometimes the adherents of these fanatics or impostors may be numbered by the thousands or hundreds of thousands. But it is perfectly plain to well-instructed Christian people that they are false prophets, one and all.

The error sometimes shows itself, however, in subtler ways. There are Christian people who have a sort of notion that God speaks in some supernatural fashion by way of direct guidance to them. I am not talking about adherents of groups or sects that obviously make light of biblical doctrine, but I am talking about people who really believe in the Bible as the only infallible rule of faith and practice, and yet when you talk to them about questions of conduct or policy they will be quite imperious to all argument and will simply tell you that they have been on their knees and that God has made his will known to them. In practice, though not in theory, these persons are assuming a position something like that of the prophets in the biblical sense of the word.

These persons, it seems to me, are rather seriously wrong. God might, of course, have chosen to guide his servants today in the manner in which these persons think he guides them, but as a matter of fact he has not done so. Instead, he guides his servants today by the Bible. He has written in the pages of that book what his will is for his people. He has written it very plainly. It is there for all to read and for all to understand. No one man and no one group of men has a monopoly in the understanding of it. The Bible's commands are to be interpreted, not in some way open only to people of special piety, but in accordance with plain, out-of-door common sense.

I do not mean, of course, that the Holy Spirit is not present with Christian people, and I certainly do not mean that his presence is not necessary if we are to understand and apply the Bible aright. But what I do mean is that, when the Holy Spirit is really present with us in our reading of the Bible, he enables us to apply the Bible to our own conduct and to the conduct of other people in a way that we can defend before all the world. It is a very dangerous thing indeed when men decline to reason about the application of the Bible to their own lives and the lives of other people, and when they say, in lieu of argument, "I have been on my knees and the Holy Spirit has made plain to me that this is God's will and that everyone who objects to it is opposing God's will."

That is the reason why it is always rather ominous when the report of an ecclesiastical committee of any kind begins by saying that the committee has been much in prayer about the matter referred to it. Do I mean by that that committees ought not to be much in prayer before they come to their decisions? I certainly mean nothing of the kind. I think they ought to be much *more* in prayer than they usually are. Do I mean, then, that it is not a good thing to ask God for his Holy Spirit that the committee may come to the right decision? I certainly do not mean that. I think it is a very necessary thing to pray for the Holy Spirit before we deliberate about any important matters.

What then do I mean? I mean that prayer is not to be made a substitute for common sense but a help to the real exercise of common sense. I mean that prayer is not to be made an excuse for evading unpalatable arguments of one's opponents in debate but is to be used rather that sound arguments may be given free scope. What we ought to pray for as individuals and as members of ecclesiastical committees is not some special supernatural guidance, but clearness of mind, receptivity of heart, and consecration of will, in order that all mists may be taken from our eyes and we may come to a decision that is in accordance with God's Word and that we can defend by perfectly plain and sound arguments.

In other words, it is a splendid thing to pray, but it is an evil thing to boast about our prayers. It is a dangerous thing to make the length and fervency of our prayers an excuse for running roughshod over things plainly taught in God's Word. The Holy Spirit does guide the servants of Jesus today; he does often give them a blessed assurance of his presence with them, and of the rightness of the decisions that he has enabled them to make. But he does that not by fresh, supernatural revelation, but by opening their minds and hearts to receive the supernatural revelation contained in the book which he, the Holy Spirit, himself has inspired.

Thus prophecy today has ceased. Like all the other supernatural gifts, and like the power of working miracles, it ceased at the close of the apostolic age. If you ask why it ceased, I cannot do better than refer you to an excellent and very learned book by Dr. B. B. Warfield, entitled *Counterfeit Miracles*.

I do not think that we ought to feel gloomy because miracles and the supernatural gifts of the Spirit do not appear in our age. That they do not appear is from one point of view the glory of the age in which we are living. Why were there miracles in Old Testament times and in New Testament times? It was because the supernatural revelation which the miracles were intended to accredit was not yet complete. Now, however, it is complete. There is a wonderful symmetry in the revelation of God which is contained in the Old and New Testaments. Nothing needs to be added to that revelation until the next great supernatural act in the drama of redemption, which will occur when our Lord returns. We can rejoice that miracles are not needed today, since the reason why they are not needed is that God has already fully made known to us his will for our salvation in the pages of the holy Book.

At any rate, whatever be the reason for the cessation of miracles, it is clear that as a matter of fact they have ceased. There are no miracles today. There are today no events in the external world which are wrought by the immediate power of God. The things that occur in the course of nature are indeed wrought by God; they are just as much wrought by him as would be the case if they were miracles. But to accomplish those events God uses means, while to accomplish the miracles of which we have accounts in the Bible he put forth directly his creative power.

There are today supernatural works of God. There is a supernatural work of God every time a sinner is born again. That is not accomplished through the course of nature. It is just as supernatural, it is just as much "above nature," as was the miracle of the feeding of the five thousand or the raising of Lazarus from the dead. But it is not done in the external world and therefore it is not properly called a "miracle."

With the cessation of the miracles has gone, as we have seen, the cessation of those special supernatural gifts of the Holy Spirit, like the gift of tongues, of which Paul speaks, for example, in the First Epistle to the Corinthians. One of those gifts, and the most important of them, was the gift of prophecy. That gift, like the other strictly supernatural gifts, has ceased.

We all ought to recognize that fact with the utmost clearness, and particularly we preachers ought to do so. We ought to recognize very clearly what our business is and what it is not. Our business is not to proclaim any word that God has given us in the night watches by dream or vision; it is not to proclaim any message which he has placed upon our lips by a supernatural impulse of which we can give no account. There were times when his Word came to men in such glorious and wonderful ways, but those times are past, and we ought very clearly to recognize the fact that they are past. We ought to honor the prophets, but in honoring the prophets we ought to be perfectly clear about the fact that we are not prophets ourselves.

Our function is a humbler function. It is the function of studying the Bible and then of setting forth what the Bible contains.

Do you think that is an unworthy function? I do not think so at all. I think it is a glorious function, and the sad thing is that men who call themselves preachers have turned aside from it to something that is far less worthy. They have turned aside to proclaim their own opinions on the subject of religion, or their own experiences, or their own views on political or social questions. In view of what much modern preaching is, I can well understand that one modern preacher has suggested that a halt be called for a number of years on the whole business. It is indeed hardly worthwhile. But very different from that sorry hubbub of voices is the voice of the real preacher. He is a man who comes forth into his pulpit from a secret place of meditation and prayer, opens the Bible upon the pulpit desk and, with his heart all aglow from the radiance of the sacred page, stands there, with dying men before him, and proclaims to them the blessed message of salvation which God in his Word has given him to proclaim. Does that view of preaching make of the preacher a mere scribe or a mere phonograph? Ah, just think of the great preachers, my friends—the great preachers who have been the first to disclaim any thought of originality in the content of their message, the great preachers who have appealed most humbly to God's written Word. Was preaching as they practiced it a cold, mechanical thing? No, my friends, it was almost the greatest privilege that could conceivably be given to mortal man. To receive God's message of salvation in the depths of one's own soul, to have it written by the Holy Spirit upon the tablets of one's own heart, and then to proclaim it to others as the Holy Spirit gives one utterance—what higher privilege can there be than that? That is the privilege of the true preacher of the gospel.

But the prophet's work was different. When he said to his hearers, "Thus says the Lord," he pointed not to the Bible open before him but to special supernatural revelation which God had given him to proclaim. He was, in the strictest possible sense, a spokesman for God.

Many passages in the Bible set forth the nature of the prophet's office, but here we shall have time to refer to only one of them. It is found in the eighteenth chapter of Deuteronomy, where we find the following verses: "And the Lord said to me, 'They are right in what they have spoken. I will raise up for them a prophet like you from among their brothers. And I will put my words in his mouth, and he shall speak to them all that I command him. And whoever will not listen to my words that he shall speak in my name, I myself will require it of him'" (Deut 18:17–19). Here the fundamental nature of prophecy is clearly set forth. A prophet is a man on whose lips God has put his Word. He is a man who speaks what God has commanded him to speak. Being thus the mouthpiece of God, his words come with divine authority. Whosoever will not hearken unto the words the prophet speaks in God's name, God will require it of him.

Just because the prophet's function is such a lofty one, the greater is the sin of any man who presumes to lay claim to it when God has not given it to him: "But the prophet [so the passage in Deuteronomy continues] who presumes to speak a word in my name that I have not commanded him to speak, or who speaks in the name of other gods, that same prophet shall die" (Deut 18:20).

Take also that great passage in the twenty-third chapter of Jeremiah, where the false prophets are described: "I did not send the prophets, yet they ran; I did not speak to them, yet they prophesied" (Jer 23:21).

Yes, very solemn is the work of the true prophet; and woe to the man who undertakes that work without command of God.

At this point, a question may arise. If there are true prophets and also false prophets, how are we to tell the true from the false? Are we just to accept as true prophecy everything that claims to be such, or are we to apply certain tests by which true prophets may be known?

The Bible tells us that the latter is the case. John tells us in his first epistle: "Beloved, do not believe every spirit, but test the spirits to see whether they are from God, for many false prophets have gone out into the world" (1 John 4:1).

If then we are to "try the spirits," if we are to apply tests to distinguish false prophets from true, just what are the tests that we are to apply?

No doubt there are various tests; but the apostle John, immediately after the verse that we have quoted, gives us one of the most important of them. No prophet, he tells us, is to be regarded as a real prophet, no spirit is to be regarded as the Spirit of God, if the prophet or the spirit tells us something that is contrary to what God has already told us regarding himself or regarding the Lord Jesus Christ. "By this you know the Spirit of God: every spirit that confesses that Jesus Christ has come in the flesh is from God, and every spirit that does not confess Jesus is not from God. This is the spirit of the antichrist, which you heard was coming and now is in the world already" (1 John 4:2–3).

So also Paul, in the First Epistle to the Corinthians, says that no man can be regarded as speaking by the impulsion of the Spirit of God if he says Jesus is anathema: "Therefore I want you to understand that no one speaking in the Spirit of God ever says 'Jesus is accursed!' and no one can say 'Jesus is Lord' except in the Holy Spirit" (1 Cor 12:3).

In these passages we find a principle which is sadly neglected in our day. It is the principle of the primacy of truth. One who comes forward as a prophet or a preacher cannot, according to the Bible, be recognized as a genuine prophet or a genuine preacher of the gospel unless the things that he says are true. It makes not the slightest difference, according to the

Bible, how fervent he is; it makes not the slightest difference how magnetic is his personality; it makes not the slightest difference what power he attains over the souls of men: he is, according to the Bible, a false prophet or a false preacher, if the things that he says about God or about Christ or about salvation are not true. Once establish what the truth is, and every man thereafter coming forward as a prophet or as a preacher must be tested by his conformity to that.

Now today the truth *is* established. It is established in the Bible. Every preacher as well as every prophet must be tested by his conformity to God's written Word. If what he says is contrary to the Bible, then it makes no difference, so far as our decision to accept him or reject him is concerned, how eloquent he is, how fervent he is, how religious he is, how spiritual (in the modern and nonbiblical sense of that misused word) he is, or how sincere he is. We are bound to reject him if what he says is not in accordance with God's Word. The true Holy Spirit does not contradict what he himself has caused to be written in the Bible; and any spirit that does contradict what the Holy Spirit has caused to be written is one of the false spirits against which we are warned in such solemn language by Paul and by John.

44

Prophecy and the Gospel

Last week we discussed the question, "What is a prophet?" and we came to the conclusion that a prophet, in the biblical sense of the word, is a person who speaks for God, who speaks what God by supernatural revelation and by definite command has commissioned him to speak.

Incidentally we observed that the popular sense of the word "prophet," in accordance with which it designates a man who predicts the future, does not do justice to the biblical sense. A "prophet," in the biblical sense of the word, may predict the future, but he may also speak of the present and of the past, and he may be just as truly a prophet when he speaks of the present and of the past as he is when he speaks of the future. Moreover, he may be just as truly a prophet when he issues commands as he is when he gives information. He is a prophet if he speaks as one who has been made, in supernatural fashion, the mouthpiece of God, so that he can say, when he comes forward, "Thus says the Lord; my voice, now, must be received as the voice of God."

It is certainly true that prophecy, according to the Bible, need not necessarily be prediction of the future. Yet in recognizing that fact, in learning not to give an entirely exclusive place to the predictive element in prophecy, men have sometimes fallen into the extreme of utterly failing to give the predictive element in prophecy that place which it does most certainly deserve. What a great discovery it was, they say, when modern biblical scholars learned that the prophets of the Old Testament were not foretellers but forthtellers, when they learned that the business of the prophet was not to predict the future but to set forth great religious truth!

Well, with regard to that allegedly great discovery, I can only say that most of those who boast about it have really made no great discovery at all, but have lost sight of an exceedingly precious truth. They have lost sight of the fact that the great prophets of the Old Testament, though they did do more than predict the future, yet did predict the future, and did make the prediction of the future a very large part of their work.

Why is it that these modern men, of whom we are speaking now, have come to deny or minimize the predictive element in prophecy? I will tell you why. It is because the predictive element in prophecy, supposing the predictions that make up that predictive element are true, exhibits with particular clearness the supernaturalism of prophecy. The future is hidden from man; and if the prophets really did predict the future accurately they could have done that only by supernatural revelation from God. But the whole idea of such supernatural revelation, as the whole idea of miracles, is abhorrent to these modern men. Therefore, they have directed their attack especially against the predictive element in prophecy because that is the element in which the supernatural nature of the prophet's work would, if only they recognized it, most clearly be seen.

Thus one of the first and one of the most important steps in the downward march of certain modern scholars as preachers was their determination to lay the emphasis upon other things in the message of the Old Testament prophets than the prediction of the future. Sometimes these scholars or preachers did not at first actually deny the predictive element in prophecy. "No doubt the Old Testament prophets," they said, "did predict the future; at least we are not at all concerned to say that they did not. Do not be alarmed, Christian readers, we are really very innocent people indeed. We are not at all concerned to deny things that you have been accustomed, in your reading of the Old Testament, to regard as precious. We are not at all concerned to deny that the Old Testament prophets may have predicted the events in the life of Christ that occurred long after their day. But we ask you just for a change to leave that element in the prophet's work out of account for the moment and consider with us another aspect of their work, an aspect which up to modern times has been sadly neglected in the church—namely, the message that the prophets had for the men of their own day. We ask you to consider those prophets primarily as great statesmen who brought to bear upon the affairs of nations certain underlying religious principles. We ask you to put yourselves back in the ancient days in which those men lived, in order that you may understand them as men who had a living message for their times. If you consider them thus, you may no longer look upon them primarily as recipients of some strange, supernatural revelation and that will perhaps at first sight seem to you to be a loss; but the loss will be compensated for by a greater gain. The prophets will become living, breathing, human figures; and since the religious principles upon which they based their lives are still valid, we shall be able to profit by their teaching more than we ever did when we looked upon them as soothsayers who predicted details about the life of Christ and the early history of the Christian church."

What shall we say about that very common way of dealing with the Old Testament prophets? I think we can say something very simple about it. I think we can just say that it is merely one expression, among the many modern expressions, of unbelief.

You see, it is all based upon the underlying assumption upon which modern unbelief is based—namely, the assumption that what man needs is simply moral guidance and the contagion of great religious experience. If that assumption is correct, then all we need from the prophets is an enunciation of great moral and religious principles and the example of men who centuries ago made those principles effective in their lives. But as a matter of fact, that assumption is radically false. What man really needs is not just the enunciation of great principles and the power of good examples, but a salvation wrought by the living God. Being utterly dead in trespasses and sins, he can do nothing whatever to save himself, no matter what fine moral instruction he receives and no matter what excellent examples of virtue are held before his eyes. If sinful man is to be saved, God must save him. The salvation of man as he actually is must be a work of the living God.

The Bible contains the blessed record of that divine work of salvation. The Bible is not just a storehouse of moral and religious instruction or an account of men's religious experiences. It is a record of events—it is a record of what God has done for the salvation of sinful men. It tells us how, when the fullness of time was come, God saved sinners by the redeeming work of Jesus Christ.

But how is that redeeming work applied to those whom God has chosen for salvation? The answer is really not obscure. The redemption purchased by Christ is applied to the individual soul by the Holy Spirit, and the means which the Holy Spirit uses to apply it is faith.

A man listens to the gospel story. He hears how Jesus died upon the cross to save sinners. At first, he does not believe. But then the Holy Spirit works faith in him. He believes and is saved.

That is true not only of those who have been saved after Jesus came, but it is also true of those who were saved before Jesus came. The Old

Testament saints, like the New Testament saints, were justified through faith. They too listened to the gospel, believed the gospel because the Holy Spirit opened their hearts, and thus were saved.

But how did the gospel come to them? How could it possibly come to them, since the events which the gospel story sets forth had in their day not yet taken place? The answer is really very plain. The gospel came to the Old Testament saints by way of promise. The redeeming work of Christ had not yet been accomplished, but God promised it, and those who received the promise in faith were saved.

Certainly, the promise was at first not at all explicit. It was not very explicit, for example, when it came to Abraham. Yet the Old Testament says that Abraham "believed the LORD, and he counted it to him as righteousness" (Gen 15:6); and the New Testament presents this faith of Abraham as an example of that same saving faith which also appears after our Lord had come. All through the Old Testament that element of promise is found. The Old Testament saints did not know how the coming salvation was to be wrought, they did not know in any great fullness—at least in the earlier stages of the promise—in what it was to consist; but God had told them to look forward to it and to trust God to accomplish it in his own way. They did trust him, and that was saving faith.

But if that be so, it will readily be seen that the predictive element in Old Testament prophecy is at the very heart of it. It is because Old Testament prophecy was prediction that it constituted a gospel. It was the gospel story told beforehand, and those who believed the gospel story, thus told beforehand, were saved.

In the great prophets such as Isaiah, the promise comes to wonderfully rich unfolding. There we find the promise of a king of David's line who should also be "Mighty God, Everlasting Father, Prince of Peace" (Isa 9:6). There also we find the meaning of the cross of Christ set forth in the fifty-third chapter of Isaiah in such explicit terms that, despite the great wealth of New Testament revelation, we love now to turn back ever again to that chapter when we think of the One who died on Calvary for our sins.

How utterly shallow, then, is the view of those who push the predictive aspect of Old Testament prophecy into the background! How utterly shallow is the view of those who regard the great prophets as being primarily statesmen and moral leaders, and lose sight of the fact that they really were men who had revealed to them by way of promise that blessed gospel through the hearing and believing of which salvation comes! If a man loses sight of that fact, that the prophets preached the gospel afore, he has not the slightest real inkling of what the prophets were raised up to do.

The prophets did indeed do more than predict the future. That is true. But they did predict the future; and the prediction of the future, far from being a merely subordinate part of their work, was quite the most important part of it—indeed, was really the part that gave meaning to all the rest. It is quite necessary, if we are to have any real understanding of the Bible, that we should get out of our minds this allegedly important discovery that the prophets were forthtellers and not foretellers, and we should get into our minds the great fact that the prophets had at the heart of their message the unfolding of that divine promise which was fulfilled in the cross and the resurrection of Jesus Christ.

The truth is that the men who deny the predictive aspect of Old Testament prophecy have really denied all prophecy. Why is it that they deny the predictive aspect? As we observed at the beginning of this talk, it is because the predictive aspect is that aspect which most obviously involves the claim on the part of the prophets to have received supernatural revelation. It is also, as we now observe, because the predictive aspect of prophecy is that aspect which most obviously shows the prophets to have been proclaimers of a piece of good news setting forth not just general principles of religion and ethics but things that God actually did at a definite point in the world's history, for the salvation of sinful men. The truth is that the denial or minimizing of predictive prophecy, so common today, is only one manifestation of that general denial of supernatural redemption which is such a marked characteristic of the life of our times.

It is not surprising, therefore, to find that those who deny to the prophets the supernatural work of predicting the future really deny to them every other supernatural work. It is not surprising to find that they regard the prophets essentially as men of extraordinary religious insight, and have not the slightest notion of the central fact that the prophets had received in supernatural fashion a message from God.

We, on the other hand, must hold on with all our souls to that great truth which these men deny. We must hold clearly to the fact that the prophets were not just men of extraordinary religious and moral insight, but were men who were, in the strictest sense, spokesmen for God—men who could truly say, as they came forward, "Thus says the Lord."

They could say that not only when they predicted the future, but also when they spoke of the present or of the past. They could say that not only when they imparted information but also when they issued commands. They could say that whenever the Spirit of God was upon them to make their word truly the Word of God.

It is with that high supernaturalistic conception of the prophet's function that we come now to speak of the prophetic office of the Lord Jesus Christ. "Christ, as our Redeemer," says the Shorter Catechism, "executeth the offices of a prophet, of a priest, and of a king" (WSC Q&A 23). I want to talk to you now about the first of these three offices which the Shorter Catechism names—Christ's office of a prophet.

The first point to notice is that we really do have a right to attribute this office to our Lord. In the passage from the eighteenth chapter of Deuteronomy, which I discussed with you, from a slightly different point of view, last Sunday, it is said: "I will raise up for them a prophet like you from among their brothers. And I will put my words in his mouth, and he shall speak to them all that I command him" (Deut 18:18), and lest we should have any doubt about our right to apply this passage to Christ, we have direct scriptural warrant for so doing in the third chapter and in the seventh chapter of the book of Acts.

Moreover, even where the word "prophet" is not actually applied to Jesus, we find Jesus represented as fulfilling functions which are very clearly those of a prophet. That is particularly prominent in the Gospel according to John. Take, for example, passages such as these: "My teaching is not mine, but his who sent me" (John 7:16); "For I have not spoken on my own authority, but the Father who sent me has himself given me a commandment—what to say and what to speak. And I know that his commandment is eternal life. What I say, therefore, I say as the Father has told me" (John 12:49–50); "For all that I have heard from my Father I have made known to you" (John 15:15). These passages, of course, present a relation between Christ and God the Father which is quite unlike the relation in which any mere man can stand toward God. But all the same they do present Christ in the clearest possible way as a prophet. "All things that I have heard of my Father I have made known unto you," "Even as the Father said unto me, so I speak"—how could the essential nature of the prophet's work, as the work of a spokesman for God, be set forth in clearer fashion than it is set forth here?

Moreover, the New Testament tells us that people, during Jesus's earthly ministry, recognized him as a prophet; and while it no doubt leads us to understand, at least in some cases, that these persons did not have a full conception of the true nature of his person, yet it does clearly at the same time lead us to understand that these persons did have a view of Jesus which was true as far as it went. Of course, Jesus was far more than a prophet, but he certainly was a prophet, as these persons saw.

There can be then no doubt whatever about the matter. The Bible does clearly teach us that Christ exercises the office of prophet. The question then arises: at what times and in what ways Christ has exercised that office?

Well, in one sense, perhaps, he may be said to have exercised that office even before he became man. The Bible does seem to teach us that the second person of the Trinity is the Revealer of God; it does seem to teach that wherever men have any knowledge of God at all they have received it from the Son.

This, however, is not that general revealing activity of the second person of the Trinity of which the Shorter Catechism is speaking when it says that "Christ executeth the office of a prophet" (WSC Q&A 24). It is speaking of that particular execution of the office of a prophet which Christ carries out as our Redeemer.

Even when so limited, however, Christ's execution of the office of a prophet seems to have begun even before the incarnation. In a passage in the first chapter of the First Epistle of Peter, for example, we are told that the Spirit of Christ testified in and through the Old Testament prophets concerning Christ's sufferings and the glory that should follow. The Old Testament prophets are represented in that passage as "inquiring what person or time the Spirit of Christ in them was indicating when he predicted the sufferings of Christ and the subsequent glories" (1 Pet 1:11). The passage does seem clearly to mean that Christ sent the Holy Spirit to give them their prophetic message regarding the salvation that was to come. If so, his prophetic office, and his prophetic office as Redeemer, began already in Old Testament times. Even in Old Testament times he was not only the substance of the gospel but also the author of it. As the author of it, as the One who sent forth the Holy Spirit to proclaim his death and resurrection beforehand, he was certainly executing the office of a prophet.

It is, however, the work of Christ after the incarnation that we think of more particularly when we speak of Christ (as our Redeemer) as executing the office of a prophet.

It is that post-incarnation work of Christ of which the Epistle to the Hebrews is speaking when, in the grand opening of the majestic epistle, it treats the coming of the Son of God as the climax of that long progress of revelation which had been carried on through the Old Testament prophets: "Long ago, at many times and in many ways, God spoke to our fathers by the prophets, but in these last days he has spoken to us by his Son" (Heb 1:1–2). I want to speak to you next Sunday afternoon about that revelation of God which was carried on and is carried on through the incarnate Son of God, that is, through him who is truly "God and man in two distinct natures, and one person, forever" (WSC Q&A 21). I want to show you wherein it is like the revelation of God that was carried on through the Old Testament prophets. But also, I want to show you the stupendous difference that separates it from the work of the Old Testament prophets and from the work of any prophet who was merely man.

45

The Teaching of Jesus

It will be remembered that we are now dealing with one of the three offices which Christ executes as our Redeemer—namely, Christ's office of a prophet.

That office is, as we observed just at the close of the last talk, very comprehensive indeed. It is not confined even to what Christ has said and done after he became man, but includes even what he said and did before that time. Even in Old Testament times, Christ was not only the substance of the gospel but also the author of it. He sent the Holy Spirit upon the Old Testament prophets that they might testify beforehand of him.

But, after all, it is the post-incarnation work of Christ as prophet of which we are most apt to think when we speak of Christ's prophetic office, and it is that post-incarnation work of which I want to talk to you this afternoon. I want to talk to you of that part of his work as a prophet which Christ our Redeemer carried on after he had become man.

In a majestic passage at the beginning of the Epistle to the Hebrews, the coming of the Son of God is put as the climax of that long progress of revelation which has been carried on through the Old Testament prophets: "Long ago, at many times and in many ways, God spoke to our fathers by the prophets, but in these last days he has spoken to us by his Son" (Heb 1:1–2). "In these last days he has spoken to us by his Son"—here this great epistle plainly has in mind that part of Jesus's execution of the prophetic office that came after the incarnation.

At the start, we observe that it may plainly be divided into two great divisions. In the first place, there is that part of it which Christ accomplished by his own words and deeds during his earthly ministry; and in the second place, there is that part of it which he has carried on after his ascension into heaven through the commission that he gave to his apostles and through the Holy Spirit whom he sent upon the apostles and upon the church.

I want you to examine now the former of these two divisions. I want you to examine that part of Christ's work as a prophet which he carried on during his earthly ministry.

It is customary to speak of that part of Christ's prophetic work as "the *teaching* of Jesus," and there is unquestionably a sense in which this designation is justified. Undoubtedly Jesus did appear to his contemporaries as a teacher, and often when they spoke to him they addressed him by that title. In the form of his discourses, in the way in which he impressed what he said upon the minds and hearts of his hearers, he used a truly pedagogic method. It is not surprising, therefore, to discover that in the Gospels the followers of Jesus are commonly called "disciples," which in the simplest sense of the word means "learners." Jesus certainly did appear, when he was on earth, in the position of a teacher surrounded by scholars in his school.

But even when he was most clearly a teacher he was also a prophet. In other cases, teaching may be contrasted with prophecy, but not in the case of Jesus. Even when he spoke most quietly, even when he sought to impress upon the minds of his hearers—by patient repetition—the great, simple, fundamental truths regarding the kingdom of God, he was speaking with a truly supernatural inspiration. He was speaking even then as the direct spokesman of God. He was speaking even then the words which God the Father had given him in supernatural fashion to speak. He was speaking, therefore, as a prophet in the high supernaturalistic sense of that word.

At this point we ought to notice the vast difference between Jesus on the one hand and all other prophets on the other. Other prophets spoke as prophets sometimes; Jesus spoke as prophet always. In the case of other prophets, the gift of prophecy was bestowed only in temporary and partial fashion; in the case of Jesus it embraced his whole life upon earth.

Other prophets were to be heard at some times as being truly God's spokesmen; their words were at some times to be treated as being truly the Word of God. At other times, they appeared just as fallible men, and their words at those other times were full of the errors that infest all ordinary human speech.

In the case of Jesus, no such limitation prevailed. His words were not merely sometimes true but always true. They were not merely sometimes but always to be received as the Word of God. In his case there is no distinction between words spoken in some private capacity and words spoken with prophetic inspiration. In his case, every word that was uttered was to be received as a message from God.

It is with that understanding that we approach the teaching of Jesus as it is recorded in the Gospels.

As we do so, we observe that two opposite errors have affected the treatment of the teaching of Jesus by modern men.

In the first place, there is the error of those who have regarded the teaching of Jesus as the sole basis of the Christian religion. We have transcended the Old Testament, they say; and we cannot agree with the doctrinal constructions of the New Testament epistles. But we are Christians because we have taken into our souls the blessed teaching of Jesus of Nazareth. We refuse to let any man interpret that teaching authoritatively for us. We refuse to let even the apostle Paul do so. His epistles may be helpful here and there; even his doctrine of the cross of Christ may contain a kernel of truth for us if we can only translate it into the forms of thought proper to the age in which we are now living. But, after all, what we ought to do ever anew is to go back to the fountainhead. And the fountainhead is found in the teaching of Jesus himself. We must return to that fountainhead ever anew for the refreshment of our souls, in order that we may not be dragged down to some lower plane of thinking and of living either by the antiquated legalism of the Old Testament or by the well-meant but mistaken theological interpretations of the apostle Paul.

Such is a very common way of thinking today. It is one of the commonest forms in which the unbelief of our day manifests itself.

We pointed out one difficulty with it when we dealt two years ago with the subject of the inspiration of the Bible. It is refuted by that very teaching of Jesus to which it itself appeals. The plain fact is that Jesus believed in the full truthfulness of the Old Testament and put that belief quite at the foundation of his teaching, so that if you reject the Old Testament you cannot possibly make good your claim to be true to what Jesus said. Moreover, if Jesus looked back to the Old Testament, he also looked forward to the New. He appointed apostles and invested them with a truly supernatural authority, in virtue of which they gave the New Testament books to the church. Be perfectly clear about one thing then: if you reject the authority of the Bible, you cannot possibly hold on to the authority of the teaching of Jesus. To reject one and try to hold on to the other involves a sheer contradiction in which a man cannot possibly rest.

In view of that fact, it is not surprising to find that those who profess to believe in the teaching of Jesus alone, as distinguished from the Bible, do not really believe in the teaching of Jesus as a whole. They believe some things that Jesus says and reject others. They pick and choose within the teaching of Jesus. In other words, it is not Jesus himself who is their authority, but some criterion that they bring with them to the study of Jesus in order that they may determine what in the teaching of Jesus is true and what is false.

Thus the first thing that is wrong with this exclusive use of the teaching of Jesus, as over against the rest of the Bible, is that it is untrue to that which is rendered by the teaching of Jesus itself.

The other thing that is wrong with it is that it treats Jesus as being simply a teacher. There have been other great religious teachers, and their followers have been called by their names. "So we are called Christians," say the men who have adopted the way of thinking that we are now dealing with, "because we are the followers of Jesus. We have made him our guide in the religious life. There are many divergent ways of thinking about God, and there are many divergent types of religious life; but we have chosen to think of God as Jesus thought of him and we have chosen to live the type of religious life that Jesus lived. That is the reason why we can be called Christians. Jesus was the first Christian, and we are Christians because we are following in his footsteps and are guided by his directions."

Two years ago, in the series of talks which I was then giving, I pointed out how erroneous is this way of looking at the matter. I pointed out in particular how untrue it is to the teaching of Jesus himself. Jesus himself presented himself as far more than a teacher and example. He presented himself as a Savior. He presented himself, not as one who came just to say something to men but as one who came to do something for them. He presented himself as one who came to give his life as a ransom for many upon the cross.

But if that is so, it follows that the teaching of Jesus is not to be put as more necessary to the Christian than the teaching of the Holy Spirit through the apostles. If Jesus came to save us by something that he did—that is, by his death and resurrection—then naturally the full meaning of what he came to do would not be fully unfolded until the thing was actually done. That is the reason why the eighth chapter of Romans is just as precious to the Christian as is the teaching of Jesus in the Gospels. Jesus did proclaim beforehand the meaning of his death. It is a great error to say that he did not. Especially did he proclaim it in the institution of the Lord's Supper. But he left a great wealth of revelation about it to be brought afterward through the apostles whom he chose. A man who depreciates the teaching of the apostles ostensibly in the interests of the teaching of Jesus, is really degrading in terrible fashion the teaching of Jesus itself. He is degrading it by taking it out of its rightful place in the grand sweep of revelation contained in the Bible from Genesis to Revelation. And if he is degrading the teaching of Jesus, he is also degrading Jesus, the author of the teaching. He is degrading him by regarding him merely as a teacher. He is degrading him by denying to him his rightful place as Redeemer and Lord.

That error we must, if we are Christians, certainly avoid. We certainly cannot take the teaching of Jesus out of its connection with the rest of the Bible, as though the teaching of Jesus exclusively could be our authority. To do so is to be untrue to the heart of the teaching of Jesus itself.

But there is also another error that we must avoid. If we must avoid attending to the teaching of Jesus to the neglect of the rest of the Word of God, we must also avoid relegating the teaching of Jesus, or any part of it, to a secondary place.

It may seem strange that any Christian men should have fallen into this latter error, but certainly some Christian men in our day seem to have fallen into it, and the reasoning by which they have fallen into it is fairly clear. Since Jesus, they have said to themselves, came into the world to die on the cross and rise again for the redemption of sinners, since those events of the death and resurrection were epoch-making events, does it not follow that what lies back of those events belongs to an era out of which we have now passed? Can we therefore take the words uttered before those epoch-making events, even the words of Jesus, as being intended directly for our guidance? Must we not regard them as belonging to a bygone era, and must we not take, instead of them, for our direct guidance *only* the teaching of the epistles that were written after the redeeming work of Jesus had already been done?

With regard to that argument, it may be said, for one thing, that it runs directly counter to the example of the early Christian church. If one thing is clear to the historian, it is that the words of Jesus were treasured by the early disciples after Jesus's death and resurrection because they provided direct and authoritative guidance for the church.

Modern skeptical historians have sometimes made wrong use of that observation. They have argued that, because the early church cited words of Jesus for a practical purpose—namely, for the purpose of settling disputes and providing comfort and giving guidance—therefore it was not citing those words with historical accuracy so that we cannot trust the record of

Jesus's words which we find included by the early church in our Gospels. I cannot follow that reasoning at all. I cannot for the life of me see why, just because the early church had certain needs with regard to which it sought the guidance of Jesus, therefore it must have put words into Jesus's mouth for the satisfaction of those needs instead of simply treasuring up the words that Jesus really uttered. But certainly, those skeptical historians are right in holding that the early church did regard anything that it held to be a word of Jesus as possessing an immediate authority for the guidance of the church. That is clear in a number of ways. It is clear, for example, through what Paul says and implies about the authority of the words of Jesus. From the very beginning, the Christian church had, as the completely authoritative guide both of its doctrine and of its life, not merely the Old Testament Scriptures but also the teaching of Jesus.

If we now adopt a different attitude toward Jesus's words we are falling into a vagary of a very deadly kind indeed. In his words recorded in the Gospels, including, for example, the Sermon on the Mount, Jesus is telling us—us of the present dispensation—what we must believe concerning God and also how we must live. If we hear his words and do not do them, we also, as well as those to whom Jesus spoke on that mountain in Galilee, are like a foolish man who built his house upon the sand (Matt 7:26–27). Only if we hear Jesus's words and do them now are we like the wise man who built his house upon the rock (Matt 7:24–25). Jesus's words in the Gospels are certainly intended for the immediate instruction and guidance of his church.

Well, we have been considering Jesus as exercising during his ministry on earth the office of a prophet. Certainly, it is true that he spoke always during his earthly ministry as one who was spokesman for God. He was truly a prophet. It is very important that this should be observed.

But if it is important that this should be observed, it is still more important that something else should be observed. If it should be observed that Jesus was a prophet, it is even more important to observe that he was infinitely more than a prophet. The prophets spoke for God; Jesus was God himself. No difference could possibly be greater than that.

That difference appears all through the Gospels. It appears all through Jesus's recorded words. It appears in the peculiar authority with which he spoke. The prophets said when they came forward, "Thus says the Lord" but no prophet could say "I say to you" as Jesus said it in the Sermon on the Mount (Matt 5–7). The deity of Christ appears also in direct utterances of Jesus, not only in the Gospel according to John but also in the Synoptic Gospels. Even where it is not made the subject of express exposition, it shines through. Everywhere, Jesus is really presenting himself not only as truly man but also as truly God.

The truth is that Jesus revealed God not only by what he said but also by what he was. The prophets had a message given them about God and from God. They spoke the truth about God. But Jesus was himself God. He was God come in the flesh. No man has seen God at any time, but Jesus revealed him. Men saw Jesus. They saw him with their eyes. And the One whom they saw was God. What a revelation was there, to be sure!

We too, as we read the Gospels, have a detailed picture of the life upon earth of one who was truly God. What a wonderful thing that is! How wonderful it is that God should have been pleased to reveal so much! But that revelation is not given us merely in order that we may know what we otherwise could not have known. It is given us in order that we may be saved.

What must we do to be saved? The Bible gives us the answer: "Believe in the Lord Jesus, and you will be saved" (Acts 16:31). But how shall we believe in the Lord Jesus Christ unless we know him? How can we trust him unless we know that he is trustworthy?

Well, the Bible answers these questions for us. It answers these questions for us by the account of Jesus which it gives in the Gospels. In his recorded words and in his recorded deeds, Jesus is presented as one who is indeed trustworthy. There is where the true uniqueness of the words of Jesus—even within the Bible—is found. The words of the apostles and prophets are true. They are inspired by the Holy Ghost. They are just as much part of God's Word as are the words of Jesus. They present things that are just as important for us to know. But the words of Jesus are unique because the speaker of the words was unique. By every recorded word of his and by every recorded deed, we have presented to us the One who is the object of our faith. We are not asked in the Bible to believe in one about whom we know nothing. Rather, we are asked to believe in one who is presented to us in the Gospels in rich and glorious fullness as one who is worthy to be believed.

Ah, surely such a one can be trusted! If only he were here with us today, how gladly would we lay before him all our troubles! How gladly would we trust him when he offers to bring us to God!

Well, my friends, we have him with us today. His prophetic work is not limited to what he said when he was on earth. After his redeeming work was done, through the cross and the resurrection, he continued to proclaim his gospel through the apostles whom he appointed and whose inspired writings we have in the New Testament. He continues to proclaim his gospel today by the Holy Spirit whom he has sent.

Christ is the substance of the gospel. The gospel sets Christ forth. It presents Christ as Savior. It tells of his death upon the cross to redeem us from our sins. It tells of his glorious resurrection. It tells of the promise of his coming again.

But Christ is not only the substance of the gospel; he is also the proclaimer of the gospel. He does not leave it to others to offer him as Savior. No, he offers himself. Whatever human instruments he uses, it is he who proclaims the good news of the salvation that he wrought for us at such infinite cost. Will you hear him, my friends? Will you hear him this afternoon when he offers himself to you as the Savior of your soul?

46

Prophet and Priest

We are now dealing with the three offices which Christ exercises as our Redeemer. They are the offices of a prophet, of a priest, and of a king.

So far, we have dealt only with the first of these—with Christ's office of a prophet. In that office of a prophet Christ reveals to us the will of God for our salvation. In other words, he proclaims the gospel to us.

We observed how he began that proclamation of the gospel even in Old Testament times. He sent the Holy Spirit upon the Old Testament prophets and they testified beforehand of him. But ordinarily when we think of Christ's office of a prophet we think of that part of the execution of the office which Christ accomplished and is accomplishing after he became man.

Last Sunday afternoon, we spent most of our time dealing with the teaching of Christ during his earthly ministry. We observed that all of that teaching is to be regarded as part of Christ's execution of the office of a prophet because in everything he uttered he had the full presence of the Holy Spirit and spoke with the full authority of the triune God. Other prophets spoke with divine authority sometimes; Jesus spoke with divine authority always. That is one great difference between Jesus and all other prophets.

We observed also that another difference is far greater still. That other difference is that, whereas other prophets spoke for God, Jesus not only spoke for God but was himself God. He revealed God not only by what God gave him to say but also by what he was. "No one has ever seen God," says the Gospel of John (1:18). But that same Gospel of John says in the very same verse that Jesus, who was God's only begotten, has revealed that unseen God. When men looked upon Jesus, they actually saw with their eyes one who was truly God. That is the marvel of the incarnation. To behold with one's bodily eyes one who was truly God—what greater wonder can there possibly be than this?

We shall one day have that wonderful privilege, as it was had long ago by the writer of the Fourth Gospel and the other eyewitnesses of the earthly ministry of Jesus. We shall have that wonderful privilege when Jesus comes again. Then we shall actually see with our very eyes one who is truly God.

Meanwhile, we can read in the Gospels about the words and deeds of the same one. By that reading we become truly acquainted with him. Much in his earthly life has not been recorded in the Gospels. We are told little about the long years which he spent at Nazareth until he was about thirty years old. Only one glimpse—a wonderful glimpse, it is true—is given us from those years. We cannot give anything like a complete biography of Jesus. We cannot trace with anything like completeness the chronological sequence of his words and deeds. But there is one wonderful thing about that which we do actually read in the Gospels. The wonderful thing about it is that it does tell us with matchless distinctness what manner of person Jesus was. If we read the Gospels in sympathetic fashion, we do come into personal contact with Jesus.

Many biographies embracing many volumes and full of the most minute and detailed information seem somehow never to present to us the real person whose life they are starting out to describe. As we read them, we learn this thing and that thing that the man said and did, but somehow the man himself seems to be hidden from us; we do not really get acquainted with him when we read the learned book that recounts his life.

It is not so with the Gospels. How marvelously lifelike is the picture that they give of Jesus of Nazareth! What wonderful insight is given into the depths of his soul! There are, indeed, mysteries there. We always feel, as we read, that we are dealing with a person so mysterious that no man can ever fathom the depths of his being. Indeed, the Gospels themselves, in the words of Jesus that they report, tell us that "no one knows the Son except the Father," says Jesus in the eleventh chapter of Matthew (Matt 11:27). But although there are depths in the person of Jesus which no mere man can know, nevertheless the devout reader of the Gospels does acquire a knowledge of Jesus which is wonderfully rich and true. It is not merely an external knowledge; it is not merely a knowledge of this detail or that regarding the things that Jesus saw and did, but it is a knowledge of the person himself.

We do rise from a reading of the Gospels, if we have read aright, with a true knowledge of the man Christ Jesus. Nay, we rise from a reading of the Gospels also with the knowledge that the man Christ Jesus is also very

God. Always the deity of Christ shines through in the gospel picture. It appears in the lofty claims of Jesus himself—his claim to do things that only God can do, his claim to forgive sins, his claim to be the final Judge of all the earth, his claim to have in his own being depths which only God the Father knows, his claim to be one with the Father. The deity of Jesus appears in the sovereign power of Jesus, substantiating his lofty claims. Yes, it is certainly true that the Gospels present one who was God and man in two distinct natures.

Yet they also just as clearly present one who was one person, and they enable us to know that person. Our knowledge of the person is given to us by the details which the Gospels tell us about him; it is entirely dependent upon those details; but it is something more than the sum of those details. If we read the Gospels aright we know more than this thing and that about Jesus. We know Jesus!

Knowing Jesus, we trust him. We could not trust any other. But when we are confronted with the majestic and yet wonderfully tender and loving person who is presented to us in Matthew, Mark, Luke, and John, then we say, "Lord, I believe," and if we also say, "Help my unbelief," we can trust him even to answer that prayer. The Bible does more than tell us, "Believe in the Lord Jesus, and you will be saved" (Acts 16:31). It also tells us who that person is in whom we are asked to believe. The Bible is not unreasonable enough to ask us to put our trust in one about whom we know nothing, but it gives us, in the Gospels, a wonderfully vivid account of the One whom it presents to us as the object of our faith. If we really read that account aright, we say that the One who is there presented to us is worthy of an utterly boundless confidence. We trust him because we know him to be trustworthy.

That knowledge of Jesus which is imparted to us in the Gospels is part of Jesus's prophetic work. He proclaims to us the will of God for our salvation not only by telling us this thing or that about the way of salvation, not only by telling us this thing or that that we should do, but also by presenting himself to us in very person as the object of our faith. He offers himself to us as our Savior, and in thus offering himself to us as our Savior he is truly executing his office as a prophet. He is revealing God to us, as a true prophet reveals God—yet in a way that goes far beyond the way in which any other prophet can reveal God. His own words make that clear. "Whoever has seen me has seen the Father," said Jesus (John 14:9). Jesus, my friends, is himself God, and his presentation to us of his own person is the very center of his prophetic office.

That presentation of Jesus to us as our Savior was, as we have seen, carried on by the words and deeds of Jesus during his earthly ministry. But it is very important to observe that it did not cease when his earthly ministry was over, and it is also very important to observe that the part of it which was carried on after his earthly ministry was over was just as truly carried on by Jesus himself as was the part of it which was carried on during his earthly ministry.

In the first place, Jesus provided even during his earthly ministry for the subsequent carrying on of his prophetic work. He did that by choosing and commissioning his apostles. He invested his apostles with a supernatural authority, and, in the exercise of that authority, they gave the New Testament books to the church. The authority of the New Testament books is not an authority independent of Jesus, but it is an authority which Jesus himself imparted.

In the second place, Jesus not only gave the apostles the commission in virtue of which they gave the New Testament books to the church, but he also empowered the writers of the New Testament books in their execution of the commission. He sent the Holy Spirit, and the Holy Spirit inspired the writers of the New Testament books so that they were preserved from error and so that the resulting books are the very Word of God. Even of the very first coming of the Holy Spirit, on the day of Pentecost, the apostle Peter said, speaking of Jesus: "Being therefore exalted at the right hand of God, and having received from the Father the promise of the Holy Spirit, he has poured out this that you yourselves are seeing and hearing" (Acts 2:33). The same thing is true of all subsequent operations of the Holy Spirit. The New Testament delights to call the Holy Spirit not only the Spirit of God but also, particularly, the Spirit of Christ, the Spirit of Jesus, or the Spirit of the Son of God. The Holy Spirit proceeds not only from the Father but also from the Son. That is true not only of the mysterious eternal relation between the persons of the Godhead, but also of the operations of the Holy Spirit in the church. So, when the Holy Spirit inspired the writers of the New Testament books so that what they wrote should be truly the Word of God, that was part of the execution of the prophetic office of Jesus Christ.

That brings us to speak of the third way in which Christ continues to execute his prophetic office after the conclusion of his earthly ministry. He executes it in the blessed ministrations of the Holy Spirit to the individual believer. We must not conceive of the relations of the persons of the Trinity to one another too much after the analogy of the relationships of finite persons. We must not apply any mechanical either/or to the question whether it is the second or the third person of the Trinity who does this or that. The New Testament does, indeed, teach the true personality of the three persons. It does make a profound distinction between them. But, at the same time, it teaches that where the Holy Spirit is present Christ is present. So close is the relationship between the Holy Spirit and the ascended Lord from whom he comes that where the Holy Spirit is present Christ himself is said to be present.

Accordingly, when the Holy Spirit enlightens the mind of some still unsaved person so that he shall receive the gospel for the saving of his soul, that is not only the work of the Spirit; it is also part of Christ's execution of his prophetic office. So also, when the Holy Spirit is graciously present with believers in their reading of the Bible, enabling them to understand in ever greater fullness the meaning of what they read and enabling them to receive it ever more profoundly in their hearts as well as in their minds, in order that they may practice it in their lives, that also is part of Christ's execution of his prophetic office.

Very comprehensive, then, is that office of a prophet which Christ executes as our Redeemer. The Shorter Catechism is quite right in saying that Christ as our Redeemer executes the office of a prophet not only by his Word but also by his Spirit. And the Larger Catechism is quite right in emphasizing, more clearly even than does the Shorter Catechism, the wonderful comprehensiveness of that prophetic work. "Christ executeth the office of a prophet," it rightly says, "in his revealing to the church, in all ages, by his Spirit and word, in divers ways of administration, the whole will of God, in all things concerning their edification and salvation" (WLC Q&A 43).

But it is time now for us to turn to the second of the three offices which Christ is said in the Catechisms to execute as our Redeemer. That is Christ's office of a priest.

As we began our discussion of Christ's office of a prophet by asking what is a prophet, so it would seem to be in the interests of logical symmetry for us to begin our discussion of Christ's office of a priest by asking what is a priest.

Fortunately, we have abundant materials in the Bible for obtaining an answer to that question. We not only have descriptions of priests and their activities from which we could ourselves derive a very clear notion of what the Bible regards as essential in the priestly function, but also in the Epistle to the Hebrews we have something almost akin to an actual definition: "For every high priest chosen from among men is appointed to act on behalf of men in relation to God, to offer gifts and sacrifices for sins. He can deal gently with the ignorant and wayward, since he himself is beset with weakness. Because of this he is obligated to offer sacrifice for his own sins just as he does for those of the people. And no one takes this honor for himself, but only when called by God, just as Aaron was" (Heb 5:1–4). Here the fundamental nature of priesthood appears very clearly. A priest is a mediator between men and God. Men, not having direct access to God, or at least not having such direct access until it is secured for them by the priest, are dependent upon the priest's mediation in their approach to God. He represents them in God's presence. They wait without. He enters in unto God and pleads their cause.

That being so, it is natural to discover that the priest's function is twofold. First, he offers sacrifice; and, second, he engages in intercession. He offers sacrifice in order to expiate sin and make God propitious, and then he uses the access to God thus secured in order to be an advocate in God's presence of the people of whom he is the representative. Sacrifice and intercession—those are the two chief functions of a priest, according to the Bible.

It may perhaps be said, with some degree of truth, that as a prophet is a representative of God in the presence of men, so a priest is a representative of men in the presence of God. But that formulation of the difference between the two offices is misleading if it is understood to mean that as a prophet is chosen by God to be his representative before men, so a priest is chosen by men to be their representative before God. The Epistle to the Hebrews, in the passage which we have just quoted, is careful to point out that a priest is not chosen by men at all. Like a prophet, he is chosen by God. He is a representative of men in the presence of God, but he does not take this honor unto himself, nor is he given it by those whose representative he is; but he is called to this honor by God, as was Aaron.

Well, then, if that is what a priest is, if a priest is one who approaches God on behalf of men by offering sacrifice and by making intercession for them, and if Christ is a priest, it follows that Christ, in the execution of the office of a priest, will be found to perform those functions. An examination of the whole Bible will show that such is actually the case, and one book of the Bible, the Epistle to the Hebrews, is concerned, almost from the beginning to the end, with showing that it is the case. Christ offered sacrifice for his people on the cross, and he makes intercession for them. He exercises, therefore, all parts of the office of a priest.

It is true, of course, that there are important differences between Christ's execution of the office of a priest and the execution of it by other priests. Other priests offer sacrifice repeatedly; Christ offered it once and for all. Other priests needed to offer sacrifice for their own sins as well as for the sins of their people; Christ, being sinless, offered sacrifice for the people's sins only. Other priests should have compassion on sinners because they are sinners too. Christ, being sinless, has compassion on sinners only because he was tempted in all points like as they are (Heb 4:15), and not at all because he himself has sinned.

Do these differences, and others, mean that the Bible is using merely a figure of speech when it calls Christ a priest? Do they mean that it is merely using an analogy taken from human life to describe, as best it may, a work of Christ which really transcends all such analogies? I do not think that is the way to look at the matter at all. Exactly the opposite is the case. Far from saying that other priests are the real priests and Christ is a priest only in a figure, what we really ought to say is that Christ is the only real priest, and other priests are at best priests only in a secondary and partial sense. Very grandly does the Epistle to the Hebrews bring that out. Even the Old Testament priests, who, unlike the priests in heathen religions, have not usurped the priesthood but are truly appointed to be priests by God, are yet priests only in a secondary and derived sense. Their priesthood brought access to God only by pointing forward to the one true Priest, who on Calvary offered the only sacrifice that can take away the guilt of sin and cause sinful men to be received by the righteous God, the one true Priest who alone has constant and untroubled access to God that he may continually make intercession for men. The priesthood of the Old Testament priests was but a shadow of what was to come, and now that the reality has been established the shadow has passed away.

We cannot possibly lay too great stress upon that fact. There is really only one priest who can bring us sinners unto God; there is only one who can present us before the throne. That one is Jesus Christ, and the means by which he presents us before the throne is his death. Then did he offer himself truly as the Lamb of God that taketh away the sin of the world.

It should be evident even this afternoon, before we go on to unfold any further what the Bible tells us about the priestly work of Christ, that in dealing with the priestly work of Christ we are dealing with the heart of the gospel. We are dealing with the heart of the gospel because we are dealing with the cross of Christ.

Will you believe that gospel this afternoon, my friends, if you have not already believed it? As Jesus knocks at the door of your heart, will you open the door and receive him as your Savior and your Lord?

47

Christ Our Redeemer

Last Sunday afternoon we began to speak of the second of the three offices which Christ executes as our Redeemer. The three offices are the offices of a prophet, of a priest, and of a king. Last Sunday afternoon we began to speak about Christ's office of a priest.

It became evident at the start that in dealing with Christ's office of a priest we are dealing with the heart of the gospel because we are dealing with the cross of Christ. By his death, the Bible teaches, Christ made the one and all-sufficient sacrifice for sin. That is the great doctrine of the atonement. Nothing, from the point of view of the Bible, can possibly be more important for mankind than that.

Well, then, in thus exalting the priestly work of Christ, are we depreciating his prophetic work, with which we have been dealing in a number of the preceding talks in this series? That is very far from being the case, and before I go further I want to show you why it is far from being the case; I want to say a few words just now upon the relation between Christ's work as a priest, with which we are now going to deal, and Christ's work as a prophet, with which we have hitherto dealt.

I think I can present the relationship in the fewest possible words by just saying that in Christ's priestly work, he died for us, and then in his prophetic work, he tells us the story of how he died for us. In his priestly work, he did the thing that forms the substance of the gospel, and then in his prophetic work he proclaims the gospel himself to us. In his priestly work, he did the thing that made it possible that there should be a gospel to preach, and then in his prophetic work he actually preaches the gospel to us in order that, through the receiving of the gospel, our souls may be saved.

How foolish, then, it is to say either that Christ's work as a priest or that his work as a prophet could possibly stand alone! No, they stand together. Without his work as a priest there would have been no gospel to preach, and without his work as a prophet there would have been no preaching of the gospel. Thank God, Christ has done both! He died on the cross that there might be a gospel to preach, and then very sweetly has he brought the gospel himself to those for whom he died.

Ignoring these simple facts, so plain in the Bible, modern unbelievers are in the habit of telling us that we ought not to be very much interested in the gospel *about* Jesus but ought instead to devote our attention to the gospel *of* Jesus. We need not be interested, they say, in the exact meaning of what Christ did when he died on the cross; we need not be much interested in the question of what is meant when we say we believe in the "deity" of Christ; we need not be much interested in the question of whether his body really came out of the tomb on the first Easter morning; we need not be much interested in the question of whether he will really in any literal sense come again.

People used to be interested in these questions, we are told. They used to set up theories of the atonement; they used to maintain, in particular, that on the cross Jesus died as a sacrifice to satisfy divine justice and reconcile us to God. They used to set up theories regarding the person of Christ; they used to maintain that Christ is "God and man in two distinct natures, and one person, forever" (WSC Q&A 21). They used to insist also on one particular view of the resurrection; they used to maintain that on the third day the tomb became empty because the body of the Lord Jesus was raised. They used to insist also on the personal return of Christ; they used to maintain, as though it were very important indeed for our souls, that at the end of the present age we shall see our Savior face-to-face.

These things, say the unbelievers about whom I am now speaking, constitute a gospel *about* Jesus. But, they say, we are no longer interested in that gospel *about* Jesus. Instead, we are interested in the gospel *of* Jesus; we are interested in the gospel that he himself actually preached. We are interested in the way of living in which he walked and in which he called on his followers to walk. We are interested, in other words, not in a gospel that sets Jesus forth, but in the gospel that he set forth, the gospel that he preached when he walked by the shores of the Sea of Galilee.

If, then, you ask the people who talk in this fashion what that gospel *of* Jesus, which they cherish in place of the gospel *about* Jesus, actually is, they will usually tell you, with more or less clearness, that it is a simple proclamation of the Fatherhood of God and the brotherhood of man, or a simple proclamation of a kingdom of God that is essentially just the realization of a high social ideal. Let us stop disputing about the meaning of the cross of Christ, they say; let us stop disputing about any other doctrinal questions; and, instead, let us just get up and obey Jesus's commands. That will honor Jesus more, they say, than all the theories of the atonement that have ever been proposed.

People who talk in this fashion seem to think that they are somehow glorifying Jesus more and are somehow getting closer to him than was done by the people who used to proclaim the old gospel. Are we not getting closer to Christ, they say to themselves, if we preach his own gospel rather than merely a gospel about him?

But a little reflection will show that is far from being the case. I may preach the gospel *of* Spurgeon or the gospel *of* D. L. Moody or the gospel *of* Calvin—that is, I may preach the same gospel as that which they preached. But what blasphemy it would be to say that I preach a gospel about Spurgeon or a gospel about D. L. Moody, or a gospel about Calvin, or even a gospel about Paul! If I should do that, I should be putting these preachers into a position which belongs only to Christ. I may preach the gospel that they preach but I certainly do not preach a gospel that has them as its content. I may preach the gospel of Calvin or the gospel of Paul, but I do not preach Calvin and I do not preach Paul. I preach Christ alone as they preach Christ alone.

It is from this unique place that these modern unbelievers are dethroning Christ when they say that they are not interested in the gospel *about* Christ and are only interested in the gospel *of* Christ. They are willing to admit that Jesus was an excellent teacher and example, and that we cannot do better than repeat his teaching and follow his example. But they have not the slightest inkling of the fact that he is the substance of the gospel. They have not the slightest inkling of the fact that the gospel consists in the good news of the way in which he saved us by his precious blood.

Well, then, in thus insisting, against these unbelievers, that the gospel is a gospel about Jesus, in thus insisting that it is a gospel that has him as its substance, that proclaims him, do we mean to say that it is not also a gospel that he himself preached? We mean nothing of the kind. On the contrary we insist that it is the gospel that he himself preached. Two winters ago, when we were treating the picture of Jesus in the Gospels, we showed how baseless is the contention of modern unbelief that Jesus kept his own person out of his gospel and merely asked people to lead the same kind of religious life as that which he himself lived. We saw how pervasive was his presentation of his own person as the divine Savior and the final Judge of all the earth. We saw how that presentation runs even through the Sermon on the Mount, to which modern unbelievers are wont particularly to appeal. We saw how utterly contrary to all our sources of historical information is this modern notion that Jesus was simply the founder of Christianity because he was the first Christian. We saw how all our sources of historical information represent Jesus as offering himself to men as the object of their faith.

Do you not see, my friends, what the real state of the case is? It is not correct to say that we Christians proclaim the gospel of Jesus in distinction from a gospel about Jesus. It is equally incorrect to say that we preach a gospel about Jesus in distinction from the gospel of Jesus. The fact is that the gospel about Jesus and the gospel of Jesus are the same. The gospel that Jesus proclaimed was a gospel about him. It was a gospel that offered him as Savior. It was a gospel that told the good news of his saving work.

He proclaimed that gospel even during his earthly ministry. He offered himself even then as Savior. He pointed forward to his atoning death on the cross and to his glorious resurrection. Then, when he had died and risen again, when his redeeming work was done, he told the story of it through the apostles whom he had chosen and through the Holy Spirit whom he sent.

Let us get this thing perfectly straight. Let us not be afraid of repeating it. *Jesus is both the author and the substance of the gospel.* Jesus died for our sins on the cross. The story of his death and of the things that go with it is the gospel. It is the good news. But after Jesus had died and risen again, did he leave it to others to bring that good news to us? Not at all. He brought us the good news himself.

That is what we mean by saying that when we now study the work of Jesus as a priest, we are not belittling or turning away from his work as a prophet. On the contrary we are just listening to what Jesus as a prophet so graciously tells us about himself. As a prophet, Jesus tells us the story of his priestly work. As a prophet, he tells us about the way in which, as the one true priest, he offered himself once-for-all as a sacrifice to satisfy divine justice and reconcile us to God, and he tells us about the way in which he is now continually making intercession for us.

Let us hear, then, what Jesus himself tells us about his priestly work. Let us hear it as it is contained in the whole Bible from Genesis to Revelation.

A priest, we observed in the last talk, is a representative of men in the presence of God. He is a mediator between God and men. He obtains access for men unto God.

Do we need a priest, in that sense of the word? That is the first question. If we do not need a priest at all, then of course all this talk about the priestly work of Christ is without practical importance. If we, in our own right, already have access to God, then we have no need that Christ should enter for us within the veil.

A great many people today take exactly that view of the matter. We are, they say, already children of God, by virtue of the fact that we are men; we already have free access to God. All that we need is to overcome our fear of God; all that we need is to have presented to us the great truth that God is our Father. Jesus, they say, has presented that great truth to us, and for that we revere him. He was the first man to make full use of the privilege which man has as man—the privilege of standing before God without fear, as a child stands before a loving father. Following Jesus, we can make use of the same privilege. But that does not mean in the slightest that Jesus is a priest whose intermediation is necessary in order that we may approach God. On the contrary, the thing that Jesus discovered was just the comforting fact that no intermediation was necessary—neither his nor anyone else's. He led the way, and we follow. But we follow in our own right, and we could have led the way ourselves if only we had had the courage. Jesus merely encouraged us to make use of a privilege which was already ours.

That is the way of looking at the matter that dominates most of the nominally Christian churches of the present day. But it is radically contrary to the Bible, and it must be radically rejected by all those who believe the Bible to be truly the Word of God.

According to the Bible, all mankind, since the fall, is under the just condemnation of God's law, subject to God's wrath and curse, utterly unable to do any good. All mankind, in other words, is lost in sin. Being lost in sin, men have no right of access unto God. On the contrary they are separated from God by a flaming sword. They are under the awful penalty of God's law, and if that penalty is treated as though it did not exist, God ceases to be God and evil has triumphed over good.

That, my friends, is the situation of fallen man. It is not presented to us just in one part of the Bible. It is presented to us in the whole Bible. From the first book of the Bible to the last, the Bible beats down men's pagan optimism; it opposes the central article of the pagan creed, which is the article: "I believe in man." It takes from us the last vestige of confidence that in ourselves we have any right of access unto God; it teaches us to fear the righteous God, and to stand in terror before the majesty of his offended law.

It teaches us, therefore, that if we are to have any access unto God, it can only be through a priest. The priest must be one of us, since he is to be our representative; but he must also be more than merely one of us. If he were merely one of us, he would have no more right of access unto God than we have. Like us he would be a sinner, subject to God's wrath and curse. But even if he were sinless, still if he were merely man he could not possibly bring us to God. Any sacrifice that he might offer for us, any punishment that he might endure for a time in our stead, would, if he were merely man, have at best only a finite value. It could not possibly be accepted instead of the eternal punishment, which was the just penalty of the law upon our sin.

If we are to have truly a priest who can bring us to God, it can only be a one who is both man and God—man that he might suffer in our stead, God that his suffering in our stead might have worth enough to satisfy the law's demands.

Such a priest, such a high priest, thank God, we have. It is Christ Jesus the Lord. He was, from all eternity, God. Through him the worlds were made. For one purpose did he humble himself; for one purpose did he become man—that he might be our priest to reconcile us to God, that he might offer on the cross for us sinners a perfect sacrifice to fulfill the law's demands and wipe out the dread handwriting that was against us. Through him and him alone we come to God; through his constant intercession alone do we stand in God's presence. In our own right, we deserve only to be cast out from God's presence and suffer to all eternity the just punishment of sin. In him alone we enter without fear unto the throne of God—not God's children in our own right but made God's children through the precious blood of Christ.

What a joy it is to search the Scriptures ever anew to see what God has told us in his Word concerning that priestly work of Christ! It is folly indeed to the men of the world; no pursuit seems to them to be more futile. What time have we, they say, to engage in these theological subtleties? But to the sinner saved by grace how sweet a thing it is to contemplate the cross of Christ! How sweet a thing it is to follow the doctrine of the shed blood that runs like a red cord through the Bible from Genesis to Revelation! How sweet a thing it is to trace the gradual unfolding of the promise from the time when sin first entered into the world! How sweet a thing it is to behold the fulfilling of the promise in those strangely simple narratives in Matthew, Mark, Luke, and John! How sweet a thing it is to explore the divine explanation of the fulfillment in the epistles of Paul! How sweet a thing it is to follow the directions there given as the Spirit applies to us the benefits of what our Savior did! How sweet a thing it is to contemplate the unity of the sacred book as it finds its center in the cross!

May that joy, my friends, be ours as we study the cross of Christ together on these Sunday afternoons! And as we have that joy, may we also have the joy of bringing others with us to the foot of the cross. May God grant that some who listen to these expositions of the Word, and who have not yet found Jesus as their Savior, may find him as he is presented to them in the Word of God!

Are you weary and heavy laden? Are you tired of a life of sin? Are you dissatisfied with the world's righteousness, which is no righteousness in God's sight? Have you some dread vision of the majesty of God's offended law? Oh, then will you not come to him who can give you rest? Will you not drink of the water of salvation? Will you not trust him who died for you?

Ah, salvation is so near! To have it you do not need to ascend into the heights or descend into the abyss:

> But the righteousness based on faith says, "Do not say in your heart, 'Who will ascend into heaven?'" (that is, to bring Christ down) "or 'Who will descend into the abyss?'" (that is, to bring Christ up from the dead). But what does it say? "The word is near you, in your mouth and in your heart" (that is, the word of faith that we proclaim); because, if you confess with your mouth that Jesus is Lord and believe in your heart that God raised him from the dead, you will be saved. (Rom 10:6–9)

May the Lord Jesus Christ, the risen Savior, attend through his Spirit the message of his cross, that precious souls may be saved!

48

The Doctrine of the Atonement

The priestly work of Christ, or at least that part of it in which he offered himself up as a sacrifice to satisfy divine justice and reconcile us to God, is commonly called the atonement, and the doctrine which sets it forth is commonly called the doctrine of the atonement. That doctrine is at the very heart of what is taught in the Word of God.

Before we present that doctrine, as we shall endeavor to do this afternoon and in a number of the talks that follow, we ought to observe that the term by which it is ordinarily designated is not altogether free from objection.

When I say that the term "atonement" is open to objection, I am not referring to the fact that it occurs only once in the King James Version of the New Testament, and is therefore, so far as New Testament usage is concerned, not a common biblical term. A good many other terms which are rare in the Bible are nevertheless admirable terms when one comes to summarize biblical teaching. As a matter of fact, this term is rather common in the Old Testament (though it occurs only that once in the New Testament), but that fact would not be necessary to commend it if it were satisfactory in other ways. Even if it were not common in either Testament, it still might be exactly the term for us to use to designate by one word what the Bible teaches in a number of words.

The real objection to it is of an entirely different kind. It is a twofold objection. The word "atonement," in the first place, is ambiguous, and in the second place, it is not broad enough.

The one place where the word occurs in the King James Version of the New Testament is Romans 5:11, where Paul says: "And not only so, but we also joy in God through our Lord Jesus Christ, by whom we have now received the atonement." Here the word is used to translate a Greek word meaning "reconciliation." This usage seems to be very close to the etymological meaning of the word, for it does seem to be true that the English word "atonement" means "at-onement." It is, therefore, according to its derivation, a natural word to designate the state of reconciliation between two parties formerly at variance.

In the Old Testament, on the other hand, where the word occurs in the King James Version not once, but forty or fifty times, it has a different meaning; it has the meaning of "propitiation." Thus we read in Leviticus 1:4, regarding a man who brings a bullock to be killed as a burnt offering: "And he shall put his hand upon the head of the burnt offering; and it shall be accepted for him to make atonement for him." So also, the word occurs some eight times in the King James Version in the sixteenth chapter of Leviticus, where the provisions of the law are set forth regarding the great day of atonement. Take, for example, the following verses in that chapter:

> And Aaron shall offer his bullock of the sin offering, which is for himself, and make an atonement for himself, and for his house. Then shall he kill the goat of the sin offering, that is for the people, and bring his blood within the vail, and do with that blood as he did with the blood of the bullock, and sprinkle it upon the mercy seat, and before the mercy seat: And he shall make an atonement for the holy place, because of the uncleanness of the children of Israel, and because of their transgressions in all their sins: and so shall he do for the tabernacle of the congregation, that remaineth among them in the midst of their uncleanness. (Lev 16:6, 15–16; KJV)

In these passages, the meaning of the word is clear. God has been offended because of the sins of the people or of individuals among his people. The priest kills the animal which is brought as a sacrifice. God is thereby propitiated, and those who have offended God are forgiven.

I am not now asking whether those Old Testament sacrifices brought forgiveness in themselves or merely as prophecies of a greater sacrifice to come; I am not now considering the significant limitations which the Old Testament law attributes to their efficacy. We shall try to deal with those matters in some subsequent talk. All that I am here interested in is the use of the word "atonement" in the English Bible. All that I am saying is that this word in the Old Testament clearly conveys the notion of something that is done to satisfy God in order that the sins of men may be forgiven and their communion with God restored.

Somewhat akin to this Old Testament use of the word "atonement" is the use of it in our everyday parlance where religion is not at all in view. Thus we often say that someone in his youth was guilty of a grievous fault but has fully "atoned" for it or made full "atonement" for it by a long and useful life. We mean by this that the person in question has—if we may use a colloquial phrase—"made up for" his youthful indiscretion by his subsequent life of usefulness and rectitude. Mind you, I am not at all saying that a man can really "make up for" or "atone for" a youthful sin by a subsequent life of usefulness and rectitude; but I am just saying that that indicates the way in which the English word is used. In our ordinary usage, the word certainly conveys the idea of something like compensation for some wrong that has been done.

It certainly conveys that notion also in those Old Testament passages. Of course, that is not the only notion that it conveys in those passages. There the use of the word is very much more specific. The compensation which is indicated by the word is a compensation rendered to God, and it is a compensation that has become necessary because of an offense committed against God. Still, the notion of compensation or satisfaction is clearly in the word. God is offended because of sin; satisfaction is made to him in some way by the sacrifice; and so his favor is restored.

Thus in the English Bible the word "atonement" is used in two rather distinct senses. In its one occurrence in the New Testament it designates the particular means by which such reconciliation is effected—namely, the sacrifice which God is pleased to accept in order that man may again be received into favor.

Now of these two uses of the word, it is unquestionably the Old Testament use which is followed when we speak of the "doctrine of the atonement." We mean by the word, when we thus use it in theology, not the reconciliation between God and man, not the "at-onement" between God and man, but specifically the means by which that reconciliation is effected—namely, the death of Christ as something that was necessary in order that sinful man might be received into communion with God.

I do not see any great objection to the use of the word in that way—provided only that we are perfectly clear that we are using it in that way. Certainly it has acquired too firm a place in Christian theology and has gathered around it too many precious associations for us to think, now, of trying to dislodge it.

However, there is another word which would in itself have been much better, and it is really a great pity that it has not come into more general use in this context. That is the word "satisfaction." If we only had acquired the habit of saying that Christ made full satisfaction to God for man that would have conveyed a more adequate account of Christ's priestly work as our Redeemer than the word "atonement" can convey. It designates what the word "atonement"—rightly understood—designates, and it also designates something more. We shall see what that something more is in a subsequent talk.

But it is time now for us to enter definitely into our great subject. Men were estranged from God by sin; Christ, as their Great High Priest, has brought them back into communion with God. How has he done so? That is the question with which we shall be dealing in a number of the talks that now follow.

This afternoon all that I can do is to try to state the Scripture doctrine in bare summary (or begin to state it), leaving it to subsequent talks to show how that Scripture doctrine is actually taught in the Scriptures, to defend it against objections, and to distinguish it clearly from various unscriptural theories.

What then in bare outline does the Bible teach about the "atonement"? What does it teach—to use a better term—about the satisfaction which Christ presented to God in order that sinful man might be received into God's favor?

I cannot possibly answer this question even in bare summary unless I call your attention to the biblical doctrine of sin with which we dealt last winter. You cannot possibly understand what the Bible says about salvation unless you understand what the Bible says about the thing from which we are saved.

If then we ask what is the biblical doctrine of sin, we observe, in the first place, that according to the Bible all men are sinners.

Well, then, that being so, it becomes important to ask what this sin is which has affected all mankind. Is it just an excusable imperfection? Is it something that can be transcended as a man can transcend the immaturity of his youthful years? Or, supposing it to be more than imperfection, supposing it to be something like a definite stain, is it a stain that can easily be removed as writing is erased from a slate?

The Bible leaves us in no doubt as to the answer to these questions. Sin, it tells us, is disobedience to the law of God, and the law of God is entirely irrevocable.

Why is the law of God irrevocable? The Bible makes that plain. Because it is rooted in the nature of God. God is righteous and that is the reason why his law is righteous. Can he then revoke his law or allow it to be disregarded? Well, there is of course no external compulsion upon him to prevent him from doing these things. There is none who can say to him, "What doest thou?" In that sense he can do all things. But the point is, he cannot revoke his law and still remain God. He cannot, without himself becoming unrighteous, make his law either forbid righteousness or condone unrighteousness. When the law of God says, "the soul who sins shall die" (Ezek 18:4), that awful penalty of death is, indeed, imposed by God's will; but God's will is determined by God's nature, and God's nature being unchangeably holy, the penalty must run its course. God would be untrue to himself, in other words, if sin were not punished; and that God should be untrue to himself is the most impossible thing that can possibly be conceived.

Under that majestic law of God man was placed in the estate wherein he was created. Man was placed in a probation, which theologians call the covenant of works. If he obeyed the law during a certain limited period, his probation was to be over; he would be given eternal life without any further possibility of loss. If, on the other hand, he disobeyed the law, he would have death—physical death and eternal death in hell.

Man entered into that probation with every advantage. He was created in knowledge, righteousness, and holiness. He was created not merely neutral with respect to goodness; he was created positively good. Yet he fell. He failed to make his goodness an assured and eternal goodness; he failed to progress from the goodness of innocence to the confirmed goodness which would have been the reward for standing the test. He transgressed the commandment of God, and so came under the awful curse of the law.

Under that curse came all mankind. That covenant of works had been made with the first man, Adam, not only for himself but for his posterity. He had stood, in that probation, in a representative capacity; he had stood—to use a better terminology—as the federal head of the race, having been made the federal head of the race by divine appointment. If he had successfully met the test, all mankind descended from him would have been born in a state of confirmed righteousness and blessedness, without any possibility of falling into sin or of losing eternal life. But as a matter of fact, Adam did not successfully meet the test. He transgressed the commandment of God, and since he was the federal head, the divinely appointed representative of the race, all mankind sinned in him and fell with him in his first transgression.

Thus all mankind, descended from Adam by ordinary generation, are themselves under the dreadful penalty of the law of God. They are under that penalty at birth, before they have done anything either good or bad. Part of that penalty is the want of the righteousness with which man was created, and a dreadful corruption which is called original sin. Proceeding from that corruption when men grow to years of discretion come individual acts of transgression.

Can the penalty of sin resting upon all mankind be remitted? Plainly not if God is to remain God. That penalty of sin was ordained in the law of God, and the law of God was no mere arbitrary and changeable arrangement but an expression of the nature of God himself. If the penalty of sin were remitted, God would become unrighteous, and that God will not become unrighteous is the most certain thing that can possibly be conceived.

How then can sinful men be saved? In one way only. Only if a substitute is provided who shall pay for them the just penalty of God's law.

The Bible teaches that such a substitute has as a matter of fact been provided. The substitute is Jesus Christ. The law's demands of penalty must be satisfied. There is no escaping that. But Jesus Christ satisfied those demands for us when he died instead of us on the cross.

I have used the word "satisfied" advisedly. It is very important for us to observe that when Jesus died upon the cross he made a full satisfaction for our sins; he paid the penalty which the law pronounces upon our sin not in part but in full.

In saying that, there are several misunderstandings which need to be guarded against in the most careful way possible. Only by distinguishing the Scripture doctrine carefully from several distortions of it can we understand clearly what the Scripture doctrine is. I want to point out, therefore, several things that we do not mean when we say that Christ paid the penalty of our sin by dying instead of us on the cross.

In the first place, we do not mean that when Christ took our place he became himself a sinner. Of course, he did not become a sinner. Never was his glorious righteousness and goodness more wonderfully seen than when he bore the curse of God's law upon the cross. He was not deserving of that curse. Far from it! He was deserving of all praise.

What we mean, therefore, when we say that Christ bore our guilt is not that he became guilty, but that he paid the penalty that we so richly deserved.

In the second place, we do not mean that Christ's sufferings were the same as the sufferings that we should have endured if we had paid the penalty of our own sins. Obviously, they were not the same. Part of the sufferings that we should have endured would have been the dreadful suffering of remorse. Christ did not endure that suffering, for he had done no wrong. Moreover, our sufferings would have endured to all eternity, whereas Christ's sufferings on the cross endured but a few hours. Plainly then his sufferings were not the same as ours would have been.

In the third place, however, an opposite error must also be warded off. If Christ's sufferings were not the same as ours, it is also quite untrue to say that he paid only a part of the penalty that was due to us because of our sin. Some theologians have fallen into that error. When man incurred the penalty of the law, they have said, God was pleased to take some other and lesser thing—namely, the sufferings of Christ on the cross—instead of exacting the full penalty. Thus, according to these theologians, the demands of the law were not really satisfied by the death of Christ, but God was simply pleased, in arbitrary fashion, to accept something less than full satisfaction.

That is a very serious error indeed. Instead of falling into it we shall, if we are true to the Scriptures, insist that Christ on the cross paid the full and just penalty for our sin.

The error arose because of a confusion between the payment of a debt and the payment of a penalty. In the case of a debt it does not make any difference who pays; all that is essential is that the creditor shall receive what is owed him. What is essential is that just the same thing shall be paid as that which stood in the bond.

But in the case of the payment of a penalty it does make a difference who pays. The law demanded that we should suffer eternal death because of our sin. Christ paid the penalty of the law in our stead. But for him to suffer was not the same as for us to suffer. He is God, and not merely man. Therefore, if he had suffered to all eternity as we should have suffered, that would not have been to pay the just penalty of the sin, but it would have been an unjust exaction of vastly more. In other words, we must get rid of merely quantitative notions in thinking of the sufferings of Christ. What he suffered on the cross was what the law of God truly demanded not of any person but of such a person as himself when he became our substitute in paying the penalty of sin. He did therefore make full and not merely partial satisfaction for the claims of the law against us.

Finally, it is very important to observe that the Bible's teaching about the cross of Christ does not mean that God waited for someone else to pay the penalty of sin before he would forgive the sinner. So unbelievers constantly represent it, but that representation is radically wrong. No, God himself paid the penalty of sin—God himself in the person of God the Son, who loved us and gave himself for us, God himself in the person of God the Father who so loved the world as to give his only begotten Son, God the Holy Spirit who applies to us the benefits of Christ's death. God's the cost and ours the marvelous gain. Who shall measure the depths of the love of God which was extended to us sinners when the Lord Jesus took our place and died in our stead upon the accursed tree?

49

The Active Obedience of Christ

Last Sunday afternoon, in outlining the biblical teaching about the work of Christ in satisfying for us the claims of God's law, I said nothing about one very important part of that work. I pointed out that Christ by his death in our stead on the cross paid the just penalty of our sin, but I said nothing of another thing that he did for us. I said nothing about what Christ did for us by his active obedience to God's law. It is very important that we should fill out that part of the outline before we go one step further.

Suppose Christ had done for us merely what we said last Sunday afternoon that he did. Suppose he had merely paid the just penalty of the law that was resting upon us for our sin, and had done nothing more than that; where would we then be? Well, I think we can say—if indeed it is legitimate to separate one part of the work of Christ even in thought from the rest—that if Christ had merely paid the penalty of sin for us and had done nothing more, we should be at best back in the situation in which Adam found himself when God placed him under the covenant of works.

That covenant of works was a probation. If Adam kept the law of God for a certain period, he was to have eternal life. If he disobeyed, he was to have death. Well, he disobeyed, and the penalty of death was inflicted upon him and his posterity. Then Christ by his death on the cross paid that penalty for those whom God had chosen.

Well and good. But if that were all that Christ did for us, do you not see that we should be back in just the situation in which Adam was before he sinned? The penalty of his sinning would have been removed from us because it had all been paid by Christ. But for the future, the attainment of eternal life would have been dependent upon our perfect obedience to the law of God. We should simply have been back in the probation again.

Moreover, we should have been back in that probation in a very much less hopeful way than that in which Adam was originally placed in it. Everything was in Adam's favor when he was placed in the probation. He had been created in knowledge, righteousness, and holiness. He had been created positively good. Yet despite all that, he fell. How much more likely would we be to fall—nay, how certain to fall—if all that Christ had done for us were merely to remove from us the guilt of past sin, leaving it then to our own efforts to win the reward which God has pronounced upon perfect obedience!

But I really must decline to speculate any further about what might have been if Christ had done something less for us than that which he has actually done. As a matter of fact, he has not merely paid the penalty of Adam's first sin, and the penalty of the sins which we individually have committed, but also he has positively merited for us eternal life. He was, in other words, our representative both in penalty paying and in probation keeping. He paid the penalty of sin for us, and he stood the probation for us.

That is the reason why those who have been saved by the Lord Jesus Christ are in a far more blessed condition than was Adam before he fell. Adam before he fell was righteous in the sight of God, but he was still under the possibility of becoming unrighteous. Those who have been saved by the Lord Jesus Christ not only are righteous in the sight of God but they are beyond the possibility of becoming unrighteous. In their case, the probation is over. It is not over because they have stood it successfully. It is not over because they have themselves earned the reward of assured blessedness which God promised on condition of perfect obedience. But it is over because Christ has merited for them the reward by his perfect obedience to God's law.

I think I can make the matter plain if I imagine a dialogue between the law of God and a sinful man saved by grace.

"Man," says the law of God, "have you obeyed my commands?"

"No," says the sinner saved by grace, "I have disobeyed them, not only in the person of my representative Adam in his first sin, but also in that I myself have sinned in thought, word, and deed."

"Well, then, sinner," says the law of God, "have you paid the penalty which I pronounced upon disobedience?"

"No," says the sinner, "I have not paid the penalty myself; but Christ has paid it for me. He was my representative when he died there on the cross. Hence, so far as the penalty is concerned, I am clear."

"Well, then, sinner," says the law of God, "how about the conditions which God has pronounced for the attainment of assured blessedness? Have you stood the test? Have you merited eternal life by perfect obedience during the period of probation?"

"No," says the sinner, "I have not merited eternal life by my own perfect obedience. God knows and my own conscience knows that even after I became a Christian I have sinned in thought, word, and deed. But although I have not merited eternal life by any obedience of my own, Christ has merited it for me by his perfect obedience. He was not for himself subject to the law. No obedience was required of him for himself, since he was Lord of all. That obedience, then, which he rendered to the law when he was on earth was rendered by him as my representative. I have no righteousness of my own, but clad in Christ's perfect righteousness, imputed to me and received by faith alone, I can glory in the fact that so far as I am concerned the probation has been kept and as God is true there awaits me the glorious reward which Christ thus earned for me."

Such, put in bald, simple form, is the dialogue between every Christian and the law of God. How gloriously complete is the salvation wrought for us by Christ! Christ paid the penalty, and he merited the reward. Those are the two great things that he has done for us.

Theologians are accustomed to distinguishing those two parts of the saving work of Christ by calling one of them his passive obedience and the other of them his active obedience. By his passive obedience—that is, by suffering in our stead—he paid the penalty for us; by his active obedience—that is, by doing what the law of God required—he has merited for us the reward.

I like that terminology well enough. I think it does set forth as well as can be done in human language the two aspects of Christ's work. And yet a danger lurks in it if it leads us to think that one of the two parts of Christ's work can be separated from the other.

How shall we distinguish Christ's active obedience from his passive obedience? Shall we say that he accomplished his active obedience by his life and accomplished his passive obedience by his death? No, that will not do at all. During every moment of his life upon earth, Christ was engaged in his passive obedience. It was all for him humiliation, was it not? It was all suffering. It was all part of his payment of the penalty of sin. On the other hand, we cannot say that his death was passive obedience and not active obedience. On the contrary, his death was the crown of his active obedience. It was the crown of that obedience to the law of God by which he merited eternal life for those whom he came to save.

Do you not see, then, what the true state of the case is? Christ's active obedience and his passive obedience are not two divisions of his work, some of the events of his earthly life being his active obedience and other events of his life being his passive obedience; but every event of his life was both active obedience and passive obedience. Every event of his life was a part of his payment of the penalty of sin, and every event of his life was a part of that glorious keeping of the law of God by which he earned for his people the reward of eternal life. The two aspects of his work, in other words, are inextricably intertwined. Neither was performed apart from the other. Together they constitute the wonderful, full salvation which was wrought for us by Christ our Redeemer.

We can put it briefly by saying that Christ took our place with respect to the law of God. He paid for us the law's penalty, and he obeyed for us the law's commands. He saved us from hell, and he earned for us our entrance into heaven. All that we have, then, we owe unto him. There is no blessing that we have in this world or the next for which we should not give Christ thanks.

As I say that, I am fully conscious of the inadequacy of my words. I have tried to summarize the teaching of the Bible about the saving work of Christ; yet how cold and dry seems any mere human summary—even if it were far better than mine—in comparison with the marvelous richness and warmth of the Bible itself. It is to the Bible itself that I am going to ask you to turn with me next Sunday afternoon. Having tried to summarize the Bible's teaching in order that we may take each part of the Bible in proper relation to other parts, I am going to ask you next Sunday to turn with me to the great texts themselves, in order that we may test our summary, and every human summary, by what God himself has told us in his Word. Ah, when we do that, what refreshment it is to our souls! How infinitely superior is God's Word to all human attempts to summarize its teaching! Those attempts are necessary; we could not do without them; everyone who is really true to the Bible will engage in them. But it is the very words of the Bible that touch the heart, and everything that we—or for the matter of that even the greatest theologians—say in summary of the Bible must be compared ever anew with the Bible itself.

This afternoon, however, just in order that next Sunday we may begin our searching of the Scriptures in the most intelligent possible way, I am going to ask you to glance with me at one or two of the different views that men have held regarding the cross of Christ.

I have already summarized for you the orthodox view. According to that view, Christ took our place on the cross, paying the penalty of sin that we deserved to pay. That view can be put in very simple language. We deserved eternal death because of sin; Jesus, because he loved us, took our place and died in our stead on the cross. Call that view repulsive if you will. It is indeed repulsive to the natural man. But do not call it difficult to understand. A little child can understand it, and can receive it to the salvation of his soul.

Rejecting that substitutionary view, many men have advanced other views. Many are the theories of the atonement. Yet I do think that their bewildering variety may be reduced to something like order if we observe that they fall into a very few general divisions.

Most common among them is the theory that Christ's death upon the cross had merely a moral effect upon man. Man is by nature a child of God, say the advocates of that view. But unfortunately, he is not making full use of his high privilege. He has fallen into terrible degradation, and having fallen into terrible degradation he has become estranged from God. He no longer lives in that intimate relationship of sonship with God in which he ought to live.

How shall this estrangement between man and God be removed; how shall man be brought back into fellowship with God? Why, say the advocates of the view of which we are now speaking, simply by inducing man to turn from his evil ways and make full use of his high privilege as a child of God. There is certainly no barrier on God's side; the only barrier lies in man's foolish and wicked heart. Once that barrier is overcome, all will be well. Once touch man's stony heart so that he will come to see again that God is his Father; once lead him also to overcome any fear of God as though God were not always more ready to forgive than man is to be forgiven; and at once the true relationship between God and man can be restored and man can go forward joyously to the use, in holy living, of his high privilege as a child of the loving heavenly Father.

But how can man's heart be touched, that he may be led to return to his Father's house and live as befits a son of God? By the contemplation of the cross of Christ, say the advocates of the view that we are now presenting. Jesus Christ was truly a son of God. Indeed, he was a son of God in such a unique way that he may be called in some sort *the* Son of God. When therefore God gave him to die upon the cross and when he willingly gave himself to die, that was a wonderful manifestation of God's love for sinning, erring humanity. In the presence of that love, all opposition in man's heart should be broken down. He should recognize at last the fact that God is indeed his Father, and recognizing that, he should make use of his high privilege of living the life that befits a child of God.

Such is the so-called moral influence theory of the atonement. It is held in a thousand different forms, and it is held by thousands of people who have not the slightest notion that they are holding it.

Some of those who have held it have tried to maintain with it something like a real belief in the deity of Christ. If Christ was really the eternal Son of God, then the gift of him on the cross becomes all the greater evidence of the love of God. But the overwhelming majority of those who hold the moral influence view of the atonement have given up all real belief in the deity of Christ. These persons hold simply that Jesus on the cross gave us a supreme example of self-sacrifice. By that example we are inspired to do likewise. We are inspired to sacrifice our lives, either in actual martyrdom in some holy cause or in sacrificial service. Sacrificing thus our lives, we discover that we have thereby attained a higher life than ever before. Thus the cross of Christ has been the pathway that leads us to moral heights.

Read most of the popular books on religion of the present day and then tell me whether you do not think that that is at bottom what they mean. Some of them speak about the cross of Christ. Some of them say that Christ's sufferings were redemptive. But the trouble is they hold that the cross of Christ is not merely Christ's cross but our cross too; and that while Christ's sufferings were redemptive our sufferings are redemptive too. All they really mean is that Christ on Calvary pointed out a way that we follow. He hallowed the pathway of self-sacrifice. We follow in that path and thus we obtain a higher life for our souls.

That is the great central and all-pervading vice of most modern books that deal with the cross. They make the cross of Christ merely an example of a general principle of self-sacrifice. And if they talk still of salvation, they tell us that we are saved by walking in the way of the cross. It is thus, according to this view, not Christ's cross but our cross that saves us. The way of the cross leads us to God. Christ may have a great influence in leading us to walk in that way of the cross, that way of self-sacrifice, but it is our walking in it and not Christ's walking in it which really saves us. Thus we are saved by our own efforts, not by Christ's blood after all. It is the same old notion that sinful man can save himself. It is that notion just decked out in new garments and making use of Christian terminology.

Such is the moral influence theory of the atonement. In addition to it, we find what is sometimes called the governmental theory. What a strange, compromising, tortuous thing that governmental theory is, to be sure!

According to the governmental view, the death of Christ was not necessary in order that any eternal justice of God, rooted in the divine nature, might be satisfied. So far, the governmental view goes with the advocates of the moral influence theory. But it holds that the death of Christ was necessary in order that good discipline might be maintained in the world. If sinners were allowed to get the notion that sin could go altogether unpunished, there would be no adequate deterrent from sin. Being thus undeterred from sin, men would go on sinning and the world would be thrown into confusion. But if the world were thus thrown into moral confusion that would not be for the best interests of the greatest number. Therefore, God held up the death of Christ on the cross as an indication of how serious a thing sin is, so that men may be deterred from sinning and so order in the world may be preserved.

Having thus indicated—so the governmental theory runs—how serious a thing sin is, God proceeded to offer salvation to men on easier terms than those on which he had originally offered it. He had originally offered it on the basis of perfect obedience. Now he offered it on the basis of faith. He could safely offer it on those easier terms, and he could safely remit the penalty originally pronounced upon sin, because in the awful spectacle of the cross of Christ he had sufficiently indicated to men that sin is a serious offense and that if it is committed something or other has to be done about the matter in order that the good order of the universe may be conserved.

Such is the governmental theory. But do you not see that really at bottom it is just a form of the moral influence theory? Like the moral influence theory, it holds that the only obstacle to fellowship between man and God is found in man's will. Like the moral influence theory, it denies that there is any eternal justice of God, rooted in his being, and it denies that the eternal justice of God demands the punishment of sin. Like the moral influence theory, it plays fast and loose with God's holiness, and like the moral influence theory, we may add, it loses sight of the real depths of God's love. No man who holds the light view of sin that is involved in these man-made theories has the slightest notion of what it cost when the eternal Son of God took our place upon the accursed tree.

People sometimes say, indeed, that it makes little difference what theory of the atonement we may hold. Ah, my friends, it makes all the difference in the world. When you contemplate the cross of Christ, do you say merely, with modern theorists, "What a noble example of self-sacrifice; I am going to attain favor with God by sacrificing myself as well as he." Or do you say with the Bible, "He loved me and gave himself for me; he took my place; he bore my curse; he bought me with his own most precious blood." That is the most momentous question that can come to any human soul. I want you all to turn with me next Sunday afternoon to the Word of God in order that we may answer that question aright.

50

The Bible's View of the Atonement

Having observed last week what are the leading views that have been held regarding the cross of Christ, we turn now to the Bible in order to discover which of these views is right.

Did Jesus on the cross really take our place, paying the penalty of God's law which justly rested upon us? That is the orthodox or substitutionary view of the atonement.

Or did he merely exert a good moral influence upon us by his death, either by giving us an exhibition of the love of God or by inspiring us to sacrifice our lives for the welfare of others as he sacrificed himself? That is the so-called moral influence theory of the atonement.

Or did he by his death merely conserve the good discipline of the world by showing that, in the interests of the welfare of the greatest number, God cannot simply allow his law to be transgressed with complete impunity? That is the so-called governmental theory of atonement.

We shall try to test these three views of the cross of Christ by comparing them with what the Bible actually says. But before we do so, there are two preliminary remarks that we ought to make.

Our first remark is that the three views of the atonement really reduce themselves to two. Both the moral influence and the governmental view of the atonement really make the work of Christ terminate upon man, rather than upon God. They both proceed on the assumption that, in order that man shall be forgiven, nothing but man's repentance is required. Both of them deny, at least by implication, that there is such a thing as an eternal principle of justice, not based merely upon the interests of the creature but rooted in the nature of God—an eternal principle of justice demanding that sin shall be punished. Both of them favor the notion that the ethical attributes of God may be summed up in the one attribute: benevolence. Both of them tend to distort the great scriptural assertion that "God is love" into the very different assertion that God is *nothing but love*. Both of them tend to find the supreme end of the creation in the happiness or well-being of the creature. Both of them fail utterly to attain to any high notion of the awful holiness of God.

No doubt the governmental theory disguises these tendencies more than the moral influence theory does. It does show some recognition of the moral chaos which would result if men got the notion that the law of God could be transgressed with complete impunity.

But, after all, even the governmental theory denies that there is any real underlying necessity for the punishment of sin. Punishment, it holds, is merely remedial and deterrent. It is intended merely to prevent future sin, not to expiate past sin. So the tragedy on Calvary, according to the advocates of the governmental view, was intended by God merely to shock sinners out of their complacency; it was intended merely to show what terrible effects sin has so that sinners, by observing those terrible effects, might be led to stop sinning. The governmental view, therefore, like the moral influence view, has at its center the notion that a moral effect exerted upon man was the sole purpose of the cross of Christ.

Very different is the substitutionary view. According to that view, not a mere moral effect upon man but the satisfaction of the eternal justice of God was the primary end for which Christ died. Hence the substitutionary view of the atonement stands sharply over against the other two. The other two belong in one category; the substitutionary view belongs in an entirely different category. That is the first remark that we desire to make before we begin to consider the biblical teaching in detail.

That remark, however, would be decidedly misleading unless we went on to make a second remark. Our second remark is that the substitutionary view of the atonement, though it makes the work of Christ in dying upon the cross terminate primarily upon God, yet does at the same time most emphatically make it terminate also upon man. What distortion of the substitutionary view it would be to say that Christ, when he died, did not die to produce a moral effect upon man?

Of course, he died to produce a moral effect upon man. If he had not died, man would have continued to lead a life of sin; but as it is, those for whom he died cease to lead a life of sin and begin to lead a life of holiness. They do not lead that life of holiness perfectly in this world, but they will most certainly lead it in the world to come, and it was in order that they might lead that life of holiness that Christ died for them. No man for whom Christ died continues to live in sin as he lived before. All who receive the benefits of the cross of Christ turn from sin unto righteousness. In holding that that is the case, the substitutionary view of the atonement is quite in accord with the moral influence theory and with the governmental theory.

Well, then, is it correct to say that the moral influence theory and the governmental theory are correct as far as they go and merely differ from the substitutionary view in being inadequate or incomplete?

No, I do not think that is correct at all. You see, the heart and core of the moral influence theory and the governmental theory is found in the denial that Christ on the cross took our place and paid the just penalty of our sins that we might be right with God. Denying that, the moral influence theory and the governmental theory are, if the substitutionary view is right, not merely inadequate but also false.

Moreover, the moral influence theory and the governmental theory are not even right in what they affirm, to say nothing of their being right in what they deny. They are indeed right in holding that Christ died to bring about a moral change in men, but they are wrong in thinking that that moral change can be brought about if the moral influence theory or the governmental theory is true. They are wrong in not observing clearly that fallen man, dead in trespasses and sins, can never be made to live a holy life merely by the introduction of new motives or new incentives to goodness, but only by the new birth which is the work of the Spirit of God. They are wrong in not observing that that new birth, which is the necessary prerequisite for any living of a holy life by fallen man, is part of the benefit purchased by Christ when he died on the cross to make sinners right with God by his payment, for them, of the penalty of sin.

I do not mean that all of the advocates of the moral influence theory or the governmental theory of the atonement deny the necessity of the new birth, but I do mean that the denial of it is part of the logical implications of their views. If Christ died on the cross merely to bring to bear a good moral influence upon men, then it does look as though a good moral influence is all that men really need; and if a good moral influence is all that they need, then it does look as though Jesus was wrong when he said, "You must be born again."

Moreover, how feeble is the moral influence exerted by the cross if the cross of Christ is only what the advocates of the moral influence theory suppose it to be! If Jesus's death on Calvary was merely a sort of exhibition of the love of God, not necessary in itself but merely necessary in order that our hearts may be touched and we may be moved to salutary tears, then, the moment we find out that that was all it was, it seems to me our tears of repentance are apt to be dried up. It is as though we had sat in some playhouse witnessing some heart-moving tragedy, entering into the struggles of the characters on the stage, imagining that it was all real. But then the curtain has fallen, and out we go into the workaday, real world again, half ashamed of the tears that we have shed over what was after all a play. The cross of Christ might exert some moral influence upon us when we thought that it was intended for something far profounder than the exertion of a moral influence upon us. But the moment we discover that after all it was but an exhibition and that Christ after all did not really do anything upon the cross that was absolutely necessary for our soul's salvation, then even that moral influence tends to disappear.

The true moral influence of the cross of Christ really comes, in other words, only when we see that the moral influence theory regarding it is false; it comes only when we see that on the cross, Christ truly bore the penalty of our sins and buried it forever in the depths of the sea. "He who is forgiven little, loves little" (Luke 7:47). If the sin for which we are forgiven is merely the light, easily forgiven thing that the advocates of the moral influence theory of the atonement think it is, then no great spring of gratitude will well up in our souls toward him who has caused us to be forgiven; but if it is the profound and deadly thing that the advocates of the substitutionary view of the atonement think it is, then all our lives will be one song of gratitude to him who loved us and gave himself for us upon the accursed tree.

From every point of view, therefore, the question with which we are now dealing is the most momentous question that could possibly be conceived. Did Christ die on the cross merely to influence us to holy and sacrificial living? Did he die on the cross merely to exhibit the necessity of some deterrent against sin in the interests of an orderly world, or did he die on the cross in order to pay the penalty of our sin and make us right with the holy God?

Which of these three views is right? That is the question which we shall seek to answer by an examination of the Word of God.

At the beginning of the examination there is one fact which stares us in the face. It has sometimes been strangely neglected. It is the fact of the enormous emphasis which the Bible lays upon the death of Christ.

Have you ever stopped to consider how strange that emphasis is? In the case of other great men, it is the birth that is celebrated and not the death. Washington's birthday is celebrated by a grateful American people on the twenty-second day of February, but who remembers on what day of the year it was that Washington died? Who ever thought of making the day of his death into a national holiday?

Well, there are some men whose death might indeed be celebrated by a national holiday, but they are not good men like George Washington; they are, on the contrary, men whose taking off was a blessing to their people. It would be a small compliment to the father of his country if we celebrated with national rejoicing the day when he was taken from us. Instead of that, we celebrate his birth. Yet in the case of Jesus it is the death and not the birth that we chiefly commemorate in the Christian church.

I do not mean that it is wrong for us to commemorate the birth of Jesus. We have just celebrated Christmas, and it is right for us so to do. Happy at this Christmas season through which we have just passed have been those to whom it has not been just a time of worldly festivity but a time of commemoration of the coming of our blessed Savior into this world. Happy have been those men and women and little children who have heard, underlying all their Christmas joys, and have heard in simple and childlike faith, the sweet story that is told us in Matthew and Luke. Happy have been those celebrants of Christmas to whom the angels have brought again, in the reading of the Word of God, their good tidings of great joy.

Yes, I say, thank God for the Christmas season; thank God for the softening that it brings to stony hearts; thank God for the recognition that it brings for the little children whom Jesus took into his arms; thank God even for the strange, sweet sadness that it brings to us together with its joys, as we think of the loved ones who are gone. Yes, it is well that we should celebrate the Christmas season, and may God ever give us a childlike heart that we may celebrate it aright.

But after all, my friends, it is not Christmas that is the greatest anniversary in the Christian church. It is not the birth of Jesus that the church chiefly celebrates, but the death.

Did you know that long centuries went by in the history of the church before there is any record of the celebration of Christmas? Jesus was born in the days of Herod the King—that is, at some time before 4 BC, when Herod died. Not till centuries later do we find evidence that the church celebrated any anniversary regarded as the anniversary of his birth.

Well, then, if that is so with regard to the commemoration of Jesus's birth, how is it with regard to the commemoration of his death? Was the commemoration of that also so long postponed? Well, listen to what is said on that subject by the apostle Paul. "For as often as you eat this bread," he says, "and drink the cup, you proclaim the Lord's death until he comes" (1 Cor 11:26). That was written only about twenty-five years after the death of Christ and after the founding of the church in Jerusalem. Even in those early days the death of Christ was commemorated by the church in the most solemn service in which it engaged—namely, in the celebration of the Lord's Supper.

Indeed, that commemoration of the death of Christ was definitely provided for by Jesus himself. "This cup is the new testament in my blood," said Jesus: "Do this, as often as you drink it, in remembrance of me" (1 Cor 11:25). In those words of institution of the Lord's Supper, Jesus carefully provided that his church should commemorate his death.

Thus the Bible makes no definite provision for the commemoration of the birth of Jesus but provides in the most definite and solemn way for the commemoration of his death.

What is the reason for that contrast, which at first sight might seem to be very strange? I think the answer is fairly clear. The birth of Jesus was important not in itself but because it made possible his death. Jesus came into this world to die, and it is to his death that the sinner turns when he seeks salvation for his soul. Truly the familiar hymn is right when it says about the cross of Christ: "All the light of sacred story, gathers round its head sublime."[1] The whole Bible centers in the story of the death of Christ. The Old Testament looks forward to it; the New Testament looks back upon it; and the truly biblical preacher of the gospel says always with Paul: "I decided to know nothing among you except Jesus Christ and him crucified" (1 Cor 2:2).

I ask you, then, which of the theories of the atonement suits this supreme emphasis which the Bible puts upon the cross?

Does the moral influence theory suit it? I think not, my friends. If Jesus died on the cross merely to give us a good example of self-sacrifice

---

1. John Bowring, "In the Cross of Christ I Glory," 1825.

or merely to exhibit, without underlying necessity, the love of God, then the Bible does seem strangely overwrought in the way in which it speaks of the death of Christ. Then indeed all the talk in the Bible about the blood of Christ and the blood of the sacrificial victims that were prophecies of him becomes just about as distasteful as so many modern men hold it to be. Some very much greater significance must be attributed to the death of Christ than a mere hallowing of some universal law of self-sacrifice or a mere pedagogic exhibition of God's love, if we are to explain the way in which the Bible makes everything to center in the event that took place on Calvary.

The case is not essentially different when we consider the governmental theory. It is true, the governmental theory does seek, as over against the moral influence theory, to do justice to the emphasis which the Bible places just on the death of Christ. It regards the tragic horror of the cross not as merely incidental to the meaning of what Christ did but as essential to it. It regards that tragic horror as being the thing that shocks sinners out of their complacency and makes them recognize the seriousness of sin. Hence it seeks to show why just the death of Christ and not some other exhibition of self-sacrificing love was necessary.

But, after all, what a short way such considerations go toward explaining the biblical emphasis on the cross of Christ! The truth is that there is just one real explanation of such emphasis. It is found in the fact that Christ on the cross did something absolutely necessary if we sinners are to be forgiven by a righteous God. Once recognize the enormous barrier which sin sets up between the offender and his God, once recognize the fact that this barrier is rooted not merely in the sinner's mind but in the eternal justice of God, and then once recognize that the cross, as the full payment of the penalty of sin, has broken down the barrier and made the sinner right with God—once recognize these things and then only will you understand the strange preeminence which the Bible attributes to the cross of Christ.

Thus even the mere prominence of the death of Christ in the Bible, to say nothing of what the Bible says about the death of Christ in detail, is a mighty argument against all minimizing theories of the significance of the death of Christ and a mighty argument in favor of the view that Christ on the cross really died in our stead, paying the dread penalty of our sin that he might present us, saved by grace, before the throne.

In presenting what the Bible says in detail about the death of Christ,

I want to speak first of all of those passages where Christ's death upon the cross is represented as a ransom, then about those passages where it is spoken of as a sacrifice, then about those passages where, without the use of either of these representations, its substitutionary or representative character is plainly brought out.

The first passage that we shall speak of, next Sunday afternoon, is that great passage in the tenth chapter of the Gospel according to Mark where our Lord says that the Son of man came to give his life as a ransom for many.

On this last Sunday of the old year, I just want to say to you who have been listening in on these Sunday afternoons how encouraged I have been by your interest and by your Christian fellowship. I trust that you have had a very joyous Christmas and I trust that the new year which is so soon to begin may be to you a very blessed year under the mercy of God.

Afterword

J Gresham Machen is rumored to have said that if he knew half as much as his Princeton Seminary colleague, Geerhardus Vos, he would be writing all the time. Even so, despite his death at the relatively early age of 55, we may be grateful for the considerable legacy of publications and publishable material he left behind, including the radio addresses collected in this volume.

Truly great biblical instruction does not become outdated. Originally addressed to specific audiences in the light of contemporary issues and problems, sound preaching and teaching also lays hold of the thinking and shapes the life of later generations of the church. Machen's radio addresses are a notable example.

What explains this enduring relevance and effectiveness? Of a number of factors that could be mentioned, two are especially important. Both may be noted here briefly for how they display Machen's awareness of his audience's context.

First, Machen's teaching and preaching is motivated and sustained, from beginning to end, by the recognition that the deepest and truest needs of human beings and, more importantly, the resolution of these needs, have remained the same since the fall. Such teaching certainly does not ignore, but rather engages the congregation within its immediate cultural, social, economic, political, and religious context. But the sermon's content is not determined by or even primarily concerned with such issues. This is in marked contrasted to much preaching in our day, with plenty of precursors in Machen's. In seeking to "contextualize" and be "missional" this kind of preaching is so occupied with immediate but ever-changing issues and problems that it soon loses whatever relevance it may have had.

Dominant in Machen's addresses is, in a word, the gospel. Their lasting value resides in the strikingly effective and memorable way he remains focused on the gospel and its primary and unchanging implications. This includes the decisive historical context the gospel has created and entails. He sought to make clear that the most important thing his early 20th century American audiences needed to understand about their circumstances—shaped by the aftermath of World War I and the tumult of the Great Depression—was precisely the same thing that the writer of Hebrews was above all concerned that his original readers understand about their own situation within the mid-first century Mediterranean world, about which he was surely aware but says virtually nothing. Decisive for both, then and now, is this: we, as well as they in their day, live in that time when Christ "has appeared once for all at the end of the ages to put away sin by the sacrifice of himself, and… having been offered once to bear the sins of many, will appear a second time, not to deal with sin but to save those who are eagerly waiting for him" (Hebrews 9:26, 28).

One of Machen's overriding concerns was that his listeners understand that what Paul observed of the Thessalonian Christians is no less true and essential for every following generation including our own: Christianity in its true essence has to do with those who have "…turned to God from idols to serve the living and true God, and to wait for his Son from heaven, whom he raised from the dead, Jesus who delivers us from the wrath to come" (1Thessalonians 1:9–10).

In this time between the times—the interim bracketed by Christ's resurrection and his return—what is "of first importance" remains his death and resurrection for the remediation of human sin (1 Corinthians 15: 3–4). Not only is the relevance of this gospel context permanent, it overrides all other contextual considerations. Keeping focused on it provides a controlling perspective that fosters preaching and teaching like Machen's, driven by the insight that in the final analysis the proper, indeed only sound approach to our immediate problems is this long-range gospel point of view. Such teaching is truly timeless in the sense that it is ever timely, today as much as in Machen's own day.

A second, more immediate contextual aspect accounts for the continuing relevance of Machen's addresses. Over the course of his ministry he was tireless in stressing that doctrine is prior to life, that life flows from doctrine. This emphasis was all the more necessary because the dominant Christianity of his day (which his *Christianity and Liberalism* effectively exposed to not be true Christianity at all, but a fundamentally different religion) was marked by a fatal doctrinal antipathy. This theological liberalism, or modernism as it is also sometimes called, advocated for religion as morality or a way of life for which essential doctrines of the Bible, such as its own entire truthfulness and the reality of the miracles and propitiatory death and bodily resurrection of Christ, were held to be dispensable or even detrimental.

Machen contended so vigorously against this doctrinally hostile moralism because he saw clearly that it denied the truth of the gospel. The life it purported to offer was devoid of salvation from sin and the eternal life in Christ offered in the gospel. So, he relentlessly countered the notion that those doctrines, perceived by many in his day as impractical abstractions irrelevant for life, were therefore better ignored or denied. Rather, his audiences must appreciate that at its heart, sound doctrine is absolutely essential biblical teaching, "as the truth is in Jesus" (Ephesians 4:21). Its centering focus is on what only God, the creator of heaven and earth, could do and has in fact done in history, in sending his Son "in the fullness of time" to save lost sinners.

Such doctrine is truly and perennially life-giving. By the accompanying power of the Holy Spirit, it is indispensable for ministering the resurrection life that Jesus came to give and to give abundantly (John 10:10; 11:25). So, Machen also observed, as an essential corollary of the priority of doctrine to life, this truth is in order to godliness, to that genuine "holiness without which no one will see the Lord" (Hebrews 12:14).

The religious liberalism of Machen's day saw the gospel as, in effect, a self-help message. It amounted to a summons to follow the example of Jesus by doing what we are supposedly able to do for ourselves. In the face of that disastrous misconception, Machen saw the paramount need of making and keeping clear that the gospel is a message of redemption, of God in Christ doing for us what we sinners are helpless to do for ourselves.

Decades later, notwithstanding all the changes in the church and world that had taken place in the meantime, Ned B. Stonehouse, Machen's colleague in New Testament at Westminster Seminary in its early days, in assessing the errant critical biblical scholarship of his own day spoke of "what may with very little exaggeration be characterized as the persistence of Liberalism." This liberalism with its serious misunderstanding of the gospel and what it means to be a Christian—the misconception of religion as the self-help moralism noted in the preceding paragraph—still persists, and remains all too widespread, at present. But then so too does the value of Machen's addresses in exposing and refuting its gospel-denying error.

A closing personal note may not be entirely amiss. Many years ago, during my college days, chapters reprinted in this volume, along with other non-academic writings of Machen were a significant influence in my life, and I have had occasion to return to them from time to time, always with great profit. I am confident that many today will benefit similarly, finding, as I have, that they have lost none of their relevance. The legacy of these writings of Machen will continue to serve the cause of the gospel and the church's wellbeing not only in our day but for generations to come.

>Richard B. Gaffin, Jr.
>Professor of Biblical and Systematic Theology, Emeritus
>Westminster Theological Seminary, Philadelphia

Index of Subjects and Names

Abishai, son Zeruiah, 171
Abraham, 22
    faith of, 370
Absalom, 171
Adam, xxxvi, 311, 315, 347, 403–4, 407–8
    sin came by, 298–99
    temptation of, 269
Addison, Joseph, 206
Alexander, Cecil Francis, 352n
Alexandria, 195, 196
Amiens Cathedral, 330
anthropomorphism, 79, 165
antinomianism, 280–81
apologetics, xxii, xxvi, xxx, xxxi, xxxv, 26, 43–44
    classical at Old Princeton, xxxi
    Tertullian, 268n
    theistic proofs, 14–15
Apostles' Creed, 141
Archimedes, 342n, 343
Aristotle, 59–60
art, 342
Arminianism, xxxiii, 338
asceticism, 274–75
Assyria, 214
Augustine, 220, 335, 343
    Confessions of, 78n
    Pelagian controversy, 310–11, 315–16

Babylon, 214
Barnabas, 132
Bartimaeus, blind, 224
Beatitudes, 100–2

Bible, 331
    authority of, xxxi, 149, 331–33, 377
    convicts reader of sin, 41–42
    defending it, 41–48
    doctrine, then life, 65, 67
    does not contain but is Word of God, 152
    God's Word, xxvi, 25–32, 35, 37, 39–40, 41–47, 49–57, 51–52, 139, 326–28, 346
    literal and figurative interpretation of, 164–65
    "spirit of Jesus" interpretation of, 53–55
    miracles in, 225
    only source of supernatural revelation, 22, 26, 32, 38, 345
    teaching about truth and doctrine, 57–58
    "teaching of Jesus" interpretation, 52–53, 67
    three theological divisions of, 348
Bible, inspiration of, 23, 26, 33–40, 41, 164, 327, 345–47, 377
    autographs only inspired, 28–29
    how inspired writers composed it, 35–36, 37, 345–46
    objections to inspiration, 29, 35–36
    misconceptions of, 33–34
    Ouija Board and dictation theory, 34
    plenary, 27–28, 33, 152
    verbal, 32, 33–34

Bible Texts
  Codex Sinaiticus, 30
  King James Version, 31, 247–48, 399–400
  reliability of Greek ones, 31
Bismarck, North Dakota, xxvii
Board for Foreign Missions, xxiii, xxx
Boettner, Lorain, 179
born again, 192, 196–97, 225, 292, 306, 308, 320–22, 363, 417
  supernatural work of God, 263
Bourget, Paul
  Le Disciple, 61–62
Bowring, John, 238n, 420
Brain Trust, 5
British Museum, 30
Browning, Robert, 15
Buddha, 106
Bultmann, Rudolph Karl, 122
Byrd, Richard, 6

Cadman, S. Parks, xxix
Calvin, Calvinism, Calvinist, xxxiii, 170, 177, 228, 320, 333–34, 335, 338, 393
  five points of, 320
  only respectable theology, 176–77
chess, 238–39
Christian schools, 284–85
Christmas, 419–20
Civilian Conservation Corps (CCC), 16
Codex Sinaiticus, 30
common sense, 121, 165, 242, 299, 318, 361–62
common sense realism, xxxiv
Confucius, 106
covenant of grace, 351, 355

covenant of life, 257–261, 263, 269, 299–300, 305, 347
  for Adam and his posterity, 258, 299, 301, 303, 305, 311, 315, 319, 347, 403, 407
  sovereignly administered, 255–56
covenant of works, 259, 261, 299, 403–404, 407
creeds, 60–61, 328–29, 331, 335, 343
  Apostles', 141, 328, 329, 335, 337, 340
  modern ones deny existence of truth, 340
  Nicene, 329, 337
  not expressions of Christian experience, 336

David, 23, 91–94, 171–72, 370
deism, 71, 207–9
Denny, James,
  Jesus and the Gospel, 96
doctrine, 63, 327–34, 335, 341, 343
  expresses truth, 57–59, 341–42
  it is wonderful, 355
  not an expression of changing experience, 58–59
  Sermon on Mount and, 100
dualism, 202, 274

Eden, 268, 270, 299
Egypt, 26, 63, 214, 231
election, see predestination
Enoch, Ethiopic book of, 108
Esau, 188
Europe, xvii, 9–10, 151, 221, 283, 333, 335
euthanasia, 273–74
evangelical, 338–39

evangelism, xxx, xxv, xxxvii, 7, 45
evolution, xxxvi, 229, 230, 231, 232, 234

Fatherhood of God-brotherhood of man, 98, 120, 392
Ferguson, Sinclair B., xix
First Cause, God, 202–3, 210–11, 214–15, 229
Ford, Henry, 8, 116
Fosdick, Harry E., xxix, xxii
Fourth Gospel, 111, 291–92, 384
fundamentalism, xxiv, xxv, xxix, xxxiv–n, 44

Galilee, 64, 126–27, 129, 231, 293, 380, 392
    Lake [Sea] of, 231
Gaffin, Richard B., Jr., 426
Gamaliel, 37
Germany, 136, 222, 283, 285
God, xxi, 74, 76–77, 78, 89, 104–5, 160–62, 199
    decrees of, 163–66, 167, 173, 179, 191, 264
    eternal purpose, 167
    freedom of 159–61
    "God" redefined, 85–86
    has spoken, 19–24
    immanence, 73, 215
    infinity, 77–78
    nothing but love view of, 416
    mysterious, 89
    not author of sin, 172, 174, 175, 264
    omniscience, 168–69
    shepherds his flock, 79
    time does not constrain, 165, 200
    transcendence, 73, 215
    unchangeable, 78
God, creator, xxxii; 67–74, 207, 217, 227, 228
    all from nothing, 201–3
    Calvin on, 228
    not continuous creation, 207–8, 217
    not deism, 207–8, 209
    time was created, 200
God, providence of, 37, 152, 201, 208, 211, 213–15, 217, 223, 227–28, 255
    governs all creatures and actions, 208, 223
    cause and effect, 209–15
gold standard, 5
gospel, the, 349–50
    about Jesus vs. *of* Jesus, 392–94
Gospels, 113, 115, 116, 380, 381, 384–85
Gospels, Synoptic, 95, 96, 97, 111, 115, 187, 292, 295, 316, 381
grace, xxix, xxxii–xxxvi, 22, 62, 112, 121, 134, 142, 149, 153, 182, 268, 280, 330–31, 348
    Christ's, 70, 81, 142
    common grace, 267, 321
    dispensation of grace, 280, 281
    divine, xxxiii, 281, 330, 335
    doctrines of, xxv–xxvi,
    electing, xxxiii
    free, 295
    mysterious, 187, 189–90, 192, 197, 348–49
    God's, xxxiin, xxxiii, 22, 153, 182, 197, 270, 281, 295, 296, 298, 306, 322–23, 330

predestination and, xxxiii
pure, 192
resistless, 349
saving, or saved by, 193, 291, 396, 408, 421
supernatural, 213
Great Britain, 283–84
Great Depression, 5, 16, 423
Greece, 231

Hart, D. G., 11n, 156n
Heber, Reginald W., 352n
Heidelberg Catechism, 335
Herod the Great, 171, 214, 420
Hodge, A. A., 149
Hodge, C. W., 149
Hodge, Charles, xxxiii, 149, 310
Hodges, collectively, xxxi
Holtzmann, H. J., 137
Holy Spirit, xxix, xxxii–n, xxxv, 35, 45, 53, 93, 102, 109, 139–45, 154, 158, 173, 248, 296, 328–29, 346, 362–66, 369, 373, 375, 382, 386–87, 394, 406, 425
   aids understanding, 165, 361, 387
   another Helper, 143
   Apostles' Creed on, 141
   at Pentecost, 386
   clearest Bible passages regarding, 143
   convicts of sin, xxxii–n, 42
   deity of, 142
   descending upon Jesus, 96
   gifts of, 45
   guidance of, 29
   inspiration of Bible, 141, 152, 386
   proceeds from Father and Son, 386
   regeneration, xxxv–n, 42–43, 192, 197, 225, 268, 281, 291, 321–22, 349, 370
   Trinity, 112, 145
   work of, 36, 81–82, 152
How, William W., 352–n
human, 6, 8, 10, 13–14, 16, 34–38, 51–56, 63, 76, 79, 120, 130, 136, 138, 159, 180, 256, 285, 292, 331, 334, 343–44, 347, 382, 412, 423
   affections, 76
   behavior, 245
   body, 73
   conduct, 271, 274
   endeavor, 210
   experience, 272
   faculties, 247
   freedom, 176
   goodness, 292
   heart, 246, 270, 292
   history, 166, 196, 241, 310
   life, 250, 257, 271
   mind, 72, 82, 143, 342
   nature, 250, 276–77, 292, 297–98, 321
   pride, 323
   race, 221–224, 230, 273, 279, 305, 319
   reason, xxxv
   responsibility, xxxvi, 210
   revelation from God needed, xxxi
   scribes, Scripture transmission, 29–30
   soul, 73, 236, 246, 248, 264, 274, 414

Index of Subjects and Names

spirit, 249, 250, 274
will, 183–88, 191, 320
idealism, 204, 239–42
    microphone illustration of, 240–42

Italy, 6, 10, 283

Jacob, 188
James, Lord's brother, 132
Jehovah, 64, 93–94
Jerusalem, 64, 82, 93–94, 134, 137
Jesus, 23, 44–45, 69, 91–93, 102, 107, 115–121, 144, 154, 297–98
    active obedience of, xxvi, xxvii, 407–10
    as "the *teaching* of Jesus," 376
    ascension of, 375
    attested to authenticity of Old Testament, 47
    author and substance of gospel, 394
    birth 233, 420
    child in the temple, 95–98, 103
    "Christ" redefined, 85–86
    condescension of, 136, 355
    crucifixion of, 175–76
    deity of, xxxi–xxxiii, 58, 83–90, 112–13, 142, 156, 158, 352, 380, 384–85
    final Judge, 107, 108–10, 113, 385, 394
    humanity of, 47–48, 68, 85, 87–90, 92–95, 106–9, 116, 120, 156, 231, 233, 329, 330, 334, 353–55, 380
    is who he claimed to be, 46–47
    "Liberal Jesus," 120
    miracles of, 85, 115–19
    Nazareth, of, 46, 47, 58, 69, 70, 71, 85, 87, 105, 110–12, 120, 124, 143, 154, 231, 270, 291, 293, 306–8, 377, 384
    New Testament on, 94–98
    humiliation of, 109, 356, 409
    incarnation of, 116–17, 154, 329, 353–54
    knowledge with Father, 111–12
    Messiah, 91–94
    necessity of Savior, 157
    not *like* God, is God, 68
    pantheizing interpretation of him, 86–87
    passive obedience of, xxvi, 409–10
    positivistic sense of, 87–88
    Redeemer, 351–52, 359, 373
    "religion of Jesus" view, 97, 135
    return of, 392
    self attestation of identity, 107–14
    Sermon on the Mount and, 99–106
    Son of God, 95, 374, 375, 411
    Son of man, 107–10, 422
    soul, his human, 232
    two distinct natures, 87, 93, 108, 117, 154, 157, 330, 351–56, 374, 385
    temptation of, 260–61, 270
    his use of "my Father," 95, 97, 103, 111, 143, 372
Jesus, atonement, xxxiv, 154, 338, 391, 392, 399–406, 407
    Christ bore elect's guilt, 302, 405, 408
    difference between debt and penalty of sin, 405

governmental view of, 413,
  415–17, 420–21
moral influence view of, 411–13,
  415–18, 420–21
occurrences of the word in Bible,
  399–402
substitutionary view of, 411,
  416–418
Jesus, offices prophet, priest, and king,
  354–58, 359, 383, 391
  prophet, 102, 359, 372–74,
    375–76, 381–82, 383
  prophetic work carried on by
    apostles, 386
  prophetic work carried on by
    Holy Spirit, 386–87
  priest, 387–90, 389, 394–97,
    399, 402
  relation of priest to prophet, 391,
    394
Jesus, resurrection of, 23, 31, 38–39,
  85, 124–30, 219, 223, 236, 258,
  281, 322, 338, 371, 373, 378–79,
  382, 392, 394, 424
  Galilean hypothesis, 127–29
  reinvigorated the disciples, 124
John the Baptist, 118, 292–94
Joseph, Jesus' father, 94, 232
Judaizers, 137
Judas Iscariot, 170–71
justification by faith, 300, 303, 333

Kaiser Wilhelm II, 8
Kant, Immanuel, 20
Keller, Tim, 37
Kuiper, R. B., 295

Law of God, 279–80, 282, 395

Christians not under curse of,
  281
"guardian until Christ came,"
  286
justice of, 284–85
moral law within man's constitution, 20
Lewis, C. S., xxii, xxx–n
liberalism, xxii, 62, 425
liberty, 6–7, 10, 62, 151, 283–85
Lippmann, Walter, 205–6
Lord's Supper, 378, 420
Luke, 35–36
Luther, Martin, 134

Machen, J. G., xxin, xxxvi–n, 149
  apologetics, xxii, xxvi
  biographical, xvii–xix
  Calvinism, xxxiii
  *Christian Faith in the Modern
    World*, xxix, 347
  The Christian View of Man, xxix,
    xxxi
  Christianity and Liberalism, xviii,
    xxii, xxiv
  Common sense realism, xxxiv
  Concern for college students, xxxi
  death of, xix, xxii, xxvii, xxx
  defrocked, xxiii
  fellowship with Arminians,
    xxxiii–n, 424
  Franconia Range and, 16
  God Transcendent, xviii, xxix
  gospel, xxiv–xxv
  "The Responsibility of the
    Church in Our New Age, 156
  Independent Board of Foreign
    Missions, xxx

classical knowledge, xxiv
Matterhorn and, 15–16, 172
mountain climbing, 15
My Idea of God, contribution to, 14
preaching, xviii, xxvi, 423
Reformed, his use of term, xxv, xxxii–xxxvii
skepticism in his day, xxxv
Virgin Birth of Christ, xviii
What is Faith?, xviii
White Mountains and, 16
man, 140, 157, 172, 196–97, 279
   created supernaturally, 228–29, 233
   body and soul, vs body, soul, and spirit, 247–50
   freedom of will of, 161–62, 168–73, 196, 317
   image of God, 79, 230, 250, 253–63, 298
   imputation of sin and righteousness, 302–4
   resurrection of body, 236, 322, 425
   soul of, 235–37, 245–46
man, fall of, 260, 264–66, 266–68, 301–5
   method of temptation, the tree, 265
   probationary period, 259–61, 263–64, 305, 408–9
   view all descendants *actually* sinned with Adam, 299
   view collective will of humanity sinned in Adam, 300–1
   view did not sin at all in Adam, 300–1
   view all sinned in Adam as representative head, 300–1, 315
man, sin, 277–78, 347, 351, 355, 402
   all people sin, 290, 295–96, 297, 319
   are children born good or bad, 289–90, 302
   dialogue between God's law and saved sinner, 408
   flesh and sin, 275–77
   hell, punishment for, 308
   knowledge of it by sinner, 296
   original, 302, 305, 308–10, 320, 347–48, 404
   repentance required, 293–94
   sin is any transgression of God's law, 278, 283, 403
   not a necessary part of human nature, 297–98
   view all people have some good, 291
   view of dualism, material impedes soul's liberation, 274
   view sin is antisocial conduct, 270–71
   view sin is triumph of man's appetites over human spirit, 274–75
   view sin impedes greatest good for greatest number, 272–73
Marsden, George M., xxxiv–n
Mary, 94, 95, 232, 353–54
materialism, 237–39, 246
Mediterranean Sea, 231, 330, 424
metaphysical, 61, 68–69, 71, 87–89, 99, 245
Mexico, 139

Micaiah, 56
Middle Ages, 231, 330–31
miracles, see supernatural,
    supernaturalism
missions conferences, 338–39
moderates, xxiii
modern age, 343–44
modernism, xxii, 62, 72, 338–40, 349,
    424–25
    its pantheism, 71–72
Monastery of St. Catherine, 30
monotheism, 137
Moody, D. L., 393
Moses, 22, 189, 280, 290
Mount Sinai, 30, 282, 287
Murray, John, xix, xxvii, xxix, xxxvii,
    149, 228
        counsel to Machen, 3
        forward to *Christian View of
            Man*, xxi–n
mystics, 75–76

National Park Service, 16
National Recovery Administration
    (NRA), 5
New Brunswick, Presbytery, xxx
The New York Times, xxiii
Newton, Joseph F., 14n
Nichols, Stephen J., xxiii–n, xxvii

Orthodox Presbyterian Church, xviii,
    xxiii

Palestine, 46, 110, 117, 154, 231
pantheism, 71–74, 203, 242
Passover, 292
Paul, 36, 127, 132–33, 135, 254, 393,
    420, 424

    Alexandria sea trip of, 195–96
    predestination doctrine, 188–90
Paulus, Heinrich, 119
Pelagianism, 309–13, 315–18, 322
    shallow view of sin, 319
Pelagianism, semi, 322
Pentecost, 65, 386
Pentecostals, xxxvii,
Persia, 214
Peter, 125, 127, 132, 137
    Pentecost sermon, 65
Pharisee, 280, 294–95
philosophy,
    Greek, 235–36
    philosophical questions, 245
    transcendent principle of right,
        19–20
Pilgrim's Progress, xxvi
polytheism, 136
Pontius Pilate, 171, 214
prayer, 56, 95–96, 361–62
    Lord's, 267–68, 297–98
    unorthodox one by a preacher,
        309
predestination, xxxiv, 183, 187–90,
    348
    doctrine divine decrees applied to
        salvation, 179, 191
    foreordaining vs. foreknowing,
        168–73, 184–87
    Israel, 187
    not arbitrary, 192
    God does not rejoice in death of
        sinner, 192
    men not saved against will, 194
    not contrary to free offer gospel,
        197
    objections to, 191–97

three imagined misconceptions, 194
Presbyterian Church, USA, 67
Presbyterian Guardian, xxix–n,29n, 357
priest, defined, 387–88
Princeton Seminary, xvi, xvii, xxi, xxii, xxiii, xxvi, xxxvii, 31, 359, 423
    Alexander Hall, xxi, xxiii, xxv
    purpose statement of, xxxv
Princeton University, 359
prophet, 22–23, 35, 37, 91–92, 101–2, 107, 109, 121, 141–42, 155, 181, 195, 227, 280, 292–93, 331, 356–59, 361–66, 367–74, 375–76, 380–88, 391, 394
    defined, 359–64, 367–68
    compared with priest, 388
    modern perspective on, 369–71
    spokesmen for God, 371–72
propitiate, 400, 424
Protestant, xxix, xxxiii, 137n, 172, 331–32
publican, 294–95

radio, xvii, xix–xxv, xxix–xxx, xxvi, 327, 423, 445
Reformation, the, 332–33, 335, 343
    importance of Bible to, 331
Reformed, 25, 32, 149, 310, 333, 334
religion, 8–10, 38–39, 51–53, 58, 68, 75, 88, 96–98, 99–100, 106, 125, 131, 135–39, 153–54, 178, 307, 331, 337, 363, 371, 377, 389, 401, 412, 425
resurrection of body, 236, 322, 425
revelation, general, 344–45
    in nature, 14–18, 25, 153
    in conscience, 19–22, 25, 153

revelation of Word, supernatural, 345
    necessary due to sin and only in the Bible, 21–22, 26, 153–54
revival, 44, 45, 337
Rian, Edwin H., xxiii, xxx, 3, 149
Rich Young Ruler, 294–95
Rome, empire, 124, 214, 231
    emperors of, 136
Roosevelt, Franklin D., 5n
Russia (Soviets), 6, 10, 139, 222, 283
    persecution in, 139
    sold Codex Sinaiticus to British Museum, 30

salvation, 40, 45, 65, 117, 137, 140, 154, 179–81, 183, 185–97, 264, 308–13, 320–22, 334, 343, 347–49, 351
    assurance of, 31, 362
    prophesied to come, 22
science, 176, 209–10, 213, 342
    modern, 167–68, 222, 230, 343, 344
    atomic energy, 221
seminaries, 45
    some are "nurseries of unbelief," 44
Sermon on the Mount, 99–106, 112, 115, 155–56, 281, 307, 380, 394
    Jesus did not set it against Old Testament, 101
Shakespeare, William, 283n
Shimei, 171
Silas, 132
social gospel, 307–8
Sockman, Ralph W., xxix
Socrates, 106
source criticism, 120

Sproul, R. C., xxv
Spurgeon, Charles H., 393
Stephen, 109
Stonehouse, Ned B., xxvi, xxxviin, 425
    wrote introduction *God Transcendent*, xxx–n, xxxi–n
Strauss, David Friedrich, 124
    Machen's critique *The Life of Jesus*, 119–20
supernatural, xxxvin, 21–23, 25–30, 30–31, 32, 33–38, 45–47, 53, 80, 92, 151–153, 197, 213, 215, 218–19, 225, 249, 252, 290, 328, 345–46, 354, 360, 362–64, 367–68, 371–72, 376–77
    attempts to remove it from Bible, 46
    Christ and, 115–19, 121–22
    critiques naturalistic explanations, 219–20
    gifts have ceased, 363
    God's acting independent of course of nature, 217–218
    man created by means of, 227–34
    miracle defined, 219, 220, 227
    miracles attest to Jesus' truth, 115
    miracles have ceased, 224, 362–63
    natural law and, 220, 223
    prophecy and, 368–71
systematic theology, xviii, 3, 228

Ten Commandments, 63–64
Tennyson, Alfred, 73n
Theism, 71, 170, 203
Thomas, Apostle, xxxii, 106
Thomson, William H., 243
Tischendorf, L. F. Konstantin von, 30

total depravity, 33, 320–22
Trinity, 80–82, 83, 93, 112, 140, 154, 251, 329, 335, 346–47, 373
    doctrine clearest in New Testament, 81–82
    human analogies and, 143
    intra–Trinitarian fellowship, 143–44
    modalism, 144
truth, 27, 57, 365–66
    always true for all, 59
Twain, Mark, 240, 331

universe, 20, 47, 68, 68–74, 75, 84, 163, 165–69, 199, 201–6, 207–10, 237, 239, 274, 282, 334, 413
    created by God, 136, 152–54, 158, 177, 207, 221–22
    God revealed in, 14, 19
    science and, 38, 77
utilitarianism, 273
unseen things, xxxi–n, 7–9
unseen world, xxi, xxv, 5–8, 13, 19

Van Til, Cornelius, xxxiv
virgin birth, xxxvi–n, 58, 85, 94–95, 232, 338, 353–54
Vos, Geerhardus, 143, 149, 423
    The Self Disclosure of Jesus, 96, 110

Ward, James, 238
Warfield, B. B., xxi–xxii, 134, 149, 204
    Augustine on Pelagian controversy, 310
    Calvin on creation, 228
    Counterfeit Miracles, 25–26, 225n, 362

predestination, 179
Trinity, 81, 93
Washington, D.C., 224–25
Washington, George, 419
Westminster Seminary, xxiii, xxx, xxvii, 3, 30, 425
  Board of Trustees, xxx, 149
  classes in, 41
  faculty of, 3, 149
  founding of, xviii, xxx
Westminster Seminary Hour, xxii, xxx, 327
Westminster Standards, 336
  Confession of Faith, 48, 235, 335–36, 337, 340, 342, 343
  Larger Catechism, 335, 343, 387
  Shorter Catechism, xvii, 32, 57, 77, 79, 144, 163, 165, 171, 175, 178, 210, 204, 208, 211, 235, 255, 257, 259, 264, 278, 299–307, 335–36, 343, 351–56, 359, 372–73, 387
Westminster Theological Journal, xxx–n
Wharton, Edith, xxi
White, Hugh G. Evelyn, 26n
White Mountains, 16
Whymper, Edward, 15
WIP radio, xxi, xxiv, xxvii, xxix, 3, 21, 149
Woolley, Paul, 149
  critiqued broadcasts by C. S. Lewis, xxii–n
World War I, 221, 342, 344, 423
  German military, 8
  residual effects of, 6–7

Yale, 359

Zacharias, 94
Zermatt, Swiss Alps, 171–72
Zeruiah, 171–72

Index of Scripture References

Genesis
1:1	63, 69
1:2	141
1:27	250, 253, 254
1:31	204, 252
2:7	230, 235
2:16–17	256–57, 265
2:17	263
3:1	265
3:2–3	265
3:3	278, 279
3:4	265
3:4–5	266
3:5	269
3:8	306
3:17–18	258
3:22	266
6:6	164
15:6	370

Exodus
20:2	63
20:13	273

Leviticus
1:4	400
16:6, 15–16	400

Deuteronomy
4:24	307
6:4–5	64
18:17–19	364
18:18	372
18:20	365

1 Samuel
15:35	164

2 Samuel
16:7–8	171
16:9	171
16:10	171, 172

1 Kings
22:14	56

Psalms
19:1	17, 153, 206
51:4	272
51:5	320
51:11	141
90:2	74
90:4	78
104:10–30	211–13
104:21	213
150	318

Isaiah
7:14	23, 94
9:6	23, 92, 370
40:6	276
40:8	151
40:11	79
40:17	79
40:22	79
40:26	70
65:17	258

Jeremiah
17:9	309
23:21	365

Ezekiel
18:4	403
33:11	193

Daniel
7:13	92, 108

Amos
7:14	37

Malachi
3:1–18	94

Matthew
1	232
3:2	294
3:14	293
3:17	96
4:17	64, 294
5:7	xxiv, 100
5:8	157
5:11	101, 156
5:17	280
5:20	280
5:21	155
5:21–22	101
5:29	105, 281
5:45	68
5:48	255, 282
6:9	73

6:12	297	**Luke**		11:25	425
6:13	267	1	232	12:49–50	372
6:19–21	308	1:16–17	94	14:9	69, 385
6:29	17	1:30–38	94	14:16	143, 144
7:11	297	2:11	23	14:23	143, 144
7:18	160, 251	2:48–49	95	15:15	372
7:21	103	3:22	96	15:26	144
7:22–23	104, 105	5:8	282	16:7	143
7:24–25	380	5:23	90, 98	17:6	187
7:26–27	380	7:47	418	17:9	187
8:20	109	7:50	97	20:28	106
10:28	235	10:27	156, 157		
10:29	68, 213	12:4–5	308	**Acts**	
10:29–30	167	12:24	213	2:23	170, 176
11:7, 9, 11	293	12:27	213	2:33	386
11:25	80	12:27–28	68, 70	2:37	65
11:25–26	113, 187	12:32	70	4:27–28	171, 214
11:27	89, 111	14:26	101	7:55–56	109
11:28–30	113	18:10–13	294	13:48	188
12:33–35	316	18:17	295	16:30–31	188
12:34	251	19:31	307	16:31	381, 385
12:36	281			20:27	xviii
19:9	307	**John**		27	xxviii
28:19	81, 142	1:1	89	27:31	195
		1:3	89		
Mark		1:13	196	**Romans**	
1:11	96	1:18	69, 383	1:18–3:20	290
2:7	110	2:23–25	292	1:20	17, 18
2:17	294	2:25	270	1:21	18, 153
8:38	101, 109	3:3	292	2	281
9:24	98	3:7	292, 320	2:14	153
9:48	307	4:18	64	2:14–15	20
10:15	295	7:16	372	3:10–12	291
10:17–22	294	8:58	89	5:11	399
10:45	109	9:25	42	5:18	300
11:27	384	10:10	425	5:18–19	303
13:26	109	10:30	144	5:19	300

8:19–20	257	3:24	286	**Hebrews**	
8:28	190, 206	5:19–21	281	1:1–2	375
8:30	190			4:15	389
8:31	70	**Ephesians**		5:1–4	388
9:5	133	1:4	166	9:26–28	424
9:11–13	188	1:12	178	10:31	176
9:15–24	189	4:21	425	11:1–2	374
10:6–9	397	4:24	254	11:4	xix
		6:12	277	12:14	425
1 Corinthians					
2:2	420	**Philippians**		**James**	
2:11	248	4:8	268	1:2	267
2:14–15	247			1:13–14	173
3:3	276	**Colossians**			
3:4	277	1:17	89	**1 Peter**	
10:26	275	2:21	275	1:11	373
11:25	420	3:10	253		
12:3	365			**1 John**	
12:11	45	**1 Timothy**		1:10	296
15:3–4	128, 424	2:4	193	3:20	296
		2:5	356	4:1	365
2 Corinthians		4:2	153	4:2–3	365
13:14	81, 142				
		1 Thessalonians		**Revelation**	
Galatians		1:9–10	424	22:13	89
1:1	133	5:23	249		

Index of Westminster Standards

Confession of Faith
1.5	48
4.2	235

Larger Catechism Questions and Answers
43	387

Shorter Catechism Questions and Answers
1	178
3	57
4	77, 79, 160
6	144
7	163, 164, 165, 171, 175, 179
8	201
9	201
10	235, 255
11	208, 211
12	255, 257, 259
13	254
14	278, 279
16	299
17	301
18	302, 304
19	306, 307, 348
21	87, 93, 117, 154, 157, 351, 352, 355, 356, 374, 392
22	355
23	102, 356, 359, 372
24	373

Notes and Acknowledgments

Machen's radio addresses, while the product of a scholarly mind, were not written as academic treatises. Rather, these brief chapters were composed with clarity and directness as their purpose. As such, despite a temptation to correct Machen in places, peculiar phrasing and "oralisms" have been preserved: These are the addresses as their author intended them. Only where Machen's meaning has been obscured by time, or where more context was thought necessary, brief notes have been added. Scripture references, unless otherwise indicated, have been updated to the English Standard Version.

Things Unseen, like each book published by Westminster Seminary Press, owes its existence to a band of extraordinary and talented people. WSP's former Director of Publishing, James Baird, set this edition of Machen's radio addresses on its feet more than three years ago, and the book still owes much of its shape and character to his vision and labors. Nate Shannon and Ben Dahlvang each offered crucial editorial expertise to the publication at critical junctures, and we are indebted to their talent and know-how.

Jessica Hiatt designed the superb cover and jacket of this book. Barry Waugh produced the indispensable indexes. Angela Messinger typeset *Things Unseen* with patience and consummate art. John Kim, Victor Kim, Josiah Pettit, and Rachel Stout each contributed their expertise to the publication, and are owed a good deal more than they received. Special thanks are due to each member of the WSP Board: David Garner, Chun Lai, Peter A. Lillback, Jim Sweet, and Jerry Timmis, for their passionate support of WSP and its mission.

Finally, we can't fully express our gratitude to Sinclair B. Ferguson, Stephen J. Nichols, Timothy J. Keller, and Richard B. Gaffin, Jr. for their grace and generosity in contributing to this project. William Dennison also crafted an illuminating essay about Machen's theology that we are grateful to have permission to publish at www.wts.edu/ThingsUnseen. Readers interested in learning more about the topics Machen introduces in this book would do well to accompany their study of scripture with the sermons, essays, and books of these authors. Each brightly reflects the gifts frequently ascribed to Machen: Faithfulness and skill in communicating and defending the mystery of faith in Jesus Christ.

> So we do not lose heart. Though our outer self is wasting away, our inner self is being renewed day by day. For this light momentary affliction is preparing for us an eternal weight of glory beyond all comparison, as we look not to the things that are seen but to the things that are unseen. For the things that are seen are transient, but the things that are unseen are eternal. (2 Cor 4:16–18)

> Westminster Seminary Press
> August, 2020

WSP

Westminster Seminary Press (WSP) was founded in 2011 by Westminster Theological Seminary in Philadelphia, Pennsylvania. WSP is a uniquely Reformed academic publisher dedicated to enriching the church, the academy, and the Christian through the printed word. WSP collaborates widely—including with faculty, staff, and students at Westminster—to publish new and classic books that foster faith in and obedience to Jesus Christ from an orthodox, Reformed perspective.

For more information, visit www.westminsterseminarypress.com, email wsp@wts.edu, or write to us at 2960 Church Road, Glenside, Pennsylvania 19038.